To Doris

from Geoff and Mary
Christmas 1971

(Returned to me by Doris
later on for my own ~~sister~~
interest)

THE BURNING HEART
John Wesley, Evangelist

THE BURNING HEART

John Wesley, Evangelist

by

A. SKEVINGTON WOOD

B.A., Ph.D., F.R. Hist.S.

A. Skevington Wood.

THE PATERNOSTER PRESS

SBN:85364 002 5

AUSTRALIA:
Emu Book Agencies Pty., Ltd.,
511 Kent Street, Sydney, N.S.W.

CANADA:
Home Evangel Books Ltd.,
25 Hobson Avenue, Toronto, 16

NEW ZEALAND:
G. W. Moore, Ltd.,
P.O. Box 29012, Greenwood's Corner,
24 Empire Road, Auckland

SOUTH AFRICA:
Oxford University Press,
P.O. Box 1141
Thibault House, Thibault Square,
Cape Town

Made and printed in Great Britain for
The Paternoster Press
Paternoster House, 3 Mount Radford Crescent
Exeter, Devon, England
by Latimer Trend & Co Ltd, Plymouth

PREFACE

ACCORDING TO BLAISE PASCAL, "THE LAST THING THAT WE DISCOVER IN writing a book, is to know what to put at the beginning." The problem still persists, but in this case it is obvious that something should be said to excuse the temerity in presenting yet another study of John Wesley. The reader might well be pardoned for questioning the need for it. An explanation is therefore required.

Surprisingly enough, in the long (and lengthening) Wesley bibliography, there is hardly a title covering his approach to evangelism. In 1905 Richard Green, formerly Governor of Didsbury Theological College, Manchester, published his *John Wesley: Evangelist*. Its stated aim was "to set forth the one chief purpose for which . . . Wesley was raised up, and to fulfil which he was especially qualified—namely, his evangelistic appeal to the heart and conscience of this nation." Despite that declaration of intent, however, what Green in the caption for Part Two called "The Great Work" was simply dealt with chronologically in a review of five decades. There was no real attempt at analysis.

Since that date, the topic has been touched on in numerous biographies of Wesley, but, so far as can be ascertained, only one serious treatment has been essayed. This was confined to Wesley's early period, and submitted as a doctoral thesis at Columbia University, New York, over thirty years ago, by Elizabeth Kristine Nottingham, who was born in the ancient city of York, England, where I now write. It was the discovery of this little-known work, through the kindness of my friend the Reverend Basil Brown, then Vicar of Holy Trinity, Heworth, York, which finally prompted me to follow up this line of research.

In an age like ours, when evangelism is placed high on the agenda of the Church, such a theme may prove to be relevant. At the same time, the current participation of Methodism in reunion conversations has accorded an even greater prominence to the figure of John Wesley, not only within the denomination of which he was perhaps the involuntary founder, but far beyond its confines. It is thus my hope and prayer that what is offered here may make some small contribution to the contemporary ecumenical dialogue. Wesley succeeded in reaching the common people with the gospel. That is still our major objective in the Church. At the moment it is also our major dilemma, for we are finding that communication is by no means easy. A look back to Wesley may help us to move forward more effectively.

Before mentioning those to whom I have been more directly indebted in the preparation of this particular volume, I must pause to salute the memory of two distinguished mentors, whose influence proved determinative. It was my first teacher in Church History, the Reverend Doctor Howard Watkin-Jones of Wesley College, Headingley, who drew me gently yet firmly to the eighteenth century as a field of specialized investigation, and encouraged me in the pursuit of intensive research. The Very Reverend Doctor Norman Sykes, sometime Dixie Professor of Ecclesiastical History in the University of Cambridge and later Dean of Winchester, not only stimulated me with his exact and balanced historical scholarship, but was also kind enough to maintain an interest in my work until his death in 1961. These two men helped to shape the course of such research as I have been privileged to undertake to date.

In connection with this present publication, I have to thank especially my former colleague, the Reverend John C. Bowmer, the official Archivist of the Methodist Church, for his unfailing patience and readiness to assist in the tracing of elusive sources, and my present District Chairman, the Reverend Doctor J. Cyril T. Downes, who loaned me the manuscript of his thesis on *Eschatological Doctrines in the Writings of John and Charles Wesley*. Mr. B. Howard Mudditt, the proprietor of The Paternoster Press, displayed generous enthusiasm for the project from the start, and has urged it forward at every stage. My obligation to the staffs of several libraries must also be recorded: the Reading Room of the British Museum, Doctor Williams' Library, and the Evangelical Library, London; the Brotherton Library, Leeds; the Rylands Library, Manchester; New College Library, Edinburgh; Wesley College Library, Headingley; and the Reference and Minster Libraries, York.

A. SKEVINGTON WOOD

York
August 1967

CONTENTS

8 CONTENTS

Chapter   *page*

INTRODUCTION

"IN ENGLAND THE FIRST HALF OF THE EIGHTEENTH CENTURY WAS a period of moral disorder."[1] With that observation of Harold Nicolson most historians today would be in substantial agreement. Neither the more balanced approach to the century which has marked recent research, nor the greater leniency with which its lapses are treated, have noticeably mitigated the gravity of the overall picture. Whilst it is never an easy matter to assess the conditions of a previous age, and unduly sweeping generalizations are to be avoided, yet it does not seem open to serious doubt that the nation was on the verge of moral disintegration. It was to this catastrophic situation that John Wesley addressed himself, under God, when in 1739, as Neville Williams puts it, he "made the vital innovation of becoming an itinerant preacher."[2]

It has been usual to assume that eighteenth-century England had recovered to some degree from the extreme libertinism of the Restoration era. There is, however, sufficient evidence to show that, in the early years at least, the entail was considerable. Contemporary vices were open and notorious, for hypocrisy was not one of them, as Canon Elliott-Binns remarked.[3] The first two Hanoverian monarchs were flagrantly dissolute. The Prime Minister for twenty years (1722–1742), Sir Robert Walpole, lived in undisguised adultery with his mistress, Maria Skellett, whom he had installed at the Old Lodge in Richmond Park.[4] Lord Chesterfield, in his letters to his son Philip, instructed him in the strategy of seduction as part of a polite education.[5] Lady Mary Wortley Montagu declared that in society the "state of matrimony is as much ridiculed by our young ladies as it used to be by young fellows: in short, both sexes have found the inconveniences of it, and the appellation of rake is as genteel in a woman as a man of quality."[6]

This prevalent moral laxity was both reflected in and fed by many of

[1] Harold Nicolson, *The Age of Reason 1700–1789* (1960), p. 369.
[2] E. Neville Williams, *Life in Georgian England* (1962), p. 135.
[3] L. E. Elliott-Binns, *The Early Evangelicals* (1953), p. 50.
[4] J. H. Plumb, *Sir Robert Walpole: The King's Minister* (1960), pp. 112–113.
[5] *The Letters of Philip Dormer Stanhope Fourth Earl of Chesterfield*, ed. Bonamy Dobrée (1932), Vol. IV, pp. 1713–1714, 15th April, 1751; pp. 1738–1739, 23rd May, 1751 *et al.*
[6] *The Letters and Works of Lady Mary Wortley Montagu*, ed. W. Moy Thomas (1861), Vol. I, p. 351. To the Countess of Mar, 31st October, 1723.

the amusements then in vogue. "The present great licentiousness of the stage" was conceded even by a man of the world like Lord Hervey.[1] Joseph Addison, writing in *The Spectator* early in the century, remarked: "It is one of the most unaccountable things in our age, that the lewdness of our theatre should be so much complained of, so well exposed, and so little redressed. . . . It is to be hoped that at some time or other we may be at leisure to restrain the licentiousness of the theatre, and make it contribute to the advancement of morality, and to the reformation of the age. . . . The truth of it is the accomplished gentleman upon the English stage is the person that is familiar with other men's wives and indifferent to his own; as the fine woman is generally a composition of sprightliness and falsehood."[2] Later, it is true, David Garrick valiantly attempted a remedy, but even his success was restricted by the fact that many playgoers preferred the rank indecency of Restoration drama. The fashionable court and subscription masquerades were scandalously sensual. "Champagne, dice, music, or your neighbour's spouse"—these were advertised on one of the invitation cards. On a royal occasion, a maid-of-honour impersonating Iphigenia was "so naked that you would have taken her for Andromeda."[3]

The popular taste in literature was no less demoralized. The notorious Minerva Press pandered to the current demand for titillation. In one of his *Edinburgh Review* essays, Lord Jeffrey complained in retrospect that "a greater mass of trash and rubbish never disgraced the press of any country than the ordinary novels that filled and supported circulating libraries. . . . The staple of our novel market was beyond imagination despicable, and had consequently sunk and degraded the whole department of literature, of which it had usurped the name."[4]

Meanwhile, the nation found itself enmeshed in the twin snares of drink and gambling. Insobriety was a vice from which no class was immune. Amongst the juvenilia of George Crabbe is to be found a satire in which he depicted the effects of intemperance on each segment of society, from "the staggering peer" to "the humble pensioner," not excluding "the slow-tongued bishop," "the easy chaplain" and the convivial vicar.[5] According to W. E. H. Lecky, the passion for gin-drinking began to

[1] Lord Hervey, *Memoirs of the Reign of King George II*, ed. Romney Sedwick (1931), Vol. II, p. 341.

[2] Joseph Addison, *The Spectator*, 1st August, 1712, No. 446. Cf. 28th April, 1711, No. 51 (Richard Steele). For the condition of the theatre in this period, see A. S. Turberville, *English Men and Manners in the Eighteenth Century* (1929), pp. 401–412; *Johnson's England*, ed. A. S. Turberville (1933), Vol. II, pp. 160–189 (W. J. Lawrence); *The New Cambridge Modern History*, Vol. VII, *The Old Regime 1713–1763*, ed. J. O. Lindsay (1957), pp. 74–75 (Sir Albert Richardson).

[3] J. Wesley Bready, *England Before and After Wesley* (1939), pp. 158–159.

[4] Francis Jeffrey, *Essays* (1853), p. 656.

[5] *The Poetical Works of George Crabbe*, ed. A. J. and R. M. Carlyle (1908), "Inebriety," pp. 3–4.

affect the masses of the population around 1724 and "spread with the rapidity and the violence of an epidemic," until it was "irrevocably implanted
in the nation."[1] The gambling craze was equally obsessive. Public gaming-
houses were officially licensed. Facilities were amply provided for faro,
bassette, ombre, dice and similar games of chance. In the two parishes of
Westminster, no less than two hundred and ninety-six tables catered for
one fashionable form of gambling alone. All classes, from members of the
royal family to city apprentices, were swept along by the prevailing tide,
with disastrous effects not only on the pocket, but on morals too. According to Sir George Otto Trevelyan, "society in those days was one vast
casino."[2] It was said that before he had reached the age of twenty-four,
Charles James Fox was in debt to Jewish money-lenders to the tune of
£100,000 which he had lost at cards and dice. Horace Walpole noted with
concern that the gaming at Almack's, which had taken precedence over
White's as the premier club, was "worthy the decline of our Empire, or
Commonwealth, which you please. The young men of the age lose five,
ten, fifteen thousand pounds in an evening there."[3] To make matters
worse, the Government itself at once exploited and inflamed the universal
desire for gain by sponsoring State lotteries.[4]

The moral decline of the nation was further indicated by widespread
indulgence in such cruel and degrading sports (if such they can be called)
as cock-fighting, cock-throwing, goose-riding, dog-tailing, bull-baiting
and badger-baiting. Meanwhile, the statistics of violent crime soared
alarmingly, and hangings became so frequent that Dr. Johnson ironically
expressed his fear lest the navy might run short of ropes.[5] There was as yet
no organized police force, and many crimes went unpunished. Prisons
were overcrowded, and tended rather to harden offenders than to reform
them. Gangs of young hooligans roamed the city streets, often clashing
with their rivals or assaulting unprotected citizens. A committee, set up by
the House of Lords "to examine into the causes of the present notorious
immorality and profaneness," discovered the existence of a club whose
members were known as "Blasters." They professed to be votaries
of the devil, addressed blasphemous prayers to him, and drank his
health.[6]

[1] W. E. H. Lecky, *A History of England in the Eighteenth Century* (1878), Vol. I, pp.
479, 481.
[2] George Otto Trevelyan, *The Early History of Charles James Fox* (1894), p. 83.
[3] *The Letters of Horace Walpole*, ed. Mrs. Paget Toynbee, Vol. VII (1904), p. 365.
To Sir Horace Mann, 2nd February, 1770.
[4] There were also private lotteries for shop goods, cf. John Ashworth, *Social Life in
the Reign of Queen Anne* (1897), pp. 86–87.
[5] Capital offences numbered over two hundred and fifty, many of them comparatively trivial.
[6] Cf. Luke Tyerman, *The Life and Times of the Rev. John Wesley* (1870), Vol. I, pp.
173–174.

This alarming and extensive lowering of moral standards stemmed from a prior indifference to the claims of the Christian faith. As Lecky commented, "a religious languour fell over England."[1] Vital Christianity was at a premium. The bulk of the populace failed to recognize its relevance. Some of them, indeed, continued to perform what the philosopher Immanuel Kant called the court-duties of religion, but comparatively few had experienced the glowing reality of personal communion with Christ. "I suppose it will be granted," wrote Dean Swift, in *A Project for the Advancement of Religion* (1709), "that hardly one in a hundred among our people of quality or gentry, appears to act by any principle of religion; that great numbers of them do entirely discard it, and are ready to own their disbelief of all revelation in ordinary discourse. Nor is the case much better among the vulgar, especially in great towns. . . ."[2]

Before his death in 1708, William Beveridge, Bishop of St. Asaph, deplored the fact that Christ's "doctrine and precepts are so generally slighted and neglected" and that "so little of Christianity is now to be found amongst Christians themselves: to our shame be it spoken."[3] In 1722 Daniel Defoe declared that "no age, since the founding and forming of the Christian Church in the world, was ever like, (in open avowed atheism, blasphemies and heresies), to the age we now live in."[4] In 1729 John Byrom, the hymn-writer and pioneer of shorthand, told his sister Phoebe he had just bought a copy of William Law's *Serious Call*, but "for Mr. Law, and Christian religion, and such things, they are mightily out of fashion at present."[5] In 1738 George Berkeley, Bishop of Cloyne, reported that morality and religion in Britain had collapsed "to a degree which was never known in any Christian country," and in the same year Thomas Secker, Bishop of Oxford, lamented that "an open and professed disregard of religion is become, through a variety of unhappy causes, the distinguishing character of the age."[6] In 1751 Joseph Butler, Bishop of Bristol and author of the famous *Analogy of Religion*, described the climate as "truly *for* nothing, but against everything that is good and sacred among us."[7] In 1753 Sir John Barnard, an outstanding Member of Parlia-

[1] Lecky, *op. cit.*, Vol. I, p. 363.

[2] *The Prose Works of Jonathan Swift*, Vol. III, ed. Temple Scott (1898), p. 29. *A Project for the Advancement of Religion, and the Reformation of Manners* (1709).

[3] *The Theological Works of William Beveridge*, ed. J. Bliss, Vol. VIII (1846), p. 297. *Private Thoughts Upon a Christian Life* (1709).

[4] Daniel Defoe, "On the death of Toland the Infidel Writer," in *Applebee's Journal*, 17th March, 1722.

[5] *Selections from the Journal and Papers of John Byrom*, ed. Henri Talon (1950), p. 105. Letter John Byrom to Phoebe Byrom, 18th February, 1729.

[6] *The Works of George Berkeley*, ed. A. A. Luce and T. E. Jessop (1953), Vol. VII, p. 211; *The Works of Thomas Secker*, ed. B. Porteus and G. Stinton (1811), Vol. V, p. 292.

[7] Joseph Butler, *Fifteen Sermons, preached at the Rolls Chapel; to which is added a Charge to the Clergy of Durham*, ed. R. Cattermole (1836), p. 279.

ment, on whom the elder Pitt conferred the title "the great commoner" (which later devolved on him), regretted the fact that "at present it really seems to be the fashion for a man to declare himself of no religion."[1]

Now, even if we concede with Dr. Roland N. Stromberg, that "the testimony of idealists, impassioned or disillusioned, is properly subject to some discounting," such a chorus of complaint can nevertheless hardly be ignored.[2] Without at all seeking to darken the night before the dawn of revival in any illegitimate manner, we are surely justified in concluding that Wesley appeared on the scene when faith and morals in England had sunk to an abnormally low ebb. For this, of course, the Church itself must shoulder a considerable share of responsibility. When every conceivable allowance has been made for the Hanoverian Establishment, it can scarcely be regarded as having brought an aggressive impact to bear on a godless and decadent age. The most that has been demonstrated by recent investigation is that eighteenth-century Anglicanism (and in particular the episcopate) was not quite as effete as it had been formerly painted. That it failed to meet the challenge of the hour in positive, heroic action is, however, an unfortunate and to some an unpalatable defect, which no amount of casuistical special pleading can amend. "It is easy to exaggerate the deadness of the Established Church in the eighteenth century," writes Dr. Dorothy Marshall, "but, apart from the non-jurors, it was not a body of martyrs."[3] Nor was it a body of evangelists, either.

"Indifference in the world," claimed Dr. Campbell Morgan, "is largely the result of passionlessness in the pulpit."[4] Here lay a major failure of the Hanoverian Church. Walpole's policy of *quieta non movere* had affected the clergy.[5] The homiletical model was Archbishop Tillotson. Enthusiasm was to be avoided at all costs. Sir Leslie Stephen said of the most celebrated preacher of the period—Hugh Blair of Edinburgh—that "he was a mere washed-out retailer of second-hand commonplaces, who gives us the impression that the real man has vanished, and left nothing but a wig and gown."[6] Oliver Goldsmith passed this judgement on the divines of his time: "Their discourses from the pulpit are generally dry, methodical, and unaffecting; delivered with the most insipid calmness, in so much that should the peaceful preacher lift his head over the cushion, he might dis-

---

[1] *Parliamentary History*, Vol. XIV (1813), p. 1389.

[2] Roland N. Stromberg, *Religious Liberalism in Eighteenth Century England* (1954), p. 3. Cf. A. R. Humphreys, *The Augustan World: Life and Letters in Eighteenth Century England* (1954), p. 158.

[3] Dorothy Marshall, *Eighteenth Century England* (1962), p. 4.

[4] G. Campbell Morgan, *Preaching* (1937), p. 54.

[5] Cf. Norman Sykes, *Church and State in England in the Eighteenth Century* (1934), pp. 260–261.

[6] Leslie Stephen, *A History of English Thought in the Eighteenth Century* (1876), Vol. II, p. 347.

cover his audience, instead of being awakened to remorse, actually sleeping over his mechanical and laboured composition."[1]

More serious than the lack of fervour in the Hanoverian pulpit was its distinct distrust of theology. Biblically-based doctrinal preaching was at a discount. Tepid, innocuous moralizing seems to have been the accepted recipe. "Evil and guilt, sin and redemption—the whole personal drama and appeal of religion—was forgotten or rationalized away and the eupeptic optimism of politicians pervaded the teaching of the Church," according to Dr. J. H. Plumb. "It was not a religion which had much appeal to the men and women living brutal and squalid lives in the disease-ridden slums of the new towns and mining villages. They needed revelation and salvation."[2] Dissent was only a little less culpable in this respect than the Church of England.[3]

It was this inculcation of a bare morality, unassociated with the evangelical truths of the Christian faith which alone can bring ethics to life, which made so pathetically little impact on the congregations that the nation drifted to the brink of moral bankruptcy. "We have preached morality so long," complained Thomas Jones of Southwark, "that we have hardly any morality left; and this moral preaching has made our people so very immoral that there are no lengths of wickedness which they are not afraid of running into."[4]

If, however, we are to trace the source of moral decline in the eighteenth century, we must go behind the indifference of the people and the ineffectiveness of the clergy to a prior and determinative factor. It used to be fashionable to depict the eighteenth century as an age of stability so far as the foundations of Christianity were concerned. The Deistic controversy, it was assumed, had turned out rather to the furtherance of the gospel, in that those who had dared to attack the revelatory basis of belief had been convincingly routed. But nowadays it is being appreciated that this was something of a Pyrrhic victory. Despite the apparent triumph of orthodoxy, severe losses had in fact been sustained. As Canon Elliott-Binns remarked, "it took long for this to be realized, for casualty lists are not issued after such warfare."[5]

In meeting the onslaught of Deism, orthodoxy "gambled on reason,"

[1] Collected Works of Oliver Goldsmith, ed. Arthur Friedman (1966), Vol. III, p. 151, "Some Remarks on the Modern Manner of Preaching" (in the Lady's Magazine, December, 1760); cf. Vol. I, pp. 480–483, The Bee, No. VII; Vol. II, pp. 49–51, "A Sublime Passage in a French Sermon," in the Weekly Magazine, 12th January, 1760—where Goldsmith complained that preachers addressed their congregations "as they would trifle at a tea table, afraid of the imputation of enthusiasm."
[2] J. H. Plumb, England in the Eighteenth Century (1950), pp. 44–45. Cf. Lecky, op. cit., Vol. I, p. 84.
[3] Cf. Elie Halévy, England in 1815 (E. T. 1924), p. 407.
[4] The Works of Thomas Jones, ed. William Romaine (1763), p. 362.
[5] Elliott-Binns, op. cit., p. 91.

so Stromberg concludes.[1] Temporarily it seemed as if this ingenious intellectual defence of the faith had paid handsome dividends. But soon it was to become apparent that in acquiescing uncritically to the purely rationalistic approach, the opponents of Deism had in fact yielded crucial ground. As a result, the entire edifice of revelation was eventually imperilled. It was not until the next century that the full extent of the damage was to be recognized, and by then it was too late; yet even in Wesley's time the presuppositions of Christianity were being increasingly questioned. A process of incipient demythologizing had already started. "Christianity was to be neither 'mysterious' nor 'miraculous,' but basically rational and humane," explains Dr. V. H. H. Green. "The attempt to bring this about, made for the most part by men of mediocre intellectual capacity, diluted the Christian faith to a ludicrous extent. It appeared no longer as a structure of dogma but a moral code, and its founder was simply a good man, neither true Saviour nor Redeemer."[2] This subtle undermining of Christian foundations lay behind the decline of faith and morals which characterized the first half of the eighteenth century.

It is against such a background that the evangelistic enterprise of John Wesley needs to be set. His task was multilateral. It was not sufficient simply to bemoan the iniquity of the age. The desiccated moralism of the contemporary pulpit had to be replaced by a passionate proclamation of evangelical truth, wherever men and women would listen to it, irrespective of ecclesiastical conventions. "Wesley did not waste his time deploring the evils of his day," asserted Richard Pyke: "he attacked them; and he attacked them by preaching repentance and conversion. He knew that the only hope of the corrupt heart was a new birth."[3] But, more than that, Wesley countered the current wave of rationalistic scepticism with a ringing reaffirmation of those fundamental and supernatural realities of the gospel which, whilst by no means incompatible with reason, nevertheless transcend and surpass it.

To the story of John Wesley's evangelism we must now turn. In concentrating on this pivotal figure, the impression must not be created, however, that Wesley was the only instrument of awakening in this era. We must be careful not to isolate his achievement. As Dr. John Walsh so discerningly reminds us: "simple chronology disposes of the stereotype of the whole Revival as a chain-reaction from the Aldersgate Street experience, and of John Wesley as a solitary Moses striking the rock of petrified Anglicanism to release a sudden stream of revival."[4] In particular, the

---

[1] Stromberg, op. cit., p. 12.
[2] Vivian H. H. Green, John Wesley (1964), p. 4.
[3] Richard Pyke, John Wesley Came This Way (1938), p. 19.
[4] Essays in Modern English Church History, ed. G. V. Bennett and J. D. Walsh (1966), p. 134.

equivalent significance of George Whitefield is not to be minimized. But this is a book about Wesley and, of necessity, the spotlight of attention must be focused on him.

PART I

THE MAKING OF AN EVANGELIST

CHAPTER I

IN A LINE

"But, so far as I can learn, such a thing has scarce been for these thousand years before, as a son, father, grandfather, *atavus*, *tritavus*, preaching the gospel, nay, and the genuine gospel, *in a line*." *Letters* 5: 76.

WITH A SHREWD FLASH OF INSIGHT, JOHN WESLEY ONCE TOLD Adam Clarke: "If I were to write my own life I should begin it before I was born."[1] That was his typically realistic way of paying tribute to the past. Ancestry has its effect on personality, and we cannot easily set aside Wesley's family tree. His preparation for the work of evangelism, to which God had destined him, began long before he came into the world. Like the prophet Jeremiah, he was aware that the divine purpose stretched back to influence his antecedents. "Before I formed thee in the belly I knew thee; and before thou camest forth out of the womb I sanctified thee, and I ordained thee a prophet unto the nations" (Jeremiah 1: 5). Referring to Wesley's untiring ministry throughout the land, Dr. Maldwyn Edwards asks: "What thrust him out on these ceaseless journeyings?"[2] "In a strict sense," he replies, "one could say 'it was in his blood.'"[3]

Wesley's pedigree is a fascinating one from a spiritual viewpoint. He himself had no interest in his genealogy for the usual reasons, since he was singularly free from any pride of class or descent. But after his evangelical conversion and when he had embarked on the mission God gave him, he realized how providentially he had been prepared for it by his family background. For, as Canon Leathem reminds us, "if we were to trace the goodly heritage of Wesley's ancestry it would be to discover Puritanism at its intellectual, cultural, and religious best."[4]

Wesley spoke of son, father and grandfather in a line of genuine gospel preaching. We can take it one stage further back, for his great-grandfather also stood in the succession. Bartholomew Westley—the 't' in the surname was not dropped until John Wesley's father went up to Oxford—was one of the recognized Puritans during the Commonwealth period who was ejected from his living in 1662. According to Calamy, he studied medicine

[1] Adam Clarke, *Memoirs of the Wesley Family* (1823), Vol. I, p. 94.
[2] *A History of the Methodist Church in Great Britain*, ed. Rupert E. Davies and E. Gordon Rupp (1966), Vol. I, p. 37.
[3] *Ibid.*
[4] William Leathem, *John Wesley 1703-1791* (n.d.), p. 32.

as well as divinity at Oxford, and this stood him in good stead when he
was driven from his parish and lost his income.[1]

Bartholomew Westley was Rector of Charmouth and Catherston in
Dorset from about 1640. In 1650 a commission of inquiry visited the
parishes to add to an inventory of incumbents and their stipends, and
Westley's name was entered.[2] In September 1651, Charles the Second
escaped to France after the battle of Worcester. The boat in which he was
to reach the vessel which lay in wait for him was delayed, and he and his
retinue stayed all night at an inn at Charmouth. Next morning, suspicions
were aroused and the ostler ran to tell the Rector. But he was reading
morning prayer in the church, and when he had finished, the defeated
King had disappeared. Westley told a friend afterwards, with a touch of
humour, that if ever Charles returned he would be certain to favour long
prayers, because "he would have surely snapt him" if the service had been
over sooner.[3] An account of this incident describes Westley as the "puny
parson."[4] He was evidently a man of small stature, like his great-grandson,
and indeed, it seems, all the Wesleys.

It was from the parish of Allington, near Bridport, that Westley was
removed in 1662.[5] When he actually took this living is not certain. After
his ejection, he threw in his lot with the persecuted nonconformists of the
area and preached in their assemblies. We are told that "he did indeed use
a peculiar plainness of speech, which hindered his being an acceptable
popular preacher."[6] He died in 1671 and "was buried in the sea-washed
cemetery," according to Prof. Martin Schmidt, "in distant view of the
little Lyme Regis valley where in the time of persecution he had held
secret services with the few faithful members of his congregation."[7]

If we can discern the shape of things to come in Bartholomew Westley,
this was even more marked in the case of his son John. The first in line to
bear the name of the great evangelist of the eighteenth century was indeed
a worthy representative. In many striking ways his story anticipated that
of his more famous grandson. John Westley was introduced by Nehemiah
Curnock as "a brave, witty, scholarly, simple-minded itinerant evangelist".[8] A portrait of him which has survived reveals his character. Although
he wears clerical dress, he looks more like a soldier than a minister: not

[1] Edmund Calamy, The Nonconformists' Memorial, ed. Samuel Palmer (1775), Vol. I.
p. 442.
  [2] William Beal, The Fathers of the Wesley Family (1833), pp. 26–27.
  [3] Gentleman's Magazine Vol. LV, (1785), p. 487.
  [4] Ibid.
  [5] Frank Baker, "Wesley's Puritan Ancestry," London Quarterly and Holborn Review,
July, 1962, p. 186.
  [6] Calamy, op. cit., Vol. I, p. 429.
  [7] Martin Schmidt, John Wesley: A Theological Biography (E.T. 1962), Vol. I, p. 36.
  [8] The Journal of the Rev. John Wesley A.M.., ed. Nehemiah Curnock (1909), (henceforward referred to as Journal), Vol. I, p. 42. Introduction.

because he appears aggressive, but by reason of a certain unyielding determination in his aspect and bearing.[1] He was a protégé of John Owen, the
Puritan divine, who was Vice-Chancellor of Oxford University. Calamy
recorded that Owen had "a great kindness" towards John Westley when
he was at New Inn Hall, where he studied oriental languages as well as
theology.[2] Amongst his contemporaries were Thomas Goodwin, Stephen
Charnock, John Howe, Philip Henry, and Joseph Alleine—all to become
shining lights in the Puritan galaxy.

On leaving the University he was associated for a time with John Janeway's "particular church" at Melcombe Regis, whilst preaching in the
district and acting as port chaplain. He became an itinerant evangelist and
saw many conversions. In 1658 he was approved by Cromwell's Triers as
minister of the parish church at Winterbourne Whitchurch, although he
was not episcopally ordained, and is even said to have preached against
episcopacy. He married the daughter of John White, one of the two
assessors at the Westminster Assembly, and a thorn in the flesh to Archbishop Laud because of his protest against Arminian doctrine and undue
ceremonialism.[3]

In 1661 charges were brought against him on the ground of his refusal
to use the liturgy of the Prayer Book. As a result, he was put into prison
and in the following year removed from his cure. Calamy recorded an
interview which John Westley had with Gilbert Ironside, Bishop of
Bristol. It was copied from Westley's own diary, which unfortunately has
been lost. John Wesley came across it in 1765, and felt it to be of such
importance that he transcribed it in full in his *Journal*.[4] It so remarkably
anticipated the position of the eighteenth-century evangelist that we must
examine it with some care.

Not unnaturally, the first question put by the Bishop concerned the
authenticity of Westley's ordination, if indeed he claimed to be ordained.
This was neatly turned as Westley simply replied that he had been sent to
preach the gospel. "By whom were you sent?" pressed the Bishop. "By a
church of Jesus Christ," was the answer. "What church is that?" "The
church of Christ at Melcombe." This was Janeway's congregation. The
Bishop dismissed it as "factious and heretical." But Westley stoutly resisted the imputation. "In what manner did the church you spake of send
you to preach? At this rate everybody might preach," the Bishop continued. "Not every one," responded Westley. "Everybody has not
preaching gifts and preaching graces. Besides, that is not all I have to offer
to your lordship to justify my preaching."

[1] Schmidt, *op. cit.*, Vol. I, p. 36.

[2] Calamy, *op. cit.*, Vol. I, p. 428.

[3] *The Letters of the Rev. John Wesley A.M.*, ed. John Telford (1931), (henceforward
referred to as *Letters*), Vol. V, p. 76. To Charles Wesley, 15th January, 1768.

[4] *Journal*, Vol. V, pp. 119–124. 25th May, 1765. Cf. Calamy, *op. cit.*, Vol. I, pp.
478 ff.

What follows is so vital that we will quote it verbatim. W. and B., of course, are abbreviations for Westley and the Bishop. "B. If you preach, it must be according to order: the order of the Church of England upon ordination. W. What does your lordship mean by ordination? B. Do you not know what I mean? W. If you mean that sending spoken of in Romans Ten, I had it. B. I mean that. What mission had you? W. I had a mission from God and man. B. You must have it according to law, and the order of the Church of England. . . . W. I am not satisfied in conscience as touching the ordination you speak of. B. What reason have you that you will not be thus ordained? W. I am not called to office, and therefore cannot be ordained. B. Why have you preached then all this while? W. I was called to the work of the ministry, though not the office. There is, as we may believe, *vocatio ad opus, et ad munus* (a call to the work, and a call to the office). B. Why may you not have the office of the ministry? W. May it please your Lordship, because they are not a people who are fit subjects for me to exercise office work amongst them. B. You mean a gathered church: but we must have no gathered churches in England, and you will see it so; for there must be a unity without divisions among us, and there can be no unity without uniformity."[1] It will be realized that the raising of such basic issues not only antedated the eighteenth century, but also our own ecumenical times.

Westley's strongest defence of his ministry lay in his appeal to its fruits amongst his converts. This was precisely the line taken by his grandson later. "W. It pleased God to seal my labour with success, in the apparent conversion of many souls. B. Yea, that is, it may be, to your way. W. Yea, to the power of godliness, from ignorance and profaneness. If it please your lordship to lay down any evidence of godliness agreeing with Scripture, and that are not found in those persons intended, I am content to be discharged the ministry. I will stand or fall on the issue thereof. B. You talk of the power of godliness, such as you fancy. W. Yea, to the reality of religion. Let us appeal to any common-place book for evidence of graces, and they are found in and upon them. B. How many are there of them? W. I number not the people. B. Where are they? W. Wherever I have been called to preach: at Radpole, Melcombe, Turnwood, Whitchurch, and at sea. I shall add another ingredient of my mission: When the church saw the presence of God going along with me, they did, by fasting and prayer, in a day set apart for that end, seek an abundant blessing on my endeavours. B. A particular church? W. Yes, my lord. I am not ashamed to own myself a member of one. B. Why, you may mistake the apostles' intent. They went about to convert heathens; you have no warrant for your particular churches. W. We have a plain, full, and sufficient rule for gospel worship, in the New Testament, recorded in the Acts of the Apostles, and in the Epistles."[2] This, however, the Bishop flatly

[1] *Journal*, Vol. V, pp. 121-122. 25th May, 1765.   [2] *Ibid.*, p. 123.

denied. He was ready to accept the precepts of the apostles as binding, but not their practice. Westley insisted on both.

The interview closed cordially. It is clear that though Dr. Ironside, as an episcopalian, could hardly have been expected to have agreed with John Westley's Puritan arguments, he nevertheless respected the integrity and also the intellectual acumen of this strange young evangelist. Here is how the conversation wound up. "B. Well, then, you will justify your preaching, will you, without ordination according to law? W. All these things, laid together, are satisfactory to me, for my procedure therein. B. They are not enough. W. There has been more written in proof of preaching of gifted persons, with such approbation, than has been answered yet by anyone. B. Have you anything more to say to me, Mr. Westley? W. Nothing; your lordship sent for me. B. I am glad to hear this from your mouth; you will stand to your principles, you say? W. I intend it, through the grace of God; and to be faithful to the King's Majesty, however you deal with me. B. I will not meddle with you. W. Farewell to you, sir. B. Farewell, good Mr. Westley."[1] Of course, if this was Westley's conviction, nothing that the Bishop might personally feel about him could prevent the law taking its course, as it did.

Professor Schmidt comments on the bearing of all this on the dilemma in which the eighteenth-century Wesley found himself when, though episcopally ordained, he exercised an itinerant ministry which involved unauthorized intrusion into other men's parishes, and employed as his assistants laymen who nevertheless had a clear call to preach. "The proud consciousness of having been sent, which yet unreservedly subjects personal activity to the judgement of the Bible, the determination to conform to primitive Christianity, the stress on visible results as the fruit and conversion as a definite aim—all this comes out again in his grandson."[2] Henceforward, John Westley was to lead the life of "a most spirituous nonconformist," as the eccentric antiquarian Mark Noble quaintly designated him.[3]

He was hunted from place to place—"oft disturbed, and several times apprehended, and four times imprisoned," as Calamy reported.[4] "He was in many straits and difficulties, but wonderfully supported and comforted, and many times very seasonably and surprisingly relieved and delivered."[5] He was only thirty-four when he died, a little before his father.[6] "The

[1] *Ibid.*, p. 124.

[2] Schmidt, *op. cit.*, Vol. I, p. 38

[3] *Reliquary*, Vol. VIII, (1867–1888), p. 188. Cf. *Proceedings of the Wesley Historical Society* (henceforward referred to as *Proc. W.H.S.*), Vol. XXVI, p. 103.

[4] Calamy, *op. cit.*, Vol. I, p. 450.

[5] *Ibid.*

[6] A. G. Matthews, *Calamy Revised* (1934), p. 13. Luke Tyerman gave the date as 1678 and his age as thirty-three or thirty-four, cf. *The Life and Times of the Rev.*

founder of Methodism was a true successor of this devoted man," declared Telford. "His itinerant ministry, his care for the fisher folk, his unflinching loyalty to his principles, his success in winning souls, and his simple godly life were all reproduced in his illustrious grandson."[1]

John Wesley's grandfather on his mother's side was one of the most distinguished of the Puritan nonconformists. Indeed, Curnock hailed him as their primate.[2] Dr. Samuel Annesley was ejected from St. Giles, Cripplegate, London, where Oliver Cromwell had been married to Elizabeth Bourchier, and by whose son Richard he had been presented.[3] The only son of a wealthy landowner, he had graduated with honours from Queen's College, Oxford and in 1648 was awarded the Doctor of Laws degree. From Calamy we learn that "he was so early under religious impressions that he declared he knew not the time when he was not converted."[4] He was ordained by presbyters in 1644 and, after a period as a naval chaplain, served as Rector of Cliffe, near Gravesend. In 1652 he was appointed to the church of St. John the Evangelist in Friday Street, and in 1658 to St. Giles. Both John Foxe and John Milton lie buried in this latter historic church. He published a volume of sermons, which Schmidt tells us "occupy an important place in the literature on the Puritan theology of conscience and the conscience-guided life."[5] His grandson was to use one of these as the basis for a discourse of his own.[6]

After his ejection in 1662, Dr. Annesley continued to fulfil his calling as a preacher, and was eventually able, with others, to found a meeting house at Little St. Helen's, Bishopsgate Street which became the focus of London nonconformity. For more than thirty years "he ruled as a patriarch

Samuel Wesley (1866), pp. 32, 50. George J. Stevenson repeated the error and criticized Calamy for an inaccuracy of which he was not guilty, cf. *Memorials of the Wesley Family* (1876), p. 33. A hitherto unpublished letter of Samuel Wesley, written from South Ormsby on 22nd August, 1692, recently reproduced by Miss H. A. Beecham, has confirmed the fact that John Westley died not long before his father, who was buried on 15th February, 1671. Samuel Wesley wrote this concerning John Westley: "He was indeed imprisoned, being taken in the year 70 preaching at a meeting, and by lying in the cold earth, whence he was not permitted to remove, as our people then told the story, he contracted a sickness, which in ten days cost him his life" (H. A. Beecham, "Samuel Wesley Senior: New Biographical Evidence," *Renaissance and Modern Studies*, Vol. VII (1963), p. 85).

[1] John Telford, *The Life of John Wesley* (1899), p. 6.
[2] *Journal*, Vol. V, p. 2. Notes.   [3] Matthews, *op. cit.*, p. 13.
[4] Calamy, *op. cit.*, Vol. I, pp. 104–105.
[5] Schmidt, *op. cit.*, Vol. I, p. 42. Samuel Annesley, *The Morning Exercises at Cripplegate, St. Giles in the Fields, and in Southwark*, ed. James Nichols, 6 Vols. (1844). It was Vol. I, first published in 1671 (delivered in 1662), to which Schmidt referred. Not all the sermons contained in it were by Dr. Annesley himself. John Wesley published many extracts from his grandfather's sermons in his *Christian Library*.
[6] Wesley's Sermon CV, On Conscience, based on the first sermon in *The Morning Exercises at Cripplegate*, and found in *The Works of the Rev. John Wesley A.M.*, 3rd Edition, ed. Thomas Jackson (1829–31) (henceforward referred to as *Works*), Vol. VII, pp. 186–194.

of Dissent in the capital," as Schmidt puts it, and it was he who dared to undertake the first public ordination of nonconformist ministers since the Great Ejectment.[1] There is a delightful picture of this venerable man conducting the sacrament of the Lord's Supper at Little St. Helen's, painted for us by Samuel Sewall, the New England judge. He went from pew to pew, as he administered the elements, "dropping pertinent expressions."[2] What he said as he gave the cup to Sewall remained with him for the rest of his life: "Stick at nothing for Christ." That was the motto of Annesley's life, as it was to be of John Wesley's.

Dr. Annesley married the daughter of another John White—a distinguished Puritan lawyer who was M.P. for Southwark. In the Long Parliament he was appointed as chairman of the "committee for scandalous ministers," which was responsible for removing those clergy whose lives were unworthy of their vocation.[3] He was one of the lay assessors at the Westminster Assembly. Thus both John Wesley's great-grandfathers on the maternal side were present at that memorable gathering.

One of the most famous of the Wesley portraits is that by the academician, John Michael Williams. When Dr. Alexander Maclaren stood before it, he exclaimed, "Now I have seen the man who moved England."[4] "No one can look at Williams' painting," claimed Dr. Simon, "without seeing Wesley's Puritan ancestors looking out from the canvas."[5] The bibliographer, Richard Green, was correct in describing Wesley's face in this portrait as being "of the Miltonic type."[6] Indeed, unnamed engravings of Wesley and Milton have sometimes been confused. Dean Hutton rightly referred to Wesley's hereditary determination, and even "conscientious obstinacy," which made him run rather against than with the current.[7] Some would conclude, he added, that Wesley "had nonconformity in his blood."[8]

On the other hand, we must take equal cognizance of the fact that both his parents were convinced Anglicans. However impressive may be Wesley's Puritan inheritance, it remains the case that his immediate legacy was one of devotion to the Church of England. It is, indeed, in this combination of influences that the clue to Wesley is to be discovered. In his make-up, Anglican and Puritan were fused—as Cadman put it, "the order and dignity of the one, the fearless initiative and asceticism of the other."[9] These elements were also integrated in the personalities of

[1] Schmidt, op. cit., Vol. I, p. 43.
[2] Horton Davies, The Worship of the English Puritans (1948), p. 210.
[3] Tyerman, Samuel Wesley, p. 123.
[4] A New History of Methodism, ed. W. J. Townsend, H. B. Workman, G. Eayrs (1910), Vol. I, p. 206.
[5] John S. Simon, The Revival of Religion in the Eighteenth Century (n.d.), p. 167.
[6] Proc. W. H. S., Vol. IV, p. 122.
[7] William Holden Hutton, John Wesley (1927), p. 5.   [8] Ibid.
[9] S. Parkes Cadman, Three Religious Leaders of Oxford (1916), p. 178.

Wesley's parents, for with all their firm attachment to the Established Church, they were no more able to sever themselves entirely from the past than their son. The roof of Epworth Rectory, where John was born on 17th June, 1703, covered two strands of English Christian tradition. As A. W. Harrison expressed it, "the Epworth parsonage had a High Church atmosphere, yet it was essentially a Puritan home."[1]

John Wesley's father, Samuel, was intended for the Dissenting ministry. He was born in the ominous year 1662, and had not reached his eighth birthday when the family was bereaved of its earthly head. His childhood reflected the deprivations endured by those who suffered for conscience's sake. Until he was fourteen he went to the free school in Dorchester, where his teacher was Henry Dolling who had made a name for himself as the translator into Latin of a Caroline manual of devotion, *The Whole Duty of Man*.[2] Through the generosity of nonconformist benefactors, Samuel Wesley was sent to a Dissenting academy in Stepney, where Edward Veal, an Oxford man, was principal. Later he moved to a similar college at Stoke Newington under Charles Morton, who eventually became Vice-President of Harvard University.[3] One of his fellow-students was Daniel Defoe, author of *Robinson Crusoe*.[4] It appeared that Samuel was all set for a vocation as a minister in the nonconformist churches.

Then came a quite unpredictable turn of events. As part of his educational exercises, he was required to refute an Anglican diatribe against the Dissenters. As he weighed the evidence, he was driven to the conclusion that the objections were valid. It was typical of the man he eventually became that as a youth he should react impetuously to this discovery. He decided to make a clean break with family tradition. With him it must be either one thing or the other. He now espoused the cause of episcopacy as earnestly as he had formerly championed Dissent. Henceforward the Church of England had no more whole-hearted protagonist than Samuel Wesley. The university was thus open to him, and he tramped off to Oxford with just enough in his pocket to pay the entrance fee.[5] He worked his way through his classes by earning money from tuition and preparing exercises for others.[6] Thus he equipped himself for orders. As Professor Schmidt makes clear, "the unusual course his life had taken explains the two features which subsequently characterized his outlook. On the one hand he always owed a great deal to the Puritan emphasis upon the importance of repentance, conversion and rebirth; on the other hand

---

[1] Archibald W. Harrison, *Arminianism* (1937), p. 137.

[2] *The Whole Duty of Man* was published in 1659. Lady Dorothy Pakington, wife of a prominent royalist, was for long credited with the authorship, but the tendency of more recent literary criticism has been to attribute it to Richard Allestree, provost of Eton from 1665.

[3] Schmidt, *op. cit.*, Vol. I, p. 40.

[4] *Ibid.*   [5] *Ibid.*   [6] *Ibid.*

he had the historical interest of the Enlightenment."[1] He was ordained deacon on 7th August, 1689 and priest on 24th February, 1690.[2]

In speaking of Samuel Wesley as a High Churchman it is important to define our terms. Although the designations Low Church and High Church had already appeared, they had not yet acquired the connotation with which we are today familiar. We must beware of interpreting early altitudinarianism in terms of nineteenth-century tractarian predilections, or even of developing theories in the later eighteenth century. Samuel Wesley's High Churchmanship was more political and ecclesiastical than doctrinal and sacerdotal.[3] He was vigorously opposed to Dissent (so strong was his reaction against his upbringing) and warmly upheld the crown, although he found no difficulty in transferring his allegiance to the house of Orange. But in his theological convictions he remained "a true friend to the Protestant cause," as Moore put it, and he did not jettison the Reformed principles which he had imbibed in his youth.[4] His abiding interest in biblical exegesis was derived from his Puritan training.

In a letter to "John Smith" in 1748, John Wesley referred to his father's views.[5] He was acquainted "with the faith of the gospel, of the primitive Christians, and of our first Reformers; the same which, by the grace of God, I preach, which is just as new as Christianity."[6] It is significant that John Wesley included his father in the line of those in the family before him who preached the genuine gospel.[7] On his deathbed, Samuel confided to John: "The inward witness, son, the inward witness; that is the proof, the strongest proof of Christianity."[8] Those words harked back to a typical Puritan emphasis, and also looked forward to John Wesley's teaching on assurance.

In many ways Susanna Wesley was the dominant personality in the Epworth household. Samuel had married her in 1688, and she brought with her a unique endowment. As the daughter of Dr. Annesley, she inherited a rich tradition. "The Annesley home was an outstanding example of a Puritan household," observes Dr. Robert C. Monk, "where demanding educational standards accompanied disciplined devotional and moral

---

[1] *Ibid.*

[2] The dates throughout are cited New Style. In actual fact, before the Calendar Act (1750) came into force in September, 1752, the legal year was reckoned from 25th March (known as Old Style). Without this explanation, Schmidt's statement that Samuel Wesley "was ordained deacon on 7th August and priest on 24th February, 1689" would be mystifying to the uninitiate (Schmidt, *op. cit.*, Vol. I, p. 41).

[3] *A New History of Methodism*, Vol. I, p. 167. Cf. *Letters*, Vol. VI, p. 161.

[4] Henry Moore, *The Life of John Wesley* (1824), Vol. I, p. 41.

[5] *Letters*, Vol. III, p. 134. 22nd March, 1748. "John Smith" is thought to have concealed the identity of Thomas Secker, Bishop of Oxford, and later Archbishop of Canterbury.

[6] *Ibid.*

[7] *Letters*, Vol. V, p. 76. To "Charles Wesley." 15th January, 1768.

[8] *Letters*, Vol. II, p. 135. To "John Smith." 2nd March, 1748.

teaching. In addition, since this was a centre of nonconformity, the children were exposed to intense theological discussion."[1] In the early years of his ministry, John Wesley still turned to his mother for advice on controverted points of doctrine. But, like her husband, Susanna was to turn from the path of Dissent and find her home in the Anglican fold. This was a decision she reached at the ripe age of thirteen, and she never went back on it.

Yet it would be a mistake to think that she forgot her nonconformist background. According to Rupert Davies, the Dissenting principles she had ostensibly renounced "never ceased to flow in her blood."[2] The distinctive features both of her personal devotions and of the instruction she gave to her children were predominantly Puritan. Although expressed within the framework of Anglicanism, her emphases were largely those which she had carried over from nonconformity. She read widely in both the Anglican and Roman divines, but she still found food for her soul in the Puritan classics. "Her spiritual life reflects at many points the impress of her Puritan upbringing," writes Dr. John A. Newton. "Her carefully ordered timetable, her regular times set apart for meditation and self-examination before God, her keeping of a spiritual journal or day-book, her observance of the strict Puritan Sabbath—these were all part of her 'method' of life, to use the Puritan key-word which was current long before John Wesley began his work."[3] It is not too much to say, therefore, with Newton, that Wesley "absorbed Puritan influences with his mother's milk."[4]

The effect of this mingled Anglican and Puritan inheritance on John Wesley was marked. He remained a Church of England man to his dying day, with a strong sense of discipline and a desire to bring about reform from within. He loved the liturgy and was persuaded that the articles and homilies enshrined the essentials of the evangelical faith. Yet as he pursued his task of mission, we find him adopting expedients more in keeping with the spirit of his nonconformist ancestors. His overriding concern was for the good of souls, and where existing church order stood in his way, he did not hesitate to set it aside. The rebel under the skin would keep bursting through.

[1] Robert C. Monk, *John Wesley: His Puritan Heritage* (1966), p. 21.

[2] Rupert E. Davies, *Methodism* (1963), p. 44. She "never lost her Puritanism even after she became an Anglican" (John A. Newton, *Methodism and the Puritans* (1964), p. 2).

[3] Newton, *op. cit.*, p. 5.

[4] *Ibid.*, p. 7.

CHAPTER II

TAKEN OUT OF THE FLAMES

"AT ABOUT eleven o'clock it came into my mind that this was the very day and hour in which forty years ago I was *taken out of the flames*. I stopped and gave a short account of that wonderful providence. The voice of praise and thanksgiving went up on high and great was our rejoicing before the Lord." *Journal* 3: 453-454.

THE NAME OF HENRY PERLEE PARKER IS FORGOTTEN, BUT A painting of his is familiar to many who have no interest in art. For it was he who depicted on canvas the scene at Epworth Rectory on 9th February, 1709, when the boy Wesley was rescued from a raging fire. Reproductions of that original by Parker are scattered all over the land, and beyond, in innumerable vestries and halls. Those who perhaps know little else about John Wesley would have some vague recollection that he was thus snatched from death as the flames closed in on him. It was a dramatic event indeed: the old building with its timbers well alight, the scorched escape of the Rector's considerable family, the face of John peering through the curtains, the resourceful villager who ran to the window and bade another climb on his shoulders to reach the lad seconds before the roof crashed in, and Samuel Wesley then inviting all to pray—"Come, neighbours, let us kneel down. Let us give thanks to God. He has given me all my eight children. Let the house go. I am rich enough."[1]

Wesley was not yet six years old when this happened, and it is not surprising that at such an impressionable age it stamped itself on his memory. It became a sign of God's hand upon him. Increasingly he realized that he had been delivered for a purpose. He referred to himself in the words of Scripture as "a brand plucked out of the fire" (Zechariah 3: 2).[2] Each succeeding year he observed the anniversary of that remarkable night. He confessed that it was "the strongest impression I had till I was twenty-three or twenty-four years old."[3] After his evangelical conversion, however, Wesley recognized himself as a brand plucked from the burning in a spiritual sense also. Henceforward he interpreted the rescue at Epworth as

[1] *Arminian Magazine*, Vol. I (1778), pp. 31-32. Susanna Wesley's account, with a postscript by John Wesley, is on pp. 32-33.
[2] Cf. also Amos 4: 11—"a firebrand plucked out of the burning." As J. E. Rattenbury observed, the words "ring out like a Greek chorus in the drama of his life" (*Wesley's Legacy to the World* (1928), p. 29).
[3] *Arminian Magazine*, Vol. VIII (1785), p. 152.

having predicted his salvation, in readiness for the mission God gave him. When he sat for his portrait by George Vertue, the background was a house in flames, with the words beneath, "Is not this a brand plucked out of the fire?"[1]

In November 1753, Wesley was so ill that he thought he was about to die. In order "to prevent vile panegyric" he composed his own epitaph.[2] It began: "Here lieth the Body of John Wesley, a brand plucked from the burning."[3] This was clearly how he wished to be known. In his *Journal*, Charles Wesley included a revealing emendation: "a brand, not once only, plucked out of the fire."[4] That was an unmistakable allusion to his conversion, and confirmed what John himself had already suggested, namely that his experience in Aldersgate Street on the 24th May, 1738, when his heart was so strangely warmed, was the spiritual counterpart of his deliverance from the fire in 1709.[5] But the imagery of burning not only expressed his own awareness of redemption from sin: it also typified the soul-saving mission to which he was divinely called. "His theology translated itself into terms of that night scene," explained W. H. Fitchett. "The burning house was the symbol of a perishing world. Each human soul, in Wesley's thought, was represented by that fire-girt child, with the flames of sin, and of that divine and eternal anger which unrepenting sin kindles, closing round it. He who had been plucked from the burning house at midnight must pluck men from the flames of a more dreadful fire. That remembered peril coloured Wesley's imagination to his dying day."[6] This was the first step in the making of an evangelist.

Wesley was imbued, even in early years, with a deep sense of vocation. As Rattenbury put it, "he was from childhood a man of destiny."[7] He knew that he had a special work to do. He did not discover what it was until after his conversion. For thirty years, then, he was in quest of a commission. It was by a hard way that he eventually arrived at his goal, but he never gave up the search. Until 1738, Wesley was an evangelist in embryo, struggling to be born through a prolonged period of gestation. In this and subsequent chapters we shall be tracing the course of these preparatory years, and picking out the salient features in his spiritual pilgrimage. We do not propose to fill in all the biographical details, for that is not our aim, but will confine ourselves to those factors which contributed to the fashioning of a missioner.

In this "era of preliminary discipline," as Dr. Bett described it, we can-

---

[1] Moore, *op. cit.*, Vol. I, p. 115.
[2] *Journal*, Vol. IV, p. 90. 26th November, 1753.
[3] *Ibid.*
[4] *The Journal of the Rev. Charles Wesley M.A.*, ed. Thomas Jackson (1849), Vol. II, p. 97.
[5] *Journal*, Vol. I, pp. 475-476. 24th May, 1738.
[6] W. H. Fitchett, *Wesley and His Century* (1906), p. 33.
[7] Rattenbury, *op. cit.*, p. 29.

not overlook the impact of Wesley's home.[1] Epworth rectory has been rightly epitomized as the cradle of Methodism. "It is no exaggeration to say of almost every later development of Wesley's character and opinions," declared James Laver, "that the seed can be found in the atmosphere of Epworth rectory and in the example of his mother."[2] It was after the fire in 1709 that Susanna determined to accord special attention to the training of John. "I do intend to be more particularly careful of the soul of this child, that Thou hast so mercifully provided for, than ever I have been," she wrote in her common-place book, "that I may do my endeavour to instil into his mind the principles of Thy true religion and virtue. Lord, give me grace to do it sincerely and prudently, and bless my attempts with good success."[3] Susanna's course of instruction was so thorough, and John was such an apt pupil, that Samuel admitted him to Holy Communion at the age of only eight.[4] We have evidence of the kind of syllabus Susanna followed in the manuscript of a *Religious Conference* which she wrote, in the form of a dialogue between a mother and her daughter.[5] The daughter was Emily, but no doubt each of the children was similarly instructed. Another conversation of Susanna's on the same plan was published by Dr. Adam Clarke.[6]

It may well have been that his mother's weekly talks with the children convinced John that the opportunity for fellowship is essential to the Christian, and thus led indirectly to the formation of the Holy Club at Oxford and, later, of the class meeting in Methodism. The gatherings she held at the rectory (begun whilst Samuel was attending Convocation in 1712) may equally have brought to John's notice the value of such groups to supplement the normal services of the Church, and thus have paved the way for the founding of his societies. In the absence of the Rector, there was no afternoon service, and the curate was a dull, unevangelical preacher whose monotonous theme was the duty of paying debts. In these circumstances, Mrs. Wesley was led to hold an informal meeting in her kitchen on Sunday evenings, primarily for her family and the servants. But soon others begged to come, and over two hundred people were crammed into the room.[7] Young John, now approaching the age of nine, and mature beyond his years, must have taken all this in. Little did he

[1] Henry Bett, *The Spirit of Methodism* (1937), p. 11.
[2] James Laver, *Wesley* (1938), p. 22.
[3] Moore, *op. cit.*, Vol. I, p. 116. The common-place book was a feature of Puritan devotion.
[4] Joseph Benson, *An Apology for the People Called Methodists* (1801), p. 1.
[5] MS at Wesley College, Headingley, Leeds. Cf. *Proc. W.H.S.*, Vol. III, p. 6.
[6] Clarke, *op. cit.*, Vol. II, pp. 38–72.
[7] Eliza Clarke, *Susanna Wesley* (1886), p. 105. Samuel Wesley founded a religious society at Epworth in 1701, on the lines of those described by Josiah Woodward in *An Account of the Rise and Progress of the Religious Societies in the City of London* (1798). Cf. *Proc. W.H.S.*, Vol. XXXV, pp. 15–17.

suspect, however, that such a scene was to be repeated scores of times in
his own itinerant ministry. After inserting an account of his mother's
funeral in his *Journal* for 1st August, 1742, John Wesley added a transcript
of a letter from Susanna to her husband in which she described these
kitchen meetings. Wesley could not refrain from commenting on the fact
that "even she (as well as her father, grandfather, her husband, and her
three sons) had been, in her measure and degree, a preacher of righteousness."[1]

Other lessons were also learned at Epworth which were assimilated by
the evangelist to be. There was always a keen interest in the incipient
missionary enterprise of the early eighteenth century. Samuel had offered
himself for work in the East Indies, perhaps for a limited period, but nothing came of it.[2] Ziegenbalg and Plützschau had written an account of
their work in Tranquebar, a region in south India, and this had been read
in its English translation by Susanna to her kitchen congregation.[3] It may
have been that what Wesley saw for himself of his father's inability to
make any real impression on his rural flock, led him to doubt the value of
the parochial system. If he was to reach the nation with the gospel, as he
was eventually called to do, traditional methods would not suffice. And,
at a severely practical level, the stringencies of parsonage life inured him to
poverty and prepared him for that hardness which he would have to endure as a good soldier of Jesus Christ. As Dr. V. H. H. Green reminds us,
"John Wesley was conditioned early to a spartan existence."[4] Yet in it all,
he saw the hand of God, and on revisiting Epworth in 1779 he confirmed
the truth of Ovid's "trite remark"—

> Nescio qua natale solum dulcedine cunctos
> Ducit, et immemores non sinet esse sui!
>
> (The natal soil, to all how strangely sweet!
> The place where first he breathed, who can forget!)[5]

Wesley's schooldays at Charterhouse need not detain us long. His
education in abstinence was evidently continued, for he revealed later:
"From ten to fourteen I had little but bread to eat, and not great plenty at
that. I believe this was so far from hurting me that it laid the foundation
of lasting health."[6] The shortage was due to the bullying of the older
boys, who commandeered the food intended for the younger. He obeyed
his father's advice to run three times round the school garden each morn-

[1] *Journal*, Vol. III, p. 32. Her grandfather was John White, the Puritan lawyer (see
above, p. 25). Samuel Wesley junior is included amongst the three sons of whom he
was the eldest.
[2] *Proc. W.H.S.*, Vol. XI, p. 3.
[3] *Journal*, Vol. III, p. 33. 1st August, 1742. Cf. Schmidt, *op. cit.*, Vol. I, p. 62, n. 4.
[4] Vivian H. H. Green, *The Young Mr. Wesley* (1961), p. 52.
[5] *Journal*, Vol. VI, p. 243. 8th July, 1779. Ovid, *Epistolae ex Ponto*, i. 3. 35, 36.
[6] *Journal*, Vol. V, p. 373. 28th June, 1770.

ing, and this too no doubt contributed to his future fitness, which was to prove so invaluable in his strenuous evangelistic campaigns.

It does not appear, on the other hand, that Charterhouse made any significant contribution to Wesley's spiritual growth. In fact, his removal from the salutary discipline of Epworth may have caused a temporary decline, although Tyerman went much too far when he claimed that Wesley "entered the Charterhouse a saint, and left it a sinner."[1] We may agree with V. H. H. Green that this latter represented "absurd special pleading."[2] Wesley's own account gave a fair indication of his state. "The next six or seven years were spent at school, where outward restraints being removed, I was much more negligent than before, even of outward duties, and almost continually guilty of outward sins, which I knew to be such, though they were not scandalous in the eye of the world. However, I still read the Scriptures, and said my prayers morning and evening. And what I now hoped to be saved by, was (1) not being so bad as other people; (2) having still a kindness for religion; and (3) reading the Bible, going to church, and saying my prayers."[3] There was one interesting link with Charterhouse in later years, apart from his frequent visits on Founder's Day and at other times.[4] In the crucial months prior to his Aldersgate Street heart-warming, he would often seek quietness there in the room of Jonathan Agutter, a Poor Brother, who was also a member of the Fetter Lane Religious Society.[5]

At the age of seventeen, Wesley went up to Oxford and matriculated from Christ Church College. We must defer until the next chapter the story of his spiritual quest, which was greatly intensified during the latter part of his residence, and content ourselves with sketching the course of his life as it moved in the direction of his ultimate vocation. Wesley was a good student, who excelled particularly in debate. His skill in logic, as it was displayed both in the oral academic exercises of the University, and in countless private discussions, was evident to all. This was no mean factor in his training as an evangelist. Within twenty years he was to be capitalizing his gains in the interest of the gospel, as he presented the case for Christianity to the masses of the people. He was often called upon to defend himself, and did so with unusual effectiveness, both verbally and in print. For this he was being prepared, albeit unconsciously, in what might otherwise have been regarded as barren years before he had even contemplated seeking orders.

We have a description of Wesley as he was in 1724 from the pen of Samuel Badcock. "He appeared the very sensible and acute collegian,

[1] Tyerman, *Life of John Wesley*, Vol. I, p. 22.

[2] V. H. H. Green, *The Young Mr. Wesley*, p. 55, n. 5. Cf. *Letters*, Vol. III, pp. 31, 302.

[3] *Journal*, Vol. I, pp. 465–466. 24th May, 1738.

[4] *Proc. W.H.S.*, Vol. XXVII, p. 56.

[5] *Ibid.*, p. 83.

B

baffling every man by the subtleties of logic, and laughing at them for
being so easily routed; a young fellow of the finest classical taste, of the
most liberal and manly sentiments."[1] Later, he was moderator of classes at
Lincoln College, and had to listen to the theses of his pupils. "I could not
avoid acquiring hereby some degree of expertness in arguing," he acknowledged many years after; "and especially in discerning and pointing out
well-covered and plausible fallacies. I have since found abundant reason to
praise God for giving me this honest art. By this, when men have hedged
me in by what they called demonstrations, I have been many times able to
dash them in pieces; in spite of all its covers, to touch the very point where
the fallacy lay; and it flew open in a moment."[2] This was an invaluable
asset, for apologetics has its essential place in biblical evangelism. Like
Paul, the missionary preacher seeks to reason from the Scriptures.

The foundation for Wesley's expository preaching may well have been
laid by his first tutor at Christ Church, George Wigan. According to
Schmidt, he was "a biblical linguist after the style of the Enlightenment,
who carried a stage farther the research into the Septuagint undertaken by
the notable German scholar, Johann Ernst Grabe (1666–1711), who had
himself gone to Oxford."[3] It is tempting to speculate as to whether it was
partly from Dr. Wigan that Wesley derived the meticulous care in the
treatment of the scriptural text which usually marked his sermons and,
even more explicitly, his *Notes* on both the Old and New Testaments.
Late in 1723 Wigan retired to a country parish, in order to concentrate on
his exegetical studies.[4] He lived there for over fifty years. Wesley's next
tutor was Henry Sherman, with whom he was more intimate, but who
does not appear to have influenced him in any special way.[5] Another
friend was Jonathan Colley, who was Chantor, or precentor, of Christ
Church. Thomas Hearne, the antiquary, dismissed him as "an apocalypti-
cal man, being much given to books upon the Revelation, reading besides
Mede, other things that he meets with upon that subject."[6] But this may
merely have reflected cultured prejudice against eschatological investigation, and Wesley's own convictions on the End perhaps began to take
shape at this time. Certainly he later read both Joseph Mead and Charles
Daubuz—also recommended by Colley.[7]

[1] *Westminster Magazine*, 1774, p. 180. Badcock was not a contemporary of Wesley,
but got his information from the daughter of Samuel, John's brother.
[2] *Works*, Vol. X, p. 353. *Some Remarks on "A Defence of the Preface to the Edinburgh Edition of Aspasio Vindicated"* (1766).
[3] Schmidt, *op. cit.*, Vol. I, p. 72.
[4] *Letters*, Vol. I, p. 5. To Susanna Wesley, 23rd September, 1723. Philip Bliss,
Reliquiae Hearnianae (1869), Vol. II, pp. 239, 279; Vol. III, pp. 83, 94.
[5] *Letters*, Vol. I, p. 5. To Susanna Wesley, 23rd September, 1723; p. 12, To the
same, 18th December, 1724.
[6] Thomas Hearne, *Collectanea* (1715), Vol. IX, p. 310; cf. V. H. H. Green, *The
Young Mr. Wesley*, p. 62.
[7] Joseph Mead, Mildmay lecturer in Greek at Cambridge, was "a scholar of

Wesley graduated in 1724 as a Bachelor of Arts, and up to the end of this year we can discern few signs of what was to come. He had as yet no thought of ordination, nor had he embarked upon the quest for reality in religion which was to be consummated in his evangelical conversion. As Schmidt has pointed out, "the first years at Oxford were similar in character to the schooldays at Charterhouse: the emphasis was upon formal instruction and education in principles and fundamentals. His tutors evidently confirmed him in the course which he had naturally taken, even to his partiality for poetry."[1] As we have tried to show, some of this acquired aptitude was to assist him in his life-work as an evangelist, but he was not to know that yet.

The year 1725 proved a turning-point. In the diary he now began to keep we read much about his spiritual condition, and we shall be tracing his pilgrimage in the next chapter. In May he discussed a theological problem with his mother for the first time, but by no means the last.[2] This new concern for Christian truth and experience coincided with a growing awareness that he was being called to be a minister of the Church. It is hard to say which preceded the other: apparently they emerged side by side. In January 1725 he went so far as to confide in his parents. Their reactions differed. Samuel counselled caution, so that there might be time to test the vocation, and also to gain some acquaintance with Greek and Hebrew. He wanted to be certain that John's motives were completely free from any admixture of self-interest—a very necessary reassurance in the eighteenth century. John must desire the office for something more than "to eat a piece of bread," like Eli's sons.[3] "The principal spring and motive, to which all the former should be only secondary, must certainly be the glory of God, and the service of the Church in the edification of our neighbour. And woe to him who, with any meaner leading view, attempts so sacred a work."[4]

Susanna was eager to see her prayers answered—for surely she must have asked God that John might become a minister—and saw no need for delay. "I approve the disposition of your mind, and think the sooner you are a deacon the better," she wrote; "because it may be an inducement to greater application in the study of practical divinity, which I humbly conceive is the best study for candidates for orders. Mr. Wesley differs

encyclopaedic knowledge" (*The Oxford Dictionary of the Christian Church*, ed. F. L. Cross (1957), p. 881). Wesley read his collected *Works*, edited by John Worthington. in 1730. In 1734 he read Charles Daubuz, *A Perpetual Commentary on the Revelation of St. John* (1720). Daubuz was Librarian of Queens' College, Cambridge, before seeking orders.

[1] Schmidt, *op. cit.*, Vol. I, p. 72.

[2] *Letters*, Vol. I, p. 15. To Susanna Wesley, 28th May, 1725.

[3] *Arminian Magazine*, Vol. I (1778), p. 29. Letter of Samuel Wesley to his son John, 26th January, 1725.

[4] *Ibid.*

from me, and would engage you, I believe, in critical earning, which, though accidentally of use, is in no wise preferable to the other. I earnestly pray God to avert that great evil from you of engaging in trifling studies to the neglect of such as are absolutely necessary. I dare advise nothing: God Almighty direct and bless you!"[1]

Wesley now began to prepare himself consciously for his ordination. He sought his father's guidance as to the most suitable Bible commentaries. He received a model reply. "You ask me which is the best commentary on the Bible? I answer, The Bible itself. For the several paraphrases and translations of it in the Polyglot, compared with the original, and with one another, are, in my opinion, to an honest, devout, industrious and humble man, infinitely preferable to any comment I ever saw. But Grotius is the best, for the most part, especially on the Old Testament."[2] He evidently followed his father's advice explicitly, for he was actually reading the *Annotationes* of Hugo Grotius, the Dutch exegete, on the very day of his examination for holy orders.[3] The Greek Testament was often in his hands. He persevered with his introduction to Hebrew and was able to read the Old Testament in the original. At the same time he managed to look into some theological works, including the Fathers.[4] Among those books more specifically related to his ordination were to be found George Bull's *Companion to Candidates for Orders* (1714); William Wake's commentary on the catechism, entitled *The Principles of the Christian Religion* (1700), and John Ellis's *Defence of the Thirty-Nine Articles* (1700).[5]

Wesley was ordained deacon in Christ Church Cathedral, Oxford, on 19th September, 1725, by John Potter, who also admitted him as priest on 22nd September, 1728. In a sermon "On Attending the Church Service," preached over fifty years later, Wesley recalled the counsel he had received from this "great and good man" after he had become Archbishop of Canterbury.[6] "If you desire to be extensively useful, do not spend your time and strength in contending for or against such things as are of a disputable nature; but in testifying against open notorious vice, and in promoting real, essential holiness."[7] That was just what Wesley sought to do. When Thomas Hayward, the Bishop's Chaplain, was examining him for priest's orders, he put one question which must often have been in Wesley's mind as he pursued his mission. "Do you know what you are about? You are bidding defiance to all mankind. He that would live a

---

[1] Tyerman, *Life of John Wesley*, Vol. I, p. 32.

[2] *Arminian Magazine*, Vol. I (1778), p. 29.

[3] Hugo Grotius, *Annotationes in Vetus et Novum Testamentum* (1642). He was one of the first to adopt the method of philological criticism.

[4] Cf. V. H. H. Green, *The Young Mr. Wesley*, p. 67.

[5] *Ibid.*, p. 306 (Appendix I). The first English version of Ellis's work appeared in 1700. It was originally published in Latin in 1660.

[6] *Works*, Vol. VII, p. 185. Sermon CIV.

[7] *Ibid.*; cf. *Journal*, Vol. II, p. 143, Diary for 21st February, 1739, and n. 1.

Christian priest ought to know that, whether his hand be against every man or no, he must expect every man's hand should be against him."[1] We can concur with the verdict of Dr. Green: "There is little doubt that his ordination was a landmark in his spiritual development."[2] But of this we shall have more to say in the following chapter.

Shortly after his reception into the diaconate, Wesley preached his first sermon. It was in the small stone-flagged parish church at South Leigh, near Witney. He must have looked up at the clock on the tower, and been impressed with the appropriateness of the words "Ye know not what hour the Lord may come." On the pulpit there is now an inscription commemorating his visit. His text was from Matthew 6: 33—"Seek ye first the kingdom of God and His righteousness, and all these things shall be added unto you." The manuscript has been preserved, and we can read the discourse in Wesley's neat and legible hand. On 16th October, 1771, he wrote in his *Journal*: "I preached at South Lye. Here it was I preached my first sermon, six-and-forty years ago. One man was in my present audience who heard it. Most of the rest are gone to their long home."[3] This was the first of many sermons delivered in the villages around Oxford in the next few years. Amongst those mentioned in Wesley's diary are Binsey, Broadway, Buckland, Combe, Fleet Marston, Pyrton, Shipton, Stanton, Thame and Winchendon.[4] He also preached in several Oxford churches.[5] He either rode, walked, or hired a horse, and went out in all sorts of weather on atrocious roads. Though he himself had no idea of it, he was in training for his evangelistic travels that were to span fifty years of his subsequent life. He was also learning the art of sermon construction. But, as Curnock commented, he did not yet know how really to *preach* what he had written, nor indeed had he found the kernel of his message.[6]

In 1726 Wesley was elected a Fellow of Lincoln College, in succession to John Thorold, who was to prove a friend of the revival in coming years. The relevance of this appointment to his vocation as an evangelist may not be immediately apparent. It was, however, another instance of how his future was being providentially shaped and secured. It was his fellowship, held until his marriage in 1751, which gave him financial security. Not only was he supported during the waiting years, until he was sure of his own position and had received his commission to evangelize; but, even more importantly, in the initial stages of his life-work he was sufficiently independent to be able to launch out regardless of the cost. This may appear to some a mundane aspect of an essentially spiritual

[1] *Works*, Vol. XII, p. 21.
[2] V. H. H. Green, *The Young Mr. Wesley*, p. 68.
[3] *Journal*, Vol. V, p. 432. 16th October, 1771.
[4] V. H. H. Green, *The Young Mr. Wesley*, p. 69.
[5] *Ibid.*
[6] *Journal*, Vol. I, p. 65. Introduction.

enterprise, but it was nevertheless a vital one. When the time came to go out to the nation, Wesley was free to do so in every sense.

It was in this period too that the Holy Club was born. It was Charles Wesley who was responsible for its inauguration, whilst John was away from Oxford serving a curacy at Wroot. But when John returned to become a tutor at Lincoln College, he began to mould it according to his own notions. Originally it had a semi-educational purpose, but this soon gave way to that of concentrated spiritual improvement. It became the channel of Wesley's own quest for faith. Yet it also anticipated the means by which the fruits of evangelism were one day to be conserved. It was not merely a self-contained fellowship group. It looked out as well as in. To devotional exercises was added charitable service amongst the underprivileged. Prisons and workhouses were visited. The sick and the poor were assisted. For the first time Wesley came face to face with the common people. They were to be his constituency throughout his long years of gospel ministry. He was to be the apostle of *hoi polloi*. Through the Holy Club he was introduced to his future clientele.

We have been noting the apparently incidental features of Wesley's career at Oxford which contributed to the making of an evangelist. In themselves they might seem to be of little account; but seen together, in the light of later events, they assume a real significance as evidence of a divine hand. But it was in Wesley's spiritual saga that this was most plainly demonstrated. We must turn to it next.

CHAPTER III

CONTINUED ENDEAVOUR

"BY MY *continued endeavour* to keep His whole law, inward and outward, to the utmost of my power, I was persuaded that I should be accepted of Him, and that I was even then in a state of salvation." *Journal* 1: 467.

I T WAS NOT UNTIL THE YEAR 1725 THAT JOHN WESLEY BEGAN TO show signs of genuine earnestness in his attitude to the Christian faith. Until then he had, as it were, gone through the motions, as he had been so ably taught at Epworth. As a schoolboy and in his undergraduate days at the University he had not made much advance towards a more personal commitment. But as he approached his ordination, he grew increasingly serious in the search for spiritual reality. This was a quest which was to occupy fully thirteen years. There were to be many twists and turns in his path, and even ups and downs, for this was no unimpeded pilgrim's progress. But at length he was brought to a vital experience of saving faith. Without this, he could never have tackled the task of mission. Before Wesley was able to offer Christ to others, he had to encounter the Master himself.

Wesley reviewed the course of his Christian life on more than one occasion. The most succinct and significant account, however, is to be found in his *Journal*. It was placed immediately before the narrative of his evangelical conversion, which in itself is an indication of how determinative he believed the latter to have been. He paid tribute to the influence of his home, where he was "strictly educated and carefully taught."[1] He had fixed, however, only on the external obligations demanded of a Christian, and had failed to grasp the heart of the matter. This was undoubtedly impressed upon him, but he did not take it in. That was his own confession: he pleaded not blindness, but neglect. "All that was said to me of inward obedience or holiness I neither understood nor remembered. So that I was indeed as ignorant of the true meaning of the law as I was of the gospel of Christ."[2]

We have noticed what Wesley had to record concerning his years at Charterhouse. When the restraints of Epworth Rectory were lifted, he grew careless even in the matter of outward observances. Nevertheless, he still read his Bible, went to church and said his prayers.[3] He expected to be saved on the basis of not being as bad as others. But the best that could be

---

[1] *Journal*, Vol. I, p. 465. 24th May, 1738. [2] *Ibid.* [3] *Ibid.*, pp. 465–466.

concluded about him was that, as he himself put it, he had "still a kindness for religion."[1] During his first five years at Oxford he remained very much in the same condition. "I still said my prayers both in public and in private, and read, with the Scriptures, several other books of religion, especially comments on the New Testament. Yet I had not all this while so much as a notion of inward holiness; nay, went on habitually, and for the most part very contentedly, in some or other known sin: indeed, with some intermission and short struggles, especially before and after the Holy Communion, which I was obliged to receive thrice a year. I cannot well tell what I hoped to be saved by now, when I was continually sinning against that little light I had; unless by those transient fits of what many divines taught me to call repentance."[2] Research into Wesley's Oxford diaries has shown that at this period he was not only engrossed in studies, largely of a secular nature, but also involved in the social life of the University. He was by no means an academic recluse, and the temptations of which he spoke were not merely those of an over-sensitive purist.[3]

As Canon Overton was right to insist, 1725 was a critical year in Wesley's spiritual odyssey. In preparing himself for orders, he was more open to the Spirit's impulse than he had ever been before, and it was in this way that God took hold of him and began to lead him step by step into the fulness of Christian experience. It was he said through "a religious friend"—whose identity he did not disclose—that, "I began to alter the whole form of my conversation, and to set in earnest upon a new life. I set apart an hour or two a day for religious retirement. I communicated every week. I watched against all sin, whether in word or deed. I began to aim at, and pray for, inward holiness. So that now, 'doing so much, and living so good a life,' I doubted not but that I was a good Christian."[4] The ironical flavour of the final remark does not escape us.

Overton, however, despite this, attempted to defend Wesley against himself. "While thoroughly believing in the reality and importance of a later change, can any one deny that from this time forward to the very close of his long life, John Wesley led a most holy, devoted life, aiming only at the glory of God, the welfare of his own soul, and the benefit of his fellow-creatures?"[5] This, of course, is perfectly true, and we are ready

---

[1] *Ibid.*, p. 466.   [2] *Ibid.*

[3] V. H. H. Green, *The Young Mr. Wesley*, pp. 101-102, 138. The unpublished diaries date from 5th April, 1725.

[4] *Journal*, Vol. I, p. 467. 24th May, 1738. The "religious friend" may have been Sarah Kirkham, daughter of Lionel Kirkham, Rector of Stanton, Gloucestershire. She was the "Varanese" of Wesley's correspondence, and not her sister Betty as was once surmised. Cf. *Proc. W.H.S.*, Vol. VIII, pp. 147-148.

[5] John H. Overton, *John Wesley* (1891), p. 14. Professor Outler discerningly refers to "a sudden focussing of faith and personal commitment" in 1725, whilst leaving room for an evangelical conversion in 1738 (*John Wesley*, ed. Albert C. Outler (1964), p. 6).

to recognize the fact. But Overton added: "And if that is not to be a good Christian, what is?"[1] Wesley himself was to find that something more was needed. However, 1725 marked the beginning of what Augustine called "the journey not of feet," which has its destination in the knowledge of God.[2]

A letter from his mother put Wesley on the right track from the start. On 23rd February, 1725, she wrote in answer to his announcement that he intended to seek ordination. She was anxious that his Christian experience should match his vocation. "The alteration of your temper has occasioned me much speculation. I, who am apt to be sanguine, hope it may proceed from the operations of God's Holy Spirit, that by taking away your relish of sensual enjoyments, He may prepare and dispose your mind for a more serious and close application to things of a more sublime and spiritual nature. If it be so, happy are you if you cherish those dispositions, and now, in good earnest, resolve to make religion the business of your life; for, after all, that is the one thing that strictly speaking is necessary, and all things else are comparatively little to the purposes of life. I heartily wish you would now enter upon a serious examination of yourself, that you may know whether you have a reasonable expectation of salvation; that is, whether you are in a state of faith and repentance or not, which you know are the conditions of the gospel covenant on our part. If you are, the satisfaction of knowing it would abundantly reward your pains; if not, you will find a more reasonable occasion for tears than can be met with in a tragedy."[3] This was the very assurance Wesley as yet lacked, and it was only after suffering real anguish of spirit that he would attain it. Tragedy was to precede triumph in the drama of his salvation.

God often approaches men along the line of their personal interests. Wesley was a scholar and an avid reader. It was in the course of his now more specifically theological studies, that he came upon three writers who were to exercise a determinative influence upon him. Before we discuss them, however, we must look at the range of Wesley's reading, and also place it in the context of his new zeal for religion. It was in pursuance of his resolve to aim at inward holiness, that he began to live by rule, both in his devotions and in his studies. From this point, leisure and he had taken leave of one another, as he so pithily expressed it.[4] It was in this period that he found the value of early rising, and from now on he seldom slept later than four a.m. "I am full of business," he told his mother; "but have found a way to write without taking any time from that. 'Tis by rising an

---

[1] Overton, *op. cit.*, p. 14.
[2] *A Companion to the Study of St. Augustine*, ed. Roy W. Battenhouse (1955), p. 404.
[3] Tyerman, *Life of John Wesley*, Vol. I, p. 32.
[4] *Letters*, Vol. I, p. 34. To his brother Samuel Wesley, 5th December, 1726. "Leisure and I have taken leave of one another: I propose to be busy as long as I live, if my health is so long continued to me."

hour sooner in a morning and going into company an hour later in the evening; both which may be done without any inconvenience."[1] In his sermon "On Redeeming the Time," he went into greater detail as to how he arrived at an estimate of his minimum requirements so far as sleep was concerned.[2] One of the cryptic comments which recurred in the cypher language of his diaries was "idleness slays."[3]

It was within the framework of such a rigid timetable that Wesley drew up a plan of study, which he nobly tried to follow. The catalogue is sufficiently daunting. Mondays and Tuesdays were to be reserved for Greek and Roman history and literature; Wednesdays for Logic and Ethics; Thursdays for Hebrew and Arabic; Fridays for Metaphysics and Natural Philosophy; Saturdays for the composition of oratory and poetry; and Sundays for Divinity. In addition to this formidable syllabus, he managed to fit in time to learn French, to acquaint himself with mathematics, and to conduct experiments in optics.[4]

In the Divinity which he read on Sundays, Wesley showed an inclination towards the Fathers. On his list we note the *Spicilegium SS. Patrum* of Johann Ernst Grabe, first published in 1698–1699 in two volumes; William Wake's *Apostolic Epistles and Fathers* (1698); William Reeves' *Apologies of Justin Martyr, Tertullian and Minucius Felix* (1716); and William Cave's *Primitive Christianity* (1672), the title of which was Wesley's nickname amongst some of his friends.[5] Wesley was encouraged in his patristic researches by John Clayton of Brasenose, who was a member of the Holy Club. He was a competent scholar, even if at times he was somewhat uncritical in his enthusiasm for the Fathers, as Green points out.[6] Wesley had evidently sought his advice even after he had left Oxford for his chaplaincy of the collegiate church in Manchester. In reply, Clayton recommended Cotelier's edition of the Apostolic Fathers as the best to begin with in "reading the ancients."[7]

This regard for the patristic authors remained with Wesley throughout his life, and constituted a prominent feature in his intellectual equipment for presenting the Christian case. Later he came to recognize more clearly the regulative criterion of Scripture as providing the proper yardstick by which all other Christian literature should be assessed, but he never ceased

[1] *Letters*, Vol. I, p. 43. To Susanna Wesley, 19th March, 1727.
[2] *Works*, Vol. VII, p. 69. Sermon XCIII.
[3] *Journal*, Vol. I, pp. 21, 54. Introduction.
[4] Tyerman, *Life of John Wesley*, Vol. I, pp. 55–56; cf. V. H. H. Green, *The Young Mr. Wesley*, p. 119.
[5] *Letters*, Vol. I, p. 50. Telford's preface to letter written to Mary Pendarves on 14th August, 1730.
[6] V. H. H. Green, *The Young Mr. Wesley*, p. 173. For Clayton, see Luke Tyerman, *The Oxford Methodists* (1873), pp. 24–56.
[7] Tyerman, *Oxford Methodists*, p. 37. Jean-Baptiste Cotelier was an outstanding French patristic scholar, whose notable edition of the Apostolic Fathers was published in 1672.

to appeal to this biblically controlled tradition. "From a child I was taught to love and reverence the Scripture, the oracles of God;" he declared, as late as December 1789; "and, next to these, to esteem the primitive Fathers, the writers of the first three centuries. Next after the primitive Church, I esteemed our own, the Church of England. . . ."[1] In the little treatise from which those words are taken, he made it clear that this was his conviction still.

But more germane to our immediate concern, namely to trace Wesley's growth in grace, is the fact that it was from his reading of the Fathers of the Church that Wesley was introduced to the normative doctrine of sanctification in classical theology. As Prof. Outler has shown, through his interest in "Macarius the Egyptian," and Ephraem Syrus, he was put in touch with Byzantine spirituality at its source.[2] "What fascinated him in these men was their description of 'perfection' ($\tau\epsilon\lambda\epsilon\iota\omega\sigma\iota\varsigma$) as the goal ($\sigma\kappa\sigma\pi\delta\varsigma$) of the Christian in this life. Their concept of perfection as a process rather than a state gave Wesley a spiritual vision quite different from the static perfectionism envisaged in Roman spiritual theology of the period and the equally static quietism of those Protestants and Catholics whom he deplored as 'the mystic writers.' The 'Christian Gnostic' of Clement of Alexandria became Wesley's model of the ideal Christian. Thus it was that the ancient and Eastern tradition of holiness as *disciplined* love became fused in Wesley's mind with his own Anglican tradition of holiness as *aspiring* love, and thereafter was developed in what he regarded to the end as his own most distinctive contribution."[3] Not only did Wesley's extensive reading in patristics help him to formulate his concept of holiness in an intellectual systematization: it led him to seek the goal as a matter of personal involvement.

We can only glance at the rest of Wesley's book-list before we consider the three devotional writers who influenced him so markedly. In the more specifically theological category we see a representation of the Caroline divines, as well as non-juring authors and the more recent anti-

[1] *Works*, Vol. XIII, p. 234. *Farther Thoughts on Separation from the Church* (1789). Cf. *Works*, Vol. X, pp. 482–484. *An Address to the Clergy* (1756) where, after insisting that biblical knowledge is the first essential in ministerial equipment, Wesley commended the study of the Fathers, "the most authentic commentators on Scripture, as being both nearest the fountain, and eminently endued with that Spirit by whom all Scripture was given" (p. 484).

[2] Cf. *The Standard Sermons of John Wesley*, ed. Edward H. Sugden (1921), (henceforward referred to as *Sermons*), Vol. II, p. 447. Sermon L; *Letters*, Vol. II, p. 387. To Dr. Conyers Middleton, 4th January, 1749. It is now known that the author of the so-called *Macarian Homilies* (J. P. Migne, *Patrologia Graeca* (1857–1866), Vol. XXXIV, pp. 446–822) was not an Egyptian of the fourth century, but a Syrian monk of the fifth century, whose conception of Christian spirituality derived almost entirely from Gregory of Nyssa (Outler, *op. cit.*, p. 9, n. 26).

[3] Outler, *op. cit.*, p. 10. Wesley's admiration for the "Christian Gnostic" was somewhat tempered in later years, cf. *Letters*, Vol. VI, p. 129. To Miss March, 30th November, 1774.

deistic controversialists.[1] He was also attracted by Christian biography, and this must have played its part in making him think about his own mission in life. Amongst these were J. B. Saint-Jure's account of Count Gaston Jean-Baptiste de Renty, who actually wrote a covenant with Christ in his own blood; the life of the Spanish-Mexican recluse Gregory Lopez, by Francisco Losa; the memoirs of Thomas Halyburton, the Scottish Presbyterian, whose works both Wesley and Whitefield later commended to their disciples; and the story of Ambrose Bonwick, a non-juror who died as a Cambridge student with his devotional books beside him.[2] All these examples must inevitably have fired Wesley's imagination and stirred his conscience.

Amongst the manuals of discipline, Wesley read Lorenzo Scupoli's *Pugna Spiritualis* (1666), in the English translation of a Spanish version by the Benedictine Juan de Castaniza. This was one of his mother's favourite books. It dealt with the call to Christian perfection, which is shown to derive solely from God. It "consists in nothing else but the knowledge of the Divine goodness and greatness, of our own nothingness, and proneness to evil."[3] Wesley also mentioned François de Sales' *Introduction to the Devout Life* (1608), Nathaniel Spinckes' *Collections of Meditations and Devotions* (1717), Peter Heylin's *Devotional Tracts* (1681), and Henry Scougal's *The Life of God in the Soul of Man* (1677).[4]

It was in his *A Plain Account of Christian Perfection* (1765) that Wesley singled out the devotional books which had meant most to him at this time of uncertainty and agonized pursuit of holiness. The first was Jeremy Taylor's *Holy Living and Holy Dying*, which he met with in 1725. "In reading several parts of this book, I was exceedingly affected; that part in particular which relates to purity of intention. Instantly I resolved to dedicate all my life to God, all my thoughts, and words, and actions; being thoroughly convinced there was no medium; but that every part of my life (not some only) must either be a sacrifice to God, or myself, that is, in effect, to the devil."[5]

---

[1] Amongst the Caroline divines we find Thomas Ken, John Pearson, George Smalridge, and George Bull; along with John Norris, the last of the Cambridge Platonists, who was of a different school. The non-jurors whose works were read by Wesley include John Kettlewell, George Hickes, Nathaniel Spinckes, William Beveridge, Thomas Deacon and, of course, William Law. The anti-deistic polemicists are *inter alia* John Rogers, Thomas Sherlock, William Wollaston and Samuel Clarke. (V. H. H. Green, *The Young Mr. Wesley*, pp. 305–319. Appendix I).

[2] This list extends to 1736.

[3] Lorenzo Scupoli, *Pugna Spiritualis* (1666), p. 16. Cf. Schmidt, *op. cit.*, Vol. I, p. 48, who compares it with Puritan classics such as Lewis Bayly's *The Practice of Piety* (1669).

[4] V. H. H. Green, *The Young Mr. Wesley*, pp. 305–319. Appendix I.

[5] *Works*, Vol. XI, p. 366. *A Plain Account of Christian Perfection* (1766). Jeremy Taylor, *The Rule and Exercises of Holy Living* (1650), and *The Rule and Exercises of Holy Dying* (1651). For the influence of Taylor on Wesley, cf. H. Trevor Hughes, *The Piety of Jeremy Taylor* (1960), pp. 175–177.

On the 18th June, 1725, Wesley wrote to his mother about what he had been reading. He was evidently impressed by what he had learned from Bishop Taylor about humility and repentance. But it is interesting that even at this stage Wesley queried what Taylor had to say about the possibility of assurance. "Whether God has forgiven us or no we know not, therefore still be sorrowful for ever having sinned."[1] Wesley refused to accept that. "If we can never have any certainty of our being in a state of salvation, good reason it is that every moment should be spent not in joy but in fear and trembling; and then undoubtedly in this life WE ARE of all men most miserable! God deliver us from such a fearful expectation as this!"[2] At least Wesley knew what he wanted, even if as yet he had not laid hold of it.

A further letter to his mother, dated the 29th July, 1725, resumed the discussion of Taylor's classic. What Wesley felt about faith is most revealing, in view of his subsequent experiences. He understood it to be "an assent to any truth upon rational grounds."[3] He was not prepared to swear that he believed anything unless it was demonstrated to him in logical fashion. This was how Wesley viewed faith at the outset of his quest. Without abandoning his conviction that faith must rest on a basis which is not repugnant to reason, he was to discover that justifying faith goes far beyond a mere subscription to propositional truth. However, what he went on to explain was something which required no revision. "I call faith an assent upon rational grounds, because I hold divine testimony to be the most reasonable of all evidence whatever. Faith must necessarily at length be resolved into reason. God is true; therefore what He says is true. He hath said this; therefore this is true. When any one can bring me more reasonable propositions than these, I am ready to assent to them; till then, it will be highly unreasonable to change my opinion."[4] In terms of apologetics, that was unexceptionable.

The second devotional manual which Wesley mentioned in *A Plain Account of Christian Perfection* was Thomas à Kempis' *De Imitatione Christi*, which he entitled *The Christian's Pattern*. He allotted his first acquaintance with it to the year 1726, but when he wrote over half a century later his recollection must have been a little at fault. It is clear, both from his

[1] *Letters*, Vol. I, p. 19. To Susanna Wesley, 18th June, 1725. Cf. Jeremy Taylor, *Holy Living*, Chapter IV, Section ix, para. 9. "A true penitent must all the days of his life pray for pardon, and never think the work completed till he dies. . . . And whether God hath forgiven us or no, we know not; and how far, we know not; and all that we have done is not of sufficient worth to obtain pardon; therefore, still pray, and still be sorrowful for ever having done it, and for ever watch against it; and then those beginnings of pardon which are working all the way, will at last be perfected in the day of the Lord" (p. 262, 1849 edition).

[2] *Letters*, Vol. I, p. 20. To Susanna Wesley, 18th June, 1725.

[3] *Ibid.*, p. 22. To Susanna Wesley, 29th July, 1725.

[4] *Ibid.*, p. 23.

diaries and the correspondence with his mother, that he read à Kempis in 1725.[1] "The nature and extent of inward religion, the religion of the heart, now appeared to me in a stronger light than ever it had done before," he confessed. "I saw that giving even all my life to God (supposing it possible to do this, and go no farther) would profit me nothing, unless I gave my heart, yea, all my heart, to Him. I saw that 'simplicity of attention', and purity of affection, one design in all we speak or do, and one desire ruling all our tempers, and indeed 'the wings of the soul,' without which she can never ascend to the mount of God.'[2]

In the *Journal* he included the reading of the *Imitation* as one of the landmarks in his spiritual pilgrimage. It was, he believed, the providence of God which directed him to it. Through it he realized that "true religion was seated in the heart, and that God's law extended to all our thoughts as well as words and actions."[3] He admitted, however, that he found à Kempis somewhat too severe for his liking, and yet he "had frequently much sensible comfort in reading him, such as I was an utter stranger to before."[4] He confided his reactions to his mother. She had to admit that she had no familiarity with à Kempis, but she was inclined to agree with her son, if indeed the book conveyed the impression that God does not desire the happiness of His creatures. As Piette remarks, John would have had difficulty in citing precise references, for not all have interpreted à Kempis in this fashion.[5] Certainly he warned against any joy that is outside Christ, but, with all his medieval austerity, he was no stranger to what Wesley seemed to miss. Samuel appended a father's verdict to Susanna's hesitations. "I have only this to add of my friend and old companion (*i.e.*, à Kempis) that, making some grains of allowance, he may be read to great advantage; nay, that it is almost impossible to peruse him seriously without admiring, and I think, in some measure imitating his heroic strain of humility, piety and devotion."[6] Despite his criticisms, Wesley was clearly moved by the *Imitation*, and in 1735 he produced a fine edition of it.

The third book to influence Wesley at this period was William Law's *A Serious Call to a Devout and Holy Life* (1729), to which must be linked his treatise *On Christian Perfection* (1726). Law, of course, was a contemporary of Wesley, who visited him at Putney more than once.[7] G. A. Wauer, the historian of the Moravians, has called Law "the father of the

[1] Cf. V. H. H. Green, *The Young Mr. Wesley*, p. 306, Appendix I; *Letters*, Vol. I, pp. 15–16, to Susanna Wesley, 28th May, 1725; p. 18, to the same, 18th June, 1725.
[2] *Works*, Vol. XI, pp. 366–367. *A Plain Account of Christian Perfection* (1766).
[3] *Journal*, Vol. I, p. 466. 24th May, 1738.
[4] *Ibid.*, p. 467.
[5] Maximin Piette, *John Wesley in the Evolution of Protestantism* (E.T. 1937), p. 252.
[6] Tyerman, *Life of John Wesley*, Vol. I, p. 35. Letter Samuel Wesley to his son John, 14th July, 1725.
[7] J. Brazier Green, *John Wesley and William Law* (1945), p. 43.

religious revival of the eighteenth century, and the grandfather of
Methodism."[1] He exercised a considerable influence on the Wesleys and
Whitefield. In *A Plain Account of Christian Perfection* Wesley referred to
these two books by Law. "These convinced me, more than ever, of the
absolute impossibility of being half a Christian; and I determined, through
His grace (the absolute necessity of which I was deeply sensible of) to be
all-devoted to God, to give Him all my soul, my body, and my substance."[2]

  In the autobiographical introduction to his conversion narrative in the
Journal, Wesley said of these volumes that "they convinced me more than
ever of the exceeding height and breadth and depth of the law of God.
The light flowed in so mightily upon my soul, that everything appeared
in a new view. I cried to God for help, and resolved not to prolong the
time of obeying Him as I had never done before."[3] It was then he added:
"And by my continued endeavour to keep His whole law, inward and
outward, to the utmost of my power, I was persuaded that I should be
accepted of Him, and that I was even then in a state of salvation."[4] He
may have laboured under this illusion then: quite clearly by 1738 he
realized that he had been deceived. But he was none the less indebted to
William Law for bringing him a stage further along the road, although
just before his Aldersgate Street experience, he rather ungraciously up-
braided his mentor for not having shown him the way of justifying faith.[5]
Yet as late as 1788 Wesley praised the *Serious Call* in a sermon, calling it a
"treatise which will hardly be excelled, if it be equalled, in the English
tongue, either for beauty of expression, or for justness and depth of
thought."[6]

  These, then, more than any others, were the three writers who, as Dr.
Maldwyn Edwards puts it, "uncovered for Wesley the riches of the in-
terior life."[7] They showed him the goal. But they did not bring him to it.
"All these writers created a want which they could not satisfy," Edwards
adds.[8] In recognizing how much Wesley owed to Taylor, à Kempis and
Law, we must be careful not to exaggerate the debt. However, we may
concur with Professor Outler when he writes of Wesley: "From his
great mentors in piety . . . he learned that faith is either in dead earnest or
just dead."[9] It was living faith he sought, and he imagined that he would
find it through his constant endeavours.

  With this end in view, Wesley broke away from unprofitable com-

[1] Gerhard A. Wauer, *The Beginnings of the Brethren's Church in England* (E.T. 1901),
p. 35.
[2] *Works*, Vol. XI, p. 367. *A Plain Account of Christian Perfection* (1766).
[3] *Journal*, Vol. I, p. 467. 24th May, 1738. [4] *Ibid.*
[5] *Letters*, Vol. I, pp. 239–240, to William Law, 14th May, 1738; pp. 241–242, to
the same, 20th May, 1738. For Law's reply, pp. 242–244.
[6] *Works*, Vol. VII, p. 297. Sermon CXVIII.
[7] *A History of the Methodist Church in Great Britain*, Vol. I, p. 43. [8] *Ibid.*
[9] Outler, *op. cit.*, pp. viii–ix.

panions and subjected himself to severe ascetic discipline. The diaries reveal the relentless pressure of his self-mortification. Sometimes he would hold an inquisition on his soul. All his most intimate motives and emotions were interrogated at the bar of his own remorseless conscience. It was Romans 7 over again. Curnock has left a vivid picture of his pitiable plight. "He binds his tortured soul to the horns of the altar, and the flames play around it. He has no mercy on himself. Not once does he excuse himself or enter a single plea in extenuation. When the record is more humiliating than usual, his only remedy is a pathetic strengthening of the outward standard or a new emphasis added to an old rule, and always with a cry to God in the sacred tongue κύριε βοήθει. More law, more methods; a new cord to the flagellant's whip, or a new knot in an old cord."[1] It is a terrifying reproduction of Bunyan's man in the iron cage. We are not surprised to learn that soon it was to culminate on the verge of despair.

Wesley had complained that à Kempis seemed to suggest that God did not mean His children to know happiness. His protest hardly sprang from his own experience, for he himself was a stranger to the peace and joy of believing. Temperamentally he was of a cheerful disposition, but thus far we can detect little of optimism in his religion. To quote Curnock once again, "his sacred song is set in a minor key. It is a wail of distress and disappointment. In the first Diary there is no rejoicing. How extraordinary the contrast between these yellow, dreary pages and St. Paul's letters to the Thessalonians or to the Philippians; or between the Wesley religion of 1725–1729 and the manuscript hymn-book which for fifteen years was his constant companion in evangelistic travel! We may even now see the thumb-marks on his favourite page—deeper, more stained with use than any other:

> O for a thousand tongues to sing
> My great Redeemer's praise!

and

> Now I have found the ground wherein
> Sure my soul's anchor may remain.

Hymns *For Believers Rejoicing* found no place in Wesley's Saturday night exercises in the year 1725."[2] Nor did they appear before 1738. It was not until then that he had something worth singing about. Meanwhile, the desperate, agonizing search went on.

[1] *Journal*, Vol. I, p. 34. Introduction.　　[2] *Ibid.*, p. 35.

CHAPTER IV

BEATING THE AIR

"I CONTINUED preaching, and following after, and trusting in that righteousness
whereby no flesh can be justified. All the time I was at Savannah I was thus
beating the air." Journal 1 : 470.

B Y 1734 THE HEALTH OF WESLEY'S FATHER HAD DETERIORATED
to such an extent that he knew that death could not be far away.
Steps obviously had to be taken accordingly with regard to the Epworth
incumbency, if it was to be kept in the family. John's eldest brother,
Samuel, was given the first opportunity to obtain the next presentation,
but declined. It was he who directed his father's attention to John. Correspondence between the three of them went on for some months. It was of
considerable importance in clarifying John Wesley's mind about the
purpose for which he had been ordained. He insisted that God had not
called him to the oversight of a parish.

Wesley stated his position in a long letter to his father, dated the 10th
December, 1734, in which he urged the argument that he could do more
good in Oxford than at Epworth.[1] On hearing of his refusal, his brother
Samuel wrote to him on Christmas Day, 1734, telling him that his ordination vows solemnly obliged him to undertake the cure of souls.[2] John
replied that he had never made a distinct resolution against such a thing,
although he did not think that he was disobeying his pledges as he exhorted and instructed the pupils under his charge.[3] Samuel maintained the
pressure in a further letter on the 8th February, 1735, in which he affirmed
categorically: "The order of the Church stakes you down, the more you
struggle, will hold the faster."[4] John vigorously resisted this implication
and even went so far as to ask Bishop Potter whether he had at his ordination in any way bound himself to seek a parish. The Bishop replied: "It
doth not seem to me that at your ordination you engaged yourself to
undertake the cure of any parish, provided you can as a clergyman better
serve God and His Church in your present or some other station."[5]

[1] *Letters*, Vol. I, pp. 166–178. To Samuel Wesley, 10th December, 1734.
[2] Joseph Priestley, *Original Letters by the Rev. John Wesley and his Friends* (1791),
pp. 17–19. Samuel Wesley junior to John, 24th December, 1734.
[3] *Letters*, Vol. I, pp. 179–180. To Samuel Wesley junior, 15th January, 1735.
[4] Priestley, *op. cit.*, p. 43. Samuel Wesley junior to John, 8th February, 1735.
[5] *Letters*, Vol. I, pp. 181–182. To Samuel Wesley junior, 4th March, 1735. Cf. pp.
180–181. To the same, 13th February, 1735.

This answer satisfied John and silenced Samuel. The controversy sub-
sided. John stayed at Oxford, and when his father died on the 25th April,
1735, the living passed into other hands. But in view of the mission that
ultimately awaited him, this apparently incidental decision was of the utmost significance. As Telford remarked: "Had he gone to Epworth,
Methodism might never have passed beyond its Oxford stage."[1] Moreover, in Bishop Potter's assurance Wesley possessed what was eventually
to be regarded as his *carte blanche* for the work of itinerant evangelism.
"Some other station" was to receive the broadest of interpretations.

Meanwhile, a further episode in Wesley's career was to play its part in
the making of an evangelist. God works in a mysterious way, and even out
of the disappointment of Wesley's mission to Georgia there emerged
factors which contributed to his Christian experience and his equipment
as a winner of souls. If nothing more, he could hardly fail to learn from
his mistakes. We must resist the temptation to write off the Georgian
fiasco merely as an unfortunate and futile interlude. That would be no
more realistic than the attempt to present it as a noble experiment which
only just fell short of success. The fact cannot be glossed over that Wesley's
venture ended in disaster and led to virtual despair. But it was out of this
human debris that God was then able to build the future of His chosen
prophet. Maldwyn Edwards is quite justified in claiming that "the underlying factors which prompted Wesley's call to his life's work stretched
from the Epworth nursery to Georgia."[2]

To construe the Georgian undertaking as a débâcle does not compel us
automatically to cast doubts on the reality of Wesley's missionary vocation. That would be an over-simplification, as Martin Schmidt and
V. H. H. Green have shown. It may well be that we have here the first
inkling given to Wesley as to what his work for God was to be. As subsequent events were to prove, he was indeed intended to be a missionary.
But his field was not to be in any far-off idealized Georgia. It lay on his
door-step in needy, pagan Britain. God does not waste time when He is
moulding a man for His use. We may take it that the call Wesley heard in
1735 was a genuine one. It was not to be fulfilled immediately, however.
It came to fruition when he himself was enabled by grace to respond.

It was through Dr. John Burton, of Corpus Christi College, Oxford,
one of Wesley's close friends, that the invitation came. Burton was a
generous supporter of the Society for the Propagation of the Gospel and a
member of the Georgia Trust. He wrote to Wesley on the 8th September,
1735, and his letter is preserved as "the oldest Methodist missionary document in existence."[3] The charter of the new colony had only been signed

[1] *Ibid.*, p. 166. Notes.
[2] *A History of the Methodist Church in Great Britain*, Vol. I, p. 52.
[3] *Wesley Studies*, Various Contributors (1903), p. 69. For the letter from John
Burton to Wesley, 8th September, 1735, see *Journal*, Vol. VIII, p. 285.

three years before. The Governor, James Oglethorpe, had taken Henry
Herbert, a son of the Lord Herbert of Cherbury, as his first chaplain, but
he died soon after disembarkation. His successor, Samuel Quincey, was
not in good health, and as his ministry was unsatisfactory, the trustees
agreed to recall him. John Wesley was appointed to take his place, and his
brother Charles went out also as Oglethorpe's secretary. It was hoped that
other members of the Holy Club might join the company, but as it was
only Benjamin Ingham and Charles Delamotte did so. Yet, in a sense, the
Georgian expedition was a somewhat naive endeavour to transport the
Holy Club to North America in order to test its effectiveness there.

Wesley made no secret of the fact, however, that his principal desire
was to advance his own spiritual life. "My chief motive, to which all the
rest are subordinate," he told Dr. Burton, "is the hope of saving my own
soul."[1] What followed indicates that Wesley entertained highly romantic
notions of what the Indians in Georgia would be like. It reflected a cult
which was to reach its peak of fashionability in the late eighteenth century,
through the advocacy of the philosopher Rousseau and the explorer Bou-
gainville, namely, that of the noble savage.[2] "I hope to learn the true sense
of the gospel of Christ by preaching it to the heathen. They have no comments to construe away the text; no vain philosophy to corrupt it; no
luxurious, sensual, covetous, ambitious expounders to soften its unpleas-
ing truths, to reconcile earthly-mindedness and faith, the Spirit of Christ
and the spirit of the world. They have no party, no interest to serve, and
are therefore fit to receive the gospel in its simplicity. They are as little
children, humble, willing to learn, and eager to do the will of God; and
consequently they shall know of every doctrine I preach whether it be of
God. By these, therefore, I hope to learn the purity of that faith which
was once delivered to the saints; the genuine sense and full extent of those
laws which none can understand who mind earthly things."[3] Wesley was
heading for disillusionment, and he soon experienced it.

Thus it came about that on the 14th October, 1735, John Wesley went
aboard the good ship *Simmonds* off Gravesend, and sailed out to exchange
"the religion of a hermit for that of a frontiersman," as Professor G. C.
Cell so graphically put it.[4] With characteristic earnestness and energy,
Wesley immediately set about organizing the Christians on board, and
also sought to influence those who were not. We hear of prayers, of religious conversation, of devotional exercises, of interviews, of preaching.

[1] *Letters*, Vol. I, p. 188. To John Burton, 10th October, 1735. Cf. *Journal*, Vol. I,
p. 109, 14th October, 1735: "Our end in leaving our native country was not to avoid
want, God having given us plenty of temporal blessings, nor to gain riches and
honour, which we trust He will ever enable us to look on as no other than dung and
dross; but singly this—to save our souls, to live wholly to the glory of God."
[2] Basil Willey, *The Eighteenth Century Background* (1940), p. 14.
[3] *Letters*, Vol. I, p. 188. To John Burton, 10th October, 1735.
[4] George Croft Cell, *The Rediscovery of John Wesley* (1935), p. 99.

On the first Sunday the day was fair and calm as the *Simmonds* still lay at anchor, through prolonged delays. A service was held on the quarter-deck, as the lounge would have been too small to contain the congregation. Here for the first time in his life, Wesley spoke in the open air.[1] It was a forecast of things to come. He also ventured to preach extemporaneously. "His surroundings inspired him," commented Dr. Simon, "and out of his heart he spoke living words."[2] One more step towards the future had been taken.

Yet, despite the reality of his missionary call and the intensity of his zeal, Wesley was still an "ecclesiastical Hamlet," to borrow the phrase of M. Daniel-Rops.[3] He had not yet sorted himself out, as we say nowadays; or, rather, allowed God to sort him out. His was a mixed-up personality: he expected Georgia to perform the miracle for him and set it straight. He was to discover that, just as Jonah could not get away from God by sailing many miles, so neither could he get nearer to God by the same expedient. As Dr. Nottingham concluded, when Wesley left for Georgia he was "a self-crippled man."[4]

A copy of an unpublished letter written by Wesley as the *Simmonds* lay off the island of Tybee has been unearthed within recent years.[5] It substantiates what has been said about his perturbed spiritual condition. "God has brought an unhappy unthankful wretch hither through a thousand dangers to renew his complaints and loathe the life which has been preserved by a series of miracles. I take the moment of my arrival to inform you of it because I know you will thank Him, though I cannot: I cannot, for I yet feel myself. In vain have I fled from myself to America: I still

[1] *Journal*, Vol. I, p. 111. 19th October, 1735. Cf. *Works*, Vol. X, p. 447. *An Answer to Mr. Rowland Hill's Tract, entitled "Imposture Detected"* (1777): "I preached in the open air in October, 1735. Mr. Whitefield had not then been ordained."
[2] John S. Simon. *John Wesley and the Religious Societies* (1921), p. 116. Despite Wesley's own statement, "I now first preached extempore" (*Journal*, Vol. I, p. 111. 19th October, 1735), it is not certain that this was his initial venture. In 1776 Wesley delivered a charity sermon in All Hallows Church, Lombard Street, London. As he entered the fact in his *Journal* (Vol. VI, p. 96. 28th January, 1776), his mind went back to an earlier visit. "In the year 1735, above forty years ago, I preached in this church, at the earnest request of the churchwardens, to a numerous congregation, who came, like me, with an intent to hear Dr. Heylyn. This was the first time that, having no notes about me, I preached extempore." Wesley was in London for three or four weeks in August, 1735, and again for a few days, including a Sunday, in September. If this was when he preached in All Hallows, when the popular John Heylin, Rector of St. Mary-le-Strand, failed to appear, then it was before he sailed for Georgia. Perhaps the entry on 19th October meant that Wesley preached extemporaneously for the first time of set purpose.
[3] Henri Daniel-Rops, *The Church in the Eighteenth Century* (E.T. 1964), p. 174.
[4] Elizabeth K. Nottingham, *The Making of an Evangelist* (1938), p. 127.
[5] It was discovered in 1944 by the daughter of the Rev. Henry Hake, Vicar of Chilvers Coton, Warwickshire. The recipient is unnamed, cf. *Proc. W.H.S.*, Vol. XXV, pp. 17-20. It is dated 5th February, 1736.

groan under the intolerable weight of inherent misery. If I have never yet repented of my undertaking, it is because I hope for nothing better in England, or paradise. Go where I will, I carry my hell about me; nor have I the least ease in anything. . . ."[1]

And then he added, in a touching paragraph: "For you I do pray continually, with an earnestness like that of Dives that you may never come into this hell of torment. I cannot follow my own advice, but yet I advise you—Give God your hearts; love Him with all your souls; serve Him with all your strength. . . . Whatsoever you speak, or think, or do, let God be your aim, and God only. Let your one end be to please and love God. In all your business, all your refreshments, all your diversions, all your conversations, as well as in all those which are commonly called religious duties, let your eye look straight forward to God. Have one design, one desire, one hope. Even yet the God whom you serve may be your God and your all in time and in eternity. O be not of double heart! Think of nothing else—seek nothing else. To love God and to be beloved of Him is enough. . . . Love which never rests, never faileth, but shall spread its flame, still goeth on conquering and to conquer, till what was but now a weak foolish, wavering creature, be filled with all the fulness of God."[2]

Now it is obvious that all this was penned in the midst of profound spiritual depression. It may not be irrelevant to remind ourselves also that Wesley had just endured a trying sea-voyage—his first crossing of the Atlantic. He himself realized later that he had laid bare the innermost of his heart in a manner which he usually reserved for his own seasons of self-examination. Yet, allowing for all these factors, we cannot escape the impression that Wesley was a man at the end of his spiritual tether. Georgia was his last resort. If it failed, he had no alternative. The house of his self-made righteousness would collapse. As we know, it did. But that was not the end, as he feared. When every trace of reliance on anything but the sheer unmerited grace of God had been removed, Wesley was ready to trust in Christ, and in Christ *alone*, for salvation.

In a continuation of this same letter, dated the 14th February, Wesley reflected on what he had previously disclosed. He recognized that it represented the nadir of his spiritual course thus far, but he decided that he would not rescind it. "I look with horror back on the desperate spirit that dictated the words above, but shall let them stand, as the naked picture of a soul. . . ."[3] But he continued in a more optimistic strain—and this is equally relevant to his future mission. "I will still call myself a 'prisoner of hope.' God is able to save to the uttermost, to break my bonds in sunder and bring deliverance to the captive. 'To what am I reserved?' is a question I am continually asking myself, though God alone can answer it. This I am persuaded will now be soon determined; for I am come to a crisis. The work I see immediately before me, is the care of fifty poor

[1] *Ibid.*, p. 17.   [2] *Ibid.*, pp. 17–18.   [3] *Ibid.*, p. 19.

families (alas for them that they should be so cared for!), some few of whom are not far from the kingdom of God. Among these I shall either be converted or *lost*. I need not ask your prayers: you both make mention of me in them continually. Obstinate pride, invincible sensuality stand between God and me. The whole bent of my soul is to be altered. My office calls for an ardent love of souls, a desire to spend and be spent for them, an eagerness to lay down my life for the brethren. May the Spirit that maketh intercession for us, direct you how to intercede for me."[1]

This recent evidence has been quoted at some length, since it bears so closely on Wesley's state of mind and soul as he made, so to speak, his last reckless throw before capitulating to the overwhelming power and love of God. Incidentally, it disposes of any doctrinaire theory about a conversion prior to 1738. But even before Wesley arrived in Georgia, he was introduced to a group of Christians who were to be the principal instruments in God's hands for his recovery. On board the *Simmonds* were some Moravian missionaries, under the charge of their Bishop, David Nitschmann. Through them Wesley was to learn of an evangelical experience to which he himself was a stranger. Not only could it give joy in life (which Wesley lacked), but peace in face of death (which Wesley had not even dared to think possible). In the midst of a violent storm, the Moravians displayed an abnormal poise. As they were singing a psalm, the sea broke over the ship, split the mainsail in pieces, and poured in between the decks "as if the great deep had already swallowed us up."[2] Panic spread amongst the rest of the passengers. But the Germans calmly sang on. Wesley asked one of them afterwards, "Were you not afraid?" "I thank God, no," he replied. "But were not your women and children afraid?" He explained quietly, "No; our women and children are not afraid to die."[3] As Prof. Philip Watson remarks: "this reply shook John Wesley even more than the storm had done."[4] When the weather had improved, Wesley made this entry in his *Journal*, over which he must have brooded. "I can conceive no difference comparable between a smooth and a rough sea, except that which is between a mind calmed by the love of God and one torn up by the storms of earthly passions."[5] Clearly he had himself in view.

On arrival off the coast of Georgia, Oglethorpe took a boat up the Savannah River and brought back the leader of the Moravian settlement, August Gottlieb Spangenberg. He was the second-in-command to Count Zinzendorf himself, and later succeeded him at the mother community in Herrnhut. It was a moment full of potential when these two men met.

---

[1] *Ibid.*
[2] *Journal*, Vol. I, p. 144. 25th January, 1736.
[3] *Ibid.*, p. 145.
[4] Philip S. Watson, *The Message of the Wesleys* (1965), p. 4.
[5] *Journal*, Vol. I, p. 145. 26th January, 1736.

They immediately took to each other.[1] The pair of them had long talks together, during the course of which Wesley's vocation was discussed. It was to prove a turning-point in his thinking. Up to now he had hoped to find the answer to his personal need in the prosecution of a practical task. Spangenberg proceeded to indicate the reverse procedure. When Wesley asked for advice concerning his work, Spangenberg instead pressed some highly personal questions. "Do you know yourself? Have you the witness within yourself? Does the Spirit of God bear witness with your spirit that you are a child of God?" Wesley was taken aback by such directness. Spangenberg was quick to spot his discomfiture, and was encouraged to multiply his inquiries. "Do you know Jesus Christ?" he asked point-blank. Wesley stalled: "I know He is the Saviour of the world." But that was not good enough for this persistent surgeon of souls. "True," Spangenberg agreed; "but do you know He has saved you?" That was the vital thing. Wesley was perceptibly hesitant: "I hope he has died to save me." Still the pressure was maintained: "Do you know yourself?" Wesley weakly mumbled, "I do," to hide his embarrassment, but he confessed in his *Journal* that they were "vain words."[2]

"In this way the question as to his own faith was posed with the most radical urgency," explains Prof. Schmidt, "and it became a goad throwing him into a state of unrest which was ultimately to bear fruit. It urged him on his way until it received effective answer in the conversion experience of 24th May, 1738."[3] Spangenberg himself gave what seems a much more favourable account of Wesley's condition: "I observed that grace really dwells and reigns in him."[4] This, however, may simply mean that Spangenberg saw the sovereign power of God already at work in Wesley's heart. He was assured that what had been thus begun, would not fail of its completion.

It is not within the scope of our intentions to rehearse the sad and complicated story of Wesley's Georgian mission. Suffice to say that disillusionment set in with remorseless rapidity. Life in the supposedly idyllic colony was no more conducive to holiness than anywhere else in this present evil world. The Indians proved singularly unresponsive on the few occasions when Wesley had the opportunity to make contact with them. Far from approximating to Dryden's "noble savage," they were almost all "gluttons, drunkards, thieves, dissemblers, liars."[5] Moreover, Wesley found them "implacable, unmerciful; murderers of fathers, murderers of mothers, murderers of their own children."[6] This was not what he had expected, and he felt cheated. We can only register our astonishment that

---

[1] Schmidt, *op. cit.*, Vol. I, p. 150.
[2] *Journal*, Vol. I, p. 151. 8th February, 1736.
[3] Schmidt, *op. cit.*, Vol. I, p. 153.
[4] *Ibid.* Spangenberg's Diary is housed amongst the Moravian Archives at Herrnhut.
[5] *Journal*, Vol. I, p. 407. 2nd December, 1737.   [6] *Ibid.*

a shrewd man like Wesley could have built up such an unrealistic conception of primitive peoples.

But these were not the worst of his troubles in Georgia. What Rattenbury did not hesitate to castigate as "his preposterous ecclesiastical discipline, and his application of a rigid and calculated ritualism," made a shambles of his ministry.[1] He even refused to administer the sacrament of the Lord's Supper to Johann Martin Bolzius, the godly pastor of the Salzburger community at New Ebenezer, near Purrysbourg, on the ground that he was not baptized by an episcopally ordained priest. "Can any one carry High Church zeal higher than this?" he asked many years later, as he looked back with shame on his uncharitable scruples. Then he added wryly: "And how well have I been since beaten with mine own staff!"[2] As Bett has fairly asserted, Wesley's missionary service was "intensely diligent, devoted and self-denying, but deplorably bigoted and tactless."[3]

Dr. Bett went on to demonstrate that all the time Wesley's "ecclesiastical prejudices were being shaken by the logic of facts. What his American experience contributed to his spiritual history was really the discipline of a progressive disillusionment."[4] Or, as Professor Outler prefers to express it, "the well furnished theologian is caught in the toils of discontent and self-reproach."[5] No amount of special pleading, following the line first laid down by Canon Overton, can circumvent this distressing yet undeniable conclusion.[6] This was what compelled Wesley to reconsider his own spiritual experience. He had begun to grasp that his soul would not be saved through a change in external environment, as he had foolishly hoped, but by an inward transformation. He realized that though he thought he was in a state of salvation, he was far from it. He returned from Georgia a sadder but a wiser man.

Wesley did not formally resign from his charge. He fled from a situation which, largely through his own clumsiness, had got completely out of hand. He was actually faced with legal proceedings, because he had repelled Sophy Williamson from Holy Communion. The matter was not alleviated by the fact that he himself had been involved with her in an unhappy love affair before her marriage. The whole atmosphere in Georgia was now uncongenial in the extreme, and eventually Wesley left in disgust and indignation. The official list of early settlers recorded his ignominious departure with the terse entry: "run away."[7]

[1] Rattenbury, op. cit., p. 39.
[2] Journal, Vol. III, p. 434. 30th September, 1749. Cf. Vol. I, p. 370. 17th July, 1737.
[3] Bett, op. cit., p. 18.   [4] Ibid.
[5] Outler, op. cit., p. 41.
[6] Overton, op. cit., pp. 51–53; cf. Piette, op. cit., p. 300, and A. B. Lawson, John Wesley and the Christian Ministry (1963), p. 16.
[7] A list of the Early Settlers of Georgia, ed. E. Merton Coulter and Albert B. Saye (1949), p. 57; cf. Outler, op. cit., p. 11, n. 36.

On the homeward journey he found that his fear of death had not been removed. He was prompted to make two observations. "1. That not one of these hours ought to pass out of my remembrance, till I attain another manner of spirit, a spirit equally willing to glorify God by life or by death. 2. That whoever is uneasy on any account (bodily pain alone excepted) carries in himself his own conviction that he is so far an unbeliever. Is he uneasy at the apprehension of death? Then he believeth not 'to die is gain.' At any of the events of life? Then he hath not a firm belief that 'all things work together for' his 'good.' And if he bring the matter more close, he will always find, beside the general want of faith, every particular uneasiness is evidently owing to the want of some particular Christian temper."[1]

As the *Samuel*, on which he had embarked, was nearing Land's End, Wesley reviewed his catastrophic experiences in Georgia. "I went to America to convert the Indians; but, oh, who shall convert me? Who, what is he that will deliver me from this evil heart of unbelief? I have a fair summer religion. I can talk well; nay, and believe myself, while no danger is near. But let death look me in the face, and my spirit is troubled. Nor can I say, 'To die is gain'!

> I have a sin of fear, that when I've spun
> My last thread, I shall perish on the shore!

. . . Oh, who will deliver me from this fear of death?"[2] On the 1st February, Wesley landed at Deal, and made a further reference to his Georgian mission in his *Journal* for that day. "It is now two years and almost four months since I left my native country, in order to teach the Georgian Indians the nature of Christianity. But what have I learned myself in the meantime? Why, what I the least of all suspected, that I, who went to America to convert others, was never myself converted to God."[3]

When Wesley set foot on English soil again, he had reached a critical juncture in his life and ministry. Up to now, as he later confessed, his entire spiritual saga was simply a "refined way of trusting to my own works."[4] He saw at last the futility of such a course. Yet where could he turn? He did not know. But God had it all in hand. This very year was to transform a despondent missionary reject into a burning evangelist, who would offer salvation to thousands in darkest Britain who were still sunk in their sins. "In Georgia the man we meet in some sense had made him-

---

[1] *Journal*, Vol. I, p. 414. 28th December, 1737.

[2] *Ibid.*, p. 418. 24th January, 1738. The couplet is from John Donne's "A Hymn to God the Father," *The Poems of John Donne*, ed. H. J. C. Grierson (1929), p. 338, st. 3, ll. 14, 15.

[3] *Journal*, Vol. I, p. 422. 1st February, 1738. Wesley added later: "I am not sure of this," cf. n. 2. The insertion first appeared in Jackson's edition of the *Works*.

[4] *Journal*, Vol. I, p. 469. 24th May, 1738.

self," wrote Rattenbury: "after Georgia, the man we meet is as God re-made him."[1]

Wesley realized that he had come to the end of a chapter. That was the positive contribution of the Georgia experience. It represented not only the *reductio ad absurdum* of his ecclesiastical rigorism. It brought him into contact with the Moravians, with their Reformed emphasis on justification by faith and the need for personal conversion. It forced him to admit that his own attempt to earn salvation had gained him nothing but near despair. It made him re-examine his missionary vocation and ask where it was to be fulfilled. "Many reasons have I to bless God, though the design I went upon did not take effect, for my having been carried into that strange land, contrary to all my preceding resolutions. Hereby I trust He hath in some measure 'humbled me and proved me, and shown me what was in my heart.' Hereby I am come to know assuredly that, if 'in all our ways we acknowledge God,' He will, where reason fails, 'direct our path' by lot or by the other means which He knoweth."[2] So Wesley wrote on the 3rd February, 1738. He was plainly ready for God's next step.

[1] Rattenbury, *op. cit.*, p. 28.
[2] *Journal*, Vol. I, p. 435. 3rd February, 1738.

CHAPTER V

THE CHANGE WHICH GOD WORKS

"ABOUT a quarter before nine, while he was describing *the change which God works* in the heart through faith in Christ, I felt my heart strangely warmed. I felt I did trust in Christ, Christ alone for salvation; and an assurance was given me that He had taken away *my* sins, even *mine*, and saved *me* from the law of sin and death." *Journal* 1: 476.

WE COME NOW TO THE CLIMAX BOTH OF WESLEY'S QUEST FOR spiritual reality, and of his preparation at God's hands for his supreme work as an evangelist. 1738 was the decisive year of his life, and the 24th May the day of his conversion. Everything had been leading up to this, and everything stemmed from it. In all his writings, Wesley looked back to his Aldersgate Street experience as the crisis and turning-point of his career. This is not to overlook other stages of development on the way, for we have already noted them. But it was what happened on the 24th May, 1738, which made Wesley an evangelist. It released him for his true vocation. For more than fifty years he valiantly fulfilled it. He had no more uncertainty then as to what God wanted him to do.

If we consult the contemporary British chronicles at this period, the only event which they record as having significance in 1738 had to do with the ear of a certain Thomas Jenkins. Bringing home the brig *Rebecca* from the Caribbean, this dashing sea-captain had a most humiliating experience. His ship was boarded by a Spanish guarda-costa, whose commander rifled the holds, and then crowned his enormities by cutting off one of Jenkins' ears. It must have been a dramatic scene in the House of Commons when, in the presence of a committee of inquiry, the Captain produced his ear in a bottle by way of evidence.[1] There is some hesitation in the minds of historians today as to whether Jenkins ever did lose his ear, or, if he did, whether it may not have been in the pillory. Be that as it may, it was this incident, blown up by the press and the Opposition, which forced the hand of the Prime Minister, Sir Robert Walpole, and precipitated a conflict with Spain which was popularly known as the war of Jenkins' ear.

The impartial observer, however, viewing the calendar in the light of later trends, is compelled to conclude that the affair of the Captain and his alleged mutilation does not bear comparison in ultimate importance with

[1] S. E. Ayling, *The Georgian Century 1714–1837* (1966), p. 139.

the conversion of John Wesley, which occurred in the same year. It is being increasingly recognized, by secular writers as well as by students of
Church history, that the rebirth of Wesley was not only the outstanding
occurrence in 1738, but one of the determinative features of the entire era.
"For, without a doubt," declared Richard Pyke, "nothing that happened
in the whole course of the century was the source of such a universal
harvest of joy, power, and life as the change which transformed Wesley
from a restless, intolerant, and poor-tempered clergyman, too sincere to
be satisfied with anything short of truth, and too earnest to dismiss the
fierce questionings that arose within him, into a radiant, confident, and
supremely happy evangelist."[1]

We must trace the way in which Wesley was brought to his climacteric
experience, as we follow him from his landing at Deal on the 1st February,
1738, to his heart-warming at the little society meeting in Aldersgate
Street on the 24th May. These were momentous months indeed. As Isaac
Taylor explained, Wesley "returned to England in a state of spiritual dis-
comfort and destitution. He had been stripped of that overweening
religiousness upon which, as its basis, his ascetic egotism had hitherto
rested. He rejoined his friends in a mood to ask and receive guidance,
rather than to afford it."[2] It was in such a frame of mind and spirit that
God could deal with him and lead him on to his desired haven.

Back once more in London, he lodged with John Hutton, a non-juring
clergyman and a friend of his father, who lived in Great College Street,
Westminster. His son, James, kept a bookshop—picturesquely advertised
as "The Bible and Sun"—in Little Wild Street, near Drury Lane. On the
first Sunday Wesley preached in the church of St. John the Evangelist,
at Millbank, Westminster, "on those strong words, 'If any man be in
Christ, he is a new creature.' "[3] He was told that his sermon had given
such offence that he was not to be allowed there again.[4] This was the pre-
cursor of many such refusals. Tuesday, the 7th February he underlined in
his Journal: "A day much to be remembered."[5] At the home of a Dutch
merchant named Weinantz he met a group of Moravians, just landed
from Germany. Amongst them was the man whom God had selected as
his pedagogue to bring him to Christ—Peter Böhler. He was destined to
continue Wesley's instruction in the evangelical faith where Nitschmann
and Spangenberg had left off. Böhler played Bilney to Wesley's Latimer.[6]

We must pause to introduce ourselves to this remarkable young man,
for at the time he was only twenty-six years of age. He had been intended

[1] Pyke, op. cit., pp. 30–31.
[2] Isaac Taylor, Wesley and Methodism (1851), p. 31.
[3] Journal, Vol. I, p. 436. 5th February, 1738.
[4] Ibid.   [5] Ibid., 7th February, 1738.
[6] It was Thomas Bilney—"little Bilney," as he was nicknamed—who led Hugh
Latimer, later Bishop of Worcester, to his evangelical conversion in 1524. Both died
as Protestant martyrs (cf. Harold S. Darby, Hugh Latimer (1953), p. 26).

for medicine, but instead studied theology at Jena. Here he was brought
into contact with an informal fellowship circle which met in the home of
Professor Walch, and was led by Spangenberg. Later Count Zinzendorf
himself came to Jena, and it was under his influence that Böhler was converted. For a time he acted as tutor to Zinzendorf's son, Christian Rena-
tus. In 1737 he was ordained to the ministry and appointed Zinzendorf's
special commissioner for England and America. He was on his way to
visit Georgia when Wesley met him in London. This was the chosen instrument who was to set the frustrated Fellow of Lincoln on the road to
peace and certainty. As Dr. C. W. Towlson has noted, "Böhler is probably
the most attractive figure in this period of the history of the Brethren.
Though he was not a born leader, like Zinzendorf and Spangenberg . . .
he possessed a certain charm which disarmed even those who disagreed
with him; and the affection of the Wesleys for him persisted when their
regard for other Moravian leaders wavered."[1]

On Friday the 17th February Wesley travelled to Oxford with Böhler,
and over the week-end was much in his company. The two had long
conversations. Wesley admitted: "I understood him not, and least of all
when he said, Mi frater, mi frater, excoquenda est ista tua philosophia: 'My
brother, my brother, that philosophy of yours must be purged away!'"[2]
Charles Wesley was also with them, and he seems to have been more
comprehending. It was, of course, Charles who preceded John in conversion. Böhler's own comments on the two brothers are of interest. "The
elder, John, is an amiable man; he acknowledges that he does not yet
rightly know the Saviour and suffers himself to be instructed. He loves us
sincerely. His brother . . . is greatly troubled in spirit and knows not how
he shall begin to know the Saviour."[3] Böhler was to be used in counselling
Charles as well as John.

What was the implication of Böhler's remark to John Wesley about the
need to be purified from "philosophy"? Professor Schmidt elucidates the
somewhat cryptic allusion. "This implied the emphatic repudiation of
natural theology, which was particularly highly esteemed and pursued
both in the tradition of English thinking from the Middle Ages and in the
contemporary Enlightenment. Like Zinzendorf Böhler rejected every
idea of God which was derived, however indirectly, from any general
principle of human reason. He would allow only the Jesus Christ of the
Bible. This was the primary thing, yet he seems in addition to have included under 'philosophy' ethics, and—again following Zinzendorf—all
ethics not derived directly from the Saviour or which did not make His
love the starting-point."[4] This would appear to be what Böhler had in

[1] Clifford W. Towlson, Moravian and Methodist (1957), p. 47.
[2] Journal, Vol. I, p. 440. 19th February, 1738.
[3] Moravian Archives, Herrnhut: cf. World Parish, Vol. II, No. 1, p. 3.
[4] Schmidt, op. cit., Vol. I, p. 235.

mind, rather than Wesley's love of logical argument, as Rigg and Impeta surmised.[1]

Wesley's reaction was to revert to his former habit and renew his previous resolutions.[2] A crucial encounter took place on the 5th March. Wesley had journeyed to Oxford again to see Charles who was ill. There he met Peter Böhler once more, "by whom (in the hand of the great God) I was, on Sunday the 5th, clearly convinced of unbelief, of the want of that faith whereby alone we are saved."[3] Wesley now knew what he lacked. From this day forward, his one desire was to experience justifying faith. He recognized his need. What he sought was the reality in his own heart. Böhler referred to the same interview. "I went walking with the elder Wesley, and asked him about his spiritual state. He said that sometimes he felt quite certain, but sometimes very fearful; he could say nothing further than, 'If that is true which stands in the Bible, then I am saved.' On this matter I talked with him very fully and besought him heartily that he might go to the opened fountain and not spoil the matter for himself."[4]

Wesley was immediately stricken with the conviction that he ought to refrain from preaching a doctrine which he had not yet embraced experimentally. How could he speak to others about a faith which was still not his own? He sought Böhler's opinion as to whether he should therefore stop preaching. The Moravian's reply proved to be perhaps the best bit of practical advice Wesley received in his life. By no means should he cease from preaching, Böhler firmly insisted. But what could he preach? "Preach faith *till* you have it," was the now classic recommendation; "and then, *because* you have it, you *will* preach faith."[5] "In this pregnant statement," according to Schmidt, "lies the deep truth that the task of the preacher is not to bring before his hearers himself or his own spiritual attainment but the authoritative Word, the greater reality of God."[6] Wesley was now satisfied that the one thing lacking in his case was saving

---

[1] James H. Rigg, *The Living Wesley* (1874), pp. 95-96; C. N. Impeta, *De leer van de heiliging en volmaking bij Wesley en Fletcher* (1913), pp. 97-98, cf. Schmidt, *op. cit.*, Vol. I, p. 236, n. 9.

[2] *Journal*, Vol. I, pp. 441-442. 28th February, 1738.

[3] *Ibid.*, p. 442. 4th March, 1738. Cf. pp. 423-424. 1st February, 1738: "The faith I want ('the faith of a *son*,' Wesley added later) is 'a sure trust and confidence in God, that, through the merits of Christ, my sins are forgiven, and I reconciled to the favour of God' (quoted from the Anglican Homily 'Of Salvation'). I want that faith which St. Paul recommends to all the world, especially in his Epistle to the Romans: that faith which enables every one that hath it to cry out, 'I live not; but Christ liveth in me; and the life which I now live, I live by faith in the Son of God, who loved me, and gave Himself for me.' I want that faith which none can have without knowing that he hath it. . . ."

[4] Moravian Archives; cf. *World Parish*, Vol. II, No. 1, p. 4.

[5] *Journal*, Vol. I, p. 442. 4th March, 1738.

[6] Schmidt, *op. cit.*, Vol. I, p. 237.

faith. Already it was an intellectual apprehension: he must go on proclaiming it to others until it became a spiritual possession for him. It may be that Böhler took a calculated risk in giving such counsel—but it paid the highest dividends. In the outcome, Wesley preached to Wesley, for it was really through his own persistent declaration that saving faith is essential that he came to lay hold on it himself.

The result of taking Böhler's advice was immediately startling. As soon as Wesley began preaching "this new doctrine" as he called it—by which he meant that up to this date it was new to him—he found that it struck a responsive chord in those who heard.[1] It was to a prisoner under sentence of death that he first offered salvation by faith alone. He would never have done such a thing beforehand, for he was sceptical about the possibility of eleventh-hour repentance. "This is one of the critical hours in Wesley's life," affirmed Richard Green. "What a revelation his words contain! He had never before preached *salvation by faith alone*. He had never before believed salvation was thus attainable. What light is thrown here upon his past efforts! He might now say truly, 'The faith I want is—this.' "[2]

Two entries in Wesley's *Journal* shortly after this marked an advance in another direction. On the 27th March he went with Charles Kinchin to the Castle at Oxford, where he preached, and afterwards prayed with a prisoner, "first in several forms of prayer, and then in such words as were given us in that hour."[3] The man there and then confessed his sins and trusted in Christ as his Saviour. On the 1st April, Wesley wrote: "Being at Mr. Fox's society, my heart was so full that I could not confine myself to the forms of prayer which we were accustomed to use there. Neither do I purpose to be confined to them any more; but to pray indifferently, with a form or without, as I may find suitable to particular occasions."[4] Telford rightly commented: "This marks a notable step in Wesley's preparation for his evangelistic work."[5] Charles also broke loose from bondage to a prayer-book at this time, and both brothers were to be severely censured by the punctilious Samuel for what he felt was a serious departure from Anglican convention.[6] We do not know precisely when Wesley began also to preach extemporaneously, as his regular habit, but it may well have been at this period. Samuel linked "extemporary expositions and extemporary prayers" in his strictures the following year.[7] As Monk points out, Wesley's use of these two leading Puritan practices would identify him with that tradition, and thus incur disapproval.[8]

[1] *Journal*, Vol. I, p. 442. 6th March, 1738.
[2] Richard Green, *John Wesley: Evangelist* (1905), p. 182.
[3] *Journal*, Vol. I, p. 448. 27th March, 1738.
[4] *Ibid.*, pp. 448–449. 1st April, 1738.
[5] Telford, *op. cit.*, p. 98.
[6] Moore, *op. cit.*, Vol. I, p. 377.
[7] Priestley, *op. cit.*, p. 96. Letter Samuel Wesley junior to John, 16th April, 1739.
[8] Monk, *op. cit.*, p. 25.

Meanwhile Wesley had met Böhler again on the 23rd March, and was more and more amazed at the account he gave of the fruits of living faith —the holiness and happiness which he claimed went with it.[1] He thereupon set himself to examine the Scriptures to see if this doctrine was of God. As we watch Wesley thus emulating the noble Bereans of Acts 17: 11, we are confident that at long last he has got on to the right track. The Protestant Reformation really began when Martin Luther sat before an open Bible high up in the Black Tower of the Augustinian monastery at Wittenberg. The eighteenth-century mission to Britain was similarly indebted to the Word, as in these crucial weeks Wesley thumbed his Greek Testament. It was to a man submissive to the magisterial revelation of Scripture that the mighty call was to come.

Once again Böhler has left his own record of this encounter on the 23rd March. Evidently both John and Charles Wesley were present. "I had a very full conversation with the two Wesleys, in order to impress upon their minds the gospel, and in order to entreat them to proclaim the same to others as they had opportunity at Oxford and elsewhere. Thereupon they confessed their doubts respecting the truth of the doctrine of free grace, through the merits of Jesus, whereby poor sinners receive forgiveness, and are set free from the dominion of sin. The Saviour, however, granted me grace to convince them from the Scriptures; and they had no way of escape, except to ask to see and converse with persons who had made the experiences of which I spoke. I told them that in London I hoped to be able to show them such Christians."[2]

This enables us to understand what occurred the next time Wesley and Böhler met, over the week-end of the 22nd–23rd March. We must transcribe Wesley's account at length, for it concerned a series of talks which clinched the issue for him. "I met Peter Böhler once more. I had now no objection to what he said of the nature of faith, namely that it is (to use the words of our Church) 'a sure trust and confidence which a man hath in God, that through the merits of Christ his sins are forgiven and he reconciled to the favour of God.' Neither could I deny either the happiness or holiness which he described as fruits of this living faith. 'The Spirit itself beareth witness with our spirit that we are the children of God,' and, 'He that believeth hath the witness in himself,' fully convinced me of the former; as, 'Whatsoever is born of God doth not commit sin,' and, 'Whosoever believeth is born of God' did of the latter. But I could not comprehend what he spoke of an *instantaneous work*. I could not understand how this faith should be given in a moment: how a man could *at once* be thus turned from darkness to light, from sin and misery to righteousness and joy in the Holy Ghost. I searched the Scriptures again touching this very thing, particularly the Acts of the Apostles: but, to my utter astonishment,

[1] *Journal*, Vol. I, p. 447. 23rd March, 1738.
[2] J. P. Lockwood, *Memorials of the Life of Peter Böhler* (1868), pp. 74–75.

found scarce any instances there of any other than *instantaneous* conversions; scarce any so slow as that of St. Paul, who was three days in the pangs of the new birth. I had but one retreat left; namely, '*Thus*, I grant God wrought in the *first* ages of Christianity; but the times are changed. What reason have I to believe He works in the same manner now?' "[1]

This brings us to the living witnesses Böhler promised to produce. On Sunday, the 23rd April, Wesley was confronted with them. Böhler reported the occasion to Count Zinzendorf. "I took with me four of the English brethren to John Wesley, that they might relate to him their guidance, how the Saviour so quickly and so mightily has mercy on sinners and accepts them. They related one after the other how it had gone with them. . . . John Wesley and the rest who were with him were as though struck dumb at these narratives.

"I asked Wesley what he now believed. He said, four examples did not settle the matter and could not convince him. I replied that I would bring him eight more here in London. After a short time he arose and said: 'We will sing the hymn, "My soul before Thee prostrate lies."' During the singing he frequently dried his eyes and immediately afterwards he took me alone with him into his bedroom and said that he was now convinced of that which I had said concerning faith and that he would ask nothing further; that he saw very well that it was not yet anything with him, but how could he now help himself and how should he attain to such faith? He was a man who had not sinned as grossly as other people. I replied that not to believe in the Saviour was sinning enough; he should only not go away from the door of the Saviour until He had helped him. I was strongly moved to pray with him; therefore I called upon the blood-covered name of the Saviour for mercy on this sinner. He said to me if once he had *this* he would certainly preach about nothing other than faith."[2] It was clear that Wesley was not far from the kingdom.

---

[1] *Journal*, Vol. I, p. 454. 22nd April, 1738. Wesley quoted again from the Homily "Of Salvation."

[2] Moravian Archives; cf. *World Parish*, Vol. II, No. 1, p. 6. The words of Christian Friedrich Richter's hymn, which Wesley had translated in Georgia, were especially appropriate (*Journal*, Vol. I, p. 299. 30th November, 1736). Three verses must have spoken particularly to his condition:

> My soul before Thee prostrate lies
> To Thee her source my spirit flies,
> My wants I mourn, my chains I see:
> O let Thy presence set me free!
>
> Lost and undone, for aid I cry;
> In Thy death, Saviour, let me die!
> Grieved with Thy grief, pained with Thy pain,
> Ne'er may I feel self-love again.
>
> When my warmed thoughts I fix on Thee
> And plunge me in Thy mercy's sea,

C

He himself admitted that, through the testimony of those four Moravians, he was "beat out of this retreat too"—that is, his demand to see contemporary proof of instantaneous conversions.[1] "Here ended my disputing," he added. "I could now only cry out, 'Lord, help Thou my unbelief!'"[2] "I was now thoroughly convinced," he explained later, in the preface to his conversion narrative; "and by the grace of God, I resolved to seek it (*i.e.*, the gift of faith) unto the end, (1) by absolutely renouncing all dependence, in whole or in part, upon *my own* works or righteousness; on which I had really grounded my hope of salvation, though I knew it not, from my youth up; (2) by adding to the constant use of all the other means of grace, a continual prayer for this very thing, justifying, saving faith, a full reliance on the blood of Christ shed for *me*; a trust in Him, as *my* Christ, as *my* sole justification, sanctification, and redemption."[3] Wesley was to verify for himself how reliable is Christ's promise: "Ask, and it shall be given you; seek, and ye shall find; knock, and it shall be opened unto you" (Matthew 7: 7). That what Wesley asked for he received is corroborated by comparing the language of his prayer at the close of the paragraph quoted above with his classic account of his converson on the 24th May. The reiteration of the personal pronouns in each is most marked.[4]

On the 26th April Böhler and Wesley had an hour's walk together, in the course of which they had another heart-to-heart dialogue. Böhler revealed that Wesley wept bitterly, but they were the tears of true repentance drawn forth by the Holy Spirit.[5] "This I can say of him; he is truly a poor sinner, who has a broken heart and who hungers after a better righteousness than he had until now, namely the righteousness of Jesus Christ."[6] Meanwhile, Wesley was still preaching "the faith as it is in Jesus."[7] He realized that it was "a strange doctrine, which some did not care to contradict, yet knew not what to make of."[8] Nevertheless, "one or two, who were thoroughly bruised by sin, willingly heard and received gladly."[9] Böhler reported that Wesley preached so effectively that "all people were astounded because one never heard like that from him. . . . Many were awakened thereby.'[10] On the 4th May Böhler left London in order to embark for Carolina. But his influence remained, and, as they

Then even on me Thy face shall shine,
And quicken this dead heart of mine.

The hymn first appeared in Freylinghausen's *Gesangbuch* in 1704.

[1] *Journal*, Vol. I, p. 455. 23rd March, 1738.
[2] *Ibid.*   [3] *Ibid.*, p. 472. 24th May, 1738.
[4] *Ibid.*, p. 476: "I felt my heart strangely warmed. I felt I did trust in Christ, Christ alone for salvation; and an assurance was given *me* that He had taken away *my* sins, even *mine*, and saved *me* from the law of sin and death."
[5] Moravian Archives; cf. *World Parish*, Vol. II, No. 1, p. 8.   [6] *Ibid.*
[7] *Journal*, Vol. I, p. 457. 26th April, 1738.   [8] *Ibid.*   [9] *Ibid.*
[10] Moravian Archives; cf. *World Parish*, Vol. II, no. 1, p. 8.

pondered what he had so faithfully insisted upon, first Charles and then John Wesley came into the experience of saving faith. John's insertion into his *Journal* on the day of Böhler's departure indicates how decisive he felt his impact had been. "Oh what a work hath God begun, since his coming to England! Such an one as shall never come to an end till heaven and earth pass away."[1]

The last word from Böhler came in a letter dated the 8th May, and written from Southampton. It contained the impassioned plea: "Delay not, I beseech you, to believe in *your* Jesus Christ; but so put Him in mind of His promises to poor sinners that He may not be able to refrain from doing for you what He hath done for so many others."[2] Not many days later, on the ever-memorable 24th May, Wesley broke the faith-barrier, as Dr. Marshall so arrestingly describes his experience.[3] The circumstances are too familiar to be rehearsed yet again. "The change which God works in the heart through faith in Christ" took place in him, even as he listened to Luther's account of it.[4] Words were translated into realities, and the doctrine came alive for him. The cardinal tenet of the Protestant Reformation, which is the root of all truly Christian belief, now not only seized his mind but touched his heart. The kindling was to be felt throughout the land as a consequence. It was indeed a strange warmth, as Wesley so accurately analysed it, for he was not a man given to emotional impressions. That this should happen to him of all people was sufficient to attest it as a work of supernatural grace.

The symbolism of fire links the upper room in Aldersgate Street with the blazing parsonage at Epworth. The brand plucked from the burning had now found his destiny. Henceforth the flame within would carry him throughout the land to ignite the tinder of revival. Wesley told Samuel Bradburn, when they were together in Yorkshire in 1781, that his Christian experience might be expressed in his brother's hymn:

> O Thou who camest from above
> The pure celestial fire to impart
> Kindle a flame of sacred love
> On the mean altar of my heart!
>
> There let it for Thy glory burn
> With inextinguishable blaze;
> And trembling to its source return,
> In humble prayer and fervent praise.
>
> Jesus, confirm my heart's desire
> To work, and speak, and think for Thee;
> Still let me guard the holy fire,
> And still stir up Thy gift in me.

[1] *Journal*, Vol. I, pp. 459–460. 4th May, 1738.   [2] *Ibid.*, p. 461. 13th May, 1738.
[3] Dorothy Marshall, *John Wesley* (1965), p. 24.
[4] *Journal*, Vol. I, p. 476. 24th May, 1738. Cf. Bett, *op. cit.*, pp. 21–22.

"Guarding the holy fire; that was what he was doing," wrote Prof. Bonamy Dobrée. "He was himself a flame going up and down the land, lighting candles such as, by God's grace, would never be put out; and as one reads the colossal *Journal* one gets the impression of this flame, never waning, never smoky, darting from point to point, lighting up the whole kingdom, till in due course it burnt out the body it inhabited."[1]

We have allowed Wesley to tell his own story largely in his own words, with interspersions from his spiritual director, Peter Böhler. This has been deliberately done, for Wesley has suffered under the weight of numerous interpreters. So many scholars have sought to enlighten us as to what actually did happen on the 24th May, 1738, that we are in danger of forgetting the fact that Wesley himself supplied very full accounts, both of the experience itself and of what led up to it. They leave us in no doubt that he regarded this as his conversion, and it is refreshing to see that recent investigators are recognizing this once again. The attempt of Piette, following Léger, Urlin and Overton, to back-date Wesley's transformation to 1725 is, as V. H. H. Green agrees, "an over-simplification."[2] "There can be no question of the contrast between the ritualist of 1737 and the evangelist of 1739", claimed Rattenbury, "and it is difficult to think of any word more fit to describe it than conversion."[3]

Other recent writers concur. "Strongly as Maximin Piette may speak of Wesley's moral conversion in 1725," declares Maldwyn Edwards, "it could not and did not supply the dynamic which came through his evangelical conversion of 1738."[4] Outler calls it "a radical change . . . a conversion if ever there was one."[5] Rupert Davies thinks it may properly be called Wesley's evangelical conversion, and sees in it a complete turning-point in his life, experientially, psychologically and theologically.[6] Prof. H. A. Hodges allows that in 1725 there was a change from laxity to serious concern for religion, which some might loosely call conversion, but he defines what occurred in 1738 as an evangelical conversion, and spends some time in analysing the phenomenon.[7] Towlson regards what happened in 1738 as something which altered the whole current of Wesley's life, and adds: "It could hardly be a new idea, a new intellectual attitude, which effected the mighty change so much as a new experience."[8] Schmidt devotes a chapter of almost one hundred pages to what he unambiguously entitles "the conversion," in which "theory had become fact, expectation had become fulfilment, desire had become possession."[9]

[1] Bonamy Dobrée, *John Wesley* (1933), pp. 96–97.
[2] V. H. H. Green, *The Young Mr. Wesley*, p. 271.
[3] Rattenbury, *op. cit.*, p. 67.
[4] *A History of the Methodist Church in Great Britain*, Vol. I, p. 43.
[5] Outler, *op. cit.*, p. 7.
[6] R. E. Davies, *op. cit.*, pp. 57–60.
[7] H. A. Hodges and A. M. Allchin, *A Rapture of Praise* (1966), pp. 13–18.
[8] Towlson, *op. cit.*, p. 58.   [9] Schmidt, *op. cit.*, Vol. I, p. 263.

Dean Carpenter considers it "one of the three most momentous conversions in Christian history," along with those of Paul and Augustine.[1] This consensus of recent scholarly opinion indicates that, after a period of scrutiny and reappraisement, the evidence for the traditional view of Wesley's experience has emerged with enhanced authority. Surely we can drop the inverted commas which have sometimes enclosed the word conversion as applied to Wesley's heart-warming, and rejoice without inhibitions in what God did by His grace on that quite literally epoch-making day, the 24th May, 1738.

[1] S. C. Carpenter, *Eighteenth Century Church and People* (1959), p. 197.

CHAPTER VI

SUCH AN INSTRUMENT

"OH WHY is it that so great, so wise, so holy a God will use *such an instrument* as me! Yea, Thou sendest whom Thou wilt send, and showest mercy by whom Thou wilt show mercy! Amen! Be it, then, according to Thy will." *Letters* I: 244–245.

WESLEY NOW STOOD ON THE THRESHOLD OF HIS UNIQUE ministry to the soul of Britain. He had "crossed his religious Rubicon," as Prof. Cell expressed it.[1] He was poised to spring into action, as God gave the word of command. This was all that was needed. In every other respect, Wesley was a man prepared. What we see in the first few months after his conversion is one who waited for God to show how his mission was to be accomplished. He had the message. He had the burning experience. The hungry multitude looked up for someone to feed them with spiritual bread. Here was his constituency, but as yet he had to be introduced to a means of reaching it. That is the clue to the period between his conversion on the 24th May, 1738, and the start of open-air preaching on the 2nd April, 1739.

Wesley was a man of destiny from birth, and, indeed, even before, as we have seen. From the night when he was rescued from the blazing rectory at Epworth, he himself was aware that somehow God had preserved his life for a purpose. Step by step he was led towards the realization of what that purpose was. Wesley firmly believed in such divine predetermination. In his treatise on *Predestination Calmly Considered* (1752), he stated that election does not only mean the appointment of some to eternal happiness, but also the appointment of some to do a particular work for God in the world.[2] In this way Paul, for example, was elected to preach the gospel to the Gentiles. This election to service, Wesley believed to be not only personal, but absolute and unconditional.[3] Increasingly, even before Aldersgate Street, Wesley became conscious that he was the subject of such a call.

We sense his own reluctance, and yet at the same time his awareness of supernatural control, as, acting on Peter Böhler's advice, he began to

---

[1] Cell, *op. cit.*, p. 28.

[2] *Works*, Vol. X, p. 210. *Predestination Calmly Considered* (1752).

[3] *Ibid.* Election to eternal bliss, however, Wesley believed to be conditional, like its corollary of reprobation.

preach saving faith, even though he himself had not experienced it.[4] This was when he first acted in direct obedience to the mysterious leading from above. The very language he employed suggests that he felt as if matters were taken out of his hands. He was not under his own volition. "I began preaching this new doctrine, though my soul started back from the work."[2] The fact that such an immediate effect was produced on one of the prisoners in the Castle must have confirmed his recognition that this was altogether of the Lord. In *A Short History of the People Called Methodists* (1781), Wesley fixed on this as the date when he first proclaimed the message which was to be his lifelong theme. Immediately after his return from Georgia, he said he occupied a number of pulpits, though he "did not yet see the nature of saving faith."[3] "But as soon as I saw this clearly," he added, "namely, on Monday, March 6th, I declared it without delay; and God then began to work by my ministry, as he never had done before."[4]

On the 25th April Wesley "spoke clearly and fully at Blendon to Mr. Delamotte's family of the nature and fruits of faith."[5] Thomas Broughton —one of the Oxford Holy Club—and Charles Wesley were present. The latter was particularly offended by the message, and roundly told John he was doing no end of harm. But John's comment in the *Journal* was most revealing: no doubt it represented an insertion at a later date in the light of after events. "And, indeed, it did please God then to kindle a fire which I trust shall never be extinguished."[6] Charles Wesley gave his own account of this incident. From what he said, it is apparent that the discussion concerned instantaneous conversion and immediate assurance: John maintained both, whilst Charles resisted them with some heat.[7] Yet within a month each of the brothers was to taste the reality, and lose all doubt or disagreement.

In *The Principles of a Methodist Farther Explained* (1746), Wesley supplied a summary of his preaching from 1729 onwards, which again demonstrates that the turning-point in effectiveness was reached when he started to concentrate on justification by faith alone. "(1) from the year 1725 to 1729 I preached much, but saw no fruit for my labour. Indeed it could not be that I should; for I neither laid the foundation of repentance, nor of believing the gospel; taking it for granted, that all to whom I preached were believers, and that many of them 'needed no repentance.'

[1] *Journal*, Vol. I, p. 442. 4th March, 1738.
[2] *Ibid.* 6th March, 1738.
[3] *Works*, Vol. XIII, p. 273. *A Short History of the People Called Methodists* (1781).
[4] *Ibid.*
[5] *Journal*, Vol. I, pp. 455-456. 25th April, 1738. Charles Delamotte had accompanied the Wesleys to Georgia, see above p. 51. His father was a London sugar merchant and a magistrate.
[6] *Ibid.*, p. 456.
[7] C. Wesley, *Journal*, Vol. I, pp. 84-85. 25th April, 1738.

(2) From the year 1729 to 1734, laying a deeper foundation of repentance, I saw a little fruit. But it was only a little; and no wonder: for I did not preach faith in the blood of the covenant. (3) From 1734 to 1738, speaking more of faith in Christ, I saw more fruit of my preaching, and visiting from house to house, than ever I had done before; though I know not if any of those who were outwardly reformed were inwardly and thoroughly converted to God. (4) From 1738 to this time, speaking continually of Jesus Christ, laying Him only for the foundation of the whole building, making Him all in all, the first and the last; preaching only on this plan, 'The kingdom of God is at hand; repent ye, and believe the gospel;' the 'word of God ran' as fire among the stubble; it 'was glorified' more and more; multitudes crying out, 'What must we do to be saved?' and afterwards witnessing, 'By grace are we saved through faith.' "[1]

This sense of being carried along in the divine plan, of which Wesley was aware even before his conversion, remained with him throughout his ministry.[2] In 1766 he could write a letter to his brother Charles, in which he confessed to a certain depression of spirit—no doubt the result of multiplied responsibilities. But, despite his temporary malaise, he still testified to his sense of mission. "And yet to be so employed of God, and so hedged in that I can neither get forward nor backward! . . . I dare not preach otherwise than I do, either concerning faith, or love, or justification, or perfection. And yet I find rather an increase than a decrease of zeal for the whole work of God and every part of it. I am φερόμενος, I know not how, that I can't stand still. I want all the world to come to ὃν οὐκ οἶδα. Neither am I impelled to this by fear of any kind. I have no more fear than love. Or if I have any fear, it is not that of falling into hell but of falling into nothing."[3] This was a most remarkable self-disclosure, not meant for anyone to see apart from Charles. If its negations bore witness to the fact that even such a man of God was not immune from periodic dejection, its affirmations indicated with contrasted vigour that the sovereign will of God was still being fulfilled through him.

This sense of destiny, then, was felt by Wesley prior to his conversion, and stayed with him after it as the motor impulse of his life. What took place in Aldersgate Street immensely strengthened his incipient consciousness of mission. Böhler's counsel had produced its desired effect. Wesley

---

[1] *Works*, Vol. VIII, pp. 468–469. *The Principles of a Methodist Farther Explained* (1746).

[2] Even the passage used as a motto for this chapter, though written on Wesley's conversion day, actually preceded the heart-warming experience which took place at "about a quarter before nine" (*Journal*, Vol. I, p. 475. 24th May, 1738). The letter, to an unknown recipient, continued with this significant affirmation, after, "Be it, then according to Thy will!"; "If Thou speak the word, Judas shall cast out devils." (*Letters*, Vol. I, pp. 244–245. 24th May, 1738.)

[3] *Letters*, Vol. V, p. 16. To Charles Wesley, 27th June, 1766. φερόμενος—"borne along." ὃν οὐκ οἶδα—"what I do not know."

did indeed preach faith *until* he had it: now he went out to preach faith *because* he had it. Beforehand, he accepted the truth but lacked the experience. After the 24th May, 1738, the doctrine was fired by the reality of a heart that had been strangely warmed. It was in this fusion of the revealed Word and the believing soul, that the Holy Spirit found a medium through which to work. Henceforth, Wesley was to exercise a catalytic influence on those he touched.

The urge to communicate was intensified by his experience. It is significant that straight away in the little society meeting, Wesley "testified openly to all there what I now first felt in my heart."[1] On the Sunday following he did the same at the home of John Hutton in Westminster, and was "roughly attacked in a large company as an enthusiast, a seducer, and a setter-forth of new doctrines."[2] Mrs. Hutton, who was as much offended as the rest, described the scene in a letter to John Wesley's eldest brother, Samuel. This was how the wife of a non-juring High Churchman viewed an evangelical conversion. "Mr. John got up and told the people that five days before he was not a Christian, and this he was as well assured of as that five days before he was not in that room, and the way for them all to be Christians was to believe, and own that they were not now Christians. Mr. Hutton was much surprised at this unexpected, injudicious speech; but only said, 'Have a care, Mr. Wesley, how you despise the benefits received by the two sacraments.'"[3] Mrs. Hutton went on to narrate how at supper Wesley "made the same wild speech," to which she replied, "If you were not a Christian ever since I knew you, you were a great hypocrite, for you made us all believe you were one." She begged Samuel "to confine or convert Mr. John while he is with you. For after his behaviour on Sunday, May 28th, when you hear it, you will think him a not quite right man."[4] If a stop was not put to it, she added, "the mischief he will do wherever he goes among the ignorant but well-meaning Christians will be very great."[5]

John Wesley, however, knew he was in good company when it was thought he was beside himself. His ministry had been impeccably sane, but lamentably ineffectual prior to his embracing this doctrine of salvation. A little apostolic madness might not come amiss. He was certainly not deterred by the attitude of his friends. "By the blessing of God, I was not moved to anger, but after a calm and short reply went away; though

[1] *Journal*, Vol. I, p. 476. 24th May, 1738.
[2] *Ibid.*, p. 479. 28th May, 1738.
[3] *Ibid.*, n. 2. Cf. Daniel Benham, *Memoirs of James Hutton* (1856), p. 34. Mrs. Hutton was obviously disturbed and annoyed by Wesley's influence on James Hutton. In a further letter, she described Wesley as "my son's Pope" (Benham, *op. cit.*, p. 39). Professor Dobrée's comment on Wesley's testimony is perceptive: "He had not been a Christian, not in the way he now was; he had been a mere nominal Christian, a poor simulacrum, so why not say so?" (*op. cit.*, p. 66).
[4] *Journal*, Vol. I, p. 479, n. 2.   [5] *Ibid.*

not with so tender a concern as was due to those who were seeking death in the error of their life."[1] It was this tender concern which was to grow with such rapidity that it soon became the master passion of his ministry. A melting pity for all who had not yet known Christ in this intimate, transforming way, was to mark his mission from this time forward. Dr. J. H. Plumb notices that Wesley's conversion was "followed by no dark night of the soul such as the great mystics have known, but by a burning determination to bring to others what he himself had felt."[2]

It was the warmed heart that made Wesley an evangelist. The fire could only spread as first of all it was kindled. The flame was lit in Aldersgate Street. That hour, as Dr. Bett believed, "was the real beginning of his unique apostolate."[3] There came to him "a spiritual energy, an evangelical zeal, an unction of the Holy One, that he had never before possessed."[4] This was his supreme equipment. Without it, he could never have accomplished the task God gave him. This new dynamic took away the nagging frustration of his previous ministry. He was completely reorientated. "In all his earlier disciplined life of holiness, and the good works to which he set his hand," writes Maldwyn Edwards, "his primary concern was on what he could do for God. But after the Aldersgate Street heart-warming, he asked only what God could do for him and through him. Thus at a stroke the old sense of strain and effort had gone. There was no longer the anxious probing of heart and conscience begetting 'the spirit of heaviness.' All was of grace through faith, and now he found he was 'always conqueror.' It was out of this experience that the ecclesiastic of Georgia could become the evangelist of the open road."[5] "He went forth from Aldersgate Street a man liberated for his work," declared Rattenbury.[6]

Wesley had only "one point of view—to promote, so far as I am able, vital, practical religion; and by the grace of God to beget, preserve, and increase the life of God in the souls of men."[7] Or, in the classic statement of his objective, "to reform the nation, particularly the Church, and to spread Scriptural holiness over the land."[8] "Henceforth he was utterly

---

[1] *Ibid.*, pp. 479–480. 28th May, 1738. The substance of Wesley's explanation has been preserved elsewhere. "When we renounce everything but faith, and get into Christ, then, and not till then, have we any reason to believe we are Christians." (Telford, *op. cit.*, p. 102.)

[2] Plumb, *England in the Eighteenth Century*, p. 92.

[3] Bett, *op. cit.*, p. 33.   [4] *Ibid.*

[5] *A History of the Methodist Church in Great Britain*, Vol. I, p. 51; cf. *Journal*, Vol. I, p. 477. 24th May, 1738: "And herein I found the difference between this and my former state chiefly consisted. I was striving, yea, fighting with all my might under the law, as well as under grace. But then I was sometimes, if not often, conquered; now, I was always conqueror."

[6] Rattenbury, *op. cit.*, p. 49.

[7] *Letters*, Vol. III, p. 192. To Samuel Walker, 3rd September, 1756.

[8] *Works*, Vol. VIII, p. 299. *Large Minutes* (1789).

convinced," says Dr. Dorothy Marshall, "that every man and woman who, conscious of their own sin and misery, turned to Christ, relying completely on His love, would be saved from hell and sin. It was the desire to spread this joyful news that turned John Wesley into a great preacher, carrying his message of hope throughout the land."[1] It is refreshing to find a distinguished secular historian who recognizes what was Wesley's real motivation. The attempt to transmogrify him into a man who was preoccupied primarily with social reform or ecclesiastical polity has singularly failed. We are realizing afresh today that first and foremost John Wesley was an evangelist. If one word must be selected to describe his calling, this is it. He was not to be an incumbent, for he never held a living. He was to leave the seclusion of Oxford behind him, for he was not to remain a tutor. What God intended him to be all along was an evangelist, and this is what He made him. The one chief purpose for which Wesley was raised up, according to Richard Green, and to fulfil which he was especially qualified, was "his evangelistic appeal to the heart and conscience of this nation."[2] Or, in the words of Pyke: "His one concern was to lead man to man's one and only Saviour. He did it from the first; and he never ceased to do so as long as he lived."[3]

This was Wesley's goal. Neither failure nor success would cause him to deviate even by a hair's breadth from his overall aim of evangelism. "You have nothing to do but to save souls," was one of his rules for preachers.[4] It was one which he himself observed with passionate fidelity. He looked out on the masses of the people, "fast bound in sin and nature's night," and had compassion on them.[5] They were as sheep without a shepherd, harassed and dejected. His heart bled for them. He saw, he came, and by God's enabling grace he conquered. For more than fifty years he rode the length and breadth of the land to offer Christ to those who needed Him most and heeded Him least. How could they hear without a preacher? He would be that preacher. Wesley was indeed an apostolic man: one sent by God with an extraordinary commission to evangelize the nation. As E. W. Thompson has argued, it was this sense of peculiar mission which prompted Wesley at times to break with established tradition, and even to set aside the normal regulations governing the Church.[6] God had given him a work to do, and nothing must stand in the way of it. Everything was subordinated to the furtherance of the gospel. This was his magnificent obsession.

---

[1] Marshall, *John Wesley*, p. 25.
[2] R. Green, *op. cit.*, p. 1.   [3] Pyke, *op. cit.*, p. 21.
[4] *Works*, Vol. VIII, p. 310. *Large Minutes* (1789). "You have nothing to do but to save souls. Therefore spend and be spent in this work. And go always, not only to those who want you, but to those that want you most." The verb "to want" in the eighteenth century carried the sense of "to need."
[5] *Wesley's Hymns*, No. 201, v. 4, l. 2.
[6] E. W. Thompson, *Wesley: Apostolic Man* (1957), pp. 53–54.

Wesley used to explain that he had two calls to the ministry in the Church of Christ. One was his *ordinary* call, which came to him through the channel of episcopal ordination. The other was his *extraordinary* call given direct from God Himself. In his extraordinary call he distinguished two elements. He was first of all to proclaim the good news of salvation to as many as would hear, in a much wider field than any parish. But he was also to care for the souls of the converts, which made him the pastor of a much larger flock than he could have found in any church.[1] We may therefore rightly describe him as missioner extraordinary to the lost sheep of the land. Wesley never received even the most modest ecclesiastical preferment. But he had a commission from God, and this he valued above all that man could have conferred upon him. Nothing could distract him from what he conceived to be his course. He could say with Paul, "This one thing I do;" and he went on doing it to the end, with astonishing concentration and unflagging zeal.

As Schmidt brings out, this strong awareness of vocation links Wesley most markedly with Martin Luther.[2] Although it was Luther who was to emancipate the concept of calling from its medieval fetters and expound the doctrine of a vocation for all believers, yet he himself nevertheless was profoundly conscious that he had been raised up by God to do a work which he personally would not have chosen. And in Luther's case, as in Wesley's, it was to be an evangelist that he was thus laid hold of by the Lord. Luther recognized and accepted this designation. He had no desire to be regarded as a national prophet, an ecclesiastical statesman, or a doctor of theology, though all these could well be claimed for him. He was content to be known as a plain preacher of the gospel. Wittenberg became a sounding-board for the Word. Luther had a mission from God to evangelize the people. "If I should want to boast," he wrote, "I should glory in God that I am one of the apostles and evangelists in German lands, even though the devil and all his bishops and tyrants do not want me to be such: for I know that by the grace of God I have taught and still teach faith and truth."[3] He described himself elsewhere as "an unworthy evangelist of our Lord Jesus."[4] As Wesley embarked on his evangelistic crusade, he shared the same sense of divine calling as the pioneer of Protestantism.

Meanwhile, before going into battle, Wesley paid a visit to the Mora-

---

[1] *Ibid.*, p. 55. Cf. *Letters*, Vol. V, p. 257. To Mary Bosanquet, 13th June, 1771: "It is plain to me that the whole work of God termed Methodism is an extraordinary dispensation of His providence. Therefore I do not wonder if several things occur therein which do not fall under the ordinary rules of discipline." The issue discussed in that particular letter was the preaching of women.

[2] Schmidt, *op. cit.*, Vol. I, p. 94.

[3] *D. Martin Luthers Werke* (Weimar Gesamtausgabe), ed. J. F. K. Knaake *et. al.* (1883 ff.), Vol. VIII, p. 683.

[4] *Ibid.*, Vol. XXX, p. 366.

vian headquarters at Herrnhut, in Saxony. It was necessary to retreat like this in order to be the better able eventually to advance. Paul retired to Arabia before plunging into his missionary programme. Wesley was led in a similar way to prepare himself for his work. This was something he had planned to do in any case, even before he left Georgia. Now he definitely decided "to retire for a short time . . ." in order to "go on from faith to faith and from strength to strength!"[1] He hoped that meeting those who were themselves living witnesses of the full power of faith would be a means, under God, of establishing his own soul.[2]

Before he left for Germany, however, Wesley preached on Sunday the 11th June, 1738, at the church of St. Mary the Virgin in Oxford. This was the stirring sermon on "Salvation by Faith," which stands as Number One in his standard collection.[3] It was printed separately not long after it had been delivered, and was the first of Wesley's publications after his conversion. Curiously enough, the *Journal* did not mention this historic occasion when, as Sugden put it, "John Wesley blew the first trumpet-call of the Evangelical Revival."[4] On Thursday the 8th June he went to Salisbury to take leave of his mother.[5] She had evidently heard about his conversion in a somewhat distorted version from the Huttons, and to set the record straight John read to her a document describing his religious experience up to and including the 24th May.[6] From Salisbury he travelled to Stanton Harcourt, Oxfordshire, to see John Gambold, a former member of the Holy Club, who was now incumbent of that parish.[7] Wesley "preached faith in Christ there" on the morning of the 11th June, and then went on to Oxford.[8] The sermon, which was in fact a manifesto of his new-found convictions, must have been the same as he had given at Stanton Harcourt. But in what different circumstances!

Instead of a village congregation, he faced the cream of the University. This was an official University service, to which he had been invited by the Vice-Chancellor. The statutes required that all doctors, masters, graduates and scholars should attend, unless they could provide a credible excuse for absence. It was a testing ordeal for any preacher, but especially so to Wesley in the flush of his conversion experience only eighteen days before. But it also afforded an unusual opportunity for him to nail his colours to the mast and proclaim in Oxford, as already he had done in

---

[1] *Journal*, Vol. I, pp. 482–483. 7th June, 1738.

[2] *Ibid.*

[3] *Sermons*, Vol. I, pp. 35–52. Sermon I. Salvation by Faith.

[4] *Ibid.*, p. 36. Notes.

[5] *Journal*, Vol. I, p. 483. 8th June, 1738.

[6] *Ibid.*, n. 1. It was this which he inserted in his *Journal*, *ibid.*, pp. 465–477. 24th May, 1738.

[7] *Ibid.*, p. 483. 10th June, 1738. For Gambold, who later became a Moravian Bishop, see Tyerman, *Oxford Methodists*, pp. 155–200.

[8] *Journal*, Vol. I, p. 483. 11th June, 1738.

London, the message of saving faith. This was not a discourse specially prepared *in toto* for the occasion: indeed, Wesley apparently preached it before the 24th May.[1] But now there was a new ring about it, and its forthright tones must have startled the academic congregation. In language strongly reminiscent of his own testimony as to what happened to him at Aldersgate Street—perhaps this was inserted into the original manuscript, or at least represents a rephrasing—he thus defined the nature of justifying faith. "Christian faith is, then, not only an assent to the whole gospel of Christ, but also a full reliance on the blood of Christ; a trust in the merits of His life, death, and resurrection; a recumbency upon Him as our atonement and our life, as *given for us*, and *living in us*. It is a sure confidence which a man hath in God, that through the merits of Christ, *his* sins are forgiven, and *he* reconciled to the favour of God; and, in consequence hereof, a closing with Him, and cleaving to Him, as our 'wisdom, righteousness, sanctification, and redemption,' or, in one word, our salvation."[2]

After three months spent on the continent of Europe, Wesley came back to England on the 17th September, 1738. His belief was considerably strengthened by what he heard and saw. In particular, the personal narratives related by one after another of the Moravians at Herrnhut took him completely by storm, as Schmidt reminds us.[3] Wesley's own faith and experience was this confirmed—which is what he had hoped when he set out. He must have found it hard to tear himself away. But he knew he had a job to do. "I would gladly have spent my life here," he wrote from Herrnhut; "but my Master calling me to labour in another part of His vineyard, on Monday 14th I was constrained to take my leave of this happy place. . . . Oh, when shall THIS Christianity cover the earth, as the 'waters cover the sea'?"[4] Despite later controversies, leading to what Monsignor Knox called "the parting of friends," Wesley never lost his regard for the Moravians and their missionary endeavours.[5] Answering the criticisms of Thomas Church, Vicar of Battersea and Prebendary of St. Paul's, in 1745, Wesley expressed the opinion that, next to the Church of England, the members of the Moravian communion were in the main the best Christians in the world.[6]

For the time being, Wesley was content to preach wherever the doors opened to him. A number of churches in London admitted him during the latter months of 1738, but, as we shall be noting in detail shortly, it

[1] Wesley "preached free salvation by faith in the blood of Christ" on 14th May at St. Anne and St. Agnes, Aldersgate, London, and the Savoy Chapel on the Strand (*Journal*, Vol. I, p. 462. 14th May, 1738).

[2] *Sermons*, Vol. I, pp. 40–41. Sermon I.

[3] Schmidt, *op. cit.*, Vol. I, pp. 294–295.

[4] *Journal*, Vol. II, p. 28. 14th August, 1738.

[5] Ronald A. Knox, *Enthusiasm* (1950), p. 459.

[6] *Letters*, Vol. II, p. 179. To Thomas Church, 2nd February, 1745.

would soon become increasingly difficult for him to find a pulpit. Had his doctrine been more acceptable, little objection would have been raised on legal grounds. But since his message was offensive, an appeal could be made to the stipulations of the Act of Uniformity (1662) which laid it down that no visiting lecturer or preacher should be received without episcopal permission.[1] Edmund Gibson, Bishop of London, had occasion to remind Charles Wesley of this in November 1738.[2] He graciously declined to use his authority, but had he chosen to do so, there could have been no redress. But where the incumbent or the vestry wished to find a hook on which to hang their protest against the Wesleys, there was no problem in discovering one. More and more, the brothers were being driven from the churches to the religious societies. In the period between September 1738 and April 1739 (when John Wesley took to open-air evangelism in Bristol), they preached less in Anglican pulpits and more in the society rooms. Except in the case of exclusively Church of England groups, on the model of those formed in the previous century by Anthony Horneck and William Smythies, the legal position with regard to these in terms of the Conventicle Act was not a little shaky. Within six months of his conversion, then, Wesley found himself skating on rather thin ice so far as ecclesiastical propriety was concerned.

As he explained in his *A Farther Appeal to Men of Reason and Religion* (1745), at this juncture he and his brother "were dragged out . . . by earnest importunity, to preach at one place, and another, and another, and so carried on, we knew not how, without any design, but the general one of saving souls, into a situation, which, had it been named to us at first, would have appeared far worse than death."[3] But, of course, the excessive rigorism of Georgia was now left far behind, and where the welfare of men and women lost in trespasses and sins was at stake, Wesley was ready to waive the regulations in the interest of evangelism. This was to be his policy throughout his ministry. But though "he had found his message," as Prof. G. R. Cragg makes clear; "he had not yet found his method."[4] That was to follow on the 2nd April, 1739.

[1] Act of Uniformity 1662, H. Gee and W. J. Hardy, *Documents Illustrative of English Church History* (1896), p. 612. 14 Charles II, cap. 4, 1662.
[2] Simon, *Religious Societies*, p. 235.
[3] *Works*, Vol. VIII, p. 227. *A Farther Appeal to Men of Reason and Religion* (1745).
[4] G. R. Cragg, *The Church and the Age of Reason 1648–1789* (1960), p. 142.

PART II
THE MISSION OF AN EVANGELIST

CHAPTER VII

EXCLUDED FROM THE CHURCHES

"IT WAS still my desire to preach in a church, rather than in any other place; but many obstructions were now laid in the way. . . . Being thus *excluded from the churches*, and not daring to be silent, it remained only to preach in the open air; which I did at first, not out of choice, but out of necessity." *Works* 13 : 273.

JOHN WESLEY WAS DESTINED TO BE AN EVANGELIST. ALONG WITH George Whitefield and his own brother Charles, he was called of God to lead the mission to Britain. Within twenty years, however, Charles was to retire almost completely from active campaigning. Whitefield died in 1770, worn out by his herculean labours. But John battled on for over fifty years, and lived to see the tide turned and a nation awakened.

He was the chosen apostle of the masses. But before he could reach his divinely appointed constituency, a way of approach had to be found. Traditional methods would never succeed in touching the thousands outside the churches. A new means of contact was needed. It was provided by open-air preaching. But Wesley did not immediately choose this medium. It was virtually forced on him. At first he exercised his evangelistic gift within the Established Church. But though a great door and effectual was opening to him, there were also many adversaries. Between his conversion in May 1738 and the launching of the mission proper in April 1739, the pulpits of London were rapidly closing on him. Being excluded from the churches, he was driven into the fields. Henceforward his was to be a predominantly extra-mural ministry.

In his *A Farther Appeal to Men of Reason and Religion* (1745) he explained the situation. As soon as he had obtained a clear view of salvation by grace through faith, he made it his only theme. He enforced it with all his might in every church where he was asked to preach, and on occasion also in the religious societies. He was overwhelmed with invitations. "Things were in this posture, when I was told I must preach no more in this, and this, and another church; the reason was usually added without reserve, 'Because you preach such doctrines.' "[1] "Be pleased to observe," he went on, "that I was forbidden, as by a general consent, to preach in any church (though not by any judicial sentence), 'for preaching such doctrine.' This was the open, avowed cause; there was at that time no other, either real or pretended, except that the people crowded so."[2]

[1] *Works*, Vol. VIII, p. 112. *A Farther Appeal to Men of Reason and Religion* (1745).
[2] *Ibid.*, pp. 112–113.

In a letter written to Samuel Walker, the evangelical curate at St. Mary, Truro, Wesley recalled the reproach he had to bear in this initial period of his work. He had known something of it at Oxford, he said. But "it was abundantly increased when we began to preach repentance and remission of sins and insist that we are justified by faith. For this cause were we excluded from preaching in the churches. (I say, for *this*: as yet there was no field-preaching.) And this exclusion occasioned our preaching elsewhere, with the other irregularities that followed. Therefore all the reproach consequent thereon is no other than the reproach of Christ."[1]

"Why were the Wesleys banned by the Established Church?" inquired J. Henry Martin, in a Wesley Historical Society lecture on *John Wesley's London Chapels*. The answer is substantiated by the facts. "In a sentence, it may be stated that the denial of the parish pulpits was due to their preaching of the Evangelical doctrines."[2] At this stage it was not an objection to methods: it was an objection to the message. The gospel itself was the scandal. Whitefield met with a similar rebuff when he returned from America towards the end of 1738. When he had been in London before, he was widely welcomed. Now he found that he was no longer allowed to enter most of the pulpits.

Wesley had a foretaste of this exclusion even before the Aldersgate Street experience. As we have seen, he began to preach justification earlier in the year, with the encouragement of Peter Böhler. This was the doctrine which caused such offence. On the 5th February, 1738, at St. John the Evangelist, Westminster, he preached "on those strong words, 'If any man be in Christ, he is a new creature.' I was afterwards informed, many of the best in the parish were so offended, that I was not to preach there any more."[3] Nor did he. The following Sunday saw him at St. Andrew, Holborn, with I Corinthians 13: 3 as his text. "Oh, hard sayings!" was his comment. "Who can hear them? Here, too, it seems, I am to preach no more."[4] He never appeared again in the very church where his father had been ordained by Henry Compton, known as "the Protestant Bishop" because of his staunch convictions.

On the 26th February Wesley preached three times: at St. Lawrence Jewry, St. Catherine Cree and St. John, Wapping. "I believe it pleased God to bless the first sermon most," he wrote, "because it gave most offence; being indeed an open defiance of that mystery of iniquity which the world calls *prudence*."[5] He was at the first two churches again on the 7th May: he

[1] *Letters*, Vol. III, p. 225. To Samuel Walker, 19th September, 1757.
[2] J. Henry Martin, *John Wesley's London Chapels* (1946), p. 21.
[3] *Journal*, Vol. I, p. 436. 5th February, 1738. The parish of St. John the Evangelist, Millbank, Westminster, was taken into St. Mary, Tothill Fields, in 1841.
[4] *Ibid.*, p. 438. 12th February, 1738. St. Andrew, Holborn, on the west side of Shoe Lane, was rebuilt by Wren in 1686. The Rector from 1734 to 1780 was Dr. Cutts Barton, who from 1763 was also Dean of Bristol.
[5] *Ibid.*, p. 440. 26th February, 1738. St. Lawrence Jewry, at the entrance to Guild-

was "enabled to speak strong words at both, and was therefore the less surprised at being informed that I was not to preach any more in either of those churches."[1] On the Tuesday of that week he "preached at Great St. Helen's, to a very numerous congregation, on, 'He that spared not His own Son, but delivered Him up for us all, how shall He not with Him also freely give us all things?' " "My heart was so enlarged to declare the love of God to all that were oppressed by the devil," he added, "that I did not wonder in the least when I was afterwards told, 'Sir, you must preach here no more.' "[2] Wesley did not occupy that pulpit again until January 1790, when he noted in his *Journal* that it was fifty years since he had been there before, and then exclaimed: "What has God wrought since that time!"[3]

On Whit Sunday he was at St. John, Wapping at three, and at St. Benet, Paul's Wharf (sometimes called St. Benet Huda) in the evening. "At these churches likewise I am to preach no more," is the sad postscript.[4] In the morning he had heard Dr. John Heylin, the popular Rector of St. Mary-le-Strand, deliver "a truly Christian sermon" on the filling of the Spirit.[5] It was after he had assisted Dr. Heylin with the administration of Holy Communion afterwards—the curate having been taken ill—that Wesley "received the surprising news" that his brother "had found rest to his soul."[6] As he had been warned, Wesley was not permitted to preach again either at Wapping or at St. Benet at this period.[7] Thus, even before his evangelical conversion, Wesley was beginning to pay the price of faithfulness to the truth.

hall Yard in Cateaton Street, was so called because the parish was occupied by Jews before their banishment by Edward I. They later settled near Aldgate: this was therefore Old Jewry. Dr. William Best was Vicar from 1729 to 1761. St. Catherine Cree, in Leadenhall Street, stood on the site of the former priory of the Holy Trinity. One of the religious societies met there. Robert Fowkes was the incumbent from 1732. The Rector of St. John, Wapping, from 1734 to 1748 was Samuel Shenton.

[1] *Ibid.*, p. 460. 7th May, 1738.

[2] *Ibid.* 9th May, 1738. St. Helen, Bishopsgate, on the site of the Black Nuns priory, had a Tuesday lectureship for which Whitefield recommended Thomas Broughton. William Butler held the living from 1713 to 1773.

[3] *Ibid.*, Vol. VIII, p. 38. 17th January, 1790.

[4] *Ibid.*, Vol. I, p. 464. 17th May, 1738. St. Benet Huda, or of the Hyth, situated on the north side of Thames Street, was a rectory in the collation of the Dean and Chapter of St. Paul. John Thomas held it from 1731 until 1757, when he became Bishop of Salisbury. He combined his parochial cure with the bishopric of Peterborough from 1746.

[5] *Ibid.*, pp. 463–464. John Heylin was the first Rector of the modern church of St. Mary, which was consecrated in 1734. He was also a Prebendary of Westminster. He died in 1759. His *Theological Lectures at Westminster Abbey, with an Interpretation of the Four Gospels* (1749) was one of the sources used by Wesley in compiling his *Notes on the New Testament* (1754), (cf. David Lerch, *Heil und Heiligung bei John Wesley* (1941), pp. 166–169).

[6] *Journal*, Vol. I, p. 464. 17th May, 1738.

[7] *Ibid.*

The first Sunday after his heart-warming gave him a further indication of what he might expect. "This day I preached in the morning at St. George's, Bloomsbury, on, 'This is the victory that overcometh the world, even our faith,' and in the afternoon at the chapel in Long Acre on God's justifying the ungodly; the last time (I understand) I am to preach at either." And then he made this significant act of obedience: "Not as I will, but as Thou wilt."[1] In point of fact, he did go again to Bloomsbury in October 1738, but that was his last visit.[2] He was not at Long Acre again. If Wesley had imagined that what happened at Aldersgate Street would usher in a period of recognition, he would have been cruelly disappointed. But it is unlikely that he entertained such sanguine hopes. He knew he had a cross to bear.

The monotonous succession of refusals began to beat out a divine communiqué to him. It was impressed upon him that wherever his sphere of witness lay, it could not be in the Anglican churches. As the door of one pulpit after another was firmly closed on him, he realized that God had another plan in store. He was ready to wait and see what it was. But meanwhile, for the rest of 1738 and into 1739, he had to endure continual obstruction. It may seem tedious to prolong the catalogue, but it is important that the relentless facts should be rehearsed. They make it clear beyond all doubt that Wesley only left the churches when they rejected him. He was brought to the point where, like Martin Luther, he could do no other. He dare not be silent. If he was to declare his new-found (though not novel) gospel, it could not as yet be in the parish pulpits.

We pick up the sad trail in September 1738, after Wesley's return from the Moravian settlement at Herrnhut. "I began again to declare in my own country the glad tidings of salvation," he wrote in his *Journal*.[3] As the diary for these days is lost, we do not know where he preached three times on the 17th September. The next Sunday he was at St. Anne and St. Agnes—the parish church of John Bray, the Moravian, with whom he was staying—and twice at St. John, Clerkenwell. "I fear they will bear me there no longer," was his laconic report.[4] His apprehension was justified in the outcome. On the 8th October he went for the last time to the Savoy Chapel, where Dr. Anthony Horneck had once ministered, who formed the religious societies of the previous century.[5]

In a letter to the Moravian brethren at Herrnhut at this juncture, Wesley

---

[1] *Ibid.*, p. 480. 28th May, 1738. The Rector of St. George from 1731 to 1761, was Edward Vernon, who also held the living of Orwell in Cambridgeshire.

[2] *Ibid.*, Vol. II, p. 95. 22nd October, 1738.

[3] *Ibid.*, p. 70. 17th September, 1738.

[4] *Ibid.*, p. 76. 24th September, 1738. St. Anne and St. Agnes in Aldersgate, on the north side of Pope Lane, was formerly known as St. Anne in the Willows, because of the trees there. The Rector from 1736 to 1764, Dr. Fifield Allen, was also Vicar of St. Paul, Hammersmith and Archdeacon both of Middlesex and St. Albans.

[5] *Ibid.*, p. 83. 8th October, 1738.

could still hold out some hope of continuing opportunities. "Though my brother and I are not permitted to preach in most of the churches in London yet (thanks be to God) there are others left where we have liberty to speak the truth as it is in Jesus."[1] But their number was quickly diminishing. On the 22nd October he paid his final visit to St. George, Bloomsbury, and appeared in St. Paul, Shadwell, where he was not to be again until 1777.[2] All Hallows-on-the-Wall heard him on the 29th October— "strange doctrine to a polite audience!" he commented.[3] Dr. William Crowe, Rector of St. Botolph, Bishopsgate, had shown no small kindness to the Wesleys, and after the first appointment of band-leaders on the 5th November, the society worshipped there, with John Wesley preaching.[4] But despite this friendliness, we do not hear of Wesley being there again. The same evening, he preached "to such a congregation as I never saw before, at St. Clement's, in the Strand. As this was the first time of my preaching here, I suppose it is to be the last."[5] It was, until 1782.[6]

One of the most hospitable churches, both to Whitefield and the Wesleys, was St. Anthony, or St. Antholin as it was known. Here Dr. Richard Venn, father of Henry Venn the Anglican Evangelical, was lecturer in charge. John Wesley was there on Wednesday the 15th November, but not again for forty years to the very day.[7] Not long afterwards, Charles Wesley was told that Dr. Venn had forbidden any Methodist to use the pulpit. The melancholy record persists to the end of the year: St. Swithin, London Stone, St. Bartholomew the Great, Christ Church, Spitalfields and St. Mary Matfellon, Whitechapel, are included.[8] In none of these do

[1] *Letters*, Vol. I, p. 261. To the Moravian Brethren, 14th October, 1738.

[2] *Journal*, Vol. II, p. 95. 22nd October, 1738. Cf. *ibid.*, Vol. VI, p. 17. 14th December, 1777.

[3] *Ibid.*, Vol. II, p. 97. 29th October, 1738. All Hallows, as its name implies, stood close to London Wall. The Rector from 1736 to 1758 was Samuel Smith.

[4] *Ibid.*, p. 99. It was Wesley's diary which mentioned the appointment of band leaders: "6½ singing; the bands met, chose leaders by lot." William Crowe was Rector from 1730 until his death in 1742. He was also Rector of St. Mary, Finchley, and Chaplain both to George II and Edmund Gibson, Bishop of London. St. Botolph, associated with the ministry of Nehemiah Rogers, the Laudian preacher, was rebuilt in 1725 by James Gold.

[5] *Ibid.*

[6] *Ibid.*, Vol. VI, p. 377. 24th November, 1782.

[7] *Ibid.*, Vol. II, p. 115. 15th November, 1738. Cf. *ibid.*, Vol. VI, p. 217. 15th November, 1778. St. Antholin, situated on Budge Row, had been rebuilt to Wren's design. It is said that the singing of psalms in Protestant Anglican worship was first introduced in this church. The parish was later united with St. John the Baptist, Walbrook.

[8] St. Swithin, London Stone "for the last time" (*ibid.*, p. 116. 17th December, 1738). Wesley did not preach there again until 2nd December, 1781 (*ibid.*, Vol. VI, p. 340), but thereafter quite often. St. Bartholomew the Great, Smithfield, was not mentioned after 24th December, 1738 (*ibid.*, Vol. II, p. 117), until 31st May, 1747 (*ibid.*, Vol. III, p. 300), but twice more in that year and twice in 1748. Christ Church, Spitalfields, may be the church mentioned in the *Journal* on 31st December, 1738

we hear of Wesley preaching again at this period, although at St. Bartholomew there was a University friend of Wesley's as incumbent, in Richard Thomas Bateman.[1] We are compelled to agree with the verdict of W. H. Fitchett that by now Wesley was "little better than an ecclesiastical outcast."[2]

The new year brought no improvement. On the 10th January St. Michael, Basingshaw, where the notorious George Lavington was Rector, was listed for the last time.[3] The entry for the 4th February ran like this: "I preached at St. Giles's on, 'Whosoever believeth on Me, out of his belly shall flow rivers of living water.' How was the power of God present with us! I am content to preach here no more."[4] On the 18th February the closure was even more drastic. He was to preach at St. Mary, Spitalfields (referred to as Sir George Wheeler's chapel, as it then was). "I did so in the morning, but was not suffered to conclude my subject (as I had designed) in the afternoon—a good remembrance that I should, if possible, declare at *every* time the *whole* counsel of God."[5] The Diary simply reads: "forbidden to preach."[6] Sir George Wheeler had married into the family of Lady Huntingdon, which makes the interruption even sadder. St. Katherine-near-the-Tower was still open and, of course, St. Mary, Islington, where George Stonehouse was Rector. Yet even at the latter, the congregation found the searching sermon rather too much for them. "Many here were, as usual, deeply offended," Wesley wrote on the 25th February. "But the counsel of the Lord, it shall stand."[7] In a letter to

(Vol. II, p. 119), for Curnock surmised some error in the text, which speaks of an unidentified "St. George's, Spitafields," cf. n. 1. On the other hand, this could have been "Sir George's," i.e. the Chapel originally built by Sir George Wheeler in 1693 for the use of his tenantry, and of which he was the curate. This is now St. Mary, Spital Square. Wesley did not preach at Christ Church until 20th February, 1785 (*ibid.*, Vol. VII, p. 52). There is no record of his appearing again at Whitechapel after his visit on 31st December, 1738 (*ibid.*, Vol. II, p. 119).

[1] Bateman went up to Jesus College, Oxford, in 1736. He is not to be confused with the "Mr. Bateman" mentioned in Wesley's first diary. Curnock copied A. C. H. Seymour, *The Life and Times of Selina, Countess of Huntingdon* (1840), Vol. I, p. 62, in describing him as "an awakened clergyman" (*Journal*, Vol. II, p. 117, n. 1), but this was not so until after his conversion later under under Howell Davies.

[2] Fitchett, *op. cit.*, p. 163.

[3] *Journal*, Vol. II, p. 128. 10th January, 1739. The church, situated in Basinghall Street, had as its Rector from 1730 to 1742 the anti-Methodist polemical writer George Lavington. He was translated to the see of Exeter in 1746.

[4] *Ibid.*, p. 139. 4th February, 1739. St. Giles-in-the-Fields, near Shaftesbury Avenue, was on the route to Tyburn, and by custom the condemned were given a bowl of ale as they passed (*ibid.*, p. 100. 8th November, 1738. Cf. n. 2). Wesley said he preached here before he went to Georgia (*ibid.*, Vol. VII, p. 219. 29th October, 1786). The Rector from 1732 to 1769 was Dr. Henry Gally, also Prebendary of Gloucester.

[5] *Ibid.*, Vol. II, p. 142. 18th February, 1739.   [6] *Ibid.*, p. 143.

[7] *Ibid.*, p. 144. 25th February, 1739. George Stonehouse was Vicar of St. Mary Islington from 1738 until he sold his living in 1740. He then retired to Woodstock,

Whitefield, Wesley confided: "I think I never was so much strengthened before."[1]

The same story was to be repeated in Bristol and Oxford, and even in his father's parish at Epworth. But all this was after Wesley had taken to the open air. Our concern in this chapter is with the exclusions in London in 1738 and early 1739, which made it evident that his mission to the nation must be conducted elsewhere than in the churches of the Anglican communion. Too many obstacles were placed in his path. He could now turn to the unchurched multitudes and meet them on their own ground with an unsullied conscience. The ecclesiastical establishment failed to recognize the day of visitation.

The pressure of restriction must have been disturbing to Wesley. He had been unmistakably called to declare the good news of salvation by grace, but it looked as if he was being gagged. If the pulpits of the metropolis were shut to him, it was unlikely that they would be opened elsewhere. His mission was in danger of being strangled at birth. As Prof. G. R. Cragg puts it, "his orbit seemed to be steadily contracting."[2] His first reaction was to go more and more to the religious societies. These gatherings afforded him an opening to expound the Word, even if mainly to the converted. Such was the power of his ministry, however, that the numbers attending were greatly increased—no doubt with some, at least, who were not yet saved. This in itself created a problem, even if it was a happy embarrassment. It was plain that the accommodation suited to the needs of a religious society—even though some of them were quite large —was totally inadequate for the purposes of mass evangelism. In the same paragraph of his *Farther Appeal* as that in which he spoke of being denied the use of churches, he added: "So much the more those who could not hear me there flocked together when I was at any of the societies; where I spoke, more or less, though with much inconvenience, to as many as the room I was in would contain."[3]

Although as yet Wesley had not discovered his evangelistic medium, it is somewhat misleading nevertheless to speak, as Prof. Piette does, about "a definite period of hesitation."[4] Doughty refers to "the valley of indecision."[5] It is true that Wesley had still to be shown the way in which the masses of the people were to be evangelized. But it is hardly accurate to say that "his position" was "very uncertain," which is what Piette would have us believe.[6] In one sense, his position was as certain as it could

where he spent the remainder of his life "in inglorious stillness" (Thomas Jackson, *The Life of the Rev. Charles Wesley* (1841), Vol. I, p. 279).

[1] *Letters*, Vol. I, p. 280. To George Whitefield, 26th February, 1739.

[2] Cragg, *op. cit.*, p. 142.

[3] *Works*, Vol. VIII, p. 112. *A Farther Appeal to Men of Reason and Religion* (1745).

[4] Piette, *op. cit.*, p. 325.

[5] W. Lamplough Doughty, *John Wesley: Preacher* (1955), p. 30.

[6] Piette, *op. cit.*, p. 325.

be, for now he was fully in the will of God, and was ready for whatever the Spirit might lead him to do. He was quite content, however, to live a day at a time, and be guided to the next step. Meanwhile, he was by no means unoccupied. We must not think of him kicking his heels, waiting for God to reveal the move ahead. Wesley was extremely busy, and his timetable left him little or no interval to nurse any misgivings.

We have only to glance at his correspondence to come across evidence of this. He wrote on the 14th October, 1738, to a physician he had met in Rotterdam—Dr. John de Koker. He had promised to transcribe some papers he had brought back from Germany. But he was compelled to confess: "I find I cannot have time for this yet, it having pleased God to give me full employment of another nature. His blessed Spirit has wrought so powerfully, both in London and Oxford, that there is a general awakening, and multitudes are crying out, 'What must we do to be saved?' So that, till our gracious Master sendeth more labourers into His harvest, all my time is much too little for them."[1] By the 22nd November he was still full of apologies. "Even to this hour I have not had one day's leisure to transcribe for you the papers I brought from Herrnhut: the harvest here also is plenteous, and the labourers so few; and it increases upon us daily. Verily the Spirit of the Lord hath lifted up His standard against the iniquity which hath overspread our land as a flood!"[2]

But a letter to George Whitefield dated the 26th February, 1739, gives an even more convincing picture of Wesley's extreme preoccupation with his God-given task. The autograph has come to light only in very recent years, and we can quote from it direct. "Our Lord's hand is not shortened among us. Yesterday I preached at St. Katherine's and at Islington, where the church was almost as hot as some of the society rooms used to be. I think I was never so much strengthened before. The fields, after service, were white with people praising God. About three hundred were present at Mr. Sims's; thence I went to Mr. Bell's, then to Fetter Lane, and at nine to Mr. Bray's, where also we only wanted more room. Today I expound in Skinner's at four, at Mrs. West's at six, and to a large company of poor sinners in Gravel Lane (Bishopsgate) at eight. The society at Mr. Crouch's does not meet till eight; so that I expound before I go to him near St. James's Square, where one young woman has been lately filled with the Holy Ghost, and overflows with joy and love. On Wednesday at six we have a noble company of women, not adorned with gold or costly apparel, but with a meek and quiet spirit, and good works. . . . At the Savoy on Thursday evening we have usually two or three hundred; most of them (at least) thoroughly awakened. Mr. Abbot's parlour is more than filled on Friday; as is Mr. Parker's room twice over; where

[1] *Letters*, Vol. I, p. 262. To John de Koker, 14th October, 1738.
[2] *Ibid.*, p. 268. To John de Koker, 22nd November, 1738.

I think I have commonly had more power given me than at any other place."[1]

This is not the report of a man groping in uncertainty as to what he should be doing. Wesley was obviously up to the eyes in the work of God. He had no time to think where it was leading, and whether there might be some new tack to be followed. As the church doors closed, the society rooms were jammed with eager hearers. For the time being, Wesley was satisfied. Indeed, it is doubtful whether he had seriously looked beyond this. He was essentially an opportunist, in the best sense of the word.[2] He did what circumstances suggested, in the belief that everything was under divine control. He scarcely had a moment to ask whether this ministry in the religious societies might not be merely a temporary expedient. Like Nehemiah, he knew he was doing a great work, and he was reluctant to leave it even when the crucial call came. It is easy for us to look back and feel that Wesley was rather slow to respond. We can see from the perspective of a later age that this was the determinative moment of his career as an evangelist. When he took to the open air, he found his channel of communication. But he was not to know this in advance. All he was concerned with in the first place was to test the proposal and discover whether it was the will of God for him. This goes far to account for his apparent backwardness.

It was George Whitefield who issued the challenge. He had left London some weeks before and had been missioning in Bristol. He had hoped that churches might be open to him there, but he found that the authorities stood in his way. The Chancellor of the diocese refused him permission to preach in any consecrated building until the Bishop had given a ruling on the matter. Impatient with the delay, Whitefield resorted first to Newgate prison, and then to Kingswood. The spiritual needs of the colliers there tugged at his heart-strings, and he felt he must reach them with the news of redemption. One Saturday afternoon, 17th February, 1739, the evangelist walked out to the village. He climbed a hill and spoke to a couple of hundred coalminers. "Blessed be God that I have now broken the ice!" he wrote afterwards. "I believe I was never more acceptable to my Master than when I was standing to teach those hearers in the open fields."[3] By the month of March the numbers had risen to as many as twenty thousand. "The fire is kindled in the country," he cried; "and, I know, all the devils in hell shall not be able to quench it."[4] This was to be the grand means of reaching the masses with the gospel. At Kingswood the die was cast.

Towards the end of March, Whitfield wrote to Wesley inviting him to

---

[1] *Proc. W.H.S.*, Vol. XXIV, p. 76. To George Whitefield, 26th February, 1739. Cf. *Letters*, Vol. I, p. 280.

[2] Cf. Ingvar Haddal, *John Wesley: A Biography*, (E.T. 1961), p. 82.

[3] *George Whitefield's Journals*, ed. Iaian Murray (1960), p. 216. 17th February, 1739.

[4] *Ibid.*, p. 223. 25th February, 1739.

Bristol to carry on the work whilst he himself went elsewhere. It was with touching and typical humility that Whitefield pleaded: "I am but a novice; you are acquainted with the great things of God. Come, I beseech you; come quickly."[1] Wesley at first appeared to be more than a little unwilling. His negative reaction, however, is not to be attributed to obtuseness. He had just come back from Oxford. London was very demanding. "During my stay here I was fully employed between our own society in Fetter Lane and many others where I was continually desired to expound," he explained; "so that I had no thought of leaving London, when I received, after several others, a letter from Mr. Whitefield, and another from Mr. Seward, entreating me in the most pressing manner to come to Bristol without delay. This I was not at all forward to do. . . ."[2]

However, after a rather discouraging exercise in scriptural sortilege (which we find hard to approve today), the project was discussed at the society in Fetter Lane. Charles Wesley was adamant against it: the rest were divided. In the end the question was settled by sacred lot. The outcome was that Wesley left for Bristol, and entered as he himself said on "a new period" in his life.[3] It was not what he would have decided if left to his own devices. It was not the unanimous choice of his Christian friends. It was the result of what the world would call chance. But who can doubt that God was in it?

Wesley arrived in Bristol on Saturday, 31st March. Though tired after his travelling, he went to hear Whitefield at the Weavers' Hall at eight and even postponed his bedtime to talk with his friend.[4] The next day he accompanied Whitefield to several of his preaching stances—the Bowling Green, Hanham Mount, and Rose Green—and saw for himself the huge crowds that gathered and the unparalleled opportunities afforded by this unusual means of communicating the gospel.[5] After Whitefield had left, Wesley took the plunge on the following day and began the open-air ministry which was to prove his principal medium for the rest of his life. "At four in the afternoon I submitted to be more vile, and proclaimed in the highways the glad tidings of salvation, speaking from a little eminence in a ground adjoining to the city, to about three thousand people."[6] The Rubicon was crossed. Wesley was an evangelist indeed. The text was prophetic in more than one sense. Not only was it taken from the book of

[1] Luke Tyerman, *The Life of the Rev. George Whitefield* (1876), Vol. I, p. 193. Letter George Whitefield to John Wesley, 22nd March, 1739.
[2] *Journal*, Vol. II, p. 156. 15th March, 1739. William Seward had accompanied Whitefield to Georgia. He joined Howell Harris in Wales, and was struck on the head while preaching at Hay. As a result of his injuries, he died on 22nd October, 1740, the proto-martyr of the Revival.
[3] *Ibid.*, p. 159. 28th March, 1739.
[4] *Ibid.*, p. 167. 31st March, 1739.
[5] *Ibid.*, p. 168. 1st April, 1739.
[6] *Ibid.*, pp. 172–173. 2nd April, 1739.

Isaiah: it also envisaged the lifework of Wesley. "The Spirit of the Lord is upon me, because He hath anointed me to preach the gospel to the poor. He hath sent me to heal the broken-hearted; to preach deliverance to the captives, and recovery of sight to the blind; to set at liberty them that are bruised, to proclaim the acceptable year of the Lord" (Isaiah 61: 1, 2).

Wesley "had come at long last to the threshold of his true vocation," as Prof. Outler expresses it.[1] Early in 1738 he had found his message, as he accepted the scriptural doctrine of justification. On that memorable 24th May he entered into the experience for himself. He had obeyed the call to proclaim what he believed and felt, but now he was shown the method by which this was to be most effectively done. "For the next half-century, in failure and triumph, tumult and peace, obloquy and fame, the picture rarely varies: a man with an overmastering mission, acutely self-aware but rarely ruffled, often in stress but always secure on a rock-steady foundation."[2]

[1] Outler, *op. cit.*, p. 17.   [2] *Ibid.*

CHAPTER VIII

THIS STRANGE WAY

"I COULD scarce reconcile myself at first to *this strange way* of preaching in the fields . . . having been all my life (till very lately) so tenacious of every point relating to decency and order, that I should have thought the saving of souls almost a sin if it had not been done in a church." *Journal* 2: 167.

IT WAS AN UNPREDICTABLE PROVIDENCE WHICH LED JOHN WESLEY to become an open-air evangelist. Field preaching was not congenial to him. Some men might have felt themselves to be in their element as they stood beneath the canopy of heaven. Not so Wesley. To him this seemed a strange way indeed. It was certainly not his own choice. He endured it only because God had called him to adopt such a means of approach to the people.

There is something ironical that such a man as Wesley should expose himself to the four winds like this. Nor did he shrink from the uncouth mob, which always surrounded him with filth and foul odours and often with heckling and violence. Wesley was a dapper little don. He was finical about his personal appearance. In company he was always as neat as a tailor's model. He was so very particular that he could not bear the slightest speck of dirt on his clerical attire. He hated noise and disturbance. He was accustomed to the academic calm of Oxford or a country rectory. That he should venture into the highways and by-ways and face the great unwashed was nothing short of a miracle. Only grace could have turned John Wesley into a missioner to the common people.

Moreover, there was nothing of the exhibitionist about him. There was no histrionic strain. Here he differed from Whitefield, who as a youth had wanted to be an actor. Wesley was no extrovert. It must have cost him more than we can imagine to run the risk of being dubbed a mountebank. We can measure the effect of his conversion, when we see this former rigorist now defying convention and abandoning all considerations of respectability in order to bring the news of salvation to those who needed it most. The Wesley we have met before the 24th May, 1738, would never have taken such a step. It may have been all right out in Georgia with the Indians: back in Britain it would have been unthinkable.[1]

Wesley revealed his own reactions often enough in his *Journal*. Here is

---

[1] In *A Farther Appeal to Men of Reason and Religion* (1745), Wesley referred to his outdoor preaching "in a warmer climate," i.e. in Georgia (*Works*, Vol. VIII, p. 112).

an entry on the 26th June, 1759, after he had been preaching outside the Keelmen's Hospital in Newcastle-upon-Tyne. "What marvel the devil does not love field preaching! Neither do I: I love a commodious room, a soft cushion, a handsome pulpit. But where is my zeal, if I do not trample all these underfoot in order to save one more soul?"[1] All this helps us to understand why Wesley spoke of submitting "to be more vile" when first he preached at Kingswood.[2] The phrase, of course, is scriptural. After David had been reprimanded by his wife Michal for dancing before the Lord when the ark was brought to Jerusalem, he told her: "And I will yet be more vile than this, and will be base in mine own eyes" (II Samuel 6: 22). The Revised Standard Version has, "I will make myself yet more contemptible." Paul described the apostles as "the filth of the world" and "the offscouring of all things" (I Corinthians 4: 13). This was the army of old contemptibles that Wesley joined when he left the churches for the open air.

In a letter to his friend James Hervey (later the evangelical Vicar of Weston Favell in Northamptonshire and formerly one of the Oxford Holy Club), dated the 20th March, 1739—just before Wesley went to Bristol—he quoted I Corinthians 4: 13 and said that it was still true, but that he rejoiced in it. "Blessed be God, I enjoy the reproach of Christ! Oh may you also be vile, exceeding vile, for His sake! God forbid that you should ever be other than generally scandalous; I had almost said universally. If any man tell you there is a new way of following Christ, 'he is a liar, and the truth is not in him.'"[3] The phrase was evidently still in Wesley's mind when on the 2nd April he recorded in his *Journal* the momentous events of the day.

The same expression was also used by Whitefield, who imagined the scorn of many self-righteous bigots to see a clergyman "venting his enthusiastic ravings in a gown and cassock upon a common." "But if this is to be vile," he added, "Lord grant that I may be more vile."[4] Wesley and Whitefield were brothers in bearing the reproach of the gospel.

Wesley was soon to realize, if he had not already anticipated it, how sharp would be the criticism of his new ministry, even from those closest to him. His own elder brother Samuel had written in real concern to Susanna declaring that he would much rather see John and Charles "picking straws within the walls than preaching in the area of Moorfields."[5] The

[1] *Journal*, Vol. IV, p. 325. 26th June, 1759.
[2] *Ibid.*, Vol. II, p. 172. 2nd April, 1739.
[3] *Letters*, Vol. I, p. 287. To James Hervey, 20th March, 1739. Hervey took the curacy of Dummer, where Charles Kinchin was Rector, in 1736. He went to Weston Favell in 1743 as curate to his father, and became Vicar in 1752. Hervey was one of Wesley's pupils at Lincoln College, Oxford. Cf. Tyerman, *Oxford Methodists*, pp. 201-333. [4] Whitefield, *Journals*, p. 265. 13th May, 1739.
[5] Priestley, *op. cit.*, p. 109. Letter Samuel Wesley junior to Susanna Wesley, 20th October, 1739.

last letter written by John to Samuel before the latter's sudden death on the 6th November, 1739, is preserved in the Lambeth Palace Library, amongst the papers connected with Archbishop Secker. It is not included in the standard edition. John pleaded for a recognition that this unconventional form of evangelism might be judged by its fruits. "O my brother, who hath bewitched you, that for fear of I know not what distant consequences, you cannot rejoice at, nor so much as acknowledge, the great power of God? How is it that you cannot praise God for saving so many souls from death and covering such a multitude of sins, unless He will begin this work within consecrated walls? Why should He not fill heaven and earth? You cannot, indeed you cannot, confine the Most High within temples made with hands. I do not despise them, any more than you. But I rejoice to find that God is everywhere. I love the rites and ceremonies of the Church. But I see, well pleased, that our great Lord can work without them. And howsoever and wheresoever a sinner is converted from the error of his ways, nay and by whomsoever, I thereat rejoice, yea and will rejoice!"[1]

For a further glimpse of what field preaching looked like to the unsympathetic we turn to the diatribe of the learned Dr. Joseph Trapp, Vicar of Christ Church, Newgate Street, London. Zachariah Pearce, Bishop of Rochester, praised him as the most diligent of all English scholars in his time, and Lord Bolingbroke favoured him with his patronage in ecclesiastical preferments.[2] Trapp delighted in controversy and the Methodists supplied a ready target. He could hardly conceal his horror at the idea of the latest evangelism. "For a clergyman of the Church of England to pray and preach in the fields, in the country, or in the streets of the city, is perfectly new, a fresh honour to the blessed age in which we have the happiness to live. I am ashamed to speak on a subject which is a reproach not only to our Church and country but to human nature itself. Can it promote Christianity to turn it into riot, tumult, and confusion? to make it ridiculous and contemptible, and to expose it to the scorn and scoffs of infidels and atheists? To the prevalence of immorality and profaneness, infidelity and atheism, is now added the pest of enthusiasm. Our prospect is very sad and melancholy. Go not after these imposters and seducers; but shun them as you would the plague."[3] And all this was in a sermon—one of a series of four preached in Christ Church, St. Lawrence Jewry and St. Martin-in-the-Fields. No wonder the pulpits of London were barred to the Wesleys and Whitefield!

[1] Proc. W.H.S., Vol. XXXIII, p. 101. Letter John Wesley to Samuel Wesley, Junior, 27th October, 1739.

[2] Tyerman, Life of Whitefield, Vol. I, pp. 207–208. Trapp became Vicar of Christ Church, Newgate Street in 1722. He also held the living of Harlington, Middlesex, and several lectureships. He had been Professor of Poetry at Oxford. Jonathan Swift caricatured him as "little parson dapper" (The Tatler, No. 66).

[3] Tyerman, Life of John Wesley, Vol. I, p. 242.

In the light of such factors, we can better appreciate what Wesley meant when he said that he "submitted to be more vile."[1] "There is a note of pathos in the words," explained Doughty, "as though he had stooped to something of which one part of him was ashamed. The Oxford scholar and don, with his inherited aristocratic instincts and ingrained respect for what was regular and constitutional, had become a 'field preacher,' a man beyond the pale of the regular ministry, knowing that the hand of authority would be increasingly heavy against him; that he would forfeit the regard and friendship of many of his own order: that he was making himself 'a fool for Christ's sake.' "[2]

That is one side of the picture. This was the price to be paid. But Wesley considered it well worth while because of the advantages gained. What was despised by men would be owned by God. And for Wesley that was the only thing that mattered. In the language of one of his brother's hymns, he had learned to

> Esteem the scandal of the Cross,
> And only seek Divine applause.[3]

It was "from a little eminence" that he spoke at Kingswood on the 2nd April, 1739.[4] But from it he could see the incalculable possibilities of this evangelistic medium. He must have felt

> . . . like some watcher of the skies
> When a new planet swims into his ken;
> Or like stout Cortez when with eagle eyes
> He stared at the Pacific. . . .[5]

An unexplored continent of opportunity was opening up before him, which was to herald "a new era in the religious history of England," according to H. W. V. Temperley.[6]

For every age God has a programme of evangelism. This was His way of reaching the masses in the eighteenth century. Whitefield was the pioneer, but Wesley was to continue the mission to the edge of the next century. Preaching in the open gave him a mobility which he could have gained in no other manner. It provided him with congregations so large that no church could have contained them. It brought him into contact with the labouring poor who would never have dared to go into a place

[1] *Journal*, Vol. II, p. 172. 2nd April, 1739.
[2] Doughty, *op. cit.*, p. 37.
[3] *Wesley's Hymns*, No. 483, v. 4, lines 5, 6.
[4] *Journal*, Vol. II, p. 172. 2nd April, 1739.
[5] John Keats, "On First Looking into Chapman's Homer," in *The Poetical Works of John Keats* (Chandos Classics) (n.d.), p. 42.
[6] *The Cambridge Modern History*, ed. A. W. Ward, G. W. Prothero, and S. Leathes (1909), Vol. VI, p. 83. "From this day, April 2, 1739, may be reckoned a new era in the religious history of England; for her greatest religious leader between Cromwell and Newman had found his way to the hearts of her people."

D

of worship with their tatters and grime. If the bulk of the people were to hear the Christian message, this was the only method. Cost what it might, the task had to be tackled. Above all, Wesley was the chosen vessel of God.

Field preaching was geared to the conditions of the age, as it turned out. "The industrial revolution paid no attention to parish boundaries," writes Dr. J. H. Plumb. "The mine ignored the parson. So that, by the middle years of the century, there were scores of industrial villages and suburbs that were without any church or priest. Ignorance of the most elementary facts of the Christian religion was astonishingly widespread. Only a fundamental constitutional reform of the Established Church could have coped with this situation, but such reform was unthinkable, for it would have disturbed the entire structure of government. Dissent, too, failed to realize its opportunities and obligations; for complex, obscure, and largely internal reasons, the old non-conformist churches were moribund. It was left to Wesley and his disciples to reap the rich harvest of neglected souls."[1]

From this day forward, Wesley's was to be the ministry of an itinerant evangelist, operating mainly out of doors, though also in hired buildings, and only occasionally in churches until the latter years. The *Journal* supplies the evidence. Almost every page reports the furtherance of the gospel. The pattern was now set for half a century to come. Wesley became an evangelist at large, the leader of a nation-wide campaign. It is noticeable how field preaching immediately assumed priority. Once he had been convinced of its value, it became central in his schedule. Tyerman has computed that of five hundred sermons delivered between April and December 1739, only eight were in churches.[2]

Numbers gradually grew in Bristol, until we read in the diary of as many as seven thousand both at the Bowling Green and Rose Green. Wesley also used the Weavers' Hall on Saturday nights, as Whitefield had done, expounding the Epistle to the Romans.[3] A series on John's Gospel was given at Newgate prison.[4] When Wesley went back to London in June, he joined Whitefield at Blackheath and addressed a crowd of twelve to fourteen thousand.[5] He took over Whitefield's stances at Moorfields and Kennington Common three days later, and thus confirmed in the metropolis what he had been led to do in Bristol.[6] He had no doubt that this was God's purpose for him.

[1] Plumb, *England in the Eighteenth Century*, pp. 89–90.
[2] Tyerman, *Life of John Wesley*, Vol. I, p. 234. Wesley's diaries were not available when Tyerman wrote, but an examination of them does not necessitate any revision of this estimate.
[3] *Journal*, Vol. II, p. 175. 5th April, 1739.
[4] *Ibid.*, p. 173. 3rd April, 1739.
[5] *Ibid.*, p. 220. 14th June, 1739.
[6] *Ibid.*, p. 223. 17th June, 1739.

Throughout his long years of evangelizing he kept commenting on the value of open-air work. "It is field preaching which does the execution still," he declared on 10th October, 1756; "for usefulness there is none comparable to it."[1] At a village in Cumberland on the 20th May, 1759, "many were there who never did and never would come to a room. Oh what a victory would Satan gain if he could put an end to field preaching! But that, I trust, he never will; at least not till my head is laid."[2] By the 25th August, 1773, his zeal had not yet abated. He saw the largest congregation on record to that date in Moorfields, but rejoiced that his voice was so strengthened that even those on the fringe could hear perfectly well. "So the season for field preaching is not yet over. It cannot, while so many are in their sins and in their blood."[3]

Although Wesley did not find this type of ministry easy, even to the end, yet he was so persuaded of its fruitfulness that he grew impatient if he was prevented by the weather or other setbacks from going out into the open. At Cork on the 3rd August 1760 he had written to the commanding officer for permission to preach near the barracks, on the south side of the city. But the C.O. had just left town, so, added Wesley with obvious disappointment, "I was obliged once more to coop myself up in the room."[4] That was an expression he often used to describe his own predicament, and also in urging the need to get outside to his societies.[5] He wrote from York on the 21st July, 1766, to James Rea, one of the four preachers from Ireland received on trial at the Conference of 1765. His advice sprang from his own experience. "Preach abroad at Newry, Newtown, Lisburn, and Carrick, if ever you would do good. It is the cooping yourselves up in rooms that has damped the work of God, which never was and never will be carried out to any purpose without going out into the highways and hedges and compelling poor sinners to come in."[6]

We have seen how field preaching aroused considerable opposition from those who objected to such an unorthodox procedure. Wesley was eventually obliged to defend his practice in print. He did so in his *A Farther Appeal to Men of Reason and Religion*, published in 1745. He explained briefly how he came to adopt this method. It was, he said, only after he had been forbidden the use of churches. He had no desire or de-

---

[1] *Ibid.*, Vol. IV, p. 188. 10th October, 1756.
[2] *Ibid.*, p. 315. 20th May, 1759.
[3] *Ibid.*, Vol. V, p. 522. 25th August, 1773.
[4] *Ibid.*, Vol. IV, p. 400. 3rd August, 1760.
[5] Cf. *ibid.*, Vol. V, p. 132. 18th June, 1765. Wesley wrote from Cork: "I had often been grieved at the smallness of the congregation here; and it could be no other, while we cooped ourselves up in the house." And again, from Bristol: "The sultry heat continuing, I would not coop myself up in the chapel, but preached again near Redcliff Parade, with much comfort and peace" (*ibid.*, Vol. VI, p. 291. 11th August, 1780).
[6] *Letters*, Vol. V, p. 23. To James Rea, 21st July, 1766.

sign to preach in the open air until after this prohibition.[1] When he did, it was a matter neither of choice nor premeditation. "There was no scheme at all previously formed, which was to be supported thereby; nor had I any other end in view than this—to save as many souls as I could."[2] Field preaching was thus "a sudden expedient, a thing submitted to rather than chosen," because he "thought preaching even thus, better than not preaching at all."[3] He was motivated by a dual concern. He was aware that a dispensation of the gospel had been committed to him, and he dare not be silent. He was also prompted by the spiritual needs of others, whom he everywhere saw "seeking death in the error of their life."[4]

In Part Three of the *Farther Appeal*, which appeared a few months later, Wesley took up the subject again and replied to more objections. "But what need is there of this preaching in fields and streets? Are there not churches enough to preach in?"[5] "No, my friend, there are not; not for us to preach in. You forget: we are not suffered to preach there, else we should prefer them to any places whatever. 'Well, there are ministers enough without you. *Ministers enough, and churches enough.*' For what? To reclaim all the sinners without the four seas? If there were, they would all be reclaimed. But they are not all reclaimed. Therefore, it is evident that there are not churches enough. And one plain reason why, notwithstanding all these churches, they are no nearer being reclaimed, is this— they never come into a church, perhaps not once in a twelve-month, perhaps not for many years together. Will you say (as I have known some tender-hearted Christians), 'Then it is their own fault; let them die, and be damned'? I grant it is their own fault; and so it was my fault and yours when we went astray like sheep that were lost. Yet the Shepherd of souls sought after us, and went after us in the wilderness. And 'oughtest not thou to have compassion on thy fellow-servants, as he had pity on thee?' Ought we not also 'to seek,' as far as in us lies, 'and to save that which is lost'?"[6]

Wesley drew an analogy from God's dealings with sinful men in the history of redemption recorded in the New Testament Scriptures. "Behold the amazing love of God to the outcasts of men! His tender condescension to their folly! They would regard nothing done in the usual way. All this was lost upon them. The ordinary preaching of the Word of God they would not even deign to hear. So the devil made sure of these careless ones: for who should pluck them out of his hand? Then God was moved to jealousy, and went out of the usual way to save the souls which He had made. Then, over and above what was ordinarily spoken in His name to all the houses of God in the land, He commanded a voice to cry in the wilderness, 'Prepare ye the way of the Lord. The time is fulfilled. The kingdom of heaven is at hand. Repent ye, and believe the Gospel.' "[7]

[1] *Works*, Vol. VIII, p. 113. *A Farther Appeal to Men of Reason and Religion* (1745).
[2] *Ibid.*   [3] *Ibid.*   [4] *Ibid.*   [5] *Ibid.*, p. 229.   [6] *Ibid.*   [7] *Ibid*, pp. 229–230.

This passage is surely one of the most moving and persuasive pleas for evangelism by all means that has ever been penned.

But Wesley came back to his own century with telling force. He drew on his own memory as he depicted the colliers of Kingswood and the shipyard workers of Newcastle as they were before the good news of Christ was conveyed to them. "Now would you really have desired that these poor wretches should have sinned on until they dropped into hell? Surely you would not. But by what other means was it possible they should have been plucked out of the fire? Had the minister of the parish preached like an angel, it had profited them nothing; for they heard him not. But when one came and said, 'Yonder is a man preaching on the top of a mountain,' they ran in droves to hear what he would say; and God spoke to their hearts. It is hard to conceive that anything else could have reached them. Had it not been for field preaching, the uncommonness of which was the very circumstance that recommended it, they must have run on in the error of their way, and perished in their blood."[1]

Then Wesley flung down the gauntlet of challenge to the indolent clergy, who sat in their comfortable arm-chairs as they dismissed this new-fangled way of preaching as unbecoming to a gentleman and a priest. "For who is there among you, brethren, that is willing (examine your own hearts) even to save souls from death at such a price? Would you not let a thousand souls perish, rather than you would be the instruments of rescuing them thus? I do not speak now with regard to conscience, but to the inconveniences that must accompany it. Can you sustain them, if you would? Can you bear the summer sun to beat upon your naked head? Can you suffer the wintry rain or wind, from whatever quarter it blows? Are you able to stand in the open air without any covering or defence when God casteth abroad His snow like wool, or scattereth His hoar frost like ashes? And yet these are some of the smallest inconveniences which accompany field preaching. Far beyond all these, are the contradiction of sinners, the scoffs both of the great vulgar and the small; contempt and reproach of every kind; often more than verbal affronts, stupid, brutal violence, sometimes to the hazard of health, or limbs, or life. Brethren, do you envy us this honour? What, I pray, would you buy to be a field preacher? Or what, think you, could induce any man of common sense to continue therein one year, unless he had a full conviction in himself that it was the will of God concerning him?"[2]

This noble passage, as Doughty rightly describes it, concludes with an appeal to his colleagues in the ministry of the Church at least not to hinder his work, even if they are disinclined to help. "Do not increase the difficulties, which are already so great, that, without the mighty power of God, we must sink under them. Do not assist in trampling down a handful of little men, who, for the present, stand in the gap between ten

[1] *Ibid.*, p. 230.   [2] *Ibid.*, pp. 230–231.

thousand poor wretches and destruction, till you find some others to take their places."[1] In this section of his *Farther Appeal* Wesley speaks not only for himself, but for the evangelist in every generation. With him, destructive criticism and lack of co-operation from those who should be the first to help is something of an occupational hazard.

Elsewhere Wesley dealt with the breach of ecclesiastical order which his itinerant evangelism was held to involve. In his correspondence with the mysterious "John Smith"—said to be the *nom de plume* of Thomas Secker, Bishop of Oxford from 1737 and later Archbishop of Canterbury —Wesley met the charge that he did "a great deal of harm by breaking and setting aside order."[2] This he was supposed to have done by preaching outside consecrated buildings and by using extemporary prayer. "I have often replied: (1) It were better for me to die than not to preach the gospel of Christ; yea, and in the fields, either where I may not preach in the church or where the church will not contain the congregation. (2) That I use the Service of the Church every Lord's Day, and it has never yet appeared to me that any rule of the Church forbids my using extemporary prayer on other occasions. But methinks I would go deeper. I would enquire, What is the end of all ecclesiastical order? Is it not to bring souls from the power of Satan to God, and to build them up in His fear and love? Order, then, is so far valuable as it answers these ends; and if it answers them not, it is nothing worth."[3] It was only by an alleged infringement of discipline that those who most needed the gospel could be enabled to hear it. It was not that Wesley was an ecclesiastical anarchist by any manner of means. He was to introduce rules into his own societies. But he had a mission to fulfil, and if existing protocol stood in the way then it would have to be set aside. Nothing must be allowed to interfere with the primary work of evangelism. "I would observe every punctilio of order," he told George Downing, chaplain to the Earl of Dartmouth, "except where the salvation of souls is at stake. There I prefer the end before the means."[4]

It was also claimed that by his intrusion into other men's parishes, Wesley was guilty of discourtesy and disobedience. More than that, he was accused of proselytism in endeavouring to steal the sheep from their lawful shepherd. Wesley had to defend himself in a letter to Edmund Gibson, Bishop of London, dated 11th June, 1747. "It is not our care, endeavour or desire to proselyte any from one man to another; or from one church (so called), from one congregation or society, to another,— we would not move a finger to do this, to make ten thousand such proselytes—but from darkness to light, from Belial to Christ, from the power

[1] *Ibid.*, p. 231. Cf. Doughty, *op. cit.*, p. 48.
[2] *Letters*, Vol. II, p. 77. To "John Smith," 25th June, 1746.
[3] *Ibid.*, pp. 77–78.
[4] *Ibid.*, Vol. IV, p. 146. To George Downing, 6th April, 1761.

of Satan to God. Our one aim is to proselyte sinners to repentance, the servants of the devil to serve the living and true God."[1]

Others again complained about the unseemliness of field preaching. It was thought to be indecorous for a service to be held under the open sky, with a rabble for a congregation. Wesley had a sharp riposte for this ill-conceived thrust. "I wonder at those who still talk so loud of the indecency of field preaching. The highest indecency is in St. Paul's Church, when a considerable part of the congregation are asleep, or talking, or looking about, not minding a word the preacher says. On the other hand, there is the highest decency in a churchyard or field, when the whole congregation behave and look as if they saw the Judge of all, and heard Him speaking from heaven."[2]

Ultimately, however, Wesley's apologia for field preaching rested on a pragmatic argument. He was prepared for it to be tested by its fruits. He knew that no one could gainsay him on that score. "A vast majority of the immense congregation in Moorfields were deeply serious," he reported in his *Journal* for the 23rd October, 1759. "One such hour might convince any impartial man of the expediency of field preaching. What building, except St. Paul's Church, would contain such a congregation? And if it would, what human voice could have reached them there? By repeated observations I find I can command thrice the number in the open air that I can under a roof. And who can say the time for field preaching is over, while, (1) greater numbers than ever attend; (2) the converting as well as convincing power of God is eminently present with them?"[3]

When "John Smith" questioned his call to "preach up and down and play the part of an itinerant evangelist,"[4] Wesley laid bare his heart in the matter of his extended parish. "I know God hath required this at my hands. To me, His blessing my work is an abundant proof; although such a proof often makes me tremble. But 'is there not pride or vanity in my heart'? There is; yet this is not my motive to preaching. I know and feel that the spring of this is a deep conviction that it is the will of God, and that, were I to refrain, I should never hear that word, 'Well done, good and faithful servant,' but, 'Cast ye the unprofitable servant into outer

[1] *Ibid.*, Vol. II, p. 289. To the Bishop of London, 11th June, 1747. Gibson had been Bishop since 1723. He seems to have ruled his diocese conscientiously. He was a High Churchman, yet reasonably tolerant towards the Methodists, and a personal friend of Isaac Watts. For his life, cf. Norman Sykes, *Edmund Gibson* (1926).

[2] *Journal*, Vol. III, p. 373. 28th August, 1748. Cf. *ibid.*, p. 536. 29th August, 1761. "There was a sermon preached at the old church before the trustees of the school. At half an hour past twelve the morning service began, but such insufferable noise and confusion I never saw before in a place of worship, no, not even in a Jewish synagogue. The clergy set the example, laughing and talking during great part both of the prayers and sermon." This was at Tiverton.

[3] *Ibid.*, Vol. IV, p. 354. 23rd October, 1759.

[4] *Letters*, Vol. II, p. 96. To "John Smith," 25th March, 1747.

darkness, where is weeping and wailing and gnashing of teeth.' "¹ The "strange way" of open-air evangelism was tolerable only because it was God's will for him. "To this day field preaching is a cross to me," he confided, as late as the 6th September, 1772. "But I know my commission, and see no other way of 'preaching the gospel to every creature.' "²

¹ *Ibid.*, pp. 96–97.
² *Journal*, Vol. V, p. 484. 6th September, 1772.

CHAPTER IX

IN THE SAME TRACK

"FROM this time, I have, by the grace of God, gone *in the same track*, travelling between four and five thousand miles a year, and once in two years going through Great Britain and Ireland." *Works* 13 : 343.

THE STAGE WAS NOW SET FOR WESLEY TO EMBARK ON THE WIDER mission which was to occupy him for the rest of his life. What had been begun in Bristol and continued in London could be extended to the country as a whole. This new method of field preaching opened up a vast potential. Wesley stood poised "to spread Scriptural holiness over the land."[1] That was his own distinctive description of his aim. Everything was ready for him to pursue it.

"He was quite clear as to the content of the gospel which he had been ordained to preach, and he had confirmed it in his own experience," explains Rupert Davies; "he had tried out his methods of preaching it, and confirming it in the lives of those to whom he preached, in Bristol and London; the situation with which he had been confronted in those two cities had shown how great was the need which the gospel was designed to meet. Henceforth no diocesan or episcopal rule was going to prevent him from doing what he conceived to be his plain duty."[2] The evangelist was eager to be about his business. His parish knew no boundaries.

It is significant that the famous letter to James Hervey, in which Wesley announced that the world was his parish, was written on the 20th March, 1739. This was before he had been to Kingswood and started his open-air experiment. But already he was prepared in mind and spirit for the step into no-man's-land. He was determined not to be restricted by ecclesiastical barriers. Hervey had inquired how Wesley could justify the invasion of other men's parishes upon catholic principles. It was a characteristic of Anglican Evangelicals like Hervey to adhere to the parochial system. Wesley's reply is a classic one. "Permit me to speak plainly. If by catholic principles you mean any other than scriptural, they weigh nothing with me. I allow no other rule, whether of faith or practice, than the Holy Scriptures; but on scriptural principles I do not think it hard to justify whatever I do. God in Scripture commands me, according to my power, to instruct the ignorant, reform the wicked, confirm the virtuous. Man

[1] *Works*, Vol. VIII, p. 299. *Large Minutes* (1789).
[2] R. E. Davies, *op. cit.*, p. 77.

forbids me to do this in another's parish: that is, in effect, to do it at all; seeing I have now no parish of my own, nor probably ever shall. Whom, then, shall I hear, God or man? 'If it be just to obey man rather than God, judge you. A dispensation of the gospel is committed to me; and woe is me if I preach not the gospel.' But where shall I preach it, upon the principles you mention?"[1]

Wesley went on to show that if he were to limit himself like this, he would have no scope "in any of the Christian parts, at least, of the habitable earth: for all these are, after a sort, divided into parishes." And then in words which represent the Magna Charta of evangelism, Wesley declared his intention. "Suffer me now to tell you my principles in this matter. I look upon all the world as my parish; thus far I mean, that in whatever part of it I am I judge it meet, right, and my bounden duty to declare, unto all that are willing to hear, the glad tidings of salvation. This is the work which I know God has called me to; and sure I am that His blessing attends it. Great encouragement have I, therefore, to be faithful in fulfilling the work He hath given me to do. His servant I am; and, as such, am employed according to the plain direction of His Word—'as I have opportunity, doing good unto all men.' And His providence clearly concurs with His Word, which has disengaged from me all things else that I might singly attend on this very thing, 'and go about doing good.' "[2]

This was the unequivocal position Wesley was unafraid to maintain even in the presence of a Bishop. In August, 1739, according to a document preserved by Dr. John Whitehead, Wesley had an interview with the Bishop of Bristol, who was none other than Dr. Joseph Butler, author of the celebrated *Analogy of Religion*. The incident is not recorded in the *Journal*, but in the account mentioned above the Bishop concluded by saying: "Since you ask my advice, I will give it you very freely. You have no business here; you are not commissioned to preach in this diocese; therefore I advise you to go hence." Wesley stoutly replied: "My lord, my business on earth is to do what good I can. Wherever, therefore, I think I can do most good there I must stay, so long as I think so. At

---

[1] *Letters*, Vol. I, pp. 285–286. To James Hervey, 20th March, 1739.

[2] *Ibid.*, p. 286. On 23rd June, Wesley wrote more briefly but on similar lines to his brother Charles. He met the objection that he must submit to the ordinances of the Church by excepting any that might be contrary to the will of God. "If any man (bishop or other) ordain that I shall not do what God commands me to do, to submit to that ordinance would be to obey man rather than God" (*ibid.*, p. 322). He distinguished between his ordinary call, received at his episcopal ordination, and his extraordinary call to evangelize the people, which came direct from God. "God bears witness in an *extraordinary manner* that my *thus exercising* my *ordinary call* is well-pleasing in His sight. But what if a bishop forbids this? I do not say, as St. Cyprian, *Populus a scelerato antistite separare se debet* (The people ought to separate themselves from a wicked bishop). But I say, God being my helper, I will obey Him still; and if I suffer for it, His will be done" (*ibid.*, pp. 322–323).

present I think I can do most good here; therefore, here I stay. As to my preaching here, a dispensation of the gospel is committed to me, and woe is me if I preach not the gospel wherever I am in the habitable world! Your lordship knows, being ordained a priest, by the commission I then received I am a priest of the Church Universal. And being ordained as Fellow of a College, I was not limited to any particular cure, but have an indeterminate commission to preach the Word of God in any part of the Church of England."[1]

With this inalienable divine authorization, Wesley calmly proceeded to implement his call by pressing on with his mission regardless of what diocesan Bishops or parochial clergy might say. He moved in the realm of the Spirit, where man-made fences must fall. For the residue of his days he was to give himself without stint to this work of God. He journeyed throughout the length and breadth of the land. He registered an incredible annual mileage, when we consider the conditions under which he travelled. And, as Augustine Birrell put it, he "contested the three kingdoms in the cause of Christ during a campaign which lasted for fifty years."[2]

Although Wesley's critics were alarmed at what appeared to be an innovation (and to them a distasteful one at that), there were in fact ample and honourable precedents for itinerant evangelism. Indeed, this was the means by which Britain was missioned in the first place. The indigenous British Church, planted it may be through Roman soldiers, had few buildings, and the early emissaries of the Cross had no alternative but to preach in the open. The pioneer missionary enterprise of Ninian and Patrick in the fifth century and of Columba in the sixth falls largely into this category. The southern Roman mission, under Augustine of Canterbury, was inaugurated as Ethelbert, King of Kent, listened to the message in the open air, and the good news was often spread in the same manner.[3] The conversion of Northumbria under Paulinus and Aidan was achieved in part by this means. Bede tells us that the latter was accustomed "to traverse both town and country on foot, never on horseback, unless compelled by some urgent necessity; and wherever in his way he saw any, either rich or poor, he invited them, if infidels, to embrace the mystery of the faith."[4] Another pedestrian evangelist of this period was Chad, a pupil of Aidan at Lindisfarne, who, first as Abbot of Lastingham and then as

---

[1] *Journal*, Vol. II, p. 257, n. 1. This was probably on 18th August, and was the second audience Wesley had with the Bishop, the first being on 16th August. Butler had been elevated to the see of Bristol in 1738. R. E. Davies mistakenly places the interview with the Bishop *before* Wesley's letter to Hervey (*op. cit.*, p. 78).

[2] Augustine Birrell, *Selected Essays 1884–1907* (1909), p. 109.

[3] Actually it was for fear of magic that Ethelbert refused to hear Augustine under cover, cf. Frank M. Stenton, *Anglo-Saxon England* (1943), p. 105.

[4] Bede, *The Ecclesiastical History of the English Nation* (E.T. John Stevens) (1910), Book III, Chapter 5, p. 110.

Bishop of Lichfield, preached the gospel in towns and in the open country-side, in castles and cottages, with unabated zeal.[1]

The coming of the friars in the thirteenth century saw a renascence of itinerant outdoor preaching. In 1224 the Grey Friars of St. Francis arrived in England, and we can picture them as they moved about the land with true gospel simplicity. In a habit of coarse brown cloth; a long, pointed hood; a short cloak; a girdle of knotted cord round their waists; and no shoes or sandals to protect their feet, they trudged the dusty lanes of summer and the muddy tracks of winter. These "religious roundsmen," as G. M. Trevelyan dubbed them, were always on the move and never tired of exalting Christ.[2] Although their provenance was different, they never-theless paved the way for Wyclif's Lollards in the following century.[3] These travelling preachers were the heralds of the Reformation, for they attacked the abuses of the Roman Church long before Luther. But their chief object was to proclaim the gospel in the language of the people. Clad in russet robes down to their bare feet, with staff in hand, and no purse from which to buy provisions, they relied on such food and shelter as was offered to them. They preached wherever they could get a hearing—sometimes in churches, but more often on the village green or by the roadside.

The same tradition of preaching in the open was carried on at the time of the English Reformation, by the Scottish Covenanters, and by George Fox and the early Quakers. When Wesley started to compass the land, therefore, he was in good company. He could claim that history vindi-cated his venture. But he was more concerned with the present and with the future. He was convinced that the only way of rousing the nation to the things of the Spirit was to extend the method with which he had ex-perimented in Bristol and London to the entire country. His goal was a mission to the masses.

Like any shrewd military commander, he knew that a base was of prime importance. If he was to attack the land as a whole, he must first plant himself in secure headquarters. London was the obvious choice. Already he had supporters there in the Fetter Lane Society and he was quick to ensure that they came under his direct control. A dispute with the Mora-vians about the doctrine of "stillness," which in itself was unfortunate, in effect turned out to be a disguised blessing. It afforded an opportunity to establish the first exclusively Methodist society. Molther's teaching was no part of official Moravian belief, and no doubt the breach could have been healed. But in terms of Wesley's mission, it was better to separate. In July

[1] *Ibid.*, Book IV, Chapter 3, pp. 165–167.

[2] George M. Trevelyan, *English Social History* (1944), p. 44.

[3] It is not altogether certain whether the Lollards were actually commissioned by Wyclif himself. K. B. McFarlane thinks they may have been despatched by some of "the younger hotheads" left behind at Oxford by Wyclif (*John Wycliffe and the Be-ginnings of English Nonconformity* (1952), p. 101).

1740 at a Sunday evening Love-feast, Wesley withdrew with eighteen or nineteen followers.[1] From this juncture, Methodists and Moravians went their several ways, each continuing to further the revival though not now in harness together. It was not, however, until two years later that Fetter Lane actually became a Moravian congregation. Although it was dominated by Moravian influences, especially after Wesley's withdrawal, it remained until 1742 what it had been from the start, namely a religious society connected with the Church of England.[2]

The withdrawal from Fetter Lane, however, was a final and calculated step in a series of moves to dissociate Wesley's disciples from the sleeping sickness of Molther's false doctrine. In his *Earnest Appeal to Men of Reason and Religion* (1744) he disclosed something which is not recorded in his *Journal*. "In November 1739 two gentlemen, then unknown to me (Mr. Ball and Mr. Watkins) came and desired me, once and again, to preach in a place called the Foundery, near Moorfields. With much reluctance I at length complied. I was soon after pressed to take that place into my own hands. Those who were most earnest therein lent me the purchase money, which was one hundred and fifteen pounds."[3] Whitehead believed that Wesley, disturbed by the situation at Fetter Lane, was already contemplating a separation.[4]

It looks as if the entry in the *Journal* for Christmas Day 1739 might mark the first meeting of the new society at the Foundery. After spending part of the night at Fetter Lane, Wesley then "went to a smaller company, where also we exhorted one another with hymns and spiritual songs, and poured out our hearts to God in prayer."[5] Of course, this is only conjectural. But it is clear that early in 1740 a society was meeting at the Foundery under Wesley's supervision.[6] Charles took charge on occasion in his brother's absence.[7] It is from him that we learn that by June 1740 there were three hundred members, so that the handful who walked out of Fetter Lane in the following month are not to be thought of as constituting the nucleus of a brand-new group. If we still accept the 23rd July, 1740, as the date when the first Methodist society met in completed

[1] *Journal*, Vol. II, p. 370. 20th July, 1739. Philip Henry Molther, an Alsatian who had been influenced by Zinzendorf, was in London on his way to missionary work in Pennsylvania. His teaching on "stillness" was intended as a curb on undue emotionalism and a warning against reliance on ordinances and piety. As Towlson explains, "though there was something of truth in Molther's general position (for there is a vague ethicalism which seeks to achieve salvation by philanthropy, and, worse, a fussiness in performing church duties which only hides spiritual poverty), he spoilt his case by exaggerating it" (*op. cit.*, p. 86).
[2] John S. Simon, *John Wesley and the Methodist Societies* (1923), pp. 14–15.
[3] *Works*, Vol. VIII, p. 37. *An Earnest Appeal to Men of Reason and Religion* (1744).
[4] John Whitehead, *The Life of the Rev. John Wesley* (1793), Vol. II, p. 125.
[5] *Journal*, Vol. II, p. 328. 25th December, 1739.
[6] Simon, *Religious Societies*, p. 329.
[7] Frederick C. Gill, *Charles Wesley* (1964), p. 98.

separation from the Moravians, we must bear these other factors in mind and recognize that in reality the break had begun sooner.

The building at the Foundery was no more than a shell when Wesley bought it. It had been used for casting cannon until a severe explosion in 1716. From that time it had been left derelict. Although he was able to buy the lease for a modest sum, nearly seven hundred pounds were spent on repairs and alterations to equip it not only as a meeting place for the society, but also as the headquarters of the mission. It was for this purpose that accommodation was provided for Wesley himself when he returned to London from his tours. There was also a bookroom to house the Christian literature to be distributed throughout the country, and stables for the preachers' horses. Here was Wesley's *pied-à-terre* from which he directed the entire campaign. Whilst he was in his journeyings (as he was for most of the year) this was the clearing house for correspondence. Until City Road Chapel was opened in 1778, the Foundery formed the operational base. Wesley might well have taken on his lips the reputed cry of Archimedes (which he does indeed quote in his *Journal*)—"Give me a place to stand and I will move the earth!"[1]

The track which he came to follow in his itinerations was in the first place triangular. Already he had London as his centre and Bristol as his second major city. The New Room in the Horsefair there was built even before the Foundery. In 1742—a year of expansion—the third point of the triangle was fixed at Newcastle-upon-Tyne. Here the Orphan House, opened in 1743, served as a kind of northern office, as well as a favourite retreat for Wesley when exhausted by his travels. This, then, was the ground-plan of the national mission.

It was through John Nelson that Wesley was drawn to the north. The Yorkshire stonemason was converted in London, and had then returned to his home in Birstall to evangelize the district. He begged Wesley to visit him and to support the crusade by preaching. Wesley reached Birstall on the 26th May, 1742, and was astonished at what he saw. "Many of the greatest profligates in all the country were now changed. Their blasphemies were turned to praise. Many of the most abandoned drunkards were now sober; many sabbath-breakers remembered the sabbath to keep it holy. The whole town wore a new face. Such a change did God work by the artless testimony of one plain man!"[2] Wesley himself preached on the top of Birstall Hill "to several hundreds of plain people; and spent the afternoon in talking severally with those who had tasted of the grace of God."[3] In the evening he preached on the side of Dewsbury Moor, about

---

[1] *Journal*, Vol. II, p. 201. 20th May, 1739. The exact words of Archimedes were: "Give me a lever long enough, and a fulcrum strong enough, and single-handed I can move the world (cf. Pliny *Historia Naturalis*, VII, 37).

[2] *Works*, Vol. XIII, p. 276. *A Short History of the People Called Methodists* (1781).

[3] *Journal*, Vol. III, pp. 12–13. 26th May, 1742.

two miles away. This initial ministry in the north bore immediate fruit. Amongst those who heard him were Nathaniel Harrison and John Murgatroyd, two stalwarts of Methodism in that area in days to come.[1] Next morning Wesley took leave of Nelson, and rode further north with his companion John Taylor.

On Friday the 28th May they arrived on the outskirts of Newcastle-upon-Tyne.[2] It was the Countess of Huntingdon who had urged Wesley to go there and bring the gospel to the colliers and keelmen. He had called at her home at Donington Park, near Ashby-de-la-Zouch, before continuing into Yorkshire.[3] After taking a meal, Wesley and Taylor walked through the town. "I was surprised: so much drunkenness, cursing and swearing (even from the mouths of little children) do I never remember to have seen and heard before, in so small a compass of time. Surely this place is ripe for Him who 'came not to call the righteous, but sinners to repentance.' "[4] Such was Wesley's immediate reaction.

Sunday saw the start of his evangelistic thrust. At seven in the morning he went down Sandgate, "the poorest and most contemptible part of the town"[5] and, taking his stance at the end of the street along with Taylor, struck up the Hundredth Psalm. Three or four people came to see what was happening. Soon there were three or four hundred curious bystanders. Then Wesley gave a message on Isaiah 53: 5, and before he had finished the crowd had grown to almost fifteen hundred. The people still stood there after he had closed the service, gaping and staring in their astonishment at such an unusual sight. Wesley, in his matter-of-fact way, made the briefest of announcements. "If you desire to know who I am, my name is John Wesley. At five in the evening, with God's help, I design to preach here again." And with that he left them.

Tyerman has graphically pieced together the elements in this drama, which inaugurated Wesley's work in the third of his key centres: "the preacher the renowned John Wesley, doubtless dressed in full canonicals, with plain John Taylor standing at his side—the time seven o'clock on a Sunday morning in the beautiful month of May—the place Sandgate, crowded with keelmen and sailors, using, says Christopher Hopper, 'the language of hell, as though they had received a liberal education in the regions of woe'—the song of praise the old hundredth psalm, which, like the grand old ocean, is as fresh and as full of music now as it was when it first was written—and the text, the very pith of gospel truth, 'He was wounded for our transgressions, He was bruised for our iniquities, the chastisement of our peace was upon Him, and with His stripes we are

[1] *Methodist Magazine*, Vol. XXIV (1801), p. 531; *ibid.*, Vol. XXXI (1808), p. 138. Cf. Tyerman, *Life of John Wesley*, Vol. I, pp. 384–385.
[2] *Journal*, Vol. III, p. 13. 28th May, 1742.
[3] *Ibid.*, p. 11. 22nd May, 1742.
[4] *Ibid.*, p. 13. 28th May, 1742.
[5] *Ibid.*, p. 14. 30th May, 1742.

healed.' "[1] It is a scene etched so vividly that, as we read of it, we seem to be there ourselves.

In the evening the numbers had swelled to incredible proportions. In Moorfields and on Kennington Common Wesley had faced congregations of up to twenty thousand, but this was more than he had ever seen. Afterwards, the poor people were ready to tread him underfoot "out of pure love and kindness."[2] It was some time before he could get away. When he reached his inn, he found a deputation waiting to press him to remain, but he had promised to be back in Birstall and so was compelled to leave. But from that day on, Newcastle was a regular stopping-place and some of his most rewarding work was done there. Not many miles away was Houghton-le-Spring, where, in the days of the Reformation, Bernard Gilpin was Rector. He was known as "the apostle of the north" as he travelled far and wide in the neglected parishes, preaching the everlasting gospel. Wesley was called in his century to follow in the steps of Gilpin, whose life he read when in Georgia.[3] The north of England figures prominently in his subsequent itineraries, Leeds and Manchester being added to Newcastle as springboards from which to evangelize whole areas.

Wesley's route back from the north was planned to bring him after many years once again to Epworth. The story of how he preached on his father's tombstone is too familiar to repeat. He had been refused permission to preach in the church by the curate, John Romley.[4] The crowd outside was considerable. No doubt the people came from many other places. "It was a wonderful scene," commented Dean Hutton: "one of the most moving in the history of the Church."[5] It is reproduced on the marble memorial to Wesley in Westminster Abbey. That was the first of many visits to Epworth, where he always seemed to draw a crowd and see results. In many ways 1742 was Wesley's *annus mirabilis* so far as breaking new ground was concerned. He reports that "in this year many societies were formed in Somersetshire, Wiltshire, Gloucestershire, Leicestershire, Warwickshire, Nottinghamshire, as well as the southern parts of Yorkshire."[6] In the following year he was unable to map out a definite plan, spending about fourteen weeks in London, ten in Bristol and district,

---

[1] Tyerman, *Life of John Wesley*, Vol. I, p. 386. Cf. Christopher Hopper in *Wesleyan Methodist Magazine*, Vol. LXXI (1848), p. 41. A granite obelisk and drinking trough now marks the site of Wesley's first preaching in Newcastle.

[2] *Journal*, Vol. III, p. 14. 30th May, 1742.

[3] *Ibid.*, Vol. I, p. 299. 27th and 28th November, 1736. Gilpin came under the influence of Erasmus' writings at Queen's College, Oxford. He was outspoken in advocating a reformation of clerical standards.

[4] *Ibid.*, Vol. III, pp. 18–19. 6th June, 1742. The Rector was the Honourable John Hay.

[5] Hutton, *op. cit.*, p. 80.

[6] *Works*, Vol. XIII, p. 277. *A Short History of the People Called Methodists* (1781).

thirteen in and about Newcastle, three in Cornwall and twelve elsewhere, chiefly in the Midlands and north. As Tyerman remarked, he was now "a thorough itinerant."[1]

Wesley was not confined to England. He had gone into Wales in October 1739, and found "most of the inhabitants . . . indeed ripe for the gospel."[2] But he was content to leave Howell Harris to push forward with the evangelization of the Principality. His first trip to Ireland was in August 1747—and twenty more were to come. This was a particularly encouraging sphere. "The overall picture is of triumphal progress," writes F. C. Gill. "Never since the days of St. Patrick had Ireland known such flaming evangelism or greeted a more fervent apostle. The soldiers to whom he preached in Athlone Barracks declared there was something superhuman about him."[3] His farewell in 1789 was "quite an ovation," according to Canon Overton.[4] In April 1751 Wesley crossed the Scottish border for the first time. He made twenty-two visits in all—the last being as late as 1790.[5] He was always received with the utmost courtesy, and had the support of distinguished ministers in the Kirk. His influence in Scotland lay not so much in the establishing of Methodist societies, of which there were comparatively few, but in quickening the existing life of Presbyterianism.[6] The Isle of Man was not reached until 1777, and the Channel Islands later still, in 1787.[7]

We have done no more than touch and glance on the broad outlines of Wesley's travel plan. To go into detail would demand a book in itself, for, as Dr. V. H. H. Green has strikingly observed, "the places that Wesley visited make his *Journal* an Evangelical Bradshaw."[8] And in all his widespread journeyings he had only one desire: it was to lead men and women to Christ. His motive was as simple as that. Evidently "John Smith" had accused him of assuming the apostolate of England. Wesley replied that he no more did that than he "assumed the apostolate of all Europe, or rather of all the world: that is, in plain terms, wherever I see one or a thousand men running into hell, be it in England, Ireland, or France, yea, in Europe, Asia, Africa, or America, I will stop them if I can: as a minister of Christ, I will beseech them in His name to turn back and be reconciled to God. Were I to do otherwise, were I to let any soul drop into the pit whom I might have saved from everlasting burnings, I am not satisfied God would accept my plea, 'Lord, he was not of my parish.' "[9]

[1] Tyerman, *Life of John Wesley*, Vol. I, p. 401.
[2] *Journal*, Vol. II, p. 296. 20th October, 1739.
[3] Frederick C. Gill, *In the Steps of John Wesley* (1962), p. 211.
[4] Overton, *op. cit.*, p. 114.
[5] *Journal*, Vol. VIII, pp. 64–68. 11th–31st May, 1790.
[6] Cf. Dugald Butler, *John Wesley and George Whitefield in Scotland* (1898), p. 217.
[7] *Journal*, Vol. VI, p. 150. 30th July, 1777; *ibid.*, Vol. VII, p. 312. 15th August, 1787.
[8] V. H. H. Green, *John Wesley*, p. 82.
[9] *Letters*, Vol. II, p. 137. To "John Smith," 22nd March, 1748.

Wesley knew that his journeys were really necessary, and he could point to the results for ample proof. In June 1755 he paused to weigh the facts. "From a deep sense of the amazing work which God has of late years wrought in England, I preached in the evening on those words (Ps. 147: 20), 'He hath not dealt so with any nation;' no, not even in Scotland or New England. In both these God has indeed made bare His arm, yet not in so astonishing a manner as among us. This must appear to all who impartially consider (1) the number of persons on whom God has wrought; (2) the swiftness of His work in many, both convinced and truly converted in a few days; (3) the depth of it in most of these, changing the heart as well as the conversations; (4) the clearness of it, enabling them boldly to say, 'Thou hast loved me; Thou hast given Thyself for me'; (5) the continuance of it. God has wrought in Scotland and New England, at several times, for some weeks or months together; but among us He has wrought for near eighteen years together, without any observable intermission. Above all, let it be remarked that a considerable number of the regular clergy were engaged in that great work in Scotland; and in New England above a hundred, perhaps as eminent as any in the whole province, not only for piety, but also for abilities, both natural and acquired; whereas in England there were only two or three inconsiderable clergymen, with a few young, raw, unlettered men; and these opposed by well-nigh all the clergy, as well as laity, in the nation. He that remarks this must needs own, both that this is a work of God and that He hath not wrought so in any other nation."[1]

By 1785 Wesley could claim that the number of those who had been brought to God in the revival was perhaps greater than in any other age since the time of the apostles: and who can deny the possibility? At his death in 1791 there were 72,000 members in his own societies alone in Great Britain, apart from those overseas. By the grace of God Wesley was enabled to go on "in the same track," and it proved to be a trail of untold blessing.

[1] *Journal*, Vol. IV, p. 122. 16th June, 1755.

CHAPTER X

THIS VAGABOND LIFE

"I saw not one whom I knew but Mr.——'s aunt, who could not long forbear telling me how sorry she was that I should leave all my friends to lead *this vagabond life*. Why, indeed, it is not pleasing to flesh and blood; and I would not do it if I did not believe there was another world." *Journal* 4: 13.

IN ORDER TO FULFIL HIS MISSION THROUGHOUT THE LAND, WESLEY had to resign himself to incessant travel. He became the great itinerant. For the sake of the gospel, he was prepared to lead a gipsy life. We catch something of the energetic momentum of the man as we dip into the *Journal*. He was in almost perpetual motion. He never had time to stay and fold his legs, as Dr. Johnson complained.[1] Canon Overton bemoaned the fact that the pace of Wesley's movements is calculated to drive a biographer to despair. "It is simply impossible to follow him step by step, although there are ample materials to enable one to do so. He seems to fly about like a meteor."[2] Wesley himself left us in no doubt as to what was the driving motive behind this unwearying haste. As late as 1781 he was still on the move: "I must go on; for a dispensation of the gospel is committed to me; and woe is me if I preach not the gospel."[3] Those two scriptural phrases (culled from I Corinthians 9, verses 17 and 16 in that order) comprised his stock answer to every question about his ministry, so often did he quote them.

It is not to be supposed that Wesley was temperamentally restless. His intense activity is not to be accounted for on purely naturalistic grounds. He had to disabuse "John Smith" about this. "To this day I have abundantly more temptation to lukewarmness than to impetuosity; to be a saunterer *inter sylvas academicas*, a philosophical sluggard, than an itinerant preacher."[4] At Oxford he wondered "how any busy man could be saved. I scarce thought it possible for a man to retain the Christian spirit amid the noise and bustle of the world. God taught me better by my own experience."[5]

[1] Johnson's comment was: "John Wesley's conversation is good, but he is never at leisure. He is always obliged to go at a certain hour. This is very disagreeable to a man who loves to fold his legs and have his talk out, as I do." *Boswell's Life of Johnson*, ed. G. Birkbeck Hill (1934), Vol. III, p. 230.

[2] Overton, *op. cit.*, p. 86.

[3] *Works*, Vol. XIII, p. 267. *A Plain Account of Kingswood School* (1781).

[4] *Letters*, Vol. II, p. 69. To "John Smith," 25th June, 1746.

[5] *Ibid.*, Vol. VI, p. 292. To Miss March, 10th December, 1777.

Now and again in the *Journal* we come across a hint that his vagabond existence was far from congenial to him. On the 9th March, 1759, he preached morning and evening at the Foundery, where he had his own rooms. "How pleasing would it be to flesh and blood to remain in this little quiet place.... Nay, I am not to consult my own care, but advancing the kingdom of God."[1] On the 4th June in the same year he wrote from Newcastle. "Certainly if I did not believe there was another world, I should spend all my summers here, as I know no place in Great Britain comparable to it for pleasantness. But I seek another country, and therefore am content to be a wanderer upon earth."[2] In 1782 he visited the home of Miss Harvey at Hinxworth in Hertfordshire. It was the month of July, when others might legitimately think of lazing in the sun. There was a pleasant garden and a shady walk round the neighbouring meadows. "How gladly could I repose awhile here! But repose is not for me in this world."[3] Soon he was addressing a congregation of villagers in the hall of the house. In more than one of his letters, Wesley had to warn his preachers against the sin of indolence. This to Brian Bury Collins has only recently been published, having come from Bishop Leete's collection in the States: "Do not creep into a quiet corner. I love as well as you do *Tacitus sylvas inter reptare salubris*. But it is not my calling. I am to save souls, and as many as I possibly can."[4]

More than once Wesley quoted the lines: "Man was not born in shades to lie!"[5] It seems to have been a motto of his life. Certainly leisure and he had now parted company with a vengeance![6] We are reminded of Whitefield's remark: "No nestling, no nestling this side of eternity!"[7] Both were men under orders, engaged in the battle for souls. There could be no letting up.

The stark statistics of Wesley's itinerations are impressive enough. Curnock was correct in claiming that he "travelled more miles and preached more sermons than any minister of his age."[8] He covered nearly a quarter of a million miles in his lifetime, delivered forty thousand sermons and yet found time to write well over two hundred books.[9] We can only marvel at his achievement. His mileage was prodigious. As Gill remarks,

[1] *Journal*, Vol. IV, p. 301. 9th March, 1759.
[2] *Ibid.*, p. 323. 4th June, 1759.
[3] *Ibid.*, Vol. VI, p. 362. 17th July, 1782.
[4] *Proc. W.H.S.*, Vol. XXXIII, p. 14. Letter to Brian Bury Collins, 27th January, 1780. Quotation from Horace, *Epistles*, Bk. I, Ep. 4, 1. 4—"to stroll silently among the health-giving woods."
[5] *Journal*, Vol. VI, p. 72. 27th August, 1775; *ibid.*, Vol. VIII, p. 10. 11th September, 1789. The source has not been traced.
[6] *Letters*, Vol. I, p. 34. To Samuel Wesley Junior, 5th December, 1726.
[7] John R. Andrews, *George Whitefield: A Light Rising in Obscurity* (1864), p. 29.
[8] *Journal*, Vol. I, p. 1. Introduction.
[9] Haddal, *op. cit.*, pp. 112–113.

Pennant and Cobbett (two of the more noted chroniclers of their travels) were "mere ramblers by comparisons."[1] Anyone who accompanied Wesley was in for a gruelling experience. Duncan Wright discovered that. He joined Wesley for part of 1765 and 1766, but he found he was unable to stand the pace. "As the exercise was too much I gave it up," he confessed.[2] There is a graphic account in the *Journal* of how Wesley and Wright nearly lost their lives on the treacherous quicksands of the Solway Firth.[3] Perhaps that was the last straw so far as Brother Duncan was concerned. Yet at this date Wright was only thirty years of age and Wesley was sixty-three.

John Wesley made it a rule never to disappoint a congregation if it could possibly be avoided. And he very rarely did. Heat and cold, rain and wind, hail and snow, bogs and flood did not prevent him from bringing the message of life and light to the people who walked in darkness. On the 14th March, 1769, he preached as usual at five a.m. to a large company in Stroud. Notice had been given that he would appear at Tewkesbury about noon, at a house not far from the town. He was hindered because the Severn floods were exceptionally high, and was tempted to make straight for Worcester where he was due later. But a messenger met him to say that a congregation gathered from all parts was waiting at Tewkesbury, so he plunged on. The people seemed earnest, so he did not regret the hardships of the journey. He admitted that the negotiation of the submerged tracks was somewhat taxing, and that he was a little tired when he reached Worcester. But when he got there, he preached at about six p.m. in the riding house and afterwards had to face shouting and jostling from the unruly crowd. He took it all in his stride. That was a typical day's work in the life of an evangelist.[4]

In May 1778 he was making his way from Castlebar to Sligo, in Ireland. There was a choice of two roads. The shorter involved some sloughs, but as they thought they had a good guide, Wesley and his colleagues decided to risk it. They crossed the first two quite well. But at the third help was needed. Seven or eight sturdy Irishmen came to the rescue. One carried Wesley on his shoulders—something he would remember with pride to his dying day. Others got the horses through and then managed to lift the chaise across. Wesley now thought the worst was past. But they came to yet another bog. Wesley was helped over and walked on. His companions stayed behind to deal with the chaise, which stuck in the mud. With much difficulty they released it, and caught up with Wesley. The evangelist, however, saw a purpose even in this delay, for on the road he met a poor

[1] Gill, *In the Steps of John Wesley*, p. 13. Cf. Thomas Pennant, *A Journey from Chester to London* (1782); William Cobbett, *Rural Rides* (1830).

[2] *Wesley's Veterans*, ed. John Telford (n.d.), Vol. II, p. 39.

[3] *Journal*, Vol. V, p. 172. 24th June, 1766.

[4] *Ibid.*, pp. 304–305. 14th March, 1769.

man whom he was able to help with the gift of a guinea and no doubt a word about Jesus.[1]

In the hard winters of the eighteenth century Wesley had many struggles in the snow. As late in the year as the 25th April in 1770 the Perthshire highlands were covered with a thickening blanket. Wesley and his friends rode from Dunkeld up into the mountains with conditions worsening as they went. They spent the night at Dalwhinnie (the dearest inn, he said, he had met with in Scotland). Next morning they were told that so much snow had fallen overnight that they would not be able to continue. Three young women had lost their lives in the drifts. "However, we resolved, with God's help, to go as far as we could. But about noon we were at a full stop; the snow, driving together on the top of the mountains, had quite blocked up the road. We dismounted, and striking out of the road warily, sometimes to the left, sometimes to the right, with many stumbles, but no hurt, we got on to Dalmigavie, and before sunset to Inverness."[2] We are reminded of something once said by Thomas Garforth, that "zealous good man" as Richard Burdsall called him.[3] The rugged old Methodist declared that he "would not give a fig for a man who would not wade snow up to the chin for Jesus Christ."[4]

Wesley was a punctual man and usually contrived to arrive at his appointments on time, despite the hazards of the weather. But on occasion arrangements were made for him, without his knowledge, which proved to be inconsiderate and inconvenient. On the 5th July, 1786, notice was given like this that he was to preach at Belper in Derbyshire. He was on his way from Sheffield to Nottingham. "I was nothing glad of this," he admitted, "as it obliged me to quit the turnpike road, to hobble over a miserable common."[5] When at last he arrived, the people were all waiting so, without time to take rest or refreshment, he went straight to the marketplace and, standing under a large tree, he testified that, "This is life eternal, to know Thee, the only true God, and Jesus Christ, whom Thou hast sent" (John 17: 3). More than once Wesley, like his Lord, had not time so much as to eat.[6]

What Wesley considered to be the longest day's journey he ever rode, is recorded in the *Journal* for the 15th June, 1750.[7] The previous day he had been on horseback, with little intermission, from five in the morning until nearly a quarter to eleven at night. At two a.m. he was disturbed by a party of friends from Waterford who had been set on by the mob. By four he was on his way, and reached Kilkenny by noon. Not surprisingly,

[1] *Ibid.*, Vol. VI, pp. 191–192. 18th May, 1778. Cf. p. 51. 25th November, 1774.
[2] *Ibid.*, Vol. V, pp. 363–364. 26th April, 1770.
[3] *Memoirs of the Life of Richard Burdsall written by Himself* (1811), p. 88.
[4] *Ibid.*
[5] *Journal*, Vol. VII, p. 185. 5th July, 1786.
[6] *Ibid.*, Vol. VI, p. 497. 19th April, 1784; Vol. VII, p. 444. 28th October, 1788.
[7] *Ibid.*, Vol. IV, pp. 478–479. 15th June, 1750.

his horse tired later and he had to borrow another. It was about eleven before he decided to stay overnight at Emo, but the good woman of the inn refused to answer and eventually let out four dogs on him. He had no option but to ride on to Ballybrittas, where he laid down to sleep just on midnight. Wesley estimated the journey at fifty old Irish miles, which he took to be the equivalent of ninety by English measurements. Actually, the distance is not quite sixty-five, but that represents a hard day's ride indeed.

Some of his consecutive journeys involved incredible mileages. In February 1745 he left London with Richard Moss, one of his converts at the Foundery. Their destination was Newcastle-upon-Tyne. They rode first through mire and water, and then over snow and ice. The last stage was the worst, as a hard frost, on top of a partial thaw, had made all the ground like glass. Then the snow began to fall again and Gateshead Fell "appeared a great pathless waste of white."[1] Even though they knew the area, they were at a loss to find the way to Newcastle until someone guided them in. They had covered 280 miles in six days—averaging close on fifty miles a day in extreme conditions. "Many a rough journey have I had before," Wesley wrote afterwards, "but one like this I never had; between wind, and hail, and rain, and ice, and snow, and driving sleet, and piercing cold. But it is past: those days will return no more, and are therefore, as though they had never been."[2]

Even at the age of eighty-four, Wesley undertook a particularly long and arduous journey from the annual conference at Manchester, to Southampton where he caught the boat to the Channel Islands. He began at midnight on Sunday, after a busy day preaching and meeting the select society. The Birmingham coach broke down several times, and when he reached the city on the Monday evening, he went straight to the meeting house to preach. The rest of the journey involved earlier rising than was usual even for him, and the taking of post-chaises which were not always easy to hire when he wanted them. On arrival in Southampton, he still had the energy to preach and even to hear Marianne Davies, who entertained the public by her performances on an instrument called the "Armonica," invented by Benjamin Franklin.[3]

Something must be said about the evangelist's means of transport. Although, of course, he used a horse for most of his ministry, he was never unwilling to walk if necessary. As Telford noticed, "Wesley was no mean pedestrian."[4] The year before he sailed to Georgia he walked over a

[1] Ibid., Vol. III, p. 165. 25th February, 1745.
[2] Ibid.
[3] Ibid., Vol. VII, pp. 308–310. 6th–10th August, 1787. The Armonica bore no resemblance to the instrument now known by the name. It consisted of a set of glasses attached to a spindle, moved by a treadle. It was tuned and played like musical glasses today.
[4] Telford, op. cit., p. 194.

thousand miles to preach in the churches around Oxford.[1] Much of his travelling on the continent of Europe in 1738 was done on foot. Wesley never lost his keenness for walking. In June 1758 he was ready to leave Castlebar in Ireland, when he found that the horse that was brought for him at four a.m. had neither bridle nor saddle. He set out on foot and eventually a man galloped after him at full speed, so anxious to catch him up that, just as they reached him, both fell down together.[2] On another occasion he walked on seven or eight miles before his servant overtook him with a carriage.[3] On the 6th September, 1788, at the age of eighty-five, he walked from Kingswood to Bristol, and complained that his friends objected to him attempting it. "It seemed so sad a thing to walk four or five miles! I am ashamed that a Methodist preacher, in tolerable health, should make any difficulty of this."[4]

But, of course, it is as a man on horseback that we rightly picture Wesley. The equestrian statue in the forecourt of the New Room at Bristol, executed by the late Gordon A. Walker, R.A., is a true representation. It is the only one in the world, strangely enough, which shows Wesley astride a horse, although a replica is found in Washington at the Wesley Theological Seminary. As we look at it, we are seeing the authentic Wesley. So inseparable are John Wesley and his horse that Dr. J. E. Rattenbury, in his whimsical way, once described him as "an evangelical centaur."[5] Not for nothing is Prof. Umphrey Lee's biography of Wesley entitled *The Lord's Horseman*. "I must be on horseback for life," Wesley himself declared.[6] And so he was for much of it.

It was early in his ministry that Wesley learned to use the saddle as a library chair. "Near thirty years ago," he wrote in March 1770, "I was thinking, 'How is it that no horse ever stumbles while I am reading? (History, poetry, and philosophy I commonly read on horseback, having other employment at other times.) No account can possibly be given but this: because then I throw the reins on his neck. I then set myself to observe; and I aver that, in riding above a hundred thousand miles, I scarce ever remember any horse (except two, that would fall head over heels any way) to fall, or make a considerable stumble, while I rode *with a slack rein*."[7]

Wesley always took the utmost care of his horses, and insisted that his preachers should do the same. Sometimes he was let down by those who serviced his steed. He left London one autumn morning in 1768 at five

[1] Whitehead, *op. cit.*, Vol. I, p. 453.

[2] *Journal*, Vol. IV, p. 269. 6th June, 1758.

[3] *Ibid.*, Vol. V, p. 294, 2nd December, 1768; cf. also Vol. II, p. 518. 18th December, 1741.

[4] *Ibid.*, Vol. VII, p. 433. 6th September, 1788.

[5] Rattenbury, *op. cit.*, p. 53.

[6] *Letters*, Vol. IV, p. 255. To Ebenezer Blackwell, 14th July, 1764.

[7] *Journal*, Vol. V, pp. 360–361. 21st March, 1770.

o'clock, only to find that his horse had scarcely a shoe on its feet. He managed to get as far as Colney, where he paid "one to shoe my horse all round, and lame him on both his fore-feet," as he sardonically put it. After hobbling on to Hockliffe, "an honest and skilful smith" remedied the matter.[2] It was as well, for further down the road the ridings through Whittlebury Forest were girth-deep.[3]

In later years Wesley resorted increasingly to his private chaise. He was no longer able to sustain extended periods in the saddle. It was no royal landau in which he rode, but "a lumbering old carriage," as an old Methodist at Yarm described it.[4] In 1772 a subscription was raised to buy him a new one. Wesley had a bookcase fitted up inside his chaise, and used it as a study, an office, a library, a bookshop and a private chapel. It was a convenient retreat when he had work to do with his papers. He would even sit in it on board ship, if the sea was calm.[5]

On occasion, Wesley would hire or borrow a carriage. A post-chaise was the eighteenth-century equivalent of a cab or taxi. But they were not always available just when wanted. In December 1782 Wesley could not procure any but an open chaise to take him from Luton to St. Albans. The frost was very keen, and as a result he caught a severe cold.[6] On his last visit to Ireland, he was heading for Tandaragee one afternoon when the iron part of the fore-axle tree on his chaise snapped. He walked on with characteristic determination, even though it was just before his eighty-sixth birthday; but eventually he was so exhausted that he was compelled to rest at an inn, and send to Banbridge for a post-chaise. His money was wasted, for within a mile or so he was met by the Rector's wife who, hearing of the breakdown, had come to collect him in her own chaise.[7]

The chief means of long-distance public transport in the eighteenth century was the stage coach. Although there was some improvement in comfort towards the end of Wesley's life, it was still quite an adventure to take the diligence, as it was also called. A German pastor, Carl Philipp Moritz, related his experiences on a ride from Leicester to London in 1782, and said that he reached his destination looking like "a crazy creature" after what he described as "hardly a journey but rather a perpetual motion, or removal, from one place to another, in a close box."[8] We read of Wesley going from London to Salisbury, from Edinburgh to

---

[1] Ibid., p. 291. 31st October, 1768.   [2] Ibid.
[3] Ibid. The "ridings" were grass tracks through the forest.
[4] Ibid., Vol. IV, p. 329, n. 1.
[5] Ibid., Vol. VII, p. 18. 15th July, 1789. On board the Princess Royal crossing the Irish Sea from Dublin.
[6] Ibid., Vol. VI, p. 380. 6th December, 1782.
[7] Ibid., Vol. VII, p. 510. 11th June, 1789. It was Mrs. Leslie, wife of Dr. Henry Leslie. (Proc. W.H.S., Vol. XXX, pp. 114–115.)
[8] Travels of Carl Philipp Moritz in England (1784), p. 214. Cf. Johnson's England, Vol. I, p. 134.

Glasgow, from Norwich to Colchester, and from Bristol to London in this way, to cite only a few examples.[1] On the 14th August, 1782, he was en route for Bristol after the conference in London, when at one a.m. the passengers were informed that highwaymen on the road ahead had stopped the coaches that had preceded and robbed the occupants. "I felt no uneasiness on the account," Wesley explained, "knowing that God would take care of us. And He did so, for, before we came to the spot, all the highwaymen were taken; so we went on unmolested, and early in the afternoon came safe to Bristol."[2] He had noted with gratitude in 1777: "I have travelled all roads, by day and by night, for these forty years, and never was interrupted yet."[3]

Wesley also travelled by boat when crossing the Irish Sea or the English Channel. He had a narrow escape from disaster when sailing to Guernsey in August 1787. The gale was so strong that the captain made for Alderney, but they were nearly shipwrecked in the bay. "When we were in the middle of the rocks, with the sea rippling all round us, the wind totally failed. Had this continued we must have struck upon one or other of the rocks: so we went to prayer, and the wind sprung up instantly. About sunset we landed; and, though we had five beds in the same room, slept in peace."[4] But whether on sea or land, Wesley was providentially preserved from serious accident throughout his fifty years of itineration.

The last reference to rather cramped sleeping quarters leads us to consider the evangelist's lodgings. Although he might have preferred and could often have commanded the comfort of a gentleman's house, or even the more uncertain facilities of an inn, he was nevertheless prepared to accept what hospitality was provided for him. Early in his itinerant ministry he had learned to rough it if need be. There is an unforgettable picture in John Nelson's *Journal* of himself and John Wesley sleeping on the floor at St. Ives, with Wesley using Nelson's top coat for a pillow and Nelson using Burkitt's *Notes on the New Testament* for his. One morning, at three o'clock, after enduring this hard bed for a fortnight, Wesley turned over, dug Nelson in the ribs and joked: "Brother Nelson, let us be of good cheer . . . for the skin is off but on one side yet."[5]

Wesley, in fact, preferred a firm bed to a soft one. On Good Friday in 1770 at Houghton, a village near Carlisle, he was given "a hard, clean bed" and "slept in peace."[6] Once when he was staying at Yarm with George Merryweather, a servant found Wesley's coachman rolling himself

[1] *Journal*, Vol. VII, p. 54. 28th March, 1785; Vol. VI, p. 19. 12th May, 1774; p. 377. 4th–5th November, 1782; Vol. VII, p. 118. 2nd October, 1785.
[2] *Ibid.*, Vol. VI, p. 365. 14th August, 1782.
[3] *Ibid.*, p. 177. 16th December, 1777.
[4] *Ibid.*, Vol. VII, p. 311. 14th August, 1787.
[5] *Wesley's Veterans*, Vol. III, pp. 80–81; cf. Tyerman, *Life of John Wesley*, Vol. I, p. 418.
[6] *Journal*, Vol. V, p. 362. 13th April, 1770.

vigorously up and down the feather bed to make it hard enough for him to sleep on.[1] However, he was not enthusiastic about sharing the room with strangers. At Besore in Cornwall he had to confess: "I was not quite reconciled to my lodging. Not but the grotto itself was very venerable, but I did not like the circumstance of having a man and his wife in the same room. I therefore willingly accepted an invitation from Mr. Painter, and walked over with him to Truro."[2]

Sometimes he was too chilly. On the 15th December, 1788, when in any case his blood must have begun to run rather thin, he was staying at Miss Teulon's school in Highgate. He rated it the coldest night ever. The house stood on the edge of a hill, and the east wind blew straight on the window, which was far from being weather-proof. He counted the strokes of eleven, twelve and one, and was then obliged to dress because the cramp was growing more and more acute.[3] Sometimes he was too stifled. At Miller's Barn in 1752 he reported: "My lodging was not such as I would have chosen, but what Providence chooses is always good. My bed was considerably underground, the room serving for both a bed-chamber and a cellar. The closeness was more troublesome at first than the coolness, but I let in a little fresh air by breaking a pane of paper (put by way of glass) in the window, and then slept sound till morning."[4]

The prophet's chamber at Terryhoogan, in Ireland, was specially built for the purpose. It was a good thing, however, that Wesley was a small man, for it was only six feet high. The floor dimensions were nine feet by seven, and it was made of mud. Yet Wesley could smile at these marble walls "vulgarly called clay."[5] But his most fragrant memory was of Polperro. "Here the room over which we were to lodge being filled with pilchards and conger eels, the perfume was too potent for me; so that I was not sorry when one of our friends invited me to lodge at her house."[6] However, if Wesley could recall his grimmer experiences, he was also invited to some of the stately homes of England and Ireland, like Barlby Hall near Selby, Portwood Hall near Stockport, and the residence of Lord Moira near Dublin.[7] Best of all, he enjoyed the fellowship of many Christians, rich and poor, up and down the land.

Reviewing his life on his birthday in 1788, Wesley claimed that he had never lost a night's sleep since he was born.[8] He added that he could com-

---

[1] *Ibid.*, Vol. IV, p. 329, n. 1.

[2] *Ibid.*, p. 238. 19th September, 1757.

[3] *Ibid.*, Vol. VII, p. 455. 15th December, 1788.

[4] *Ibid.*, Vol. IV, p. 32. 9th June, 1752. The warmest atmosphere Wesley ever experienced was when the house went on fire (*Proc. W.H.S.*, Vol. XXV, p. 86).

[5] *Journal*, Vol. IV, p. 379. 28th May, 1760. Cf. pp. 263–264. 9th May, 1758.

[6] *Ibid.*, Vol. V, p. 487. 16th September, 1768.

[7] *Ibid.*, Vol. VII, p. 407, 26th June, 1778, cf. n. 2; Vol. V, p. 20, 17th June, 1763, cf. n. 1; p. 423, 6th July, 1771.

[8] *Ibid.*, Vol. VII, p. 408. 28th June, 1788.

mand sleep whenever he was weary, day or night.[1] This ability to dose off for a few minutes at will was the secret of other men of action besides Wesley, of whom Sir Winston Churchill was a notable instance. These factors must have contributed to Wesley's astonishingly clean bill of health over the busy years, especially in view of the fact that as a young man he was thought to be far from strong.

In view of his incomparable record of evangelistic endeavour, we find it hard to believe that he was once criticized for taking life too easily. Of course, his accuser was a crank. She claimed to have a message from the Lord to the effect that Wesley was laying up treasures on earth, living at leisure and interested only in eating and drinking. Wesley's reply was characteristic. "I told her, God knew me better; and, if He had sent her, He would have sent her with a more proper message."[2] The prayer of "that good man, Bishop Stratford" was more than once on Wesley's lips and abundantly answered in his ministry: "Lord, let me not live to be useless!"[3]

No tribute is more fitting than that which Fletcher paid in 1771, whilst Wesley was still in full orbit. Fletcher saw him flying "with unwearied diligence through the three kingdoms, calling sinners to repentance and to the healing fountain of Jesus' blood. Though oppressed with the weight of near seventy years, and the cares of nearly 30,000 souls, he shames still, by his unabated zeal and immense labours, all the young ministers in England, perhaps in Christendom. He has generously blown the gospel trumpet, and rode twenty miles, before most of the professors who despise his labours, have left their downy pillows. As he begins the day, the week, the year, so he concludes them, still intent upon extensive services for the glory of the Redeemer and the good of souls."[4]

[1] *Ibid.* Gill tells how as an old man Wesley once arrived very tired at the Old Cross inn at Penrith. He asked how long it was to service time and was informed that he had ten minutes to spare. He immediately leaned back in his chair and dropped off to sleep. He woke refreshed and ready for action. (*In the Steps of John Wesley*, p. 183.)

[2] *Journal*, Vol. IV, p. 364. 16th January, 1760.

[3] *Ibid.*, 8th December, 1764. Nicholas Stratford was Bishop of Chester from 1689 until his death in 1707.

[4] Frederick W. MacDonald, *John W. Fletcher* (1885), p. 118.

CHAPTER XI

A CONVENIENT PLACE

"AT FOUR in the afternoon there were above three thousand, *in a convenient place* near Bristol, to whom I declared, 'The hour is coming, and now is, when the dead shall hear the voice of the Son of God, and they that hear shall live.' "
Journal 2: 182.

ONE OF THE MAJOR PROBLEMS OF OPEN-AIR PREACHING IS TO find a suitable stance. A great deal depends on the right location. Wesley was as much aware of this as any modern evangelist. As the years passed and he returned again and again to the same towns, he made for some familiar spot which had already been tested by use. But in the pioneer days, or whenever even at a later period he ventured to break new ground, the choice of a preaching place exercised him considerably.

Sometimes changed circumstances in an often-visited area raised the matter again. "The question was, where I should preach," he wrote in his *Journal* for the 27th May, 1787. He was on his farewell tour of Ireland, and he had come to Clones once more. Church service was over on this Sunday afternoon, and he was looking for a stand. The weather conditions ("furious wind and violent rain") made it impracticable for him to preach in the market-place as he had planned. Eventually he stood in a doorway to address the people.[1]

In May 1756, on an earlier tour, he had reached Clonmel, which he described as "the pleasantest town, beyond all comparison, which I have yet seen in Ireland."[2] That evening he proclaimed the gospel in a large loft, capable of holding five or six hundred people. It was not full, however, because there were doubts about its safety. This was obviously not the best place for a meeting, and in any case the owner forbade its use on the next day. An approach was made to the commanding officer of the militia in the town with a view to securing the barrack-yard. He replied that it was unavailable for such a purpose. "Not that I have any objection to Mr. Wesley," he quickly added. "I will hear him if he preaches under the gallows." In the end, Wesley decided to preach in the street, and as a result the congregation was more than doubled. Both officers and men were amongst them, as well as the mayor. The latter proved an asset in restraining a drunk who tried to disturb the service.[3]

[1] *Journal*, Vol. VII, p. 281. 27th May, 1787.
[2] *Ibid.*, Vol. IV, p. 161. 10th May, 1756.　　　[3] *Ibid.*

The choice of a site was sometimes left to the local Methodists, and was not always a happy one. "I was desired to preach at Worksop," Wesley noted on the 29th July, 1780; "but when I came, they had not fixed on any place. At length they chose a lamentable one, full of dirt and dust, but without the least shelter from the scorching sun. This few could bear; so we had only a small company of as stupid people as ever I saw."[1] If Wesley's comments now and then tended towards acidity, it was because he was jealous for the work of God. His impatience with inefficient arrangements was a reflection of his concern to ensure that only the best was offered in the Master's service.

In this chapter we propose to review Wesley's preaching stations—not as they later appeared on the Methodist plans when meeting houses were erected, but as they originally were in the open air or in some borrowed building. Most of Wesley's sermons, especially in the earlier years of his itinerant ministry, were preached neither in church nor chapel, but in some convenient place where the people could easily gather. An analysis of these, as they are indicated in the *Journal*, has not been fully attempted before, so far as can be ascertained, and if what follows sounds rather like a catalogue it is because only so can we grasp the range of Wesley's improvised pulpits. We shall begin with the outdoor stances and then list those inside.

Quite often all we are told is that Wesley stood in the street, or, as at Adwalton, "in a broad part of the highway."[2] Some of the streets are actually named: Prince Street in Bristol, Barrack Street in Tullamore, Ship Street and Marlborough Street in Dublin, and Sandgate in Newcastle.[3] In other instances it is simply "in the main street," as at Pocklington, Pembroke, Builth Wells and Wakefield amongst others.[4] Later references often clarify this more general statement by pinpointing the exact spot. Open squares were common gathering-places, not only for the purpose of evangelism but for political or other demonstrations too. Among those specifically mentioned are Charles Square in Hoxton, Ratcliffe Square near Stepney, Blake Square in York (better known now as St. Helen's Square), and the Linen Hall, Lisburn, "so called, a large square, with piazzas on three sides of it," as Wesley explained.[5] Others can be identified: St. Martin's Square, Chester; King Square, Bristol; St. George's Square, Portsmouth; and Paradise Square, Sheffield.[6]

[1] *Ibid.*, Vol. VI, p. 288. 29th July, 1780.   [2] *Ibid.*, Vol. III, p. 17. 3rd June, 1742.
[3] *Ibid.*, Vol. V, p. 30. 18th September, 1763; Vol. IV, p. 175. 15th July, 1756; Vol. III, p. 338. 25th March, 1748; p. 14, 30th May, 1742.
[4] *Ibid.*, Vol. IV, p. 227. 15th July, 1757; Vol. V, p. 229. 1st September, 1767; Vol. III, p. 317. 30th August, 1747; p. 368, 20th August, 1748.
[5] *Ibid.*, Vol. II, p. 461. 7th June, 1741; Vol. III, p. 4. 25th May, 1742; Vol. IV, p. 224. 11th July, 1757; Vol. V, p. 113. 4th May, 1765.
[6] *Ibid.*, Vol. IV, pp. 35–36. 22nd June, 1752; Vol. V, p. 29. 4th September, 1763; Vol. VII, p. 105. 11th August, 1785; Vol. VI, p. 287. 28th June, 1780.

One of the fascinating items in the collection of Wesley relics housed in Brunswick Chapel, Newcastle-upon-Tyne is a colour engraving of the evangelist standing in Hospital Square in that city. He has just finished preaching from the stone steps which lead to the upper storey of the Guildhall. He is being protected from the mob by a fishwife. She was "a muckle woman," we are told, and afforded an ample screen for the diminutive Wesley. She flung her arms around him and shouted in broad Tyneside: "If ony yen o' ye lifts another han' to touch ma canny man, A'll floor ye direckly." She ran by the horse's side down Sandgate as Wesley left, crying: "Noo touch the little man, if ye dare !"[1]

Wesley's most frequently-used post was in the market-place—the most natural focus in an eighteenth-century town. Often he used the steps of the market cross, as he did at Epworth.[2] As he exhorted the people there, did his mind go back to the day when he caught the coach from that very spot to go to school at Charterhouse? The cross was recently damaged, and there is talk of removing it. Wesley often preached at Bolton cross, and a photograph from a reconstructed model shows that the top of the steps rose to quite a height. It faced the parish church, and behind are the stocks. On one occasion the champion prize-fighter in Lancashire climbed up on the cross to quell the unruly crowd by threatening those who were causing the disturbance.[3]

Other spots close to the market were also utilized. In Newark Wesley preached in the covered shambles, or meat-market, with one end open to the street and the other abutting on Middle Gate. Two or three thousand people managed to squeeze in.[4] The Town Hall now occupies the site. In Truro, Wesley once preached in the piazza next to the Coinage Hall.[5] He probably stood under the arches whilst the people listened in a square off Powder Street. At Skipton he preached "near the bridge," and a cottage at the foot of Chapel Hill marks the site of what was called "John Wesley's Forum."[6]

One of the most famous of Wesley's open-air pulpits was at Wednesbury, and is still preserved. He preached thirty or forty times in the High Bullen—so called because here the cruel sport of bull-baiting was staged. The Black Country was notorious for its addiction. Wesley stood on a flight of steps outside a malthouse. Carts would back up to unload. This horse-block now stands in front of the Spring Head Mission. The lower steps are of brick, and have clearly been restored, but the top stones are original. We can safely say that they were trodden by the soles of Wesley's trim black shoes.

---

[1] Gill, *In the Steps of John Wesley*, p. 148.

[2] *Journal*, Vol. III, p. 174. 21st April, 1745, p. 280. 22nd February, 1747; Vol. IV, p. 121. 9th June, 1755, *et. al.*   [3] *Ibid.*, Vol. III, p. 373, n. 3.

[4] *Ibid.*, Vol. VI, p. 284. 12th June, 1780.   [5] *Ibid.*, p. 124. 27th August, 1776.

[6] *Ibid.*, Vol. V, p. 79. 26th June, 1764. Cf. Gill, *In the Steps of John Wesley*, p. 180.

The evangelist often preached in the precincts of a castle. We hear of him in the court at Fonmon, on the steps at Cardiff, and in the yard at Lincoln, Cockermouth and Dungannon.[1] At Aberdeen he stood on the paved stones at the gate and at Castletown, in the Isle of Man, just outside.[2] At Corfe he preached in front of Well Court under the shadow of the castle and at Swansea on one of the lawns "surrounded by high old walls."[3] Rougemont Castle in Exeter, the seat of the Anglo-Saxon kings, provided an ideal venue. There "were gathered together (as some imagined) half the grown persons in the city. It was an awful sight. So vast a congregation in that solemn amphitheatre! And all silent and still as I explained at large, and enforced, that glorious truth, 'Happy are they whose iniquities are forgiven, and whose sins are covered.' "[4]

Moving from town to the countryside, Wesley would find that a hill was an obvious vantage point for a speaker. Since the days of our Lord's sermon on the mount, the messengers of the Cross have sought out similar eminences, though often on a smaller scale than the traditional setting in Galilee. Natural contours combined to form an auditorium. At South Biddick, a mining village near Newcastle-upon-Tyne, the spot where Wesley spoke "was just at the bottom of a semi-circular hill, on the rising sides of which many hundreds stood; but far more on the plain beneath."[5] He was so impressed with it that weekly preaching was started there. Down in Falmouth he used Pike's Hill with its smooth top; up in Edinburgh he went both to Calton Hill and the Mound.[6] At Otley he preached at the foot of the Chevin.[7] At Helston he occupied "a rising ground about a musket shot from the town," and at Gaulksholme "the congregation stood and sat, row above row, in the sylvan theatre" on a mountain-side.[8] There was a similar scene at Heptonstall, not far away, where the place where Wesley preached was, he said, "an oval spot of ground, surrounded with spreading trees, scooped out, as it were, in the side of the hill, which rose like a theatre."[9] It was known as Dickey Brown Hey.

In Cornwall the downs were frequently used, and in Yorkshire the moors. In Gateshead Wesley preached on "a smooth part of the fell," and a large stone is preserved at one of the nearby Methodist Chapels on which

---

[1] *Journal*, Vol. III, p. 318. 2nd September, 1747; Vol. IV, p. 284. 1st September, 1758; Vol. VI, pp. 284–285. 13th June, 1781; Vol. IV, p. 30. 19th June, 1752; Vol. VII, p. 511. 14th June, 1789.

[2] *Ibid.*, Vol. V, p. 257. 1st May, 1768; Vol. VI, p. 151. 30th June, 1777.

[3] *Ibid.*, Vol. VI, p. 126. 5th September, 1776; Vol. IV, p. 283. 27th August, 1755.

[4] *Ibid.*, Vol. III, p. 87. 28th August, 1743.   [5] *Ibid.*, p. 72. 22nd March, 1743.

[6] *Ibid.*, Vol. VIII, p. 3. 18th August, 1789; Vol. V, p. 71. 27th May, 1764; p. 225. 2nd August, 1767.

[7] *Ibid.*, Vol. IV, p. 331. 17th July, 1759. It is hardly "a high mountain."

[8] *Ibid.*, p. 132. 3rd September, 1755; p. 332. 21st July, 1759.

[9] *Ibid.*, Vol. III, p. 372. 26th August, 1748. Cf. Vol. IV, p. 211. 18th May, 1757.

he is supposed to have stood.[1] At Matlock Bath, he took his stand under
the hollow of a rock, and at Crich he preached from an outcrop on the
Tors ridge above the town.[2] On the edge of Dartmoor he preached from
the White Rock on the Mount near Sticklepath, and through the years the
granite boulder has been treated with an annual coat of whitewash to
mark the site.[3] At St. Ives on one windy day he found a little enclosure on
rising ground, with native rock ten or twelve feet high. "A jutting out of
the rock, about four feet from the ground, gave me a very convenient
pulpit," he reported.[4]

On other occasions, a hollow formed his auditorium. There was one
called Holloway Bank at Wednesbury, near the bridge over the Teme. It
could hold four or five thousand people, according to Wesley's estimate.
They stood in a semicircle one above another.[5] There was another near
Limerick, near the old camp. The ground sloped upwards so that the
congregation sat on the grass, row above row.[6] A third at Morvah, in
Cornwall, was just like a theatre.[7] The hollow at Birstall was evidently the
largest of all, for Wesley imagined that it might contain sixty thousand,
and that a strong, clear voice could command them all.[8] But, of course,
the most famous was at Gwennap, although this was only partly natural,
the grass having grown over disused mine workings. Wesley considered
it to be "far the finest I know in the kingdom. It is a round, green hollow,
gently shelving down, about fifty feet deep; but I suppose it is two hundred across one way, and near three hundred the other."[9] On that visit he
calculated the congregation to be "full twenty thousand people," but
some years later he took it to be over thirty thousand.[10] It fell into dis-
repair after Wesley's death, but was restored in 1806. Each Whit Monday
a well-attended service is held there. Its present measurements are somewhat smaller than those Wesley gave.

Wesley's first open-air preaching in London was at Whitefield's sites at
Moorfields, Blackheath and Kennington Common.[11] These were far from
reputable places in the eighteenth century. Moorfields had once been very
fashionable, with gravel walks lined with elms. It was known as the "city
mall." But by Wesley's time it had become a general recreation ground,
where all sorts of social undesirables resorted.[12] Kennington Common was

[1] Ibid., Vol. III, p. 68. 8th March, 1743. Cf. Vol. IV, p. 115. 18th May, 1755.
[2] Ibid., Vol. IV, p. 473. 27th July, 1761. Cf. Gill, In the Steps of John Wesley, p. 172.
[3] Journal, Vol. III, p. 126. 1st April, 1744. Cf. Gill, In the Steps of John Wesley, p. 85.
[4] Journal, Vol. IV, p. 407. 10th September, 1760.
[5] Ibid., Vol. III, p. 63. 9th January, 1743.
[6] Ibid., Vol. IV, p. 277. 2nd July, 1758.
[7] Ibid., pp. 235–236. 11th September, 1757.
[8] Ibid., p. 114. 4th May, 1755.
[9] Ibid., Vol. V, p. 187. 14th September, 1756.   [10] Ibid.
[11] Ibid., Vol. II, p. 223. 17th June, 1739; p. 220. 14th June, 1739; p. 223. 17th June,
1739.   [12] Walter Besant, London in the Eighteenth Century (1892), p. 124.

E

even worse. It was a neglected waste and the place of execution most in use after Tyburn. It was not unusual to see men hanging there in chains.[1] Not surprisingly it was, as Tyerman described it, "the rendezvous of London riff-raffs."[2] Blackheath, on the other hand, was in a much more respectable neighbourhood. It is typical of Wesley that he concentrated on the disreputable spots.

In the villages he was to be found most often on the green. He also used the parks and common land in the towns or cities which bore this name. Bedminster Green, Bristol; Southernhay Green, Exeter (now covered with Georgian houses); Carr Green, Stockport; St. Peter's Green, Bedford; and Oxmantown Green, Dublin are all mentioned.[3] At Colchester he preached on St. John's Green "at the side of a high old wall (a place that seemed to be made on purpose)."[4] In his rural tours Wesley frequently held his service in a field, or a meadow as he normally described it. One at Clyro in Wales was "large" and "smooth."[5] At Durham it was pleasantly situated "near the riverside."[6] At Week St. Mary the grass was newly mown.[7] At Cullompton the people stood in a half moon.[8] At St. Ives they sat on the hedges—which in that district would be broad stone walls.[9] It was in Richard Merchant's field at Bath that Wesley was interrupted by Beau Nash, and got the better of him in a battle of words.[10] At Tiverton many stood in the gardens and orchards flanking the meadow.[11]

Derryanvil, near Portadown in Ulster, was depicted as "a small village surrounded by a bog, but inhabited by lively Christians."[12] There Wesley "preached in a shady orchard to an exceeding large congregation" on a June morning.[13] At Stanley, close to Winchcombe, there was not enough room in Farmer Finch's house, so the meeting was held in his orchard.[14] On one of his many visits to Bristol, Wesley preached in the Old Orchard, which was part of what had been a Dominican Friary. The estate fell into

[1] Ibid.
[2] Tyerman, Life of George Whitefield, Vol. I, p. 207.
[3] Journal, Vol. IV, p. 137. 5th October, 1755, cf. n. 7; p. 526. 29th August, 1762; p. 311. 29th May, 1759; p. 87. 16th October, 1753; Vol. III, p. 347. 24th April, 1748.
[4] Ibid., Vol. IV, p. 289. 27th October, 1758
[5] Ibid., Vol. III, p. 317. 30th September, 1747.
[6] Ibid., Vol. IV, p. 222. 4th July, 1757.
[7] Ibid., p. 240. 2nd October, 1757.
[8] Ibid., p. 99. 7th September, 1754.
[9] Ibid., Vol. V, p. 381. 21st August, 1770.
[10] Letters, Vol. I, p. 320. To James Hutton, 7th June, 1739. After Wesley had turned the tables on Nash, an old woman in the crowd addressed him: "Sir, if you ask what we come here for, we come for the food of our souls. You care for your body: we care for our souls." At that, Nash walked away with never a word.
[11] Journal, Vol. III, p. 493. 2nd September, 1750.
[12] Ibid., Vol. VII, p. 92. 15th June, 1785.
[13] Ibid.
[14] Ibid., Vol. III, p. 359. 27th July, 1748.

the Penn family, through William's marriage, and the site was popularly known as Quakers' Friars.[1] In Ireland Wesley once stood on a pedestal from which a statue of Patrick had fallen. It was in the middle of the Grove at Downpatrick, which formed a perfect setting, with the summer sun glimmering through the trees.[2]

Wesley preached in many gardens, both private and public. Amongst those referred to by name are James Mears' at Oxford and John Stovin's at Crowle.[3] The latter belonged to a Justice of the Peace and that fact helped to restrain "so wild a congregation."[4] Some of the gardens were attached to the Methodist meeting houses, which were springing up throughout the land.[5] In London, Wesley held services in the Great Gardens off Whitechapel Road.[6]

In the heat of summer Wesley would seek the shade of a convenient tree, and scores of these are remembered up and down the land. Perhaps the most famous is that which survived until 1842 in the ground of Kingswood School. It was a sycamore, and on the 26th June, 1739, Wesley sheltered under it from a violent storm as he spoke. Work on the original school for colliers' children had been started only a few days previously.[7] It was beneath this same sycamore that John Cennick stood not long before, waiting for a preacher to arrive from Bristol. When he failed to appear, Cennick was prevailed on to take his place, and thus began his evangelistic ministry.[8] John Wesley's garden and walk are still shown to visitors, with a row of elms which he is reputed to have planted.

At Derriaghy Wesley preached "under a venerable old yew, supposed to have flourished in the reign of King James, if not of Queen Elizabeth," so he noted.[9] At Chrome Hill (formerly Lambeg House, a residence of the Gayer family with whom Wesley stayed) there are two beech trees growing into each other. Local legend has it that they were intertwined as saplings by Wesley, as a symbol of hope that Methodism and the Church of Ireland would be united.[10] The vestry of the parish church at Bishop Burton, in the East Riding of Yorkshire, houses a most unusual bust of Wesley. It is carved from the trunk of a huge elm, under which he once preached on the village green. Wesley's last open air sermon was delivered at the age of eighty-seven at Winchelsea. He has left an account of the

[1] *Ibid.*, p. 303. 23rd June, 1747, cf. n. 2.
[2] *Ibid.*, Vol. VI, pp. 198–199. 13th June, 1778.
[3] *Ibid.*, Vol. V, p. 345. 17th October, 1769; Vol. III, p. 361. 8th July, 1748.
[4] *Ibid.*, Vol. III, p. 361.
[5] *Ibid.*, Vol. IV, p. 99. 8th September, 1749 (Tiverton); p. 309. 18th April, 1759 (Selby).
[6] *Ibid.*, Vol. III, p. 45. 12th September, 1742.
[7] *Ibid.*, Vol. II, pp. 228–229. 26th June, 1739.
[8] John Cennick's *Journal*, in *London Quarterly Review*, July, 1955, p. 209.
[9] *Journal*, Vol. VI, p. 109. 16th June, 1778.
[10] Gill, *In the Steps of John Wesley*, p. 217.

occasion. "I stood under a large tree . . . and called to most of the inhabitants of the town, 'The kingdom of heaven is at hand; repent, and believe the gospel.' It seemed as if all that heard were, for the present, almost persuaded to be Christians."[1] The tree has been replaced, but an inscription recalls the facts, and identifies it as an ash. The old chapel at Winchelsea proudly displays a collection box made from the wood.

Wesley often preached in a yard: sometimes attached to a house, sometimes to a shop, sometimes to an inn. Sometimes it was the more genteel enclosure of a gentleman's residence. Sometimes it was a churchyard, as at Epworth and a number of other places. He stood on a tombstone at Leominster and Osmotherley and Staveley, as well as on the resting-place of his father's remains.[2] At Zennor it was "under the churchyard wall."[3] At Haworth a scaffold had to be erected on the south side of the church.[4] Services in the churchyard were sometimes held as the only option when the church itself was overfull. This happened, for example, at Codshaw, in Lancashire, when Wesley led the congregation outside after the prayers, as he could see that many could not get in. He mounted the churchyard wall and pressed home the word of life from there.[5]

We cannot complete the list. Wesley preached in such unexpected places as a bowling green, a prehistoric mound, a shooting range, and a brickyard (his first open-air gathering on Hanham Mount, Kingswood).[6] He preached on the beach when visiting Alderney; on the cliffs at Whitby, Penzance and St. Ives; and down at the quay in Bridlington, Robin Hood's Bay, Bristol and Plymouth.[7]

That brings us, more summarily, to Wesley's indoor preaching places. The weather would at times drive him to seek cover. As the years passed, he was well respected in the towns he included in his regular itinerary, and was able to hire accommodation. Occasionally he was even offered it. His chief resorts were the market houses, or the town halls. The latter were not always very attractive. At Bodmin he encountered the most dreary he ever saw.[8] There was hardly any light to relieve the encircling gloom. Others were historic, like the Old Hall at Gainsborough, dating from the

[1] *Journal*, Vol. VIII, p. 102. 7th October, 1790.

[2] *Ibid.*, Vol. III, p. 251. 13th August, 1746; p. 290. 20th April, 1747; Vol. VI, p. 282. 4th June, 1780; Vol. III, p. 319. 6th June, 1742.

[3] *Ibid.*, Vol. III, p. 307. 12th July, 1747.

[4] *Ibid.*, Vol. V, p. 180. 3rd August, 1766.

[5] *Ibid.*, Vol. III, p. 373. 28th August, 1748.

[6] *Ibid.*, Vol. IV, p. 455. 14th May, 1761 (Berwick-upon-Tweed); Vol. VI, p. 193. 23rd May, 1778 (Clones); Vol. IV, p. 100. 2nd October, 1754 (Old Sarum); Vol. II, pp. 172–173. 2nd April, 1739.

[7] *Ibid.*, Vol. VII, p. 312. 14th August, 1787; Vol. IV, p. 465. 23rd June, 1761; p. 411. 17th September, 1760; Vol. VI, p. 170. 23rd August, 1777; Vol. V, p. 372. 20th June, 1770; Vol. IV, p. 65. 8th May, 1753; Vol. V, p. 29. 4th September, 1763; Vol. VI, p. 125. 1st September, 1776.

[8] *Ibid.*, Vol. VI, p. 37. 31st August, 1774. Cf. *Proc. W.H.S.*, Vol. IV, p. 193.

fifteenth century, with its impressive battlemented frontage, its beautiful oriel window and two fine Tudor towers.[1]

Wesley also used a courthouse, or session-house—mainly in Ireland, where he had the fullest co-operation from the civic authorities. Galway he rated the neatest by far.[2] At Waterford a file of musketeers, ordered by the mayor, guarded the door.[3] The local assembly room also figures prominently amongst Wesley's preaching centres. These were usually in the hands of the gentry and reserved for social functions. It was a concession indeed that they should be given over to evangelistic purposes. But, as Wesley asked himself at Wexford, "Were ever assembly rooms put to better use?"[4] At Kilkenny meetings were held in the Custom House, or tholsel, and at the tolbooth, or tolsey, at Gloucester.[5] At Newcastle-upon-Tyne he also used the old Custom House, "a large commodious room near the quayside, the grand resort of publicans and sinners."[6] In Ireland he preached in more than one exchange.[7] Other public buildings included a library, at Inverness and Yarmouth; a school, at Exeter, Coventry, Southampton and Highgate; and a university, in the Hall of Marischal College, Aberdeen.[8]

Wesley preached in a workshop at Newbury, a forge at Alpraham, a malt-room (which he found very draughty) at Ashton, in the cornmarket at Leominster and Newport, Isle of Wight, and the buttermarket at Canterbury.[9] He went not only where work was done but where leisure was enjoyed. He was not above taking a playhouse if it suited him. Some had fallen on lean days and were not in use. The New Wells in London (not to be confused with Sadler's Wells) was closed in 1750, and Wesley had it in May 1752.[10] At Sheerness the old playhouse was "filled from end to end."[11] At Kendal what was the theatre is now a furniture store. It was used not only by Wesley, but by Whitefield and some of Lady Hunting-

[1] *Journal*, Vol. IV, p. 343. 3rd August, 1759. Cf. *Proc. W.H.S.*, Vol. VI, pp. 67–68.
[2] *Journal*, Vol. V, p. 413. 27th May, 1771.
[3] *Ibid.*, Vol. VII, p. 270. 1st May, 1787.
[4] *Ibid.*, 30th April, 1787.
[5] *Ibid.*, Vol. IV, pp. 512–513. 10th July, 1762. Cf. *Proc. W.H.S.*, Vol. VII, p. 121; Vol. VII, p. 250. 20th March, 1787, cf. n. 1.
[6] *Journal*, Vol. V, p. 264. 21st May, 1768.
[7] *Ibid.*, Vol. III, p. 474. 28th May, 1750 (Kinsale); Vol. V, p. 133. 28th June, 1765 (Youghal).
[8] *Ibid.*, Vol. V, p. 364. 27th April, 1770; Vol. VI, p. 132. 18th November, 1776, cf. n. 1; p. 252. 31st August, 1779; p. 362. 15th July, 1782; Vol. VII, p. 309. 9th August, 1787; p. 455. 15th December, 1788; Vol. IV, p. 450. 4th May, 1761.
[9] *Ibid.*, Vol. V, p. 355. 5th March, 1770; Vol. II, p. 520. 4th April, 1751, cf. n. 1; Vol. V, p. 346. 24th October, 1769; Vol. III, pp. 251–252. 14th August, 1746; Vol. IV, p. 287. 6th October, 1758; *Wesleyan Methodist Magazine*, Vol. LX (1837), p. 421.
[10] *Gentleman's Magazine*, Vol. XXII (1752), p. 238. Cf. *Journal*, Vol. IV, pp. 93–94. 29th April, 1754: "I am glad when it pleases God to take possession of what Satan esteemed his own ground."
[11] *Journal*, Vol. V, p. 349. 5th December, 1769.

don's preachers too. They evidently spoke from the window overlooking the marketplace, rather than to an audience inside.[1] At Newbury Wesley wished to hire the playhouse, but, as he explained caustically, "the good mayor would not suffer it to be so profaned."[2] In Cavan he actually gave his message in a ballroom.[3]

When we come to consider Wesley's congregations we shall be seeing how he visited prisons, workhouses, hospitals and asylums. But much of his indoor preaching was done in private houses. Many rooms are still indicated as having been the scene of one of Wesley's services. Sometimes it was a cottage, like Digory Isbell's at Trewint.[4] Sometimes it was a fashionable residence, like Lady Huntingdon's London home.[5] Sometimes it was a rectory, like Charles Caulfield's at Killyman.[6] Sometimes Wesley simply used the house as a pulpit for an open-air meeting, speaking from the doorway, a window, or a balcony.[7] Sometimes it was only a loft, like the one at Merryweather's home in Yarm.[8] Anyone with whom the evangelist stayed was liable to find his house turned into a chapel.

When Wesley spent the night at an inn, he would invariably use the yard or the door as a pulpit. It would be an intriguing exercise to trace all these hostelries. Many of them are still in business, though not always under the same sign. The most nauseating experience in this connexion was when Wesley preached in an upper chamber of a fifteenth-century building, which formed part of the George Inn at Bedford. "We had a pretty large congregation, but the stench from the swine under the room was scarce supportable. Was ever a preaching place over a hog stye before? Surely they love the gospel who come to hear it in such a place?"[9] John Walsh had been there the previous year, and found that "many had left off hearing."[10] No wonder! More than once Wesley preached in a

[1] Ibid., Vol. IV, p. 60. 9th April, 1753. Cf. Gill, In the Steps of John Wesley, p. 181.

[2] Journal, Vol. V, p. 355. 5th March, 1770.

[3] Ibid, Vol. VII, p. 84. 28th May, 1785.

[4] Ibid., Vol. III, pp. 126–127. 2nd April, 1744, cf. n. 1; p. 194. 15th July, 1745; Vol. IV, p. 530. Cf. Methodist Magazine, Vol. XXXII (1809), p. 165. Digory and Elizabeth Isbell were the first-fruits of John Nelson's ministry in Cornwall. The cottage was rescued from demolition in 1947 by Mr. Stanley Sowton, and restored by Sir George Oatley.

[5] Journal, Vol. VIII, pp. 157–159. 7th, 9th, 11th August, 1748; Vol. IV, p. 300. 27th March, 1769.

[6] Ibid., Vol. VII, p. 511. 14th June, 1789.

[7] Ibid., Vol. IV, p. 28. 19th May, 1752 (Whickham); Vol. V, p. 25. 19th August, 1763 (Brecknock); p. 369. 11th June, 1770 (Stockton-on-Tees); Vol. VI, p. 36. 18th August, 1774 (Llanelly); Vol. III, p. 340. 1st April, 1748 (Athlone); Vol. IV, p. 475. 8th August, 1761, cf. n. 1 (Winterton); p. 466. 25th June, 1761 (Scarborough); Vol. VI, p. 124. 21st August, 1776 (Penzance).

[8] Ibid., Vol. IV, p. 329. 6th July, 1759, cf. n. 1.

[9] Ibid., pp. 358–359. 23rd November, 1759.

[10] Arminian Magazine, Vol. III (1780), p. 104.

stable: one at Stafford was "a deplorable hole."[1] He also made use of an army riding school, not only in Ireland, but in Worcester and Northampton.[2] He often found himself in a farmhouse, or an adjoining barn. At Godmanchester he preached in a barn where John Berridge and Henry Venn had often been before.[3] Near Chertsey, he held a service in a large summer-house, even though it was February. It was supported by a wooden frame which split. The congregation left without any panic and stood in the garden.[4]

Throughout his evangelistic ministry, and more especially as the years passed, Wesley preached in churches whenever they were open to him. He preferred to go to the parish church if possible, but he was increasingly prepared to take advantage of dissenting chapels when they were offered. A long list could be produced to show that his initial reluctance to preach in nonconformist places of worship was overcome. We find him in Presbyterian, Independent, Baptist and Quaker meeting-houses.[5] Denominational boundaries were gladly crossed when the opportunity afforded itself. He even preached in the Seceder chapel in Armagh, and the Calvinist chapel at Carmarthen (where Peter Williams was pastor).[6] And as the new Methodist buildings were erected, of course he employed them too, though not all were large enough for the purposes of evangelism. On a number of occasions, he preached in the shell of a chapel which was in the process of erection.

[1] *Journal*, Vol. VI, p. 488. 29th March, 1784; cf. Vol. III, p. 329. 25th January, 1748, when Wesley is said to have preached in the stables of the Green Dragon inn at Fisherton, near Salisbury.
[2] *Ibid.*, Vol. IV, p. 377. 17th April, 1760 (Dublin); Vol. VI, p. 184. 16th August, 1778 (Tullamore); Vol. VII, p. 488. 19th April, 1789 (Athlone); Vol. V, p. 305. 14th March, 1769 (Worcester); p. 236. 28th November, 1767 (Northampton).
[3] *Ibid.*, Vol. VI, p. 52. 25th November, 1774.
[4] *Ibid.*, Vol. III, p. 353. 5th February, 1750.
[5] Presbyterian: *ibid.*, Vol. IV, pp. 325-326. 29th June, 1759 (Swalwell); Vol. V, p. 236. 27th November, 1767 (Weedon); Vol. VI, p. 193. 23rd May, 1778 (Cootehill); Vol. VII, p. 33. 24th November, 1784 (Banbury); p. 36. 6th December, 1784 (Tunbridge Wells); p. 93. 16th June, 1785 (Newry); p. 123. 1st November, 1785 (Northampton); p. 230. 24th December, 1786 (London, Old Jewry); p. 287. 8th, 9th June, 1787 (Ballymena and Antrim); p. 311. 13th August, 1787 (Yarmouth); p. 391. 23rd May, 1788 (Berwick-on-Tweed); p. 508. 8th June, 1789 (Belfast). This latter—the first Presbyterian meeting house in Rosemary Street—Wesley described as "the completest place of public worship" he had ever seen (*ibid*).
Independent: Vol. V, p. 433. 17th October, 1771 (Chesham); p. 523. 15th August, 1773 (Plymouth); Vol. VI, pp. 271-272. 7th April, 1780 (Delph); p. 294. 12th September, 1780 (Trowbridge); Vol. VII, p. 449. 26th November, 1788 (Sandwich, Isle of Wight); Vol. VIII, pp. 7-8. 1st September, 1789 (Tiverton); p. 25. 25th November, 1789 (Towcester); p. 75. 24th June, 1790 (Bridlington).
Baptist: Vol. VI, pp. 285-286. 17th June, 1780 (Boston).
Quaker: Vol. III, p. 234. 24th February, 1746 (Skircoat Green, near Halifax); Vol. IV, p. 187. 10th September, 1756 (London).
[6] *Ibid.*, Vol. VII, pp. 292-291. 17th June, 1767; Vol. V, p. 332. 11th August, 1769.

But with all this, it still remains the fact that by far the majority of Wesley's mission sermons were preached elsewhere than in a building designed for worship. His real pulpit was where the people were. His evangelism was not of the passive sort (if that is worthy of the name), which waits for unbelievers to come to church. His was essentially an outgoing ministry to take the gospel, as the Saviour did, to the man and woman in the street.

CHAPTER XII

THE PEOPLE GATHERED

"I STOOD in the street and cried, 'Now God commandeth all men everywhere to repent.' *The people gathered* from all sides and, when I prayed, kneeled down upon the stones, rich and poor, all around me." *Journal* 5: 203.

WESLEY BECAME AN ITINERANT EVANGELIST, PREACHING IN THE open, because only in this way could he reach those who were out of touch with God. His congregations were made up largely of those who were beyond the range of the usual ministrations of the Church. This in itself was an indictment of the Church's failure to fulfil its proper function, for, considered in terms of the New Testament, it exists primarily for the purpose of bringing Christ to the people and the people to Christ. That this should be regarded as at all abnormal in the eighteenth century was an indication of how far the contemporary Church had fallen from its original standards. Unless the Church is an outgoing society, is it untrue to its own nature.

The study of Wesley's congregations, their composition, character and behaviour, is at once engrossing and revealing. It helps us to appreciate a further aspect of John Wesley's evangelism. It is in this person-to-person confrontation that we see the sparking-point of effective soul-winning. The crowds surrounding Wesley's improvised pulpits represented a fair cross-section of eighteenth-century society in Britain. Almost every class of the community was to be found amongst them at some time. But the bulk of the congregation consisted of the poor. Wesley was supremely the apostle of what the Marxists called the proletariat. It was the common people who heard him gladly.

In his *Memoirs*, James Hutton has left a vivid account of these audiences. They "were composed of every description of persons, who, without the slightest attempt at order, assembled, crying 'Hurrah!' with one breath, and with the next bellowing and bursting into tears on account of their sins; some poking each other's ribs, and others shouting 'Hallelujah.' It was a jumble of extremes of good and evil. . . . Here thieves, prostitutes, fools, people of every class, several men of distinction, a few of the learned, merchants, and numbers of poor people, who had never entered a place of worship, assembled in crowds and became godly."[1] The final comment is determinative for our judgement on this curious hotchpotch.

[1] Benham, *op. cit.*, p. 42.

This was why Wesley felt it all to be worth while. He too, no doubt, was as hesitant at first as any of his critics about the mixed multitude which flocked to hear him, and the emotional outbursts almost inevitably associated with such large-scale gatherings; but the fact that many "became godly" was enough for him. The pragmatic test was his vindication.

We have no means of calculating with any precision how big these congregations really were. Modern methods of computation with a convenient instrument were unknown. No turnstiles registered the incoming "gate." We have to rely on Wesley's own estimates, checked occasionally by others who were present. Like preachers in later generations than his own, Wesley was apt to exaggerate the numbers attending his services. It is strange that one who in so many matters was noted for dispassionate exactitude should fall a prey to inaccuracy here. But in his enthusiasm for the work God had given him to do, it seems that he rather overdid the statistics of attendance.[1] It is therefore wise to treat Wesley's figures with some caution.

In March 1748, Wesley inquired into the state of the society in Dublin. He found that the progress reports he had received from time to time were far too optimistic. He expected to meet six or seven hundred members. Actually since he was last there the numbers had increased from three hundred and ninety-four to three hundred and ninety-six. "Let this be a warning to us all how we give in to that hateful custom of painting things beyond the life," he added. "Let us make a conscience of magnifying or exaggerating anything. Let us rather speak under than above the truth. We, of all men, should be punctual in all we say, that none of our words may fall to the ground."[2] Wesley himself certainly observed this principle in his own accounts of the societies, and of the converts from his campaigns. Only in the matter of attendances did he tend to err. We can conclude that this was not through a desire to give a false impression, which would be his last thought, but because of the real difficulty involved in attempting to assess numbers running into thousands. He may sometimes have been misled by others.

On the 21st September, 1773, Wesley claimed to have preached to over thirty-two thousand at Gwennap pit—the largest crowd he had ever seen there.[3] As the amphitheatre is now, anything near such a number is out of the question. But then we know that the present auditorium dates from 1806 and just what it was like before it was altered we cannot tell. There are those who are prepared to defend Wesley's estimate.[4] Elsewhere in the *Journal*, we learn that Wesley's method was to judge the dimensions of the packed preaching-ground, and then to arrive at a total from the assump-

[1] *Journal*, Vol. II, p. 285, n. 1; Vol. V, p. 45, n. 4.
[2] *Ibid.*, Vol. III, p. 338. 16th March, 1748.
[3] *Ibid.*, Vol. V, p. 524. 21st September, 1773.
[4] *Proc. W.H.S.*, Vol. IV, p. 86.

tion that five could stand in a square yard.[1] That would hardly satisfy a surveyor, and the margin of error was considerable.

Yet even allowing for involuntary exaggeration, the congregations must have been colossal in comparison with what any church could hold. Perhaps even more astonishing is the fact that they kept coming, year after year, in the same places, and invariably increasing rather than otherwise. "John Smith" dismissed these huge attendances at Wesley's meetings by ascribing them to "the very novelty and irregularity" of his methods, akin to those of "a dispenser of physic who dances on a slack rope."[2] But Wesley was no quack. Mere novelty soon loses its appeal. Nothing but the gospel could have drawn such ever-growing multitudes over the space of half a century. Returning to Moorfields in 1775, Wesley found an even larger congregation than usual. "Strange that their curiosity should not be satisfied yet," was his comment, "after hearing the same thing near forty years."[3]

Often there were counter-attractions which might well have reduced the attendance at the preaching. It would be a market-day or a fair.[4] The races would be on, as at Chester.[5] It might be Assize Week, as in Clonmel.[6] Or a general election might threaten to interfere, as in 1768 at Cockermouth.[7] Sometimes strolling players were in town.[8] At Devizes there was a pantomime.[9] But most of these events brought extra people to the town, and tended to swell Wesley's congregation rather than diminish it. He was never slow to seize an evangelistic opportunity. At Berwick-upon-Tweed there was a funeral of a young man, who was the heir to a large fortune,

[1] *Journal*, Vol. V, p. 181. 10th August, 1766. "I judged the congregation closely wedged together, to extend forty yards one way, and about a hundred the other. Now, suppose five to stand in a yard square, they would amount to twenty thousand people."

[2] Moore, *op. cit.*, Vol. II, pp. 537–538. Letter "John Smith" to John Wesley, 11th August, 1746.

[3] *Journal*, Vol. VI, p. 79. 8th October, 1775.

[4] *Ibid.*, Vol. III, p. 428. 8th September, 1749 (Morpeth); Vol. VII, p. 364. 19th March, 1788 (Tewkesbury); Vol. IV, p. 22. 25th April, 1752 (Pocklington); Vol. V, p. 142. 5th September, 1765 (Camelford); Vol. VII, pp. 155–156. 17th April, 1786 (Blackburn).

[5] *Ibid.*, Vol. IV, pp. 311–312. 2nd May, 1759.

[6] *Ibid.*, p. 401. 18th August, 1760. Cf. p. 152. 20th March, 1756. At Carrickfergus the Quarter Sessions coincided with Wesley's visit (Vol. V, p. 308. 6th April, 1769). On 27th May, 1760 at Castlebar, a notable trial was being held. Many of the gentry came to attend. "It was to be heard in the court house where I preached; so they met an hour sooner and heard the sermon first. Who knows but even some of these may not be found of Him they sought not?" (Vol. IV, p. 390).

[7] *Ibid.*, Vol. V, p. 255. 14th April, 1768. Cf. Vol. VI, p. 185. 21st April, 1778 (Kilkenny).

[8] *Ibid.*, Vol. III, p. 400. 15th May, 1749 (Limerick); Vol. VII, p. 392. 26th May, 1788 (Morpeth).

[9] *Ibid.*, Vol. III, p. 275. It was advertised as "obnubilative," *i.e.* containing veiled references and examples of *double entendre*.

cut down in his prime. Almost the whole population was in the church-yard. Wesley stood by the grave when the committal was over and preached about Christ, who is the resurrection and the life. He remarked afterwards that he "had full as many attendants as the corpse, among whom were abundance of fine gay things, and many soldiers."[1]

Some of the distractions were deliberate. At Priestdown, near Bristol, two men, hired for the purpose, began singing a ballad, but were silenced when Wesley stopped his sermon and invited the congregation to drown them with a psalm.[2] At Athlone "a man with a fine curvetting horse drew off a large part of the audience."[3] This was in the middle of the message. Wesley paused for a second and then, raising his voice, threw out this challenge: "If there are any more of you who think it is of more concern to see a dancing horse than to hear the gospel of Christ, pray go after them." "They took the reproof," Wesley was able to report in his *Journal*; "the greater part came back directly and gave double attention."[4] At Bristol the sermon was interrupted by the arrival of the press-gang, who seized one of the hearers.[5]

Accidents will happen, and more than once a meeting was disturbed by some unforeseen occurrence, which might have proved disastrous in view of the numbers, but which providentially never did. At Stonesey Gate, in the Pennines, the six a.m. congregation filled both the yard and the road for a considerable distance. Many were seated on a long wall, constructed of loose stones. In the midst of the sermon, it collapsed. But no one was hurt. No one screamed and hardly any even altered their posture. They simply sank slowly together and "appeared sitting at the bottom just as they sat at the top."[6]

At Turner's Hall, in Deptford, a dissenters' meeting house, the capacity of two thousand was stretched to the limit when Wesley preached there on the 27th October, 1739.[7] Soon after he had started to expound the Word, the main beam supporting the floor gave way. There was a vault below and the floor began to subside. But a day or two before a man had filled the basement with hogsheads of tobacco, so after sinking a foot or more, it rested on them in perfect safety, and Wesley proceeded without interruption. At Stanhope in 1788 (7th June), it was thought that the preaching-house would contain the congregation at five a.m. It was a large upper room. Before Wesley started to speak, the main beam broke and the floor began to collapse. There was a cry: "The room is falling!" But the only one to panic was a man who jumped out of the window. The

[1] *Ibid.*, p. 522. 23rd April, 1751.
[2] *Ibid.*, Vol. II, p. 213. 7th June, 1739.
[3] *Ibid.*, Vol. III, p. 468. 6th May, 1750.
[4] *Ibid.*
[5] *Ibid.*, Vol. II, p. 245. 22nd July, 1739.
[6] *Ibid.*, Vol. III, p. 294. 5th May, 1747.
[7] *Ibid.*, Vol. II, pp. 282–283. 27th October, 1739.

sole casualty was a dog on which he dropped with all his weight. The rest left quietly, and Wesley preached in the open air to a congregation enlarged by those who had come to see what was happening.[1]

So much, then, for rival attractions and rude interruptions. We shall look at the more serious of the latter when we come to deal with mob violence. Meanwhile we turn to the composition of the congregations who listened to Wesley. As we have already stressed, they consisted mainly of the poor. This was the evangelist's principal constituency. He did what is always the most difficult thing in communicating the gospel: he reached the common man. He had the ear of the working classes. In the eighteenth century poverty was abject. The lower strata of society lived at a bare existence level. And their numbers were very considerable indeed. They formed a high proportion of the populace. A German pastor, Friedrich August Wendeborn, could report as late as 1791, that "in no other country are more poor to be seen than in England."[2]

"It is difficulty today to imagine how low the standard of life of the average worker was," writes Dr. Marshall, "how brutish, ignorant and violent the poor, especially the urban poor, were. . . . Conditions made it difficult for the mass of the people to live by any strict moral code. Overcrowding made every kind of sexual laxity almost normal. Extreme poverty made thieving and bullying the only alternatives to starvation. . . . It was a hard, harsh world for the mass of the English people, and one singularly devoid of pity."[3] But God had pity, and sent a man named John to preach the gospel to the poor. It is fashionable nowadays to dismiss Wesley's contribution with a cynical sneer. All he did, it is suggested, was to offer a soporific of heavenly prospects to persuade men to endure their unjust lot. Wesley is almost regarded as a kind of spiritual drug-pedlar. This is, in the first place, to overlook the very considerable practical social work that Wesley and his helpers did. It was he who set up dispensaries for the sick and helped the poor to guard their meagre savings in a mutual benefit society.[4] It was he who started the school for colliers' children at Kingswood and the orphan house at Newcastle. It was he who promoted co-operative industry amongst the underprivileged and encouraged the Strangers' Friend Society to provide relief.[5] Wesley did what lay in his power at the physical and material level. But modern

---

[1] *Ibid.*, Vol. VII, p. 396. 7th June, 1788.

[2] F. A. Wendeborn, *A View of England* (1791), Vol. I, p. 384.

[3] Marshall, *The Eighteenth Century*, p. 243.

[4] *Journal*, Vol. III, p. 273. 4th December, 1746; p. 301. 6th June, 1747; p. 329. 17th January, 1748. Cf. Bready, *op. cit.*, pp. 270–271.

[5] *Journal*, Vol. II, p. 403. 25th November, 1740; p. 323. 21st January, 1740; Vol. VIII, p. 49. 14th March, 1790. The Strangers' Friend Society was started in London in 1785 by John Gardner, a retired soldier. A similar organization was set up in Bristol the next year, cf. Bready, *op. cit.*, pp. 271–272.

critics tend to undervalue the effect of Wesley's message on the personality. The spiritual factor is minimized today. Yet what Wesley did by the grace of God for the souls of the poor is not lightly to be set aside. He helped to keep hope alive in a miserable age.

Wesley made no secret of the fact that he felt that his main mission was to the poor. "I bear the rich and love the poor," he declared; "therefore I spend almost all of my time with them."[1] "I love the poor," he repeated; "in many of them I find pure, genuine grace, unmixed with paint, folly, and affectation"—and he was not using "grace" there in its theological sense, but rather to indicate a natural dignity and charm.[2] But there were none to care for their welfare. They were the neglected sector of English society. The Church was either unwilling or unequipped to reach them. They were as sheep without a shepherd. Wesley pressed them to his heart. There, more than anywhere, lies the key to his evangelistic success. He loved the people. So, as Dr. Marshall puts it, he became "the pastor of the mob."[3] That is why he has been called the St. Francis of the eighteenth century.

His first concern was for the coal miners at Kingswood. This was his introduction to the plight of the poor. Those grimy faces haunted him. He longed to tell them of One whose hands were hardened with toil before they were pinned to a Cross. Conditions in the pits were unbelievably crude and dangerous. Coal was still hewn manually and the Davy lamp had not yet been invented to bring a measure of safety. The men themselves were coarse in the extreme, and even the rest of the poor were afraid of them because they were so black and rough. When Wesley was led to offer Christ to the colliers, he was touching the most unlikely group in the kingdom. But they listened—and many of them turned to the Lord. If the gospel could move them, it could move anyone. This initial encounter in April 1739 convinced Wesley that the good news was meant for the outcasts of men. The mining areas of Britain were Wesley's best-loved preaching places. Gateshead he called "the very Kingswood of the north."[4] Plessey was his "favourite congregation," although at first he was not accustomed to being clapped on the back by way of appreciation.[5] One of the finely reproduced engravings in *Johnson's England* shows the mouth of a coal pit near Broseley, which Wesley must have known well, for he had been there and told a story about one of the miners.[6]

Other workers mentioned by Wesley include lead miners at Nenthead and St. Ives, iron smelters at Burton Forge, brass workers at Bristol, copper workers at St. Helen's and Hayle, glassmen at Ballast Hills,

[1] *Letters*, Vol. IV, p. 266. To Ann Foard, 29th September, 1764.
[2] *Ibid.*, Vol. III, p. 299. To Dorothy Furly, 25th September, 1757.
[3] Marshall, *John Wesley*, p. 31.
[4] *Journal*, Vol. III, p. 68. 8th March, 1743.
[5] *Ibid.*, p. 81. 17th July, 1743; cf. p. 71. 17th March, 1743.
[6] *Ibid.*, Vol. VI, p. 33. 31st July, 1774. Cf. *Johnson's England*, Vol. I, facing p. 240.

quarrymen at Shipham, and shipyard workers on Wearside and Tyne-side.[1] Nor did he overlook farm labourers, and female spinners and weavers.[2] He referred to fishermen and bargemen too.[3]

Wesley visited the workhouses and prisons, as he had done at Oxford. Conditions in both were indescribable, but this did not deter him. He was one of the first to expose the need for reform. On the 3rd February, 1753, he went to Marshalsea prison, which he described as "a nursery of all manner of wickedness." His further comment was significant: "O shame to man, that there should be such a place, such a picture of hell, upon earth! And shame to those who bear the name of Christ, that there should need any prison at all in Christendom!"[4] His ministry to the doomed at Tyburn, along with helpers like Silas Told and Sarah Peters is a story in itself. "I preached the condemned criminal's sermon in New-gate," he wrote on the 26th December, 1784, from London. "Forty-seven were under sentence of death. While they were coming in there was something very awful in the clink of their chains. But no sound was heard, either from them or the crowded audience, after the text was named: 'There is joy in heaven over one sinner that repenteth, more than over ninety and nine just persons that need not repentance.' The power of the Lord was eminently present, and most of the prisoners were in tears. A few days after twenty of them died, at once, five of whom died in peace."[5]

The *Journal* often mentions the presence of soldiers in Wesley's congregations, and quite often he would go to the barracks to preach specially to them. He had a practical concern for their welfare, and once actually wrote to the Mayor of Newcastle-upon-Tyne about them.[6] Most of all he longed to lead them to Christ. He found it hard to get across to them at times, as he confessed after addressing them on the Town Moor at New-castle. "None attempted to make the least disturbance, from the beginning to the end. Yet I could not reach their hearts. The words of a scholar did not affect them like a dragoon or a grenadier."[7] In Salisbury in 1759, the Hampshire militiamen in the congregation listened to the message,

[1] *Journal*, Vol. VI, p. 276. 5th May, 1780; Vol. III, p. 89. 3rd September, 1743; Vol. IV, p. 109. 7th April, 1755; p. 477. 13th October, 1761; Vol. VI, p. 348. 13th April, 1782; Vol. VII, p. 110. 27th August, 1785; Vol VI, p. 29. 26th July, 1774; pp. 371–372. 6th September, 1782; p. 29. 26th July, 1774.
[2] *Ibid.*, Vol. VII, p. 112. 31st September, 1785 (Cathanger); Vol. VI, p. 352. 14th May, 1782 (Epworth); p. 358. 17th June, 1782 (Rothbury), cf. Gill, *In the Steps of John Wesley*, p. 153.
[3] *Journal*, Vol. IV, p. 330. 8th July, 1759 (Robin Hood's Bay); Vol. III, p. 321. 2nd November, 1747 (Reading).
[4] *Ibid.*, Vol. IV, p. 52. 3rd February, 1753.
[5] *Ibid.*, Vol. VII, p. 41. 26th December, 1784.
[6] *Letters*, Vol. II, pp. 52–53. To the Mayor of Newcastle-upon-Tyne, 26th October, 1745. More troops than usual were quartered there because of the Jacobite Rebellion.
[7] *Journal*, Vol. III, p. 218. 31st October, 1745.

but Wesley had to admit that "it was as music to a horse."[1] Yet it was not always like that, and Wesley had many converts amongst the soldiery. As Vulliamy points out, he was always popular with them, for they "admired his pluck and his neat, manly bearing."[2]

Wesley had a particularly soft spot for children and delighted to see them present at his meetings.[3] Again and again he made mention of them. Occasionally they were noisy and tended to disturb the preaching, but in most cases he commented on their excellent behaviour and attentiveness to the Word. He was obviously not one of those who supported the theory that boys and girls ought not to hear the truth of God at too early an age. He even held children's meetings at five in the morning.[4] He realized that an unusual gift was needed for this work.[5]

Although Wesley's mission was directed chiefly to the labouring classes, it must not be thought that he was altogether indifferent to the rest, or that they were absent from his meetings. But they formed only a small part of the whole, and he was more concerned to touch the majority. Quite often, however, the gentry would appear on the fringe of the crowd, though they preferred to remain in the comfort of their carriages. At Moorfields on the 14th June, 1739, he "was greatly moved with compassion for the rich that were there, to whom I made a particular application. Some of them seemed to attend, while others drove away their coaches from so uncouth a preacher."[6] On the whole, he does not seem to have been impressed by their attitude. At Bandon in 1775, "all behaved well, except three or four pretty gentlemen, who seemed to know just nothing of the matter."[7] He was not afraid to rebuke aristocratic irreverence if need be. At Kirton in Lincolnshire he had a large and serious congregation. "Only before me stood one, something like a gentleman, with his hat on even at prayer. I could scarce help telling him a story. In Jamaica, a Negro passing by the Governor, pulled off his hat; so did the Governor; at which one expressing surprise, he said, 'Sir, I should be ashamed if a Negro had more good manners than the Governor of Jamaica.' "[8]

Wesley was not always flattering in his comments about the ladies in his congregation. Some of the younger ones were evidently attractive but empty-headed. He was apt to refer to them as "pretty butterflies."[9] At

[1] *Ibid.*, Vol. IV, p. 355. 25th October, 1759.

[2] C. E. Vulliamy, *John Wesley* (1931), p. 191.

[3] Knox (*op. cit.*, p. 443) was sceptical about this, but there are many references in the *Journal*

[4] *Journal*, Vol. VII, p. 97. 17th July, 1785.

[5] *Ibid.*, Vol. V, p. 285. 31st September, 1768: "a work which will exercise the talents of the most able preachers in England."

[6] *Ibid.*, Vol. II, pp. 220–221. 14th June, 1739.

[7] *Ibid.*, Vol. VI, p. 61. 3rd May, 1775.

[8] *Ibid.*, p. 283. 11th June, 1780.   [9] *Ibid.*, Vol. IV, p. 529. 14th September, 1762.

Liverpool on the 6th April, 1768, there was a vast listening multitude, "but some pretty, gay, fluttering things did not behave with such good manners as the mob at Wigan."[1] At Manorhamilton in the following year, all in the session house behaved well "except one young gentlewoman, who laughed almost incessantly. She knew there was nothing to laugh at, but she thought she laughed prettily."[2]

Space forbids us to do more than note that others in Wesley's audiences included farmers, lawyers, clergymen and nonconformist ministers, university undergraduates and civic leaders. We must not overlook those from foreign lands—especially the Germans in Newcastle-upon-Tyne, Bedford and in the Palatine colony at Ballingrane in Ireland, from whom came Barbara Heck and Philip Embury to take Methodism to North America.[3]

Wesley was usually quick to sum up a congregation. He could soon tell whether it was likely to be responsive. Some of his terse comments were more than a little caustic. At Tanfield Lea he expounded the first part of Romans 5 to "so dead, senseless, unaffected a congregation" as he had scarce ever seen. "Whether gospel or law, or English or Greek, seemed all one to them!"[4] Yet a few days later one of the hearers, John Brown, was "waked out of sleep by the voice that raiseth the dead" and witnessed to his faith for over sixty-five years.[5] At Athlone most of the hearers were "as bullocks unaccustomed to the yoke, neither taught of God nor man."[6] At Andover he preached "to a few dead stones," and in the chapel at Rotherhithe a handful of people "appeared to be just as much affected as the benches they sat upon."[7] On the quay at Plymouth he marvelled at "the exquisite stupidity of the hearers, particularly the soldiers, who seemed to understand no more of the the matter than so many oxen."[8] He did not hesitate to tell them so, and some were ashamed. The nadir was reached at Kilkenny in the spring of 1775, where he was compelled to concede: "Of all the dull congregations I have seen, this was the dullest."[9]

Wesley does not seem to have been put off by such apathy. Indeed, it stirred him to intensified forcefulness in his presentation of the message. It is rare to find him refusing to speak in such circumstances, as he did at

[1] *Ibid.*, Vol. V, p. 254. 6th April, 1768.
[2] *Ibid.*, p. 316. 5th May, 1769.
[3] *Ibid.*, Vol. III, p. 219. 3rd November, 1745; Vol. IV, p. 349. 27th August, 1759; pp. 168–169. 16th June, 1756; p. 397. 9th July, 1760; cf. Vol. IV, pp. 275–276. 23rd June, 1758 (Courtmatrix).
[4] *Ibid.*, Vol. III, p. 53. 28th December, 1742.
[5] *Ibid.* Brown joined Christopher Hopper in some of his evangelistic campaigns.
[6] *Ibid.*, Vol. IV, p. 391. 8th June, 1760.
[7] *Ibid.*, p. 418. 7th November, 1760; Vol. VI, p. 264. 7th December, 1779.
[8] *Ibid.*, Vol. VI, p. 125. 1st September, 1776.
[9] *Ibid.*, p. 60. 24th April, 1776.

Ulverston on the 5th June, 1752.[1] By far the majority of his observations referred to the keen attentiveness of the congregation. Preaching was Wesley's constant cordial, and in most cases the people caught his infectious spirit and were in rapport with him throughout. They knew he loved them in Christ, and they loved him too. Those are conditions in which the Spirit does His own distinctive work. That was Wesley's greatest desire. He was content to be the channel through whom the grace of God was mediated to the needy masses of the land.

[1] *Ibid.*, Vol. IV, p. 31. 5th June, 1752: "Few people had any desire to hear, so I went quietly back to my inn."

CHAPTER XIII

DECLARING THE GRACE OF GOD

"THE sun was very hot, and shone full on my head; but the wind was very high and very cold, so that the one tempered the other while I was *declaring the grace of God* to a well-meaning multitude, who knew little as yet, but are willing to know 'the truth as it is in Jesus.' " *Journal* 4: 326.

IN HIS PERCEPTIVE LITTLE CAMEO OF JOHN WESLEY'S CHARACTER William Wakinshaw noted many facets of his genius. Scholar, wit, writer, philanthropist, organizer and leader—Wesley was all these. But "it is supremely as a preacher that he will be had in everlasting remembrance."[1] That is a just judgement. Wesley was first and foremost an evangelist, and as such he was aware that his commission was to preach the gospel. He held the view that the primary means of evangelism is proclamation. There may be room for ancillary methods in connexion with this, but for Wesley there was no substitute for the preaching of the Word. It is by this apparent foolishness, as the world regards it, that God designs to save.

More than once Wesley himself confessed that this was his ruling passion. "About noon I preached at Woodseats," he wrote on the 28th August, 1757; "in the evening at Sheffield. I do indeed live by preaching!"[2] And there was no doubt in his mind about the aim of his message. In his *Earnest Appeal*, he recalled an encounter he once had with a confessed atheist. He said to Wesley: "I hear you preach to a great number of people every night and morning. Pray, what would you do with them? Whither would you lead them? What religion do you preach? What is it good for?" Here is Wesley's reply: "I do preach to as many as desire to hear, every night and morning. You ask what I would do with them: I would make them virtuous and happy, easy in themselves and useful to others. Whither would I lead them? To heaven; to God the Judge, the lover of all, and to Jesus the Mediator of the new covenant. What religion do I preach? The religion of love; the law of kindness brought to light by the gospel. What is this good for? To make all who receive it enjoy God and themselves: to make them like God; lovers of all; contented in their lives; and crying out at their death, in calm assurance, 'O grave, where is

---

[1] William Wakinshaw, *John Wesley* (1928), p. 31.
[2] *Journal*, Vol. IV, p. 231. 28th August, 1757.

thy victory! Thanks be unto God, who giveth me the victory, through my Lord Jesus Christ.' "[1]

Wesley constantly reminded his preachers that they had "nothing to do but to save souls."[2] What he impressed on others he first exemplified himself. He was not only a preacher, but essentially a gospel preacher. In a letter to his brother Charles, dated 26th April, 1772, he put the matter quite bluntly. "Your business as well as mine is to save souls. When we took priests' orders, we undertook to make it our *one business*. I think every day lost which is not (mainly at least) employed in this thing. *Sum totus in illo* (I am completely committed to this)."[3]

In view of all this, we may be surprised to learn that in Wesley's day there were those who nevertheless considered that he failed to preach the gospel. On Sunday the 8th August, 1742, he was "constrained to separate from the believers some who did not show their faith by their works."[4] This was at the Foundery. Amongst them was Samuel Prig, who was most displeased and made some harsh comments before leaving in disgust. Next morning he called on John Wesley and told him that neither he nor Charles preached the gospel or knew what it meant. Wesley asked, "What do we preach then?" The astonishing answer was: "Heathen morality: Tully's *Offices* and no more. So I wash my hands of you both. We shall see what you will come to in a little time."[5] The critic was clearly no prophet, and he seems to have been a religious crank with antinomian inclinations. His strictures can be safely discounted.

Wesley came under fire, no doubt, because he did not conform to what he himself disparagingly referred to as "a luscious way of talking."[6] This was what passed for a gospel message in some circles, and Wesley repudiated it. The derogatory expression may have been borrowed from John Worthington, one of the Cambridge Platonists of the previous century. He once wrote: "It pleases men to be entertained with a luscious preaching of the gospel made up all of promises, and these wholly unconditional; it gratifies them to hear what is done without them, rather than what is done with them, and the sincere and entire obedience to our Saviour's precepts."[7] Wesley was very much of the same mind as Worthington on this matter, as some of his correspondence makes obvious.

On the 4th November, 1772, for instance, he wrote from Colchester to

[1] *Works*, Vol. VIII, p. 8. *An Earnest Appeal to Men of Reason and Religion* (1744).
[2] *Ibid.*, p. 310. *Large Minutes* (1789).
[3] *Letters*, Vol. V, p. 316. To Charles Wesley, 26th April, 1772. Cf. Horace, *Satires*, Book I, ix. 2—*Totus in illis*. "One business"—an allusion to "The Form and Manner of Ordering of Priests", in the *Book of Common Prayer*.
[4] *Journal*, Vol. III, p. 39. 8th August, 1742.
[5] *Ibid.* "Tully's *Offices*"—i.e. Marcus Tullius Cicero, *De Officiis*, drawn mainly from Stoic sources.
[6] *Letters*, Vol. V, p. 84. To John Fletcher, 20th March, 1768.
[7] *A New History of Methodism*, Vol. I, p. 213.

his brother Charles, apropos some discussion with James Rouquet, the evangelical curate at St. Werburgh, Bristol, where Richard Symes was the incumbent. "If we duly join faith and works in all our preaching, we shall not fail of a blessing. But of all preaching, what is usually called gospel preaching is the most useless, if not the most mischievous; a dull, yea or lively, harangue on the sufferings of Christ or salvation by faith without strongly inculcating holiness. I see more and more that this naturally tends to drive holiness out of the world."[1]

In a similar strain Wesley had this to say on the 18th October, 1778 (probably addressed to Mary Bishop): "I find more profit in sermons on either good temper or good works than in what are vulgarly called gospel sermons. That term is now become a mere *cant* word. I wish none of our Society would use it. It has no determinative meaning. Let but a pert, self-sufficient animal, that has neither sense nor grace, bawl out something about Christ and His blood or justification by faith, and his hearers cry out, 'What a fine gospel sermon!' Surely the Methodists have not so learned Christ. We know no gospel without salvation from sin."[2] That Wesley regularly instructed his hearers on this subject was indicated by an entry in his *Journal* for the 14th November, 1776, which is representative of others. He was at Norwich, where there had been a good deal of trouble in previous years because one of the preachers, James Wheatley, had brought the cause into disrepute by his immoral conduct. He had continued to preach the gospel, as he regarded it, though living in sin. This sort of disgrace was still in mind when Wesley visited the society some years later. "I showed in the evening what the gospel is, and what it is to preach the gospel. The next evening I explained, at large, the wrong and the right sense of, 'Ye are saved by faith.' And many saw how miserably they had been abused by those vulgarly-called gospel preachers."[3]

About the same period, Wesley set down his *Thoughts Concerning Gospel Ministers*. He had noted the fact that the term was often bandied about with an almost complete lack of understanding. Some rejoiced that they had a gospel minister in their church, whilst others deplored the absence of one from theirs. But all too often such talkative advocates of a gospel ministry had little or no idea of what it really was. "What then is the meaning of the expression?" Wesley inquired. "Who is a gospel minister? Let us consider this important question calmly, in the fear and in the presence of God."[4] He began by dismissing the negatives, after his logical fashion: not every one who preaches the eternal decrees, who speaks much

[1] *Letters*, Vol. V, p. 345. To Charles Wesley, 4th November, 1775.

[2] *Ibid.*, Vol. VI, pp. 326–327. To Mary Bishop, 18th October, 1778. Some think the recipient may have been Mary Bosanquet.

[3] *Journal*, Vol. VI, p. 131. 14th November, 1776. It was Wheatley who had disturbed Ebenezer Blackwell, or whoever received the letter of 20th December, 1751 (*Letters*, Vol. V, p. 85).

[4] *Works*, Vol. X, p. 455. *Thoughts Concerning Gospel Ministers* (n.d.).

about the sovereignty of God, of free distinguishing grace, of dear elect-
ing love, of the infallible perseverance of the saints, can make the claim.
"A man may speak of all these by the hour together; yea, with all his
heart, and with all his voice; and yet have no right at all to the title of a
gospel minister."[1] Not every one who speaks much about the blood and
righteousness of Christ, or who deals with the promises of the Word, or
who bends all his strength to coax sinners to Christ with tender appeals,
is necessarily to be considered a gospel minister. Not even one who insists
on justification by faith—which is the very crux of the saving message—
is worthy of the title, unless he goes further than that.

Wesley showed that all these things are in themselves partial and in-
complete, if we are to declare the whole counsel of God as it is revealed in
His Word. There must be a clear association of God's sovereignty with
man's responsibility; of Christ's sufferings on the Cross with man's involvement in what was purchased there for him; of the precious promises
with the terrors of God's wrath; of the invitation to receive Christ with a
deep conviction of sin; and of justification by faith with its scriptural
corollary in newness of sanctified living. Only when all these are held
together and proclaimed together, is the whole gospel set forth. Otherwise, said Wesley, evangelism will be no more than a futile endeavour "to
heal those that never were wounded."[2] This little-known tractate of
Wesley's supplied a pungent corrective in his day and will in ours, if
taken to heart.

A further letter of Wesley on the 20th December, 1751, clarified the
issue.[3] The recipient may have been Ebenezer Blackwell, as Telford surmised, but more recent scholars are inclined to think otherwise.[4] Wesley
spoke from his own experience as an evangelist and described the kind of
preaching he had found to be most effective in leading to conviction of
sin and genuine repentance. Wheatley was evidently in mind, and the
man to whom Wesley wrote had been captivated by this insubstantial
gospel preaching. In fact, he confessed that after listening to Wheatley and
his colleagues, he lost his taste for the more solid messages of Wesley and
Nelson. This did not surprise Wesley. "Why, this is the very thing I
assert," he replied: "that the 'gospel preachers' so called corrupt their
hearers; they vitiate their taste, so that they cannot relish sound doctrine;
and spoil their appetite, so that they cannot turn it into nourishment; they,
as it were, feed them with sweetmeats, till the genuine wine of the kingdom seems quite insipid to them. They give them cordial upon cordial,
which make them all life and spirit for the present; but meantime their
appetite is destroyed, so that they can neither retain nor digest the pure
milk of the Word. Hence it is that (according to the constant observation

[1] *Ibid.*   [2] *Ibid.*, p. 456.
[3] *Letters*, Vol. III, pp. 78–85. To Ebenezer Blackwell(?), 20th December, 1751.
[4] *Ibid.*, p. 79, Notes.

I have made in all parts both of England and Ireland) preachers of this kind (though quite the contrary appears at first), spread death, not life, among their hearers. As soon as the flow of spirits goes off, they are without life, without power, without any strength or vigour of soul; and it is extremely difficult to recover them, because they still cry out, 'Cordials, cordials!' of which they have had too much already, and have no taste for the food which is convenient for them. Nay, they have an utter aversion to it, and that confirmed by principle, having been taught to call it husks, if not poison."[1] This is so relevant still, that we find it hard to believe that it was written two hundred years ago and more.

As we now go on to look at Wesley as a gospel preacher, we must realize that he was so in the scriptural sense, and not according to the all-too-common image. Wesley was far from being what so many imagine an evangelist is like. He was equally far from being what unfortunately some who have assumed the name of evangelist are like. He was a gospel preacher in the line of Peter and Paul, of Augustine and Chrysostom, of Bernard and Francis, of Luther and Calvin, of Baxter and Bunyan, of Wishart and Welsh.

If we are to reconstitute the picture of Wesley the evangelist in action, we must say a word about his pulpits. We have already listed the many places where he preached. Often his pulpit was a purely natural one. But whenever practicable he preferred that something should be prepared for him. It was necessary for him to be raised above the level of the congregation, especially in view of his tiny stature. If he was not on a hillside or a rock, or speaking from a window, a balcony, a gallery, or on the steps of a building or a market cross, he required elevation.

This was most frequently supplied by a chair, on which he would stand. At Nenagh in Ireland one spring day in 1749 he was urged to preach by one of the dragoons stationed in the town. "I ordered a chair to be carried out and went to the market-place," he reported.[2] In Edinburgh in 1786 on Castle Hill, "the chair was placed just opposite the sun."[3] After the mob had attacked the house where Wesley was staying at Bolton in 1749, John Bennett and David Taylor succeeded in pacifying them. Then Wesley himself walked down into the thick of the crowd. "I called for a chair. The winds were hushed, and all was calm and still. My heart was filled with love, my eyes with tears, and my mouth with arguments. They were amazed, they were ashamed, they were melted down, they devoured every word. What a turn was this!"[4]

[1] *Ibid.*, p. 84. In the same letter Wesley described Wheatley's preaching as "an unconnected rhapsody of unmeaning words," and likened it to Sir John Suckling's

Verses, smooth and soft as cream

In which was neither depth nor stream (p. 83).

[2] *Journal*, Vol. III, p. 399. 12th May, 1749.

[3] *Ibid.*, Vol. VII, p. 165. 28th May, 1786.

[4] *Ibid.*, Vol. III, p. 442. 18th October, 1749.

Some of these chairs still survive. There is one in the pulpit at Wesley Chapel, Bloxwich, from which the evangelist is reputed to have preached at Oldbury in 1773. It is strongly built, with club feet at the front. There is another at Mellor, used when Wesley was at Bongs (i.e. the Banks), on the slopes of Cobden Edge in Cheshire. The square-backed wooden chair from which he preached "in Mr. M'Geogh's avenue" at Armagh is preserved in the Argory there.[1] At Thorne, Wesley borrowed a kitchen chair from Martha Meggitt to use when preaching in the market-place.[2] It was she who also ironed his cuffs and ruffles whenever he came there. It is thought that a chair now to be found in the Chapel at Muston, not far from Filey, built by one of the Meggitt family, is the same as Wesley stood on.[3] The chair from Wesley's last open-air service at Winchelsea on the 7th October, 1790, was carefully kept as a relic.[4] One of the Wesley chairs has actually been taken as far as New Zealand. It was utilized on the Green at Stockport in 1765, and is now to be seen in the Methodist church, Pukekohe.[5]

On other occasions Wesley stood on a table. The first time he went to Wolverhampton—"this furious town," as he described it, because of the wild mobs—he "ordered a table to be set in the inn yard."[6] From this improvised pulpit, commandeered from the Angel hotel, he faced the seething multitude and preached the grace of God. At Guisborough he went into the market-place and "there a table was placed" for him.[7] At Bunklody in Ireland—"a little, ugly scattered town, but delightfully situated"—he had a somewhat discouraging experience in July 1769. "I did not find five persons in the town would come a bowshot to hear. So I ordered a table to be set in the street; and a few slowly crept together. They were as quiet, and seemed as much affected, as the trees."[8] It was altogether different at Cockhill in 1778. "I preached here at the bottom of the garden: the table was placed under a tree, and most of the people sat on the grass before it; and everything seemed to concur with the exhortation, 'Acquaint thyself now with Him, and be at peace.' "[9] Sometimes the mob threatened to overturn the table, as happened on Southernhay Green in Exeter.[10] Wesley felt it prudent to withdraw. At Osmotherley in Yorkshire, he spoke from the ancient five-pillared barter-table in the market-place.[11]

[1] Ibid., Vol. V, p. 204. 15th April, 1767.   [2] Ibid., p. 377. 17th July, 1770.
[3] Gill, In the Steps of John Wesley, p. 128.
[4] Journal, Vol. VIII, p. 102, n. 4; Proc. W.H.S., Vol. III, p. 114.
[5] Journal, Vol. V, p. 141. 25th September, 1765; Proc. W.H.S., Vol. XXV, p. 80.
[6] Journal, Vol. IV, p. 442. 17th March, 1761.
[7] Ibid., p. 465. 22nd June, 1761.
[8] Ibid., Vol. V, p. 328. 13th July, 1769.
[9] Ibid., Vol. VI, p. 200. 19th June, 1778.
[10] Ibid., Vol. IV, p. 527. 29th September, 1762.
[11] Gill, In the Steps of John Wesley, p. 139.

A desk is mentioned in a few instances in the *Journal*, and in others a platform.[1] At Seaton, a mining village near Whitehaven in Cumberland, Wesley described how "the poor people had prepared a kind of pulpit for me, covered at the top and on both sides and had placed a cushion to kneel upon of the greenest turf in the country."[2] On one of his Irish tours, he preached near the ancient fort at Kinsale. The soldiers soon cut a place with their swords for Wesley to stand on the grassy slopes of a hollow, screened from both wind and sun.[3] In Glasgow he had the use of a small tent—"a kind of moving pulpit, covered with canvas at the top, behind, and on the sides."[4] At Terryhoogan the people erected a similar wind-break, and the same was done at North Shields.[5]

How did Wesley attract his congregation? As time went on, he was so well known that it was enough that word was passed round that he was due to preach. But in the pioneering days it was sometimes hard to gain a hearing and even to draw a reasonable company. Wesley had none of the advantages of twentieth-century publicity techniques—and none of their disadvantages either. "For the gathering of these crowds Wesley employed none of the familiar modern devices," explained Dr. W. H. Fitchett. "There were no advertisements, no local committees, no friendly newspapers, no attractions of great choirs. It is a puzzle still to know how the crowds were induced to assemble, for Wesley gives no hints of any organization employed. His hearers seemed to wait for him, to spring up before him as if at the signal of some mysterious whisper coming out of space."[6] It must be remembered that this was evangelism in the context of revival, and the Spirit Himself was moving everywhere.

There were, however, problem situations now and then. Wesley does not seem to have been deterred by them. At six a.m. on the 10th June, 1757, he and his comrade William Coward went to the market-house at Kelso. "We stayed some time, and neither man, woman, nor child came near us. At length I began singing a Scotch psalm, and fifteen or twenty people came within hearing, but with great circumspection, keeping their distance as though they knew not what might follow. But while I prayed their number increased, so that in a few minutes there was a pretty large congregation."[7] At Wooler next day Wesley wrote: "I stood on one side of the main street, near the middle of the town. And I might stand, for no creature came near me till I had sung part of a psalm. Then a row of children stood before me and in some time about a hundred men and

[1] *Journal*, Vol. III, p. 4. 20th April, 1742 (Brentford); p. 93. 16th September, 1743 (St. Ives); Vol. IV, pp. 332–333. 22nd July, 1759 (Haworth).
[2] *Ibid.*, Vol. IV, p. 30. 2nd June, 1752.
[3] *Ibid.*, p. 42. 25th September, 1752.
[4] *Ibid.*, p. 62. 19th April, 1753. Cf. p. 216, 1st June, 1753.
[5] *Ibid.*, Vol. V, p. 308. 5th April, 1769; Vol. VII, p. 168. 7th June, 1786.
[6] Fitchett, *op. cit.*, p. 202.
[7] *Journal*, Vol. IV, p. 219. 10th June, 1757.

women."[1] These were rare occasions, and it is noticeable that they took place in the border country, where reticence was a trait.

If we ask when Wesley preached, the only comprehensive answer would be "in season, out of season" (II Timothy 4: 2). Introducing the third volume of the *Journal*, which starts in 1742—the year of expanding mission for Wesley—Curnock announced, by way of preview, that "he preaches, often every day of the week, morning, noon, and night, wherever a crowd can gather or his voice can be heard."[2] We cannot but be struck by the contrast between Wesley's incessant ministry and the vegetable existence of a Parson Woodforde, who found one sermon each Sunday more than enough. Wesley habitually preached at five a.m. and at least once if not twice more during the day. Only by such early meetings could he catch the workers before they went off to the mine or the forge, the mill or the farm. The morning preaching he cherished as "the glory of the Methodists," and he was convinced that should it be abandoned, Ichabod would soon be inscribed over his societies.[3] At Stroud in 1784 he was distressed to discover that there was no early meeting. "If this be the case while I am alive, what must it be when I am gone?" he asked sadly. "Give up this, and Methodism too will degenerate into a mere sect, only distinguished by some opinions and modes of worship."[4]

Can we recapture something of Wesley's manner in preaching? We cannot doubt that, as T. E. Brigden put it, "his personal endowments contributed to his power—his magnetic presence, his expressive features, his vivid eye, his clear voice."[5] The latter was a prominent feature. In 1749 Wesley published a penny tract entitled *Directions Concerning Pronunciation and Gesture*, the first part of which is on, "How we may speak so as to be heard without difficulty, and with pleasure." It is full of good advice, which Wesley observed himself. The first business of a speaker, he insisted, was that he might be heard and understood with ease. A clear, strong voice was an asset, but even those not naturally endowed could cultivate distinctness by paying attention to the basic rules of elocution. Wesley warned against the chief faults of speaking either too loud or too low; too fast or too slow; "in a thick cluttering manner" or, worst of all, "speaking with a tone"—squeaking, singing, theatrical or whining as the case might be.[6]

Wesley's own voice was as clear as a bell, and endowed with unusual carrying powers. After preaching once on Brown Hill, Birstall, he asked someone to measure the ground, for he had noticed that some of his

[1] *Ibid.*, p. 219. 11th June, 1757.
[2] *Ibid.*, Vol. III, p. ix. Prefatory Note.
[3] *Letters*, Vol. VII, p. 84. To John Bredin, 22nd September, 1781.
[4] *Journal*, Vol. VI, p. 485. 15th March, 1784.
[5] *A New History of Methodism*, Vol. I, p. 209.
[6] *Works*, Vol. XIII, pp. 479–480. *Directions Concerning Pronunciation and Gesture* 1749).

hearers were sitting on the side of the opposite ridge. It was no less than
eighty-four yards. Yet no one had missed a word he said.[1] At St. Ives one
windy September day, he was afraid that the roaring of the sea might
drown his voice. But he was enabled to make everyone hear.[2] At Leominster he was preaching from a tombstone in the churchyard. "The
multitude roared on every side, but my voice soon prevailed, and more
and more of the people were melted down, till they began ringing the
bells; but neither thus did they gain their point, for my voice prevailed
still. Then the organs began to play amain."[3] Eventually Wesley withdrew to the cornmarket, but not before demonstrating that he could compete vocally with most distractions. At Freshford, near Frome, he
conquered the church bells again, and an old man who was extremely
deaf, told his neighbours with delight that he had heard every word.[4] At
Chapel-en-le-Frith, the miller near whose pond the congregation were
standing, tried to drown Wesley's voice by letting out the water with a
tremendous gurgle, but even that failed to prevent the people hearing.[5]
Yet all this was achieved without undue strain or shouting. Wesley repeatedly warned his preachers against the perils of "screaming."[6]

In the little tract already referred to, Wesley went on to deal with gesture, which he strikingly described as "the silent language of face and
hands."[7] He gave detailed instructions which made it clear that he had
little use for windmill preachers, who attempted to recompense their lack
of unction with gesticulation. As Doughty assumed, "the tract is a bit of
self-portraiture," and from it we can learn how Wesley himself managed
his gestures.[8] He once went to hear one of the Huguenot preachers. He
clearly disapproved of his Gallic animation. "I have sometimes thought
Mr. Whitefield's action was violent; but he is a mere post to Mr. Cail-
lard."[9]

There are several "preaching portraits" of Wesley by eminent artists,
one of the most notable being by the academician John Russell. In his
monumental survey of Church history, M. Daniel-Rops gives us a verbal
picture of Wesley which is true to life. "Wesley was a man of small
stature, thin and pale, with steely eyes and an expression that was often

[1] *Journal*, Vol. IV, p. 17. 5th April, 1752.
[2] *Ibid.*, p. 407. 13th September, 1760.
[3] *Ibid.*, Vol. III, p. 251. 14th August,1746.
[4] *Ibid.*, Vol. V, p. 232. 25th September, 1767.
[5] *Ibid.*, Vol. III, p. 176. 28th April, 1745.
[6] *Letters*, Vol. VI, p. 167. To John King, 28th July, 1775: "Scream no more at the
peril of your soul. . . . I often speak loud, often vehemently; but I never scream, I
never strain myself." Vol. VIII, p. 190. To Sarah Mallet, 15th December, 1789:
"Never scream. Never speak above the natural pitch of your voice: it is disgustful to
the hearers."
[7] *Works*, Vol. VIII, p. 484. *Directions Concerning Pronunciation and Gesture* (1749).
[8] Doughty, *op. cit.*, p. 150.
[9] *Journal*, Vol. III, p. 479. 24th June, 1750.

supercilious; but he exuded a mysterious and pervasive charm. Disdaining the periwig he let his black hair grow long and fall in curls upon his shoulders. When speaking he would often raise his slender hands to heaven. Was that because, while preaching to the crowds, he was examining himself with fear and trembling? Be that as it may, all who heard him bore witness to the fact that he was disturbing, moving and persuasive."[1] He normally wore his gown and cassock, with Geneva bands. If he had appeared without them, even in the open air, it might have been thought that the rumour was correct that he had been hounded out of the Established Church. In his hand he would hold his Field Bible—so called because it was printed by John Field in the seventeenth century.[2] It is this which is presented to each incoming Methodist President as he assumes his office.

Wesley's style was marked by simplicity and sincerity. His sermons were meant for the people, and they were couched in language which the people could grasp. To contrast the printed discourses of the learned eighteenth-century divines with the lucid messages of Wesley is in itself a lesson in the art of communication. His main concern was not to overshoot the congregation, as he graphically put it.[3] With it all, he was obviously a man in earnest. "I felt what I spoke," he declared with reference to a sermon at Alnwick: that was usual with him.[4] Like Bunyan, he could have testified: "I preached what I felt; what I smartingly did feel."[5] John Newton once said he did not deal in unfelt truths.[6] Wesley was of the same school. As Dean Hutton remarked, his sermons "came straight from his heart as well as from his sound, strong head."[7] In this combination of heat and light lay the secret of Wesley's power as a gospel preacher. It was in the tension of the two that the Spirit worked so mightily.

[1] Daniel-Rops, op. cit., p. 173.
[2] Journal, Vol. VI, p. 372. 8th September, 1782, n. 1. Cf. Proc. W.H.S., Vol. XXIV, pp. 13–15; Vol. XXV, pp. 46–47.
[3] Journal, Vol. VII, p. 490. 24th April, 1789.
[4] Ibid., Vol. III, p. 428. 8th September, 1748.
[5] John Bunyan, Grace Abounding to the Chief of Sinners, ed. Hannaford Bennett (1924), p. 132.
[6] The Works of John Newton, ed. Richard Cecil (1808), Vol. I, p. 655.
[7] Hutton, op. cit., p. 75.

CHAPTER XIV

INVITING ALL SINNERS

"WHILE I was earnestly *inviting all sinners* 'to enter into the holiest' by the 'new and living way,' many of those that heard began to call upon God with strong cries and tears." *Journal* 2: 221.

IN A PENETRATING CHAPTER OF HIS PAYTON LECTURES ON *The Preacher's Portrait*, John R. W. Stott insists, after a close examination of the New Testament evidence, that in distinctively Christian preaching proclamation and appeal are inseparable.[1] Whilst there should be no appeal without proclamation, there should equally be no proclamation without appeal. The invitation is the necessary outcome of the declaration. "It is not enough to teach the gospel; we must urge men to embrace it."[2]

Wesley might not have expressed it in precisely the same terms, but he subscribed to the principle. His was true biblical preaching, if this is to be taken as one of the criteria. As an evangelist, he knew that his main task was to persuade men. However faithfully the message might be delivered, he realized that it was not enough to leave it there. The appeal had to be pressed home in a personal manner, so that every hearer was left feeling that the protective covering of neutrality and indifference had been stripped off, and that a decisive moment had arrived. In other words, Wesley's preaching possessed an existential quality, although such philosophical jargon had not yet been minted in his day.

The comprehensiveness of Wesley's aims was reflected in a compendious statement in the *Large Minutes*. In answer to the question, "What is the best general method of preaching?" this reply is given. "(1) To invite. (2) To convince. (3) To offer Christ. (4) To build up; and to do this in some measure in every sermon."[3] What has been called "the preaching of conquest" was admirably exemplified in Wesley.[4] He was out for a verdict. He was not content to present the gospel in any detached or exclusively objective fashion. He sought to exercise an influence on the conscience and the will. In all this he recognized the primacy of the Spirit's operation, but he did not allow any inhibitions of subjectivity to prevent him from pressing home the appeal to the full.

[1] John R. W. Stott, *The Preacher's Portrait* (1961), pp. 48–51.
[2] *Ibid.*, p. 50.
[3] *Works*, Vol. VIII, p. 317. *Large Minutes* (1789).
[4] W. M. Macgregor, *The Making of a Preacher* (1945), p. 77.

On Sunday the 13th June, 1779, Wesley attended worship in a Presbyterian church in Aberdeen. Here is his comment. "This very day I heard many excellent truths delivered in the kirk; but, as there was no application, it was likely to do as much good as the singing of a lark. I wonder the pious ministers of Scotland are not sensible of this. They cannot but see that no sinners are convinced of sin, none converted to God, by this way of preaching. How strange is it, then, that neither reason nor experience teaches them to take a better way!"[1] Wesley himself preached twice that same day, "and made a pointed application to the hearts of all that were present."[2] Again and again in the *Journal* he recorded a similar conclusion to his message. "I applied the words as closely as possible;" "I applied it to the conscience of each person;" "I had a fair opportunity of closely applying that weighty question, 'Lord, are there few that be saved?' "—these are sample entries.[3] Yet throughout he knew that this was not his work, but the Lord's. "May God make the application!" he would add.[4] Or, "again the Spirit applied the Word."[5]

Wesley had no doubt about the value of such an appeal. "There is always a blessing when we cut off all delay, and come to God now by simple faith," he declared.[6] It was at this point that the Spirit probed deepest, bringing conviction and leading to repentance and faith. Those who had resisted the Word or tried to ignore it were often broken down by the application. At Dublin in 1756 a German woman stumbled into the service whilst Wesley was expounding, "Is Christ the minister of sin?" This was evidently in the preaching-house. "For a time she seemed greatly diverted; but the application spoiled her mirth. She soon hung down her head, and *felt* the difference between the chaff and the wheat."[7]

Even unsympathetic observers like Benjamin Kennicott realized that Wesley's sermons had an arrow running through them, and that the appeal was the intended climax. Kennicott, who was to become a distinguished Old Testament scholar, heard Wesley preach his last sermon before the University of Oxford at St. Mary the Virgin. He was then an undergraduate at Wadham College. In handling his text Wesley, in Kennicott's view, had "expressed himself like a very good scholar, but a rigid zealot."[8] "Then he came to what he called his plain, practical conclusion. Here was what he had been preparing for all along; and he fired his address with so much zeal and unbounded satire as quite spoiled what

[1] *Journal*, Vol. VI, p. 239. 13th June, 1779.
[2] *Ibid.*
[3] *Ibid.*, p. 314. 29th April, 1781; Vol. VII, p. 93. 16th June, 1785; Vol. IV, p. 20. 22nd April, 1752.
[4] *Ibid.*, Vol. VII, p. 38. 16th December, 1784.
[5] *Ibid.*, Vol. V, p. 453. 13th April, 1772.
[6] *Ibid.*, Vol. IV, p. 490. 28th February, 1762.
[7] *Ibid.*, p. 158. 25th April, 1756.
[8] *Wesleyan Methodist Magazine*, Vol. LXXXIX (1866), p. 14.

might have otherwise been turned to great advantage."[1] Horace Walpole noted the same regrettable feature, as he regarded it, in Wesley's preaching. He heard the evangelist at Lady Huntingdon's Chapel in Bath on the 5th October, 1766. Five days later he wrote to John Chute: "Wesley is a lean, elderly man, fresh-coloured, his hair smoothly combed, but with a *soupçon* of a curl at the ends. Wondrous clean, but as evidently an actor as Garrick. He spoke his sermon, but so fast and with so little accent, that I am sure he has often uttered it, for it was like a lesson. There were parts and eloquence in it; but towards the end he exalted his voice and acted very ugly enthusiasm. . . ."[2] Walpole was, of course, looking on with a jaundiced eye, but at least he saw what Wesley was driving at, even if in his superior way he strongly disapproved.

François de Sales once told his father: "My test of the worth of a preacher is when his congregations go away saying, not, 'What a beautiful sermon,' but, 'I will do something.' " That was Wesley's conception too. As a result, as Telford put it, the application was "never slurred."[3] There was no uncertainty as to what Wesley wanted his hearers to do. It was to receive Christ. That is clear from the way in which he epitomized his preaching in the *Journal*. "I there offered Christ," he said, with reference to a service at Bradford-on-Avon—and scores of entries are simply variations on that theme.[4] "I offered the grace of God;" "I offered the redemption that is in Christ Jesus;" "I proclaimed the name of the Lord;" "I proclaimed Christ crucified;" "I proclaimed 'the grace of our Lord Jesus Christ' "; "I proclaimed free salvation;" "I declared to them all the grace of our Lord Jesus Christ;" "I declared the free grace of God;" "I exhorted 'the wicked to forsake his way;' " "I began to call sinners to repentance;" "I invited all guilty, helpless sinners."[5] It is obvious from these crisp descriptions that Wesley believed that the chief end of preaching was to offer Christ.

Wesley invariably assessed his congregations in terms of their potential responsiveness to the gospel appeal. This was his overriding concern. What he wanted was not simply quiet and attentive hearing, but a readiness to open the heart to the Saviour. It was said of Richard Cameron, the Scottish Covenanter evangelist, that "the bias of his heart lay to the proposing of Christ and persuading men to close with Him."[6] That was

---

[1] *Ibid.*

[2] *The Letters of Horace Walpole*, Vol. VII, p. 50. To John Chute, 10th October, 1766.

[3] Telford, *op. cit.*, p. 318.

[4] *Journal*, Vol. II, p. 243. 17th July, 1739.

[5] *Ibid.*, p. 174. 4th April, 1739; Vol. III, p. 429. 15th September, 1749; p. 444. 24th October, 1749; Vol. IV, p. 202. 17th April, 1757; Vol. III, p. 522. 17th April, 1751; Vol. IV, p. 440. 11th March, 1761; Vol. III, p. 281. 24th February, 1747; Vol. II, p. 185. 29th April, 1739; Vol. IV, p. 56. 28th March, 1753; Vol. III, p. 334. 21st February, 1748; p. 88. 30th September, 1783. [6] Macgregor, *op. cit.*, p. 79.

Wesley's burning preoccupation too. "I am amazed at this people," he confessed after preaching in Edinburgh. "Use the most cutting words, and apply them in the most pointed manner, still they *hear*, but *feel* no more than the seats they sit upon!"[1] It was Wesley's aim to get his congregation to feel the truth of God's Word, as well as to hear it. Yet this was not merely a psychological attack on the emotions, as Dr. William Sargant would have us believe. The sections in his widely publicized book, *Battle for the Mind*, which deal with Wesley are not only historically inaccurate but also unreliable even from a scientific viewpoint.[2]

Sometimes Wesley's audiences seemed to be receptive, but were in fact not so. At Athlone, for example, in April 1748 the people apparently took in the Word with seriousness, "I preached once more at five, and a great part of the congregation was in tears. Indeed almost all the town appeared to be moved, full of good-will and desires of salvation. But the waters spread too wide to be deep. I found not one under any strong conviction, much less had any one attained the knowledge of salvation, in hearing about thirty sermons. So that, as yet, no judgement could be formed of the future work of God in this place."[3] At Morvah in Cornwall Wesley had to admit: "But still I could not find the way into the hearts of the hearers, although they were earnest to hear what they understood not."[4] The next day at Zennor he had a congregation of two or three hundred, and "found much good-will in them, but no life."[5]

Sometimes, however, the response was better than expected. On the 19th June, 1777, Wesley did not reach Leicester until the people had waited some time for his arrival. He immediately began to enforce his text from Acts 16: 31—"Believe on the Lord Jesus Christ, and thou shalt be saved." "I had designed not to call here at all, supposing it would be lost labour," he confided. "But the behaviour of the whole congregation convinced me that I had judged wrong. They filled the house at five in the morning, and seemed determined to 'stir up the gift of God which was in them.' "[6] One of the converts was William Reeve, pioneer of Methodism in the village of Gaddesby.[7]

The most significant fact to emerge from an exhaustive scrutiny of Wesley's *Journal* is that, whilst the evangelist never failed to conclude his

[1] *Journal*, Vol. VI, p. 499. 25th April, 1784.

[2] William Sargant, *Battle for the Mind: A Physiology of Conversion and Brain-Washing* (1957). Cf. D. Martyn Lloyd-Jones, *Conversions Psychological and Spiritual* (1959); A. Skevington Wood, "Dr. Sargant and Mr. Wesley," in *Faith and Thought*, Vol. XCII, pp. 39–46.

[3] *Journal*, Vol. III, p. 341. 4th April, 1748.

[4] *Ibid.*, p. 89. 6th September, 1743.

[5] *Ibid.*, 7th September, 1743.

[6] *Ibid.*, Vol. VI, p. 157. 19th June, 1777. Cf. Vol. III, p. 444. 25th October, 1749: "I rode to Birmingham. This had been long a dry, uncomfortable place: so I expected little good here: but I was happily disappointed."

[7] *Ibid.*, Vol. VI, p. 157, n. 1.

sermon with an appeal for response to the offer of Christ, there is no indication that he prescribed any external form which this should take. We
do not read of him asking inquirers to come forward or remain behind.
There is no trace at all of any such suggestion. The meeting apparently
closed with prayer, in which no doubt Wesley besought the Lord to work
on the hearts of those who had been affected by the Word, but after that
the people dispersed. He preferred them to do so quietly and reverently,
as became those who had been faced with the solemn issues of spiritual life
and death. If this did not happen, he commented adversely and even
acidly. The congregation on St. Stephen's Down in Cornwall listened to
him in commendable silence. "But the moment I had done," Wesley
went on, "the chain fell off their tongues. I was really surprised. Surely
never was such a cackling made on the banks of the Cayster or the Common of Sedgemoor."[1]

More often the presence of the Spirit was so manifest that a hush fell on
the vast crowd at the close. At Newcastle on the 12th December, 1742, the
congregation stirred neither hand nor foot. "When the sermon was done,
they divided to the right and left, none offering to go till I was past; and
then they walked quietly and silently away, lest Satan should catch the
seed out of their hearts."[2] Again, at Miller's Barn in Rossendale on the
27th August, 1748: "When I had finished my discourse, and even pronounced the blessing, not one person offered to go away, but every man,
woman, and child stayed just where they were till I myself went away
first."[3] One cannot fail to be impressed with such a report.

As to the results of his gospel preaching, Wesley was fully content to
leave these with the Lord. He was persuaded that the Word would not fail
in its effect, but he displayed what almost amounted to an aloofness so far
as immediate evidence was concerned. He left the scene as one who had
discharged his commission in proclaiming the good news and offering
Christ. Now he knew that only God could work, and he was satisfied
with that. "All the hearers were deeply attentive," he was able to say
concerning a meeting at Birstall; "whom I now confidently and cheerfully committed to 'the great Shepherd and Bishop of souls' "[4] "Many
were deeply affected, and all received the Word 'with all readiness of
mind,' " he reported from Sligo. "But which of these will 'bring forth
fruit with patience'? God only knoweth."[5] "If they hear no more, I am
clear of their blood," he wrote again from Birstall, "I have declared the
whole counsel of God."[6] "I spoke as plain as possibly I could," he said of a

[1] *Ibid.*, Vol. III, p. 377. 18th September, 1748.
[2] *Ibid.*, p. 55. 12th December, 1742.
[3] *Ibid.*, p. 373. 27th August, 1748. Wesley said that he had only seen this once
before.
[4] *Ibid.*, p. 17. 4th June, 1742.
[5] *Ibid.*, Vol. IV, p. 390. 18th May, 1760.
[6] *Ibid.*, Vol. VII, p. 384. 4th May, 1788.

F

sermon in Grimsby (at St. James' Church); "but God only can speak to the heart."[1] Wesley recognized that it was the prerogative of God Himself to break up the fallow ground of the soul, and implant the seed of new life.

It was his habit to insert into his *Journal* some concise observation, but he was most cautious in his expression and made it clear that he was merely recording a personal judgement. At Epworth he could say; "I believe many in that hour began to cry out, 'God be merciful to me a sinner.' "[2] At Biddick: "They seemed all, even some who had long drawn back, to be melted down as wax before the fire. So strong and general influence on a congregation I do not remember to have seen for some years."[3] At Bristol: "I believe many found desires of coming to Him. O that they may be brought to good effect!"[4] Such prayerful ejaculations recurred: "My subject was, 'By grace are ye saved through faith.' Oh that all who heard might experience this salvation!"[5] "O what shoals of half-awakened sinners will be broad awake when it is too late!" was his more solemnizing observation at Cork, after seeing "many of the gay and honourable" almost persuaded to be Christians.[6]

It will be realized that Wesley was far from prone to pronounce a hasty, optimistic verdict on the consequences of his preaching. He was not interested in what might lie on the surface. It was a deep work of the Spirit which he expected. Hence his repeated emphasis on the Divine initiative in evangelism. "God gave an edge to His Word, both this evening and next morning," he wrote from Ireland. "He can work, even among these dry bones."[7] "I believe God applied His Word. Some trembled, others wept. Surely some of these shall know there is balm in Gilead," was another entry.[8] "God made some impression on the stony hearts;" "I believe God confirmed the Word of His grace;" "He bore witness to His Word in a very uncommon manner"—these were some of Wesley's observations.[9] His very language revealed that he looked to God alone to bring about conversions.

At times he seemed to be almost sceptical in his attitude. This arose, however, not from any lack of faith, but from long experience, in which he had learned not to jump to evangelistic conclusions. It is so fatally easy

[1] *Ibid.*, p. 411. 1st July, 1788.
[2] *Ibid.*, Vol. III, p. 23. 9th June, 1742. He had preached on the story of the Pharisee and the Publican.
[3] *Ibid.*, Vol. IV, p. 28. 20th May, 1752.
[4] *Ibid.*, p. 355. 30th October, 1759.
[5] *Ibid.*, Vol. III, p. 63. 9th January, 1743.
[6] *Ibid.*, Vol. VII, p. 272. 7th May, 1787.
[7] *Ibid.*, Vol. IV, p. 393. 16th June, 1760.
[8] *Ibid.*, p. 394. 27th June, 1760.
[9] *Ibid.*, Vol. V, p. 314. 28th May, 1769 (Brickkilns); Vol. VI, p. 271. 2nd April, 1780 (Warrington); p. 288. 29th July, 1780 (Sheffield).

to be misled by surface symptoms. Wesley was always on his guard against any such superficiality. As a result, he tended if anything to err in the opposite direction. "All were moved a little," he wrote from Alnwick, "but none very much."[1] "Never did I see a fairer prospect of good here," he reported from Sligo. "But blossoms are not fruit."[2] And again, in a similar strain, from Wallingford: "How pleasant it is to see the dawn of a work of grace! But we must not lay too much stress upon it. Abundance of blossoms! But when the sun is up, how many of these will wither away?"[3] And after preaching at Plymouth: "God uttered His voice; yea, and that a mighty voice insomuch that the stout-hearted trembled; and it seemed as if He would send none empty away; but of these, too, though many were called, I fear few were chosen."[4] And at Great Marlow: "Many were surprised and perhaps in some measure convinced (but how short-lived are many of these convictions!)."[5]

These are not the remarks of an evangelist liable to live in a fantasy world of wishful thinking. There is a certain healthy realism about Wesley's sober comments. One suspects that he would rarely be required to eat his own words. His only concern was with a genuine work of grace, and for this he was ready to bide God's time. He combined urgency in bringing the gospel to the people with restraint in prejudging its effect. The occasions when he actually reported an on-the-spot conversion were comparatively rare. But equally they bore all the marks of Divine power. On a September day in 1739 he preached in Plaistow on "Blessed are those that mourn" (Matthew. 5: 4). "It pleased God to give us in that hour two living instances of that piercing sense both of the guilt and power of sin, that dread of the wrath of God, and that full conviction of man's inability either to remove the power, or atone for the guilt, of sin (called by the world, despair); in which properly consisted that poverty of spirit, and mourning, which are the gate of Christian blessedness."[6]

Writing to James Hutton on the 4th June, 1739, Wesley gave an account of a typical day's ministry in Bristol. "I began preaching in the morning at Weavers' Hall, where two persons received remission of sins; as did seven in the afternoon at the Brickyard, before several thousand witnesses; and ten at Baldwin Street in the evening, of whom two were

---

[1] *Ibid.*, Vol. III, p. 363. 19th July, 1748.

[2] *Ibid.*, Vol. IV, p. 394. 24th June, 1760.

[3] *Ibid.*, Vol. V, p. 345. 17th October, 1769.

[4] *Ibid.*, Vol. VII, p. 245. 3rd March, 1787. Wesley distinguished between a general gospel call and an effectual call leading to conversion, on the basis of the dominical apothegm in Matthew 20: 16.

[5] *Journal*, Vol. III, p. 47. 28th September, 1742. Cf. p. 217, 28th October, 1745 at Biddick: "Many appeared to be cut to the heart; but it is well if these convictions also do not pass away as the morning cloud."

[6] *Ibid.*, Vol. II, p. 279. 17th September, 1739.

children."[1] From the parallel entry in the *Journal* we learn that the after-noon converts received salvation "during the sermon."[2] But it was not often that Wesley gave statistics like this. Most of his reports were in personal terms, as where he spoke of a girl of thirteen or fourteen at Rose Green, Bristol, who along with others was deeply convinced of sin and called on God for deliverance; and of an old man at Shackerley, at whose house he preached, who was groaning for redemption, and on whom the power of God fell almost as soon as Wesley parted from him after the service.[3]

Sometimes, more especially in the earlier years of the revival and during the remarkable awakening at Everton in 1759, there were outward mani-festations during the delivery of the message. Those under conviction of sin would fall to the ground, convulsed with sighs and sobs, or cry out in the agony of their souls. Wesley would call on the rest to bow in prayer whilst he pleaded for the release of the captives. Often it was as a hymn was sung that victory was given. Whilst he was speaking at Epworth, "several dropped down as dead, and among the rest such a cry was heard of sinners groaning for the righteousness of faith as almost drowned my voice. But many of these soon lift up their heads with joy, and broke out into thanksgiving, being assured they now had the desire of their soul— the forgiveness of their sins."[4] During a sermon at Norwich a young woman, after trying to contain herself as long as she could, sank down and cried aloud. The women around her gave her water and hartshorn, but all to no avail. At the close of the service, Wesley came up and asked her, "What do you want?" She immediately replied, "Nothing but Christ." "And indeed what physician beside Him is able to heal that sickness?" inquired Wesley.[5] Although the danger of mass hysteria can never have been far away in such gatherings, it must be remembered that where the Spirit is in control, emotions which otherwise might cause harm can be touched for the purposes of grace.

In some cases, those in spiritual need would seek out the evangelist when the meeting was over. After preaching at Snowsfields, London, Wesley went into a friend's house nearby. "A poor sinner indeed followed me," he wrote afterwards, "one who was broken in pieces by the con-vincing Spirit, and uttered such cries as pierced the hearts of all that heard. We poured out our souls before God in prayer, and light sprung up in her heart."[6] At St. Agnes in Cornwall, Wesley was sought out after the service by a young woman who was weeping bitterly, and crying out, "I

[1] *Letters*, Vol. I, p. 317. To James Hutton, 4th June, 1739. Cf. *Journal*, Vol. II, pp. 205–206. 28th May, 1739.
[2] *Journal*, Vol. II, p. 205.
[3] *Ibid.*, p. 227. 24th June, 1739; Vol. IV, p. 33. 15th June, 1752.
[4] *Ibid.*, Vol. III, p. 23. 12th June, 1742.
[5] *Ibid.*, Vol. IV, p. 363. 3rd January, 1760.
[6] *Ibid.*, Vol. III, p. 454. 17th February, 1750.

must have Christ; I will have Christ. Give me Christ, or else I die!" There
and then Wesley and two or three others knelt down to claim the promise
on her behalf. Soon, he said later, she was filled with peace unspeakable,
and they left her rejoicing in the Saviour.[1]

Often it was the next day before Wesley heard of results. A soldier
stood up after the society meeting in Athlone, and gave his testimony. "I
was going to a woman last night, when one of my comrades met and
asked me if I would go to the watchnight. Out of curiosity I came; but for
half the sermon I minded nothing that was said. Then God struck me to
the heart, so that I could not stand, but dropped down to the ground. I
slept none last night, and came to you (i.e., Wesley) in the morning; but I
could not speak. I went from you to a few of our brethren, and they
prayed with me till my burden dropped off. And now, by the grace of
God, we will part no more."[2] No sooner had the society praised God for
this and the benediction been pronounced for the second time, when another soldier intervened with a second and similar word of witness. The
news was not always conveyed so promptly as that. On many occasions
Wesley had left town too soon to hear of all that had happened. He might
be told by letter, or not know until he passed that way again.

One of the signs that encouraged Wesley to think that a real work of
grace had been begun in a sinner's heart was his presence at the early
morning meeting. If he saw some of those who had been moved the previous evening still concerned about their souls the next day, he had reason
to hope that they would soon find what they sought. He preached at Rye,
for instance, one evening. When he had finished, he read over the rules of
the Methodist society in the open congregation, as he was in the habit of
doing from time to time. "The number of those who came at five in the
morning showed that God had touched many hearts," he observed.[3] It
was a fair test, and a straight answer to the charge of undue emotionalism.
It takes more than titillated feelings to induce someone to stand in the open
air early on an autumn morning, listening to a clergyman. If he was not
compelled to leave, Wesley might arrange to meet any who had been
under conviction the night before. We hear of twenty-six who were so
affected and promised to call on him the following day. Only eighteen
turned up, however, and even with these Wesley showed characteristic
caution. After talking closely with them, he went so far as to admit that
some of them may have gone home to their house justified.[4]

Occasionally Wesley would hold what we would nowadays call an
after-meeting. He once preached in the market-place at Whitehaven from
II Corinthians 8:9. "I saw they were moved, and resolved to improve the

---

[1] *Ibid.*, Vol. VI, p. 77. 3rd September, 1775.
[2] *Ibid.*, Vol. III, p. 483. 3rd July, 1750.
[3] *Ibid.*, Vol. IV, p. 288. 13th October, 1758.
[4] *Ibid.*, Vol. II, p. 222. 15th June, 1739.

opportunity. So, after preaching, I desired those who determined to serve God to meet me apart from the great congregation. To these I explained the design, nature, and use of Christian societies."[1] We also hear of him asking those who were interested in joining the Methodist society to tell him so the next morning. This seems to be the nearest Wesley approached to making a call for decision.

Wesley was careful to ensure that any converts would be properly cared for. As we shall be discovering from a later chapter, much of Methodist organization was directed to this end. On the 17th July, 1743, Wesley preached to his favourite congregation of miners at Plessey. He added: "I then joined a little company of them together who desire 'repentance and remission of sins.' "[2] It was in the fellowship of such informal groups that the effectiveness of his appeal was to be tested. Those who had truly trusted in Christ now had every opportunity to grow in grace.

[1] *Ibid.*, Vol. III, p. 430. 21st September, 1749.
[2] *Ibid.*, p. 81. 17th July, 1743.

CHAPTER XV

THE MANY-HEADED BEAST

"WHILE I was enforcing that great question with an eye to the spiritual resurrection, 'Why should it be thought a thing incredible with you that God
should raise the dead?' *the many-headed beast* began to roar again. I again proclaimed deliverance to the captives; and their deep attention showed that the
word sent to them did not return empty." *Journal* 2: 395.

SO FAR WE HAVE ONLY HINTED IN PASSING AT THE OPPOSITION
Wesley met. Now we must consider it more fully. It was hardly to be
expected that such an aggressive work for God would be allowed to go on
unhindered. At the outset, Wesley encountered resistance within the
Church: this was what drove him into the open air. But even there he was
not left undisturbed. Indeed, especially in the early years, there were many
adversaries. He seems to have anticipated this, and accepted it as an inevitable accompaniment of effective evangelism. "Such is the general
method of God's providence," he wrote: "where all approve, few
profit."[1] He was thinking in that instance about those who rejected his
message because it was so uncompromising: and for this very reason
others were impressed by it. But the same principle obtained when disapproval exhibited itself in something more than closed ears and hardened
hearts. There were times when hostility to the gospel led to violent mass
attacks on Wesley and his colleagues.

Wesley frequently referred to these uncontrolled mobs as "the beasts of
the people," or "the sons of Belial."[2] In the *Journal* entry for the 26th
October, 1740, where he spoke about "the many-headed beast," it would
appear that he was personifying the vicious crowd as a single entity under
the direction of Satan himself.[3] In other cases he alluded to "a rude rout,"
"abundance of rabble," and those "possessed by Moloch."[4] If this sounds
strong language, it must be recollected that the eighteenth-century mob
was a terrible phenomenon. No one knew that better than Wesley, for he

[1] *Journal*, Vol. V, p. 492. 14th December, 1772.
[2] *Ibid.*, Vol. II, p. 523. 26th January, 1742; Vol. V, p. 53. 27th March, 1764; p. 129.
5th June, 1765; p. 341. 19th October, 1769; Vol. III, p. 77. 7th May, 1742; Vol. VI,
p. 462. 1st April, 1750. Wesley was no doubt recalling Paul's allusion to fighting
with "beasts at Ephesus" (1 Corinthians 15: 32), and the several Old Testament
references to the "sons of Belial."
[3] *Journal*, Vol. II, p. 395. 26th October, 1740.
[4] *Ibid.*, p. 521. 9th January, 1742; Vol. III, p. 264. 25th September, 1746; Vol. IV,
p. 21. 24th April, 1752.

had to face it perhaps more often than any man of his time. He earned the right to comment by the hard way of experience.

It must not be imagined that only the Methodists were the victims of such violence in this period.[1] "The mob was a persistent and violent element in the Georgian scene," explains S. E. Ayling; "and in an age whose characteristic freedom was underlined by its almost total absence of police a riot was never far below the political surface. There were pro-Jacobite riots in 1715, anti-Jewish riots in 1753, anti-Catholic riots in 1780, and anti-Methodist riots on numerous occasions, riots against Walpole and his Excise Bill in 1733, riots in Edinburgh in 1736 against the hanging of convicted smugglers, riots in London against the attempt to regulate gin-drinking in 1736, riots arising out of the imposition of turnpike tolls or import duties, or from taxes on Scottish beer, or the introduction of labour-saving machinery, or industrial strikes, or unpopular wage-fixing, or parliamentary elections, or a hundred and one matters, great and small."[2]

Horace Walpole wrote ironically of "our supreme governors, the mob," and Henry Fielding referred to it as "the Fourth Estate," along with King, Lords, and Commons.[3] In Smollett's *Humphrey Clinker* (1771), the testy squire, Matthew Bramble, depicts the mob as "a monster I never could abide, either in its head, tail, midriff, or members; I detest the whole of it, as a mass of ignorance, presumption, malice, and brutality."[4] It is understandable that this "many-headed beast" was profoundly feared.[5] It was made up from the dregs of society, and constituted a constant menace. Most of the cities and larger towns were threatened by such a mob, as Wesley discovered to his cost.

The most serious opposition was raised in Staffordshire. Wednesbury was the centre. Wesley arrived there on the 20th October, 1743. There had been anti-Methodist riots earlier in the year, but he had not been present. He preached at noon in the High Bullen on "Jesus Christ, the same yesterday, and today, and for ever" (Hebrews. 13:8). "I believe every one present felt the power of God," he declared: "and no creature offered to molest us, either going or coming; but the Lord fought for us, and we held our peace."[6] This, however, proved to be the lull before the storm. Wesley was attending to his correspondence in Francis Ward's house in the afternoon, when the mob surrounded the building. Inside the Chris-

---

[1] Cf. Outler, *op. cit.*, p. 20, n. 69. Max Beloff, *Public Order and Popular Disturbances 1660–1714* (1938), presents a revealing account of the general unrest in the period before Wesley.

[2] Ayling, *op. cit.*, p. 52.

[3] *The Letters af Horace Walpole*, Vol. I (1903), p. 377. To Sir Horace Mann, 7th September, 1743. *The works of Henry Fielding*, ed. Leslie Stephen, (1882), Vol II, p. 129.

[4] Tobias G. Smollet, *The Expedition of Humphrey Clinker*, ed. Lewis M. Knapp (1966), p. 37.

[5] *Journal*, Vol. II, p. 395. 26th October, 1740.

[6] *Ibid.*, Vol. III, p. 98. 20th October, 1743.

tians knelt in prayer. The crowd left, but then returned with reinforcements. They demanded that Wesley should come out to them. Instead, he invited the ringleader inside, and very soon had won him over. Some Wednesbury men then undertook to escort Wesley as he went to visit the Justice of the Peace to claim protection. Unfortunately, the magistrate was in bed and refused to get up to intervene. It was decided to seek out Mr. Justice Persehouse at Walsall. He likewise declined to assist.

At this point the Walsall mob set on one whom they regarded as an intruder. The men from Wednesbury tried to screen him in vain. That Wesley escaped with his life was nothing less than a miracle. As he was carried through the town, successive cries were raised of, "Drown him!" "Hang him!" and even, "Crucify him!" Some shouted, "Strip him, tear off his clothes!" to which he mildly answered, "That you need not do: I will give you my clothes, if you want them." "In the intervals of tumult," wrote Charles Wesley later, "he spoke, the brethren assured me, with as much composure and correctness as he used to do in their societies. The Spirit of glory rested upon him. As many as he spoke to, or but laid his hands on, he turned into friends. He did not wonder (as he himself told me) that the martyrs should feel no pain in the flames; for none of their blows hurt him, although one was so violent as to make his nose and mouth gush with blood."[1]

Eventually, he was rescued by the man who had led the mob. "Sir, I will spend my life for you," he said. "Follow me, and not one soul here shall touch a hair of your head." He lifted Wesley on his shoulders and waded through the river to safety. The evangelist reached Wednesbury, having lost only a flap of his waistcoat and a little skin from one of his hands. Looking back on his adventures, he exclaimed: "I never saw such a chain of providences before; so many convincing proofs that the hand of God is on every person and thing, overruling all as it seemeth Him good."[2] It was certainly a night to be remembered. It confirmed Wesley's sense of destiny. He knew that only God could have preserved him, and that this was for His purpose. Perhaps the most touching incident of all was when a rough lout came rushing at the preacher, with his arm raised to strike. Suddenly he let it drop and only stroked Wesley's head, saying, "What soft hair he has!"[3]

This was by no means the only time Wesley was in danger of losing his life. Both at Bolton and at Rochdale the stones flew plentifully, but whilst they damaged some of the other assailants, Wesley himself was untouched. At Hull, clods and stones were hurled on every side without harming him. He had difficulty in reaching his coach afterwards, however, and then found that the driver had thought it safer to quit the scene.

[1] C. Wesley, *Journal*, Vol. I, p. 339.
[2] *Journal*, Vol. III, p. 100. 20th October, 1743.
[3] *Ibid.*, p. 101.

However, he was offered a seat in another coach, where he was amply protected from the missiles by "a large gentlewoman," who deposited herself in his lap.[1] At Falmouth, the house where he was staying was "beset on all sides by an innumerable multitude of people. A louder or more confused noise could hardly be at the taking of a city by storm."[2] The rabble roared, "Bring out the Canorum! Where is the Canorum?" This was a term used to denote a Methodist in Cornwall.[3] Wesley faced the mob alone when they broke down the door and rushed into the room. "Here I am," he coolly announced. "Which of you has anything to say to me? To which of you have I done any wrong? To you? Or you? Or you?" He went on speaking until he came bareheaded, so that all might see his face, into the street. There he continued to pacify the angry crowd until he was rescued by the local clergyman, one of the aldermen, and some gentlemen of the town.

It was Wesley's "rule, confirmed by long experience, always to look a mob in the face."[4] His frankness, his poise and his unruffled speech went far to quench inflamed passions and to bring the rabble under control. It was his superb courage and composure, combined with his evident good humour and friendliness to all, which finally overcame even the bestial savagery of the eighteenth-century mob. "Wesley, the evangelist, was a man possessed of amazing grace," comments Dr. Bready. "Never did he lose his temper; and always was he prepared to endure a blow, if the dealing of it would relieve the hysteria of the assailant. Repeatedly, when struck by a stone or cudgel, he quietly wiped away the blood and went on preaching without so much as a frown on his face. He loved his enemies; and do what they would, they could not make him discourteous or angry."[5]

Wesley was wise enough, however, not to court trouble unnecessarily. He arrived in Pocklington on a Fair day in the spring of 1752. The unusual bitterness of several who met him in the street gave warning of what might follow. A yard which was suggested as a preaching place seemed to be suitable, save for one feature. "It was plentifully furnished with stones—artillery ready at hand for the devil's drunken companions."[6] Just then it started to rain, so Wesley withdrew to a large barn and held his service in peace. Sometimes he abandoned the attempt to preach at all if it appeared to be lost labour. At Cowbridge "the sons of Belial gathered themselves together, headed by one or two wretches called gentlemen; and continued shouting, cursing, blaspheming, and throwing showers of

---

[1] *Ibid.*, Vol. IV, p. 21. 24th April, 1752.

[2] *Ibid.*, Vol. III, p. 189. 4th July, 1745.

[3] It may have been derived from the Cornish "canor" (a singer), and thus be connected with the Methodist love of singing (cf. *ibid.*, n. 2).

[4] *Ibid.*, p. 250. 6th August, 1746.

[5] Bready, *op. cit.*, p. 211. Cf. *Journal*, Vol. III, p. 45. 12th September, 1742.

[6] *Journal*, Vol. IV, p. 22. 25th April, 1752.

stones, almost without intermission."[1] After spending some time in prayer for them, Wesley deemed it best to dismiss the people. At Derby interrupters "lifted up their voice, hallooing and shouting on every side."[2] Finding it impossible to make himself heard, Wesley walked unobtrusively away. An "innumerable retinue" followed him, but only a few pebbles were thrown.[3]

All kinds of diversions were introduced to distract the attention of the people from the Word. Animals figure prominently in the accounts. At Charles Square, in London, "many of the rabble had brought an ox, which they were vehemently labouring to drive in among the people. But their labour was in vain; for in spite of them all, he ran round and round, one way and the other, and at length broke through the midst of them clear away, leaving us calmly rejoicing and praising God."[4] At Pensford "a great company of rabble" (hired for the purpose it turned out) brought a bull, which they had been baiting, and tried to force it into the congregation. "But the beast was wiser than his drivers: and continually ran on one side of us or the other, while we quietly sang praise to God, and prayed for about an hour. The poor wretches, finding themselves disappointed, at length seized upon the bull . . . and by main strength, partly dragged and partly thrust him in among the people. When they had forced their way to the little table on which I stood, they strove several times to throw it down, by thrusting the helpless beast against it; who of himself, stirred no more than a log of wood. I once or twice put aside his head with my hand, that the blood might not drop upon my clothes; intending to go on as soon as the hurry should be a little over. But, the table falling down, some of our friends caught me in their arms and carried me right away on their shoulders; while the rabble wreaked their vengeance on the table, which they tore bit from bit. We went a little way off, where I finished my discourse without any noise or interruption."[5] At the Great Gardens, in London, a herd of cows was used to create a disturbance, but once again without preventing the continuance of the meeting.[6]

The mob did not always act on its own initiative. In some cases it was incited by Wesley's enemies amongst the gentry, and even, sadly enough, amongst the clergy. "It was unquestionably the attitude of the clergy and of the landed classes which gave the mob its privilege and excuse, even when it was not led in person by gentlemen or curates," affirmed C. E. Vulliamy.[7] Wesley was preaching once in Halifax when a gentleman got some of the rabble together, and began to throw money amongst them,

[1] *Ibid.*, Vol. III, p. 77. 7th May, 1743.
[2] *Ibid.*, Vol. V, p. 53. 27th March, 1764.
[3] *Ibid.*
[4] *Ibid.*, Vol. II, p. 475. 12th July, 1741.
[5] *Ibid.*, pp. 534-535. 19th March, 1742.
[6] *Ibid.*, Vol. III, p. 45. 12th September, 1742.
[7] Vulliamy, *op. cit.*, p. 232.

which not unnaturally caused quite a commotion. Finding that he could not compete with it, the evangelist led the people to a meadow about half a mile away, and there they concluded the service in peace.[1] But the disturbances encouraged by the gentry were by no means all as mild as that. Some of the most violent assaults were incited by those of the upper classes. The Shrove Tuesday riots in Wednesbury in 1744 were deliberately provoked by mine owners who threatened to sack any collier who did not take part.[2] In Cornwall, some of the gentlemen magistrates set themselves against Wesley, and their hostility to him accounted for the attacks of the mob.[3]

There were occasions when the gentry intervened in person. At Gwennap, Wesley was reading his text when a gentleman (so called, as Wesley invariably underlined) came riding into the thick of the crowd and seized three or four of the men. A second appeared on the scene and did the same. As the congregation started to sing a hymn, the leader, one Francis Beauchamp, later Sheriff of Cornwall, actually tried to lay hands on Wesley himself and impound him for the service of the Crown.[4] At Bradford-on-Avon, "the beasts of the people were tolerably quiet till I had nearly finished my sermon. They then lifted up their voice, especially one, called a gentleman, who had filled his pocket with rotten eggs; but, a young man coming unawares, clapped his hands on each side, and mashed them all at once. In an instant he was perfume all over; though it was not so sweet as balsam."[5] Wesley must have relished that case of the biter bit.

At other times, the gentry ordered their servants to break up the meeting. Coming to St. Ives in 1750, Wesley was careful to seek permission from the mayor to preach in the market-place. Despite this, he was rudely interrupted when the notorious John Stephens of Trevalgan sent his man to ride a horse to and fro through the midst of the congregation.[6] Although some of the chief citizens urged him to continue and guaranteed protection, Wesley decided to transfer the service to the society room. But he saw good in this as in all things, adding: "Oh the wisdom of God, in permitting Satan to drive all these people together into a place where nothing diverted their attention, but His word had its full force upon their hearts!"[7]

The persecution from the clergy must have been particularly hard for

[1] *Journal*, Vol. III, pp. 368–369. 22nd August, 1748.
[2] *Ibid.*, p. 118. 6th February, 1744.
[3] *Ibid.*, p. 188. 3rd July, 1745.
[4] *Ibid.*
[5] *Ibid.*, Vol. V, p. 341. 19th October, 1769.
[6] *Ibid.*, Vol. III, p. 491. 23rd August, 1750. He was known locally as John à Court, from his house. Cf. p. 185 'a famous man of the town" (24th June, 1745); *Proc. W.H.S.*, Vol. IV, p. 188.
[7] *Journal*, Vol. III, p. 492. 23rd August, 1750.

Wesley to bear. He sought to be a loyal churchman wherever this did not conflict with his conscientious convictions, or impede the work to which he was called by God. He genuinely loved his brethren in the ministry, and desired only to strengthen their hands where they were concerned for the kingdom. He must have been pained beyond measure when some of them turned against him, and actually stirred up the mob. The most virulent of his clerical opponents was George White, incumbent at Colne in Lancashire. Tyerman dubs him, rather dramatically, "a popish renegado," because he was educated at Douai and intended for the Roman priesthood.[1] In August 1748 he issued a proclamation in these terms: "Notice is hereby given, that if any men be mindful to enlist into His Majesty's service, under the command of the Rev. George White, commander-in-chief, and John Bannister, lieutenant-general of His Majesty's forces, for the defence of the Church of England, and the support of the manufactory in and about Colne, both of which are now in danger . . . let him now repair to the drumhead at the cross, where each man shall have a pint of ale for advance, and other proper encouragements."[2] Shortly afterwards, Wesley came to preach nearby at Roughlea, with William Grimshaw. He was half-way through his message, when the mob "came pouring down the hill like a torrent."[3] They were armed with clubs and staves, and had evidently been plied with more than the promised pint of ale.[4] Wesley was taken off to the constable at Barrowford, who tried to make him promise not to come to Roughlea again. This, of course, he could not be persuaded to do, although he agreed to leave then without holding another meeting. Wesley was allowed to go, with an assurance that the mob would be silenced. The constable spoke a few half-hearted words to them, and disappeared. Wesley and his colleagues were left to their mercy. He himself was beaten to the ground, and when he attempted to get up, the whole horde made for him "like lions."[5] Grimshaw and Thomas Colbeck, a grocer from Keighley, were tossed to and fro, thrown down and "loaded with dirt and mire of every kind."[6] William Mackford, a trustee of the Orphan House at Newcastle, was dragged about by the hair of his head. And all this time neither the constable nor those who had recruited the disreputable army lifted a finger to intervene. White soon drank himself first into gaol and then to death.

Another clerical inflamer of mobs was Dr. William Borlase, Rector of Ludgvan and Vicar of St. Just, the noted antiquarian. As a magistrate, he

[1] Tyerman, *Life of John Wesley*, Vol. II, p. 15.
[2] William Myles, *The Life and Writings of the late Rev. William Grimshaw* (1806), p. 114. The proclamation was issued in August, 1748.
[3] *Journal*, Vol. III, p. 369. 25th August, 1748.
[4] *Letters*, Vol. II, p. 153. To James Hargrave, 26th August, 1748. Hargrave was the constable at Barrowford, and the letter is now thought to have been addressed to him and not to White as formerly supposed.
[5] *Ibid.*, p. 155.   [6] *Ibid.*

harried the Methodist preachers relentlessly and refused their appeals for protection. One James Dale applied to him for redress, after the mob had broken into his house and stolen some of his goods. "Thou conceited fellow!" thundered Borlase. "What, art thou too turned religious? They may burn thy house if they will; it is no concern of mine."[1] There is little doubt that the attitude of this scholarly yet unreasonable clergyman helped to provoke the anti-Methodist riots in Cornwall at the time.

At Buckland, near Frome, Wesley preached in a meadow owned by Jeremiah Emblem. "The curate had provided a mob, with horns and other things convenient, to prevent the congregation's hearing me. But the better half of the mob soon left their fellows, and listened with great attention. The rest did no harm, so that we had a comfortable opportunity."[2] At Shepton Mallet the incumbent "had hired a silly man, with a few other drunken champions, to make a disturbance. Almost as soon as I began, they began screaming out a psalm; but our singing quickly swallowed up theirs. Soon after, their orator named a text, and, as they termed it, preached a sermon; his attendants meantime being busy, not in hearing him, but in throwing stones and dirt at our brethren."[3] It ought to be added, however, that in other places the local clergyman dissociated himself from the persecutions, even though he himself did not subscribe to Wesley's views. After the mob had pulled down the house where Wesley had preached on a previous visit to Chester, the Vicar, John Baldwin, publicly expressed his regret.[4] At Falmouth, as we have seen, it was a clergyman, Thomas by name, who came to Wesley's rescue.[5]

There were others whose position ought to have taught them better who nevertheless joined in the fashionable pastime of baiting the Methodist evangelist. An attorney who happened to be in Heptonstall when Wesley was speaking there one evening, endeavoured to interrupt by "relating some low, threadbare stories with a very audible voice."[6] He threatened to spoil the service with his interminable narratives. Eventually some of the earnest hearers "cut him short in the midst by carrying him quietly away."[7] We can imagine his discomfiture at being removed so unceremoniously, but he got no more than he deserved. At Taunton,

---

[1] Vulliamy, op. cit., p. 236. Cf. p. 150: "It is deplorable to find a man of culture like Dr. Borlase, one of the most respectable inventors of Druid antiquities, persecuting the Wesleys and their preachers with idiotic anger and a villainous disregard of justice."

[2] Journal, Vol. IV, p. 82. 10th September, 1753.

[3] Ibid., Vol. III, pp. 249–250. 6th August, 1746. In addition to the instances cited, it must be remembered that the worst persecution of all, at Wednesbury, was encouraged by the Vicar, Edward Egginton (Letters, Vol. II, pp. 76–77. To "John Smith," 25th June, 1746).

[4] Journal, Vol. IV, pp. 36–37. 5th July, 1752.

[5] Ibid., Vol. III, p. 189. 4th July, 1745.

[6] Ibid., Vol. IV, p. 31. 8th June, 1752.

[7] Ibid.

Wesley planned to preach in the yard of the Three Cups (now the County Hotel). But before he had even named his text, having uttered only two words, "Jesus Christ," he was interrupted. A tradesman of the town—who turned out to be the mayor-elect—made such a commotion that in the end it was judged best to yield him the ground. Wesley led the people to a large room elsewhere, and there continued the service without further incident.[1]

Other individual disturbers of the peace of unspecified class are also mentioned. Some of them were quickly dealt with by the bystanders. At Newcastle-under-Lyme "one buffoon laboured much to interrupt; but, as he was bawling, with his mouth wide open, some arch boys gave him such a mouthful of dirt as quite satisfied him."[2] In some cases, those who came to scoff and make themselves a nuisance were strangely subdued. As Wesley came out to face a large congregation in the rain at St. Mewan, a huge man ran full tilt into him. He thought it was accidental until it happened a second time. Then the man began to curse and swear as he followed Wesley through the crowd. He planted himself right at the preacher's side. Wesley feared further outbursts, but as he proceeded with his sermon, his face grew serious and he slipped off his hat. At the close, he squeezed Wesley earnestly by the hand, and went away as meek as a lamb.[3]

Another big man appeared at Newark, when Wesley was speaking in the covered shambles. He was exceedingly drunk and as a result very noisy and turbulent. It seemed that he might ruin the meeting, when his wife seized him by the collar, gave him two or three hearty boxes on the ear, and dragged him away like a calf. Eventually he eluded her, crept in among the people and stood as quiet as could be.[4] That is reminiscent of an incident at Burnley, when the town crier "began to bawl amain," which no doubt he could do with more volume than most. However, his wife got hold of him with one hand and clapped the other over his mouth, so that he could not give vent to another word.[5]

Mob violence against Wesley seems to have been at its fiercest in England. Only occasionally do we read of attacks in Wales, as at Llaner-chymedd in 1750. Wesley observed that he could just understand the oaths and curses, which were in broad English, but the rest of the language was lost on him, as his was on them. There were severe riots in Cork, but apart from that Wesley was comparatively free from molestation in Ireland. It was a country he loved and which learned to love him. "If we except a few abnormal outbreaks accounted for by special incite-

---

[1] *Ibid.*, Vol. III, p. 95. 23rd September, 1743.
[2] *Ibid.*, Vol. VI, p. 57. 17th March, 1775.
[3] *Ibid.*, Vol. III, p. 489. 6th August, 1750.
[4] *Ibid.*, Vol. VI, p. 282. 12th June, 1760.
[5] *Ibid.*, p. 526. 13th July, 1784.

ments," claimed Curnock, "Wesley was almost as immune from persecution in Ireland as in Scotland."[1] In Scotland he was received with the
utmost respect, though the response to his message disappointed him. All
that was ever thrown at him there was a potato—in Aberdeen.[2]

The most serious aspect of the mass onslaughts on Wesley was undoubtedly the fact that some of them were clearly organized. The gentry
collaborated with the clergy in opposing a movement which they feared
would upset the *status quo*. Their apprehension was justified to a certain
extent, for the spread of the Christian gospel did more to emancipate the
labouring classes than has been recognized by some materialistically conditioned sociologists. "It is not difficult to understand why the mobs were
often such pliant material in designing hands," writes Brian Greaves.
"They loved the loose living that the Methodists condemned; many of
their erstwhile comrades had deserted the tavern for the meeting-house;
there was abundant emotional energy in the eighteenth-century mobs
which could easily be channelled. The chief reason, however must be the
economic dependence of the populace on the 'squarsons' and the landed
gentry in rural areas, and the industrialists who feared working-class un-
orthodoxy in the towns.... That the landlords and the clergy were closely
allied in the matter of persecuting the Methodists is beyond doubt, and one
can perceive why this was especially so in eighteenth-century England. The
vestry was an important tool in persecution's hand. It was here that land-
lord and clergy, constable and alehouse-keeper met to determine much
that went on in eighteenth-century England. One need hardly point out
that here was a channel by which religious differences could be translated
into physical force."[3]

[1] *Ibid.*, Vol. V, 126. Notes.
[2] *Ibid.*, p. 257. 1st May, 1757.
[3] *Proc. W.H.S.*, Vol. XXXI, p. 111.

CHAPTER XVI

LIVING WITNESSES

"So many *living witnesses* hath God given that His hand is sill 'stretched out to heal' and that 'signs and wonders are even now wrought by His holy child Jesus.' " *Journal* 2: 180.

THE MINISTRY OF AN EVANGELIST MUST ULTIMATELY BE JUDGED in terms of his converts. Its effectiveness is reflected in the renewed lives of those who have been led to Christ through him. Where there has been an undeniable transformation of character, and men and women who formerly served self and sin now devote themselves to pleasing God and helping their fellows, then the work of an evangelist is vindicated, even in the eyes of those who may not altogether approve of his methods. This pragmatic test is entirely legitimate. It has to do not so much with the number of converts, for this may vary, but with their quality.

Assessed by such a yardstick, John Wesley emerges as a highly successful missioner. His converts were many over the course of the years, and they stood. These living witnesses up and down the land were the best testimonial to the value of his ministry. He in turn rejoiced in them. These abiding seals of God's favour brought him comfort in the midst of much that might have depressed him. He could echo the apostle Paul: "For what is our hope, or joy, or crown of rejoicing? Are not even ye in the presence of our Lord Jesus Christ at his coming? For ye are our glory and joy" (I Thessalonians 2: 19, 20).

The very first open-air sermon that Wesley ever preached bore fruit in the life of at least one of his listeners. It was as if God chose to put His mark on this daring venture in evangelism from the start. The man who was thus affected was William Webb of Bristol, then about thirty years old. Here is his own account of what happened. "I went to the place appointed, out of curiosity, and heard that great and good man; but with much uneasiness all the time, not knowing what was the matter with me; nor could I relate any part of the sermon, being much confused in my mind and filled with astonishment at the minister. For I had never seen such proceedings before, it being quite a new thing to preach in the open air and not in a church or chapel. This was the first sermon Mr. Wesley preached in Bristol. When it was ended I was induced to follow him, but, at the same time, knew not why I did so, being shut up in ignorance and gross darkness, through the multitude of my sins and the hardness of my

177

heart. . . . But oh how great was the goodness of God to me, who drew
my heart with love to follow that dear minister of Jesus Christ, whose
name I revere and esteem."[1] Thus quickened by the Spirit through
Wesley's preaching of the Word, Webb soon afterwards found salvation
and entered into the peace and joy of believing. He survived to the age of
ninety-seven, and bore a consistent Christian witness throughout those
many years.

In the first apologia Wesley offered for his unusual ministry, he appealed
to the miracle of multiplied conversions as the sufficient proof that it was
owned by God. He insisted that this was not the work of man, but the
Lord's doing which was marvellous in the eyes of those who truly belonged to Him. "Such a work as this hath been, in many respects as
neither we nor our fathers had known. Not a few whose sins were of the
most flagrant kind—drunkards, swearers, thieves, whoremongers, adul-
terers—have been brought 'from darkness unto light, and from the power
of Satan unto God.' Many of these were rooted in their wickedness, having long gloried in their shame, perhaps for a course of many years—yea,
even to hoary hairs. Many had not so much as a notional faith, being
Jews, Arians, Deists, or Atheists. Nor has God only made bare His arm in
these last days in behalf of open publicans and sinners; but many 'of the
Pharisees' also 'have believed on Him,' of 'the righteous that needed no
repentance;' and, having received 'the sentence of death in themselves,'
have then heard the voice that raiseth the dead: have been made partakers
of an inward, vital religion, even 'righteousness, and peace, and joy in the
Holy Ghost.' The manner wherein God hath wrought this work in many
souls is as strange as the work itself. It has generally, if not always, been
wrought in one moment. 'As the lightning shining from heaven,' so was
'the coming of the Son of Man,' either to bring peace or a sword; either
to wound or to heal; either to convince of sin or to give remission of sins
in His blood. And the other circumstances attending have been equally
remote from what human wisdom would have expected. So true is that
word, 'My thoughts are not your thoughts, neither are your ways my
ways.' "[2]

It was on such lines that Wesley sought to meet the objection of those
who considered his ministry too unconventional. They argued that because they had never seen anything like it, therefore it could not be of God.
He invited them to draw the opposite inference. It was of our Lord's
miracle of healing and forgiveness that the astonished onlookers declared, "We never saw it on this fashion," and thereupon glorified God
(Mark 2: 12).

This was Wesley's repeated line of defence. On the 11th June, 1747, he
wrote to Edmund Gibson, Bishop of London, to refute misrepresentations

[1] *Methodist Magazine*, Vol XXX (1807), p. 416.
[2] *Journal*, pp. 67-68. Preface to the Third Extract.

made in his visitation charge of that year.[1] Wesley as usual was content to appeal to plain fact. "What have been the consequences (I would not speak, but I dare not refrain) of the doctrines I have preached for nine years last past? By the fruits shall ye know those of whom I speak; even the cloud of witnesses, who at this hour experience the gospel which I preach to be the power of God unto salvation. The habitual drunkard that was is now temperate in all things; the whoremonger now flees fornication; he that stole, steals no more, but works with his hands; he that cursed or swore, perhaps at every sentence, has now learned to serve the Lord with fear and rejoice unto Him with reverence; those formerly enslaved to various habits of sin are now brought to uniform habits of holiness. These are demonstrable facts: I can name the men, with their places of abode. One of them was an avowed Atheist for many years; some were Jews; a considerable number Papists; the greatest part of them as much strangers to the form as to the power of godliness. My Lord, can you deny these facts? I will make whatever proof of them you shall require. But if the facts be allowed, who can deny the doctrines to be in substance the gospel of Christ? 'For is there any other name under heaven given to men whereby they may thus be saved?' or is there any other word that thus 'commendeth itself to every man's conscience in the sight of God'?"[2]

Wesley wrote in a similar strain to George Lavington, Bishop of Exeter, one of the most vitriolic critics of the revival. His lengthy diatribe, *The Enthusiasm of Methodists and Papists Compared*—a surprising combination—appeared in 1749. Much of it was mere abuse and hardly deserved a serious reply, but Wesley nevertheless wrote courteously to the Bishop and tried to set the record straight. Lavington had concluded that "this new dispensation is a composition of enthusiasm, superstition and imposture."[3] This is how Wesley responded. "It is not clear what you mean by a new dispensation. But the clear and undeniable fact stands thus: A few years ago Great Britain and Ireland were covered with vice from sea to sea. Very little of even the form of religion was left, and still less of the power of it. Out of this darkness God commanded light to shine. In a short space He called thousands of sinners to repentance. They were not only reformed from their outward vices, but likewise changed in their dispositions and tempers; filled with 'a serious, sober sense of true religion,' with love to God and all mankind, and with an holy faith, producing good works of every kind, works both of piety and mercy."[4]

Wesley's converts represented as wide a range of age and class as the congregations themselves. We hear of the young and of the old. "The number of children that are clearly converted to God is particularly re-

[1] The charge has not survived, cf. Sykes, *Edmund Gibson*, p. 321.
[2] *Letters*, Vol. II, p. 290. To the Bishop of London, 11th June, 1747.
[3] George Lavington, *The Enthusiasm of Methodists and Papists Compared* (1749), p. 81.
[4] *Letters*, Vol. III, pp. 270-271. To the Bishop of Exeter, 1st February, 1750.

markable," Wesley reported from Dublin in 1785. "Thirteen or fourteen little maidens, in one class, are rejoicing in God their Saviour; and are as serious and stayed in their whole behaviour as if they were thirty or forty years old. I have much hopes that half of them will be stedfast in the grace of God which they now enjoy."[1] Teenagers were often amongst the converts. At Bristol in 1739, for example, "a girl of thirteen or fourteen, and four or five others persons, some of whom had felt the power of God before, were deeply convinced of sin, and, with sighs and groans, which could not be uttered, called upon God for deliverance."[2] In the same year, Rebecca Mason of Shadwell, aged sixteen, was invited by a friend to hear Wesley preach at the Foundery. "They waited some time at the door, in the midst of a great crowd, before Mr. Wesley arrived," so we learn from an account in the *Methodist Magazine*.[3] "The delay led her to think of the parable of the ten virgins, and was the occasion of exciting a serious desire that she at last might be found ready to enter into the marriage supper of the Lord. The approach of the minister was announced by, 'Here he comes!' As soon as they entered and the congregation was settled (for seats they had none), Mr. Wesley gave out the following hymn:

> Behold the Saviour of mankind
> Nailed to the shameful tree.

These words were accompanied with a divine influence and fixed her attention to that man of God, whom, from that time, she never ceased highly to esteem. When she returned home, being asked by her mother how she liked the preacher, she replied, 'I never saw such a people; I will go again.' "[4] So she did, and lived to be a burning and a shining light for the Lord until she died at eighty. At the other end of the age scale, we have already met the old man at whose house Wesley preached at Shackerley, and who soon afterwards found the redemption for which he groaned.[5] His was by no means an isolated case.

All sorts and conditions were brought to a knowledge of Christ. But since Wesley's mission was directed mainly to the masses of the common people, it is understandable that we hear most of these. Wesley went into a barber's shop in Bolton just after Easter in 1751. As he attended to his customer, the proprietor said, "Sir, I praise God on your behalf. When you were at Bolton last, I was one of the most eminent drunkards in all the town; but I came to listen at the window, and God struck me to the heart. I then earnestly prayed for power against drinking; and God gave me more than I asked: He took away the very desire of it. Yet I felt myself

---

[1] *Journal*, Vol. VII, p. 68. 12th April, 1785.
[2] *Ibid.*, Vol. II, p. 227. 24th June, 1739.
[3] *Methodist Magazine*, Vol. XXVII (1804), p. 126.
[4] *Ibid.*
[5] *Journal*, Vol. IV, p. 33. 15th June, 1752.

worse and worse, till on the 5th of April last, I could hold out no longer. I knew I must drop into hell that moment unless God appeared to save me. And He did appear. I knew He loved me, and felt sweet peace. Yet I did not dare say I had faith, till yesterday was twelve-month, God gave me faith; and His love has ever since filled my heart."[1] What an encouraging testimony for an evangelist to hear so spontaneously as he sat in a barber's chair!

Wesley more than once received delightful surprises of this nature. He was leaving Nafferton, on the Yorkshire wolds, after preaching at one o'clock, when a woman stopped him on the road and said: "Sir, do you not remember, when you were at Prudhoe two years since, you break-fasted at Thomas Newton's? I am his sister. You looked upon me as you were going out, and said, 'Be in earnest.' I knew not then what earnestness meant, nor had any thought about it; but the words sunk into my heart, so that I could never rest any more till I sought and found Christ."[2] How an evangelist is uplifted when bread cast on the waters is found after many days!

When preaching at Epworth in 1742 Wesley was surprised to see in his outdoor congregation one of the local gentry "who was remarkable for not pretending to be of any religion at all."[3] He had not been at public worship of any kind for upwards of thirty years, so Wesley was informed. After the service was closed, the man still stood in his place, as motionless as a statue. Wesley went straight to the point. "Sir, are you a sinner?" he inquired. With a broken voice the man replied, "Sinner enough." He continued to stare upwards, until eventually his wife, and some of his servants, who were all in tears, got him to his chaise to go home.[4] There was a sequel to the story. Almost ten years later, Wesley called on him and was agreeably surprised to find him strong in faith, though weak in body. For some time, he told Wesley, he had been rejoicing in God, without either doubt or fear, and was now waiting for the welcome hour when he should "depart and . . . be with Christ" (Philippians 1: 23).[5]

Another member of the gentry whom Wesley evidently influenced came from Leicester. He rode with Wesley and Richard Moss one day as they headed north—clearly with a view to finding solace for his soul. He was a victim of depression and although he had taken "abundance of physic," he was no better for it.[6] Wesley "explained his case to him at large, and advised him to apply to that Physician who alone heals the broken in heart."[7] If this was indeed John Coltman, as is surmised, then a

[1] Ibid., Vol. III, pp. 520–521. 11th April, 1751.
[2] Ibid., Vol. IV, pp. 324–325. 21st June, 1759.
[3] Ibid., Vol. III, p. 23. 12th June, 1742.
[4] Ibid., pp. 23–24.
[5] Ibid., Vol. IV, p. 19. 17th April, 1752.
[6] Ibid., Vol. III, p. 164. 20th February, 1745.
[7] Ibid.

notable convert was thus gained, for he became a leading Methodist light in the city.[1]

Such an incident as this reminds us that Wesley's evangelism was not confined to preaching. He seized every possible opportunity to commend his Saviour to others. He was a true hunter of souls, who never allowed himself to go off duty. He once fell into conversation with "a serious man" as he was leaving Newport Pagnell.[2] They had a lively discussion about theological opinions, until the unidentified traveller lost his patience. He told his companion that he was wide of the mark in his views, and that he must be a follower of John Wesley. "No," was the reply. "I am John Wesley himself." At this, the unfortunate debater was so discomfited that he would gladly have accelerated out of sight. But, Wesley said, "being the better mounted of the two, I kept close to his side, and endeavoured to show him his heart, till we came into the street of Northampton."[3] That is an unforgettable picture, and it shows us how genuine was Wesley's zeal in evangelism.

It was no doubt this transparent concern for souls which communicated itself to those who heard him preach, and which explains (so far as can be) his extraordinary magnetism. Ultimately, of course, this has to be ascribed to the indwelling Spirit. The testimony of those who listened to him is so unanimous as to this that we cannot overlook it. We can quote only one or two samples. One of the aged Methodist saints in Bristol whom Adam Clarke met in 1789 was Dame Summerhill. She was one hundred and four years old. She told Clarke that John Wesley was her father in the gospel. "When he first came to Bristol, I went to hear him preach; and, having heard him, I said, 'This is the truth.' I inquired of those around, who and what he was. I was told that he was a man who went about everywhere preaching the gospel. I further inquired, 'Is he to preach here again?' The reply was, 'Not at present.' 'Where is he going to next?' I asked. 'To Plymouth,' was the answer. 'And will he preach there?' 'Yes.' 'Then I will go and hear him. What is the distance?' 'One hundred and twenty-five miles.' I went, walked it, heard him, and walked back again!"[4]

Matthias Joyce was a native of Dublin and reared as a Roman Catholic. He was to become one of Wesley's preachers. He first heard the evangelist in 1773, when he was a lad of nineteen and still unenlightened. But the impression made was lasting, and started him on the road to conversion. It was merely out of curiosity that Joyce went one Sunday morning to the place where Wesley was preaching. But, he testified later, "as soon as I saw him, my heart clave to him; his hoary hairs and grave deportment

[1] *Ibid.*, Vol. II, p. 463, n. 1.
[2] *Ibid.*, Vol. III, p. 10. 20th May, 1742.
[3] *Ibid.*, pp. 10–11.
[4] J. W. Etheridge, *The Life of the Rev. Adam Clarke, LL.D.* (1859), pp. 120–121.

commanded my respect, and gained my affections. What endeared him still more to me was seeing him stoop to kiss a little child that stood on the stairs. However, though this prepared me for receiving the word of life, so great was my darkness that I could not understand what he said; and therefore went away as ignorant as I came."[1]

No account of Wesley's preaching illustrates this remarkable combination of Spirit-filled attractiveness and penetrating power than that supplied by John Nelson. It enables us to realize what an exceptional aura surrounded the evangelist. The Birstall stonemason confessed that he was "like a wandering bird, cast out of the nest," until Wesley came to preach his first sermon at Moorfields.[2] "Oh that was a blessed morning to my soul! As soon as he got upon the stand, he stroked back his hair, and turned his face towards where I stood, and I thought fixed his eyes upon me. His countenance struck such an awful dread upon me, before I heard him speak, that it made my heart beat like the pendulum of a clock; and, when he did speak, I thought his whole discourse was aimed at me. When he had done, I said, 'This man can tell the secrets of my heart: he hath not left me there; for he hath showed the remedy, even the blood of Jesus.' Then was my soul filled with consolation, through hope that God for Christ's sake would save me; neither did I doubt in such a manner any more, till within twenty-four hours of the time when the Lord wrote a pardon on my heart."[3]

A similar testimony was given by a soldier convert whose name has not been recorded. He was "desperate in wickedness, and did not put a restraint on any lust or appetite" until he heard Wesley on Kennington Common.[4] He wanted to discover what he might say, for rumour had it that he was beside himself. "But when he began to speak, his words made me tremble. I thought he spoke to no one but me, and I durst not look up; for I imagined all the people were looking at me. I was ashamed to show my face, expecting God would make me a public example, either by letting the earth open and swallow me up, or by striking me dead. But before Mr. Wesley concluded his sermon, he cried out, 'Let the wicked forsake his way, and the unrighteous man his thoughts; and let him return unto the Lord, and He will have mercy upon him; and to our God, for He will abundantly pardon.' I said, 'If that be true, I will turn to God today.' "[5]

Undoubtedly such conversions, multiplied a thousandfold, covering the three kingdoms and spanning half a century, constituted Wesley's strongest vindication. As we have seen, it was to this that he invariably appealed when assailed by his detractors. It was from this supernatural transformation of individual lives that the renewal of the nation sprang. "Wesley swept the dead air with an irresistible cleansing ozone," wrote

[1] *Wesley's Veterans*, Vol. VII, p. 191.   [2] *Ibid.*, Vol. III, p. 11.
[3] *Ibid.*, pp. 11–12.   [4] *Ibid.*, p. 13.   [5] *Ibid.*, pp. 13–14.

Sir Charles Grant Robertson. "To thousands of men and women his preaching and gospel revealed a new heaven and a new earth; it brought religion into soulless lives and reconstituted it as a comforter, an inspiration, and a judge. No one was too poor, too humble, too degraded to be born again. . . . Wesley wrestled with the evils of his day and proclaimed the infinite power of a Christian faith based on personal conviction, eternally renewed from within, to battle with sin, misery, and vice in all its forms. The social service he accomplished was not the least of his triumphs."[1]

The evidence of changed lives could not be suppressed or denied, and gradually the sheer pressure of facts began to persuade even those who had been unsympathetic to admit the truth. A wagon-load of Lincolnshire Methodists were hauled before the Justice of the Peace at Crowle. When he asked what they had done wrong, there was a long silence, for in their agitation the objectors had failed to frame a charge. At last one of them said, "Why, they pretended to be better than other people; and besides, they prayed from morning to night." The Justice asked, "But have they done nothing besides?" "Yes, sir," said an old man, "an't please your worship, they have *converted* my wife. Till she went among them, she had such a tongue! And now she's as quiet as a lamb." "Carry them back, carry them back," ordered the J.P., "and let them convert all the scolds in the town."[2]

In many places Wesley could point to the evident alteration. As early as 1744 he could report from Cornwall: "It is remarkable that those of St. Just were the chief of the whole country for hurling, fighting, drinking, and all manner of wickedness; but many of the lions are become lambs, are continually praising God, and calling their old companions in sin to come and magnify the Lord together."[3] Of Epworth he was able to say in 1748: "God has wrought upon the whole place. Sabbath-breaking and drunkenness are no more seen in these streets; cursing and swearing are rarely heard. Wickedness hides its head already. Who knows but, by-and-by, God may utterly take it away?"[4] He came to Arbroath in 1772, and noted: "In this town there is a change indeed! It was wicked to a proverb; remarkable for Sabbath-breaking, cursing, swearing, drunkenness, and a general contempt of religion. But it is not so now. Open wickedness disappears; no oaths are heard, no drunkenness seen in the streets. And many have not only ceased to do evil, and learned to do well, but are witnesses of the inward kingdom of God, 'righteousness, peace, and joy in the Holy Ghost.' "[5] At Eyre Court in Ireland it could be stated: "A great awakening

[1] C. Grant Robertson, *England Under the Hanoverians* (1911), p. 210.
[2] *Journal*, Vol. III, p. 20. 9th June, 1742.
[3] *Ibid.*, p. 129. 7th April, 1744.
[4] *Ibid.*, p. 360. 3rd July, 1748.
[5] *Ibid.*, Vol. V, p. 458. 5th May, 1772.

has been in this town lately; and many of the most notorious and profligate sinners are entirely changed, and are happy witnesses of the gospel salvation."[1] Wigan used to be called "wicked Wigan," but the town took on "a softer mould" as a result of the missions there.[2] At St. Ives the improved lives of the converts had convinced most of the town that there was truth in the gospel preached by Wesley and his helpers.[3] The behaviour of Sir Thomas Stepney's servants at Llanelly House not only broke down their master's prejudices, but also impressed the entire community.[4] Colley, the butler, was allowed to hold preaching-services in the kitchen of the mansion.[5]

The cumulative effect of such multiplied conversions was enormous. Not only did it remove misgivings and silence criticism, but also provided living channels through which the work of evangelism could be furthered. Converts became witnesses, and so the good news was spread. Many of Wesley's preachers were led to Christ under his own ministry, and then went out to reach countless thousands of others. Men like John Nelson, Alexander Mather, William Hunter, Joseph Cownley, Thomas Tennant, Thomas Rutherford, Jasper Robinson and Richard Moss were the fruit of Wesley's evangelistic labours, and they in their turn became itinerant preachers themselves. Others of Wesley's converts assumed the leadership of the society where they lived, and pioneered the outreach in their district. Dean Carpenter was not exaggerating when he claimed that "no Christian evangelist since St. Paul, Luther and Calvin could look back on more concrete results of his ministry."[6]

When John Wesley came to die, he had little to bequeath in the way of property. The profits from the sale of his books were to go into the funds of Methodism. A few personal belongings were distributed amongst his friends. He really had nothing to leave except his books, his clothes, his chaise and his loose cash. His true legacy lay in the realm of the Spirit. He left behind him a host of converts, to carry on his mission to the nation and the world. This was something no will could list. It represented Wesley's most substantial bequest.

[1] *Ibid.*, p. 501. 13th April, 1773.
[2] *Ibid.*, Vol. VIII, p. 58. 9th April, 1790.
[3] *Ibid.*, Vol. III, p. 378. 20th September, 1748.
[4] *Ibid.*, Vol. V, p. 333. 17th August, 1769.
[5] *Ibid.*, n. 2.
[6] Carpenter, *op. cit.*, p. 216.

CHAPTER XVII

THE CHIEF CARE

"This is the great work: not only to bring souls to believe in Christ but to build them up in our most holy faith. How grievously are they mistaken who imagine that as soon as the children are born they need take no more care of them! We do not find it so. *The chief care* then begins." *Letters* 5: 344.

WE LIVE IN AN AGE WHICH IS FAMILIAR WITH ADVANCED TECH-niques in the realm of evangelism. The twentieth-century Church is aware that a haphazard approach to this most vital of all tasks is inadequate and indeed unworthy. At every stage the most careful planning is demanded if the harvest of souls is to be reaped. And once the wheat is in the barn, further attention needs to be given to its storage. New-born Christians, to change the metaphor, cannot be left without after-care, any more than new-born babies. The post-natal programme is as important as the ante-natal. What we now know as follow-up is an integral part of effective evangelistic enterprise.

This was not always so, and sometimes the results of mission have been lost in consequence. One of the pioneers of follow-up in evangelism was John Wesley, though, of course, the term would have not been used by him. But what it stands for represents one of his major concerns. Wesley was ahead of his time in realizing that the evangelist cannot abandon his converts once they have been brought to the birth. Although the Holy Spirit will Himself watch over them, and increase the life He has implanted, yet nevertheless means must be devised to ensure that on the human level steps are taken to nurse the little one in the early months. For this purpose Wesley evolved a highly developed organization. Some believe that this is where his real genius lay. Certainly, what he set up by way of supervision was vindicated in the endurance of his converts. Inevitably, some will fall away, as our Lord's parable of the soils leads us to expect, but in Wesley's missions the proportion was not large, so far as we can ascertain.

There was a characteristic phrase in one of Wesley's letters to Lady Maxwell, soon after she had decided to join the Methodist society. He issued a warning that not all who professed to be followers of Christ—even amongst the Methodists—were fully in earnest. He begged her not to be put off by these semi-Christians. "Do not mind them who endeavour to hold Christ in one hand and the world in the other. I want you to be all a Christian; such a Christian as the Marquis de Renty or Gregory Lopez was; such as one as that saint of God, Jane Cooper, all sweetness, all gentleness, all love."[1] Now that affords an insight into what lay at the heart of Wesley's programme for the care of souls. The emphasis on holiness was something more than a matter of sound doctrine or even of right living. Wesley recognized that it was only as Christians grew in grace and went on to maturity, that they would be kept from falling. Paradoxically, to stand still is to be in danger of slipping back.

It was here that the streak of what might be described as evangelical asceticism in Wesley came to the surface. His stress on justification by faith, apart from all works of the law, did not lead him in the direction of antinomianism. No man was more aware than he that, once the new life in Christ had been kindled in the experience of regeneration, it required to be nurtured by a strong regulative system. Hence the insistence in Methodism on what Wesley himself called "our discipline."[2] "It is a great mistake to suppose that original Methodism had as its inspiration either a rollicking 'revival service,' or an informal 'group-fellowship,' " writes John Lawson. "Methodism was altogether more severe and less 'popular.' It was in every part a religion of exact discipline."[3]

This element in Wesley's organization stemmed from Scripture and the primitive Church, as did so much else in his teaching. He quoted the saying: "The soul and body make a man; the Spirit and discipline make a Christian."[4] But, more directly, Wesley derived his emphasis from the Puritans. As Monk brings out, the hallmark of both Puritanism and Methodism was a call to "a true, pure, consistent, and dynamically active life of love modelled after the life of Christ."[5] One of the reasons why Wesley and his followers were attacked so bitterly, was that they seemed to be reviving the spirit and practice of the despised separatists of the seventeenth century. The title of an eighteenth-century diatribe is revealing in this respect: *Methodism Unmasked: or the Progress of Puritanism*.[6] Wesley's own estimate of the Puritan contribution to the teaching on the progressive Christian life is worth quoting. It is the "peculiar excellency" of the Puritan divines that they instruct us "how to use the faith which God has given, and to go from strength to strength. They lead us by the hand in the paths of righteousness, and show us how, in the various cir-

---

[1] *Letters*, Vol. IV, pp. 263–264. To Lady Maxwell, 22nd September, 1764. De Renty and Lopez were Christians whose lives Wesley had read in his Oxford days (cf. above, p. 44). Jane Cooper had died in 1762 and Wesley published her letters in 1764. He called her "a pattern of all holiness" (*Letters*, Vol. IV, p. 311).

[2] Cf. *Works*, Vol. VIII, p. 328. *Large Minutes* (1789).

[3] *A History of the Methodist Church in Great Britain*, Vol. I, p. 188.

[4] *Journal*, Vol. III, p. 490. 17th August, 1750. Wesley had regretted that "through all Cornwall I find the societies have suffered great loss from want of discipline."

[5] Monk, *op. cit.*, p. 139.

[6] T. E. Owen, *Methodism Unmasked: or the Progress of Puritanism* (1803).

cumstances of life, we may most surely and swiftly grow in grace, and in the knowledge of our Lord Jesus Christ."[1]

Early in his evangelistic ministry Wesley was convinced that much of his effort would be wasted unless a scheme was devised whereby his converts could be properly cared for. It was plain that by and large the churches of the land were in no position to do this, even if the clergy were inclined. Unless the babes in Christ were to be exposed to the elements, like the unwanted children of the Roman empire, then some plan would have to be drawn up for their oversight. In 1743 Wesley visited Tanfield, not far from Newcastle. "From the terrible instances I met with there (and indeed in all parts of England), I am more and more convinced that the devil himself desires nothing more than that the people of any place should be half-awakened and then left to themselves to fall asleep again. Therefore I determine, by the grace of God, not to strike one stroke in any place where I cannot follow the blow."[2]

This became a principle with him, and also led to the formation of the united societies shortly afterwards. He had now been preaching in Northumberland for almost a year, without forming societies everywhere, and had found that "almost all the seed had fallen by the wayside."[3] In future he would go only where he knew he could return, and in each place he determined to leave societies. At Mullingar in Ireland, he stopped for an hour in passing to have a meal. But the sovereign, as the governor of the town was called, came to the inn and pressed him to hold a service. He could do no other than accede to the request. He added, however: "I had little hopes of doing good by preaching in a place where I could preach but once, and where none but me could be suffered to preach at all."[4]

From Haverfordwest he wrote in 1763: "I was more convinced than ever that the preaching like an apostle, without joining together those that are awakened and training them up in the ways of God, is only begetting children for the murderer (*i.e.*, the devil). How much preaching has there been for these twenty years all over Pembrokeshire! But no regular societies, no discipline, no order or connexion; and the consequence is that nine in ten of the once-awakened are now faster asleep than ever."[5] Whitefield, who lacked the aptitude for such a task, acknowledged Wesley's discretion in this matter. "My brother Wesley acted wisely. The souls that were awakened under his ministry he joined in class, and thus preserved the fruit of his labour. This I neglected, and my people are as a rope of sand."[6] No doubt that was a pessimistic self-judgement on the

---

[1] *Christian Library*, Vol. IV, pp. 107–108.

[2] *Journal*, Vol. III, p. 71. 13th March, 1743.

[3] Abel Stevens, *The History of the Religious Movement in the Eighteenth Century Called Methodism* (1858–1861), Vol. I, p. 324.

[4] *Journal*, Vol. III, p. 485. 10th July, 1750.

[5] *Ibid.*, Vol. V, p. 26. 25th August, 1763.

[6] Cf. R. Denny Urlin, *The Churchman's Life of Wesley* (1874), p. 188.

part of Whitefield, but certainly Wesley's organization paid dividends. It may have been the case that differences of theological outlook caused these two leaders of the revival to react as they did.

We must not, however, overestimate the originality of Wesley, nor misconstrue the exact nature of his gifts. He was not so much an innovator as an adapter. He knew how to suit a plan to the occasion. He improvised measures as the need arose. Fascinating though it is to compare his methods with those of the early Christians, the Reformers or the Puritans, by whom he was clearly influenced, we should be wrong to regard him as a calculated copyist. Rather he was guided by the Spirit to shape an instrument to meet the exigencies of the situation with which he was faced. "How was he competent to form a religious polity so compact, and permanent?" inquired his Irish friend, Alexander Knox, who understood him better than most. "I can only express my firm conviction that he was totally incapable of *preconceiving* such a scheme. . . . That he had an uncommon acuteness in fitting expedients to conjunctures, is most certain: this, in fact, was his great talent."[1]

What prompted the setting up of Wesley's organization was the care of souls. It was a direct outcome of evangelism. He had no ulterior intention. He was not deliberately founding a new communion, although, of course, this was the eventual and some would feel the inevitable outcome. But for the moment his sole concern was for the converts God had given him. How were they best to be nurtured? This was all that motivated Wesley as he established the first Methodist societies. What was lacking in the Church of the day was the opportunity for Christian fellowship in prayer, in searching the Scriptures, and in sharing Christian experience. The complaint was made against Wesley that he caused a schism in the Church, and destroyed existing fellowship. He strongly repudiated the charge. "I answer, That which never existed, cannot be destroyed."[2] It was said that there were Christians already in the parishes, and to set up societies was to break with them. Wesley inquired pointedly what such nominal believers had done to care for his converts. "Who watched over them in love? Who marked their growth in grace? Who advised and exhorted them from time to time? Who prayed with them and for them, as they had need? This, and this alone is Christian fellowship. But, alas! where is it to be found? Look east or west, north or south; name what parish you please: is this Christian fellowship there? Rather, are not the bulk of the parishioners a mere rope of sand? What Christian connexion is there between them? What intercourse in spiritual things? What watching over each other's souls? What bearing of one another's burdens? What a mere jest is it then, to talk so gravely of destroying what never was! The real truth is just the

---

[1] Cf. George Herbert Curteis, *Dissent in its Relation to the Church of England* (1873), p. 345, n. 6.

[2] *Works*, Vol. VIII, p. 251. *A Plain Account of the People Called Methodists* (1748).

reverse of this. We introduce Christian fellowship where it was utterly destroyed. And the fruits of it have been peace, joy, love, and zeal for every good word and work."[1]

The first distinctively Methodist society was that at the Foundery.[2] Wesley's own accounts of its inception showed that it arose from the demands of the situation in London as the mission was pressed forward. He referred to the fruits of his ministry at this time, along with that of his brother. "Many sinners were changed both in heart and life. But it seemed, this could not continue long; for every one clearly saw, these preachers would quickly wear themselves out; and no clergyman dared to assist them. But soon one and another, though not ordained, offered to assist them. God gave a signal blessing to their word. . . . Some of them were learned; some unlearned. Most of them were young; a few middle-aged. Some of them were weak; some, on the contrary, of remarkable strong understanding. But it pleased God to own them all; so that more and more brands were plucked out of the burning."[3] It is clear from this that the formation of the first Methodist society sprang from the needs not only of Wesley's converts, but also of his lay helpers in the work of evangelism. On both counts, it was born out of the demands of mission.

"It may be observed," Wesley continued, "that these clergymen, all this time, had no plan at all. They only went hither and thither, wherever they had a prospect of saving souls from death. But when more and more asked, 'What must I do to be saved?' they were all desired to meet together. Twelve came the first Thursday night, forty, the next; soon after, a hundred."[4] "This was the rise of the United Society, first in London, and then in other places," Wesley explained elsewhere. "Such a society is no other than 'a company of men having the form and seeking the power of godliness, united in order to pray together, to receive the word of exhortation, and to watch over one another in love, that they may help each other to work out their own salvation.' "[5]

Only one condition was laid down for those who wished to join these societies—"a desire 'to flee from the wrath to come, to be saved from their sins.' But, wherever this is really fixed in the soul, it will be shown by its fruits. It is therefore expected of all who continue therein, that they should continue to evidence their desire of salvation."[6] This they would achieve by avoiding evil of every kind, by doing good, and by attending on all the ordinances of God—public worship, the ministry of the Word, the Lord's Supper, family and private prayer, Bible study, and fasting or abstinence.[7]

[1] Ibid., pp. 251–252.

[2] See above, pp. 109–110.

[3] Works, Vol. VII, pp. 206–207. Sermon CVII. On God's Vineyard. Cf. Vol. VIII, p. 269. The Nature, Design and General Rules of the United Societies (1743).

[4] Ibid., Vol. VII, p. 207. Sermon CVII.

[5] Ibid., Vol. VIII, p. 269. Rules of United Societies (1743).

[6] Ibid., p. 270.   [7] Ibid., pp. 270–271.

"These are the General Rules of our societies," the document concluded; "all which we are taught of God to observe, even in His written Word, the only rule, and the sufficient rule, both of our faith and practice. And all these, we know, His Spirit writes on every truly awakened heart. If there be any among us who observe them not, who habitually break any of them, let it be known unto them who watch over that soul as they that must give an account. We will admonish him of the error of his ways; we will bear with him for a season. But then if he repent not, he hath no more place among us. We have delivered our own souls."[1] Such were the rules governing a Methodist society, finalized in the year 1743.

It will be seen that they provided for just the kind of disciplined fellowship which a new convert needed. It is only under such conditions that spiritual growth can be fostered. The mortality rate in evangelism would be much reduced, if such pains were always taken to ensure that babes in Christ are properly fed. Wesley saw to it that his societies were kept up to the mark. On his visits he reminded them of their obligations. At Newcastle in March 1743 he "read over in the society the rules which all our members are to observe; and desired every one seriously to consider whether he was willing to conform thereto or no."[2] Wesley added: "That this would shake many of them I knew full well; and therefore, on Monday 7th, I began visiting the classes again, lest 'that which is lame should be turned out of the way.' "[3]

This leads us to notice briefly the subsidiary groups within the Methodist societies. Of these the class meeting was the core. In Wesley's eye this was the keystone of the entire Methodist edifice, as Piette rightly reminds us.[4] At first Wesley attempted to examine the classes himself, but soon he had to delegate the supervision to leaders, and thus the organization of under-shepherds to the flock was inaugurated. As a system of pastoral care, especially for the newly-converted, it was ideal. The class was the disciplinary unit of the society. It was the responsibility of a leader "to see each person in his class, once a week at least, in order to inquire how their souls prosper; to advise, reprove, comfort, or exhort, as occasion may require; to receive what they are willing to give toward the relief of the poor."[5] He also kept the preacher informed as to the sick, or the disorderly. Thus "evil men were detected, and reproved. They were borne with for a season. If they forsook their sins, we received them gladly; if they obstinately persisted therein, it was openly declared that they were not of us. The rest mourned and prayed for them, and yet rejoiced, that, as far as in us lay, the scandal was rolled away from the society."[6]

[1] Ibid., p. 271.
[2] Journal, Vol. III, p. 68. 6th March, 1743.   [3] Ibid.
[4] Piette, op. cit., p. 476.
[5] Works, Vol. VIII, p. 253. A Plain Account of the People Called Methodists (1748).
[6] Ibid.

If the class meeting was the disciplinary cell of Methodism, the band was the confessional. These inner groups were continued in the form in which they had been taken over from the Fetter Lane Society, with its predominantly Moravian stamp. The bands met weekly for the purpose of recounting current Christian experience, and telling each other's faults "and that plain and home."[1] This mutual confession to one another, based on the scriptural injunction of James 5: 16, was the Methodist equivalent of auricular confession to a priest, and was designed to bring the same sense of relief and catharsis. The leader of each band was required to describe "his own state first, and then to ask the rest, in order, as many and as searching questions as may be, concerning their state, sins, and temptations."[2] Within the bands were the select bands, an even more intimate and searching fellowship. Whilst, as Dr. Towlson brings out, we can see here a borrowing from Moravian sources, we must not overlook the Puritan influence in the societal basis of Wesley's organization.[3] Professor Horton Davies has claimed that it may be "an amalgam of two great Puritan concepts, namely 'the gathered church' and 'the priesthood of all believers.' "[4]

Together with the recognized means of grace, these distinctive groups provided the convert with the very thing that was most needed to ensure steady growth in grace. This was the goal in sight throughout. At Dublin in 1750, Wesley "exhorted the society to stand fast in the good old Bible way and not to move from it, to the right hand nor to the left."[5] He commended the Methodists in New Mills, Derbyshire, because "they go straight forward, knowing nothing of various opinions, and minding nothing but to be Bible Christians."[6] Nothing was more calculated to keep Christians on the path mapped out in Scripture than the system of supervision which Wesley was led to design.

Although in the interests of evangelism, Wesley had been compelled to take steps which could only be interpreted as exceeding what was allowed by existing ecclesiastical order, yet nevertheless he tried not to alienate his converts from the Church. He decreed that Methodist services should not be held during the normal hours of worship on the Lord's Day, although towards the end of his life this command was increasingly ignored. Despite the treatment he himself received at the hands of the clergy, he still attended the services when that was possible, and communicated regularly. Often he would comment on the sermon, and always in a charitable manner, even when he disagreed with its contents. More usually, how-

---

[1] *Ibid.*, p. 272. *Rules of the Band Societies* (1738).
[2] *Ibid.*
[3] Towlson, *op. cit.*, pp. 184–195.
[4] *The Livingstonian* (1960), p. 6, quoted in Monk, *op. cit.*, p. 211.
[5] *Journal*, Vol. IV, p. 463. 8th April, 1750.
[6] *Ibid.*, Vol. VI, p. 100. 3rd April, 1776.

ever, he could report that it was "exceeding useful," "strong and weighty," or "solemn and affecting."[1] The church of St. Luke, Old Street, Clerkenwell, he referred to as "our parish church," since the Foundery stood within its bounds.[2] On the 3rd August, 1740, he wrote, with obvious delight: "At St. Luke's, our parish church, was such a sight as, I believe, was never seen there before: several hundred communicants, from whose very faces one might judge that they indeed sought Him that was crucified."[3] As Dr. Simon remarked, "that beautiful scene might have been reproduced throughout the country if the Church of England had only known 'the time of her visitation.' "[4]

It was always the aim of Wesley's societies "to challenge and rebuke the general body of the Church and nation by its earnestness in the pursuit of holiness," as Lawson insists.[5] In the *Large Minutes*, the design of Methodism was succinctly stated: "Not to form any new sect; but to reform the nation, particularly the Church; and to spread scriptural holiness over the land."[6] It was assumed that the majority within the societies belonged to the Church of England, which was no doubt nominally true. These were advised to attend their parish churches, just as dissenters presumably were expected to go to their meeting-houses. The original Methodist societies were inter-denominational rather than non-denominational in character: in this they bore a certain resemblance to the early Brethren assemblies of the next century. They were meant to afford a focus of fellowship for Christians of varying affiliations. In contradistinction from the old religious societies of Horneck and Smythies, there was nothing in the rules of Methodism which tied a member to the Church of England.[7] "The Methodists are to spread life among all denominations," declared Wesley; and then added, in a sadly prophetic postscript: "which they will do till they form a separate sect."[8] That was in 1790, when the course was irrevocably set. It could well be argued that Wesley's societies were most useful when they remained independent of ecclesiastical control, whether Anglican or eventually Methodist.

---

[1] *Ibid.*, Vol. III, p. 489. 12th August, 1750 (Redruth); p. 212. 22nd September, 1745 (Newcastle); Vol. IV, p. 111. 13th April, 1755 (Hayfield).

[2] *Ibid.*, Vol. II, p. 373. 3rd August, 1740; Vol. VIII, p. 34. 27th December, 1789. The church was built in 1733 by James, a pupil of Wren, and was "one of the largest parish churches in London" (Vol. VII, p. 127. 27th November, 1785). The Rector until 1774 was Dr. William Nicholls, also Vicar of St. Giles, Cripplegate, and President of Magdalene College, Cambridge. He was followed by Henry Waring.

[3] *Ibid.*, Vol. II, p. 373. 3rd August, 1740.

[4] Simon, *Methodist Societies*, p. 22.

[5] *A History of the Methodist Church in Great Britain*, Vol. I, pp. 194–195.

[6] *Works*, Vol. VIII, p. 299. *Large Minutes* (1789).

[7] For the rules of the religious societies, cf. J. Wickham Legg, *English Church Life from the Restoration to the Tractarian Movement* (1914), pp. 308–313.

[8] *Letters*, Vol. VIII, p. 211. To Thomas Taylor, 4th April, 1790.

G

But whilst it may have been true that most of the early Methodists were technically members of the Church of England by reason of their baptism, if not always through episcopal confirmation, yet their attachment was tenuous in the extreme. Many of them had no vital link. From this point of view, to speak of the Methodist societies as being any more than very loosely Anglican, is to go beyond the evidence. In a letter written in 1829 to Humphrey Sandwith of Bridlington, Adam Clarke assessed the situation with reasonable accuracy and moving eloquence. "Our societies were formed from those, who were wandering upon the dark mountains, that belonged to no Christian Church; but were awakened by the preaching of the Methodists, who had pursued them through the wilderness of this world to the highways and the hedges—to the markets and the fairs—to the hills and the dales; who set up the standard of the Cross in the streets and lanes of the cities, in the villages, in barns and farmers' kitchens. And all this in such a way, and to such an extent, as never had been done before, since the apostolic age. They drew their drag-net into the troubled ocean of irreligious society, and brought in to shore both bad and good: and the very best of them needed the salvation of God."[1]

We have contented ourselves with examining the way in which Wesley's organization was geared to the after-care of his converts. It stemmed from evangelism. To complete the picture, however, we would also need to show how it led to evangelism. Converts were trained to become soul-winners themselves. Many enlisted as lay preachers—some itinerant and others local. Many more were appointed as leaders in their own society, and, in addition to watching over the flock, engaged in evangelistic activity in the neighbourhood. In this way, over the years, Wesley was surrounded by a huge army of helpers to sustain the work as it expanded. "Oh for labourers," he cried in 1758; "for a few γνήσια τέκνα, desirous only to spend and be spent for their brethren!"[2] His plea was eventually to be answered there in Ireland, from which country he wrote, as already it had been by that time in England. Only Scotland disappointed him in this respect.[3]

This was a lasting legacy. Long after Wesley's death, his work went on by means of the system he had set up. The mission was prolonged because its harvest was fully gathered, and then used to sow further seed. This is perhaps the most impressive proof of his genius, as J. E. Rattenbury underlined. "His organizations were to become the model for all sorts of social and political organizers in the near future, as Halévy's new history of England shows, but, most important of all, they were great roadways of evangelical traffic in the eighteenth and nineteenth centuries, and were

[1] *Proc. W.H.S.*, Vol. XVIII, p. 26.
[2] *Journal*, Vol. IV, p. 268. 28th June, 1758.
[3] *Ibid.*, Vol. V, p. 14. 25th May, 1763.

as valuable as the Roman roads of the first century for spreading the good news of Jesus the Crucified. By means of them the Word of the Lord had free course and was glorified."[1]

[1] Rattenbury, *op. cit.*, p. 103.

CHAPTER XVIII

AN HONOURABLE MAN

"I PREACHED again at Allhallows Church morning and afternoon. I found great liberty of spirit; and the congregation seemed to be much affected. How is this? Do I yet please men? Is the offence of the Cross ceased? It seems, after being scandalous for nearly fifty years, I am at length growing into *an honourable man! Journal* 6: 137.

IT WAS ON SUNDAY THE 26TH JANUARY, 1777, THAT JOHN WESLEY occupied the pulpit at the church of All Hallows, in Lombard Street, London, and was led to comment on the fact that he now seemed to have developed into "an honourable man."[1] The Rector was Thomas Broughton, one of his colleagues in the Holy Club at Oxford, who in addition to his parochial duties had rendered distinguished service since 1743 as the secretary of the Society for the Promotion of Christian Knowledge.[2] He died in December of the same year. No doubt it was this previous link which made it possible for Wesley to preach in Broughton's church both in 1776 and 1777.[3] It was the first time he had been there since 1735, as a last minute substitute for Dr. John Heylin, who failed to appear.[4] From 1776 onwards we find him here several times. Obviously, there had been a change of attitude towards him.

This ties in with other evidence at this period. Gradually the prejudice against him began to subside. Persecution virtually ceased. The violence of the mob was no longer hurled at his person. Even those in high places in Church and State realized that Wesley was not the fanatic his detractors had made him out to be, and that his contribution to the spiritual recovery of the land had been notable. We may date this improvement in what we nowadays call public relations from approximately 1770. The last twenty years of his life were comparatively free from serious interference, although the literary campaign against him was unabated, and indeed reached a new intensity.[5] As Richard Green remarked, "his influence in the kingdom had become very great, so that his periodical visits were seasons of great interest, and created no little excitement in many parts of

[1] *Journal*, Vol. VI, p. 137. 26th January, 1777.
[2] Tyerman, *Oxford Methodists*, pp. 349, 359. Broughton was appointed Lecturer at All Hallows in 1741 and Rector in 1755.
[3] *Journal*, Vol. VI, p. 96. 28th January, 1776.
[4] See above, p. 52, n.2
[5] Albert M. Lyles, *Methodism Mocked* (1960), pp. 18–19.

the country. The churches, too, were gradually recognizing the greatness of his service in the interests of religion throughout the land. Not only had antagonism to a great degree died down, but even honours were being conferred upon him. He was made a Burgess of Perth, and the Freedom of Arbroath was granted to him. But what he prized more was the opening of the churches to him, which was not merely a token of respect, but a sign of a great change in the spirit of the clergy, and the first indication of that gracious revival of religion within the Church as a whole which the last century was permitted to witness."[1]

A paragraph from *Lloyd's Evening Post* for the 20th January, 1772, reflected this more appreciative estimate of Wesley. A section of the *Journal* had recently been published, and was favourably reviewed. "In this interval, between 27th May, 1765, and 5th May, 1768, this zealous and truly laborious missionary of the Methodists, who seems to consider the three kingdoms as his parochial cure, twice traverses the greater part of Ireland and Scotland, from Londonderry to Cork, from Aberdeen to Dumfries, besides making a progress, chiefly on horseback (in many places more than once), through the great part of Wales, and almost all the counties in England, from Newcastle to Southampton, from Dover to Penzance. Those who expect to find in this *Journal* only the peculiar tenets of Methodism will be agreeably disappointed, as they are intermixed with such occasional reflections on men and manners, on polite literature, and even on polite places, as prove that the writer is endued with a taste well cultivated by reading and observation; and above all with such a benevolence and sweetness of temper, such an enlarged, liberal, and truly Protestant way of thinking towards those who differ from him, as clearly show that *his heart*, at least, is right, and justly entitle him to that candour and forbearance, which, for the honour of our common religion, we are glad to find he now generally receives."[2]

It was in 1777 that the foundation stone of the new chapel at City Road was laid, and preaching on this occasion Wesley permitted himself a review of his ministry and the astonishing advance of the revival. It was factors like these which could not be ignored, and which account for the revised attitude to Wesley on the part of those who were formerly unsympathetic. "This revival of religion has spread to such a degree, as neither we nor our fathers had known. How *extensive* has it been! There is scarce a considerable town in the kingdom, where some have not been made witnesses of it. It has spread to every age and sex, to most orders and degrees of men; and even to abundance of those who, in time past, were accounted monsters of wickedness. . . . We may likewise observe the *depth* of the work so extensively and swiftly wrought. Multitudes have

---

[1] R. Green, *op. cit.*, pp. 491–492. Cf. *Journal* Vol. V, p. 456, 28th April, 1772, p. 458 6th May, 1772.

[2] *Lloyd's Evening Post*, 20th January, 1772. Cf. R. Green, *op. cit.*, p. 492.

been thoroughly convinced of sin; and, shortly after, so filled with joy and love, that whether they were in the body, or out of the body, they could hardly tell; and, in the power of this love, they have trampled under foot whatever the world accounts either terrible or desirable, having evidenced, in the severest trials, an invariable and tender goodwill to mankind, and all the fruits of holiness. Now, so deep a repentance, so strong a faith, so fervent love, and so unblemished holiness, wrought in so many persons in so short a time, the world has not seen for many ages."[1]

Later in the same significant discourse, Wesley touched on another feature of his ministry which contributed to the welcome reappraisal of his work. As we have seen, Wesley had always tried to keep faith with the Church of England in which he had been ordained, and his desire was to reform and awaken that existing body. At certain points, where the urgency of his mission required it, he sat loose to some of the conventions of Anglicanism, but, whilst many of his followers never really regarded themselves as bound to the national Church, he himself remained a staunch loyalist, despite his association with Dissenters. We have noted how careful he was to attend the parish church when he could, and to co-operate with the clergy wherever they were ready to co-operate with him. Even when there were few of his fellow-ministers to stand with him, he nevertheless refused to abandon the Church of England to its fate. His aim was to revive it rather than to reject it.

This wise, long-term policy ultimately brought its rewards. The eighteenth-century awakening not only created Methodist societies up and down the land, but also affected the Church as a whole, so that by the end of Wesley's life evangelical influence, if not predominant, was exceptionally strong.[2] In a large measure, Wesley's personal fidelity to the Church opened the way for the years of recognition, not only with respect to his own societies, but to the Evangelicals within the parishes too.

In his sermon at the City Road stone-laying, Wesley dwelt on this feature at some length. It is so crucial that the passage must be quoted in full. "It may throw considerable light upon the nature of this work, to mention one circumstance more, attending the present revival of religion, which, I apprehend, is quite peculiar to it. I do not remember to have either seen, heard, or read of any thing parallel. It cannot be denied that there have been several considerable revivals of religion in England since the Reformation. But the generality of the English nation were little profitted thereby; because they that were the subjects of those revivals, preachers as well as people, soon separated from the Established Church, and formed themselves into a distinct sect. So did the Presbyterians first;

[1] *Works*, Vol. VII, pp. 425–426. Sermon CXXXII.
[2] Elliott-Binns, *op. cit.*, pp. 446–457.

afterwards, the Independents, the Anabaptists, and the Quakers. And after this was done, they did scarce any good, except to their own little body. As they chose to separate from the Church, so the people remaining therein separated from them, and generally contracted a prejudice against them. But these were immensely the greatest number; so that, by that unhappy separation, the hope of a general, national reformation was totally cut off.

"But it is not so in the present revival of religion. The Methodists (so termed) know their calling. They weighed the matter at first, and, upon mature deliberation, determined to continue in the Church. Since that time, they have not wanted temptations of every kind to alter their resolution. They have heard abundance said upon the subject, perhaps all that can be said. They have read the writings of the most eminent pleaders for separation, both in the last and present century. They have spent several days in a General Conference upon this very question, 'Is it *expedient* (supposing, not granting, that it is *lawful*) to separate from the Established Church?' But still they could see no sufficient cause to depart from their first resolutions. So that their fixed purpose is, let the clergy or laity use them well or ill, by the grace of God to endure all things, to hold on their even course, and to continue in the Church, maugré men or devils, unless God permits them to be thrust out."[1]

Although we may conveniently take the year 1770 as a turning-point in the general attitude to Wesley within the Church, and beyond, there was nevertheless no dramatic change-over, and for some time before this signs of amelioration were discernible. As early as 1747 Wesley could write from Cornwall, where he had met with rough treatment in the past: "We came to St. Ives before morning prayers, and walked to church without so much as one huzza. How strangely has one year changed the scene in Cornwall! This is now a peaceable, nay, an honourable station. They give us good words almost in every place. What have we done, that the world should be so civil to us?"[2] There were, in fact, extenuating circumstances to explain the vigorous reaction to Wesley on his earlier visits to Cornwall. As Canon Colliss Davies reminds us: "The time coincided with the arrival of the Young Pretender in England, and more than once John Wesley himself, or one of his followers, was mistaken for the usurper. It was not unnatural that appeals to the degraded miners should have been regarded as attempts to sow sedition among those most likely in any case to be discontented with their living conditions. The rioting which John Wesley encountered at Falmouth, for example, was directly attributable to fear of the young Prince Charles."[3] The unfriendly clerics were few, and in the group which gathered round Samuel Walker of Truro the

---

[1] *Works*, Vol. VII, pp. 427–428. Sermon CXXXII.
[2] *Journal*, Vol. III, p. 305. 30th July, 1747.
[3] G. C. B. Davies, *The Early Cornish Evangelicals 1735–1760* (1951), p. 27.

revival found true supporters, though not all favoured the Methodist societies as such.[1]

In the following year, Wesley was back at St. Bartholomew the Great in London, and was able to report: "How strangely is the scene changed! What laughter and tumult was there, among the best of the parish, when we preached in a London church ten years ago! And now all are calm and quietly attentive, from the least even to the greatest."[2] Actually, Wesley had preached three times at St. Bartholomew in 1747, and this was his second appearance in 1748.[3] The incumbent, Richard Thomas Bateman, who had received Wesley in 1738, had since then undergone an evangelical conversion through the ministry of Howell Davies in Wales, and as a result became an active coadjutor of Wesley and Whitefield. This evidently offended some of the parish officials, for the churchwardens complained to Edmund Gibson, Bishop of London, on the score that their Rector invited Wesley to preach at St. Bartholomew. The Bishop replied, "And what would you have me do? I have no right to hinder him. Mr. Wesley is a clergyman regularly ordained and under no ecclesiastical censure."[4] This was the only parish church in London which received Wesley until a much later period.

Even at Oxford, Wesley found the tension eased. "I was much surprised, wherever I went, at the civility of the people—gentlemen as well as others," he noted in 1751. "There was no pointing, no calling of names, as once; no, nor even laughter. What can this mean? Am I become a servant of men? Or is the scandal of the Cross ceased?"[5] But he was never again asked to preach before the University, or in any church in the city. The expulsion of six undergraduates from St. Edmund Hall in 1768, on a charge that they were enthusiasts "who talked of regeneration, inspiration, and drawing nigh unto God," was not calculated to further the evangelical cause in Oxford either amongst town or gown.[6] "Whatever the Wesleys may have done towards the reformation of morals," observed A. D. Godley, "they certainly had not broadened the sympathies of Oxford Heads of Houses."[7] Wesley was no longer harried: it can hardly be said that he was cherished.

In the north, too, there were some indications that the storm was abat-

[1] Professor Davies names Hoblyn of St. Ives, Borlase of Madron, and Symonds of Lelant as the most inimical (op. cit., p. 28).

[2] Journal, Vol. III, p. 356. 15th June, 1748.

[3] Ibid., p. 300. 31st May, 1747; p. 301. 4th June, 1747; p. 302. 21st June, 1747; p. 355. 12th December, 1748.

[4] Letters, Vol. III, p. 132. To the Bishop of London, 23rd June, 1755. This was a letter to the then Bishop, Dr. Thomas Sherlock, reminding him of Gibson's toleration. Sherlock was Bishop from 1748 to 1761.

[5] Journal, Vol. III, pp. 511–512. 31st January, 1751.

[6] J. S. Reynolds, The Evangelicals at Oxford (1735–1871) (1953), pp. 34–40; S. L. Ollard, The Six Students of St. Edmund Hall (1911).

[7] A. D. Godley, Oxford in the Eighteenth Century (1908), p. 275.

ing. "Who would have expected to see me preaching in Wakefield Church to so attentive a congregation a few years ago," Wesley wrote in 1752, "when all the people were as roaring lions, and the honest man (*i.e.*, Francis Scott) did not dare to let me preach in his yard lest the mob should pull down his houses!"[1] This parish church which accepted him would be All Saints, now the cathedral. The incumbent was Benjamin Wilson, who had been instituted the previous year.

Although such early signs as these appeared that the situation was beginning to alter, it was not until the last two decades of Wesley's life that the improvement was marked. This was particularly noticeable in the London area. In 1783 Wesley could exclaim: "The tide has now turned; so that I have more invitations to preach in churches than I can accept of."[2] He returned to several pulpits where he had been in 1738 and 1739, prior to his exclusion: such as St. Antholin; St. Clement Dane; Christ Church, Spitalfields; St. Helen, Bishopsgate Street; St. John, Clerkenwell; St. John, Wapping; St. Luke, Old Street; St. Paul, Shadwell; and St. Swithin, London Stone.[3] Other churches opened to him for the first time: St. Matthew, Bethnal Green; St. Dunstan and All Saints, Stepney; St. Ethelburgha; St. George, Southwark; St. John, Horsleydown; St. Leonard, Shoreditch; St. Margaret Pattens; St. Paul, Covent Garden; St. Peter upon Cornhill; St. Sepulchre, Holborn; St. Thomas, Southwark; and St. Vedast, Foster Lane.[4]

[1] *Journal*, Vol. IV, p. 18. 12th April, 1752. Cf. Vol. VI. 24th April, 1774.

[2] *Ibid.*, Vol. VI, p. 387. 19th January, 1783. Cf. Vol. VIII, p. 34. 27th December, 1789. "So the tables are turned and I have now more invitations to preach in churches than I can accept of."

[3] St. Antholin, *ibid.*, Vol. VI, p. 217. 15th November, 1778; St. Clement Dane, p. 377. 24th November, 1782; Christ Church, Spitalfields, Vol. VII, p. 52. 20th February, 1785; St. Helen, Vol. VIII, p. 38. 17th January, 1790. St. John, Clerkenwell, Vol. VII, p. 348. 16th December, 1787; St. John, Wapping, Vol. VI, p. 302. 14th January, 1781; p. 340. 18th December, 1781; St. Luke, Old Street, Vol. VI, p. 217. 29th November, 1778; Vol. VII, p. 127. 27th November, 1785; Vol. VIII, p. 34. 27th December, 1785. St. Paul, Shadwell, Vol. VI, p. 177. 14th December, 1777; p. 261. 24th November, 1779; Vol. VII, p. 28. 24th October, 1784; Vol. VIII, p. 110. 24th October, 1790; St. Swithin, London Stone, Vol. VI, p. 340. 2nd December, 1781; p. 387. 19th January, 1783; p. 465. 14th December, 1783; p. 466. 21st December, 1783; p. 473. 8th February, 1784; Vol. VII, p. 131. 18th December, 1785; p. 237. 21st January, 1787.

[4] St. Matthew, Bethnal Green, *ibid.*, Vol. VI, p. 83. 12th November, 1755; Vol. VII, p. 126. 20th November, 1785; p. 420. 27th August, 1788; Vol. VIII, p. 115. 5th December, 1790. St. Dunstan and All Saints, Stepney, Vol. VII, p. 53. 27th February, 1785; St. Ethelburgha, Vol. VII, p. 52. 20th February, 1785; St. George, Southwark, Vol. VI, p. 473. 25th January, 1784; p. 475. 8th February, 1784; St. John, Horsleydown, Vol. VII, p. 141. 19th February, 1786; St. Leonard, Shoreditch, Vol. VII, p. 125. 13th November, 1785; St. Margaret Pattens, Vol. VI, pp. 174-175. 16th November, 1777; p. 217. 29th November, 1778; St. Paul, Covent Garden, Vol. VII, p. 34. 28th November, 1784; St. Peter upon Cornhill, Vol. VI, p. 223. 28th March, 1779; p. 264. 28th December, 1779; p. 268. 4th February, 1780; St. Sepulchre, Holborn, Vol. VI, p. 221. 25th December, 1778; St. Thomas (Southwark?), Vol. VI, p. 387. 19th January, 1783; St. Vedast, Vol. VI, p. 130. 10th November, 1776.

The situation was similarly encouraging in Bristol. After 1770 we find Wesley at St. Werburgh, where Richard Symes was incumbent; at St. James, Barton; and at St. Mark, College Green—the Mayor's Chapel.[1] But most frequently Wesley preached at the Temple Church, which he described as "the most beautiful and the most ancient in Bristol."[2] This double superlative has been queried, for St. James is certainly the most ancient and St. Mary Redcliffe generally regarded as the most beautiful. Wesley's comments on the worship at the Temple Church are of interest. "The congregation here is remarkably well-behaved; indeed, so are the parishioners in general. And no wonder, since they have had such a succession of rectors as few parishes in England have had. The present incumbent truly fears God. So did his predecessor, Mr. Catcott, who was indeed as eminent for piety as most clergymen in England."[3] Further back in the line was "Mr. Arthur Bedford, a person greatly esteemed fifty or sixty years ago for piety as well as learning."[4]

Up in the north, the scene was changing, too. Wesley was able not only to communicate at the parish church of Epworth, but also to conduct the service and deliver the sermon.[5] Sir William Anderson was Rector from 1757 to 1784, and was succeeded in the incumbency (and the baronetcy) by his son, Charles.[6] The curate was Joshua Gibson, who was not too keen on having a Methodist in the pulpit, but who was overruled by the explicit command of the Rector.[7] Wesley's entry in the *Journal* for the 6th July, 1788 shows how his own attachment to the Church of England could not compel his followers to copy his example. There were scarcely twenty communicants, half of whom he had brought. He was told that barely fifty attended the Sunday services in normal circumstances. "I would fain prevent the members here from leaving the church; but I cannot do it. As Mr. G(ibson) is not a pious man, but rather an enemy to piety, who frequently preaches against the truth, and those who hold and love it, I cannot with all my influence persuade them either to hear him, or to attend the sacrament administered by him. If I cannot carry this point even while I live, who then can do it when I die? And the case of Epworth is the case

---

[1] *Ibid.*, Vol. VI, p. 140. 16th March, 1777; Vol. V, p. 425. 4th August, 1771; p. 430. 15th September, 1771; Vol. VII, pp. 362–363. 16th March, 1788.

[2] *Ibid.*, Vol. VI, p. 340. 2nd December, 1781; p. 387. 19th January, 1783; p. 465. 14th December, 1783; p. 466. 21st December, 1783; p. 475. 8th February, 1784; Vol. VII, p. 131. 18th December, 1785; p. 237. 21st January, 1787; p. 333. 14th October, 1787.

[3] *Ibid.*, Vol. VII, p. 305. 18th March, 1781. "The present incumbent" was Joseph Easterbrook, educated at Kingswood School before going to Emmanuel College, Cambridge. He was Vicar of Holy Cross (or Temple as it was known) from 1779 to his death.

[4] *Ibid.* Cf. n. 3. *Proc. W.H.S.*, Vol. III, pp. 157–158.

[5] *Journal*, Vol. VI, p. 287. 25th June, 1780.

[6] *Proc. W.H.S.*, Vol. V, p. 204.

[7] *Journal*, Vol. VI, p. 287. 25th June, 1780.

of every church where the minister neither loves nor preaches the gospel.
The Methodists will not attend his ministrations. What then is to be
done?"[1] We can see here the factors which ultimately compelled seces-
sion. Although Wesley himself continued to display a firm adherence to
the Anglican Church, and exhorted his disciples to do the same, if that
was where their original association lay, yet he must have been aware that a
break was bound to come. As we have seen, he was convinced in principle
that the fruits of the revival could best be preserved within the framework
of the national Church. But where in practice, as in the instance of Epworth, the good of souls was best served otherwise, he could hardly
object. In the last analysis, it was the spiritual welfare of his converts
which determined the issue.

Wesley's relationship with official Anglicanism eased somewhat with
the passing of the years. In the pioneering period, he had amicable but in-
conclusive conversations both with the Archbishop of Canterbury (John
Potter) and the Bishop of London (Edmund Gibson).[2] The former
"showed us great affection," according to Charles Wesley; "spoke
mildly of Mr. Whitefield; cautioned us to give no more umbrage than
was necessary for our own defence; to forbear exceptional phrases; to
keep to the doctrines of the Church."[3] The latter inquired more precisely
what they taught about assurance, admitted that the religious societies
could not be classed as conventicles (since these, as distinct from the
Methodist societies, were not open to Dissenters), and assured them that
they could have free access to him at all times.[4] We have already taken
notice of John Wesley's protracted correspondence with the mysterious
"John Smith," who is generally assumed to have been Thomas Secker,
then Bishop of Oxford, and later Archbishop of Canterbury.[5] He had
been educated at a Dissenting Academy and had been an occasional
preacher in the Dissenters' meeting houses before offering for orders in the
Established Church. It might have been imagined that, with this background, Secker might have understood something of Wesley's dilemma
with regard to the irregularity (as some held it) of his own intrusion into
other men's parishes, and of his use of unordained helpers. But in his
letters he did not betray even a hint of his previous connexion with Dissent. Secker was perhaps the one man on the episcopal bench who might
have grasped what Wesley was about, but apparently he failed to do so.[6]

---

[1] *Ibid.*, Vol. VII, p. 414. 6th July, 1788.

[2] *Ibid.*, Vol. II, p. 143. 21st February, 1739 and n. 1; p. 94. 20th October, 1738;
C. Wesley, *Journal*, Vol. I, p. 133.

[3] C. Wesley, *Journal*, Vol. I, p. 133.

[4] *Ibid.*

[5] See above, p. 102.

[6] Simon, *Methodist Societies*, pp. 272–280. Dr. Simon contrasted the narrow-
mindedness of "John Smith" with the breadth of Secker's *Lectures on the Church
Catechism* (1769), and was led to question the generally accepted identification.

Wesley's later contacts with the episcopate were uniformly happy. On the 24th November, 1777, he spent the afternoon with the newly-appointed Bishop of London, Robert Lowth. He was Professor of Poetry at Oxford, and had been transferred from that see. "His whole behaviour was worthy of a Christian bishop," declared Wesley, "—easy, affable, courteous; and yet all his conversation spoke the dignity which was suitable to his character."[1] One incident, however, Wesley's modesty preventing him from relating. On going in to dinner, the Bishop refused to sit above Wesley at the table. With real emotion he added, "Mr. Wesley, may I be found at your feet in another world!" Wesley declined the higher seat until the Bishop requested that, as a favour, Wesley would occupy it, because his hearing was bad and he did not wish to miss a word of what the evangelist said.[2] Nothing more movingly indicates the honour in which Wesley was now held than this story. It also serves to remind us that the Georgian bishops were not as black as they have sometimes been painted.

Sunday, the 18th November, 1782, saw Wesley in Exeter yet again. He worshipped at the cathedral and was pleased both with the behaviour of the congregation and the fine music at the post-communion.[3] The organist at this time was William Jackson, whose setting of the *Te Deum* in F is so well known. The Bishop, John Ross, invited Wesley to the Palace for dinner. Wesley approved of the plain but sufficient food and the simple furniture. He also marked the propriety of the company, consisting of five clergymen and four aldermen, and "the genuine, unaffected courtesy of the bishop, who, I hope, will be a blessing to his whole diocese."[4] Twenty years before Wesley had rejoiced to partake of the Lord's Supper in Exeter Cathedral with his old opponent, George Lavington, who was then Bishop.[5] "Oh may we sit down together in the kingdom of our Father!" was his prayer.[6]

On the 21st March, 1787, Wesley "had the satisfaction of spending an hour" with the Bishop of Gloucester, Samuel Hallifax, whom he believed to be a sensible, candid and pious man.[7] Hallifax had been a Professor at Cambridge and had already showed himself sympathetic to the revival.[8] One of Wesley's friends was William Barnard, Bishop of Londonderry, formerly Dean of Rochester. It was he who ordained Thomas Maxfield in 1762 to be an associate evangelist with Wesley. "Sir, I ordain you to assist that good man," the Bishop had told Maxfield, "that he may not

---

[1] *Journal*, Vol. VI, pp. 175–176. 24th November, 1777. It was through Ebenezer Blackwell that the meeting took place. His second wife, Mary (*née* Eden), was a niece of Mrs. Lowth.

[2] Thomas Jackson, *The Centenary of Wesleyan Methodism* (1839), p. 201.

[3] *Journal*, Vol. VI, p. 365. 18th November, 1782.   [4] *Ibid.*

[5] *Ibid.*, Vol. IV, p. 527. 29th September, 1762.   [6] *Ibid.*

[7] *Ibid.*, Vol. VII, pp. 250–251. 21st March, 1787.

[8] Cf. A. Skevington Wood, *Thomas Haweis (1734–1820)* (1957), pp. 147, 154–155.

work himself to death."[1] Dr. Barnard retired to Bath, and there became friendly with the Countess of Huntingdon. He was one of those who on occasion occupied the curtained seats just inside the door of her chapel, reserved for the distinguished visitors who wished to preserve their incognito when attending such a place of worship.[2]

Civic as well as ecclesiastical leaders were now eager to greet Wesley. At Bristol, the mayor invited him to preach in his chapel, and then to dine with him at the Mansion House. Most of the aldermen were present in the congregation. Wesley seized the opportunity to expound the story of Dives and Lazarus.[3] At Macclesfield the Mayor invited Wesley to join him in procession to the parish church: he was John Ryle, grandfather of Bishop J. C. Ryle.[4] At Newark he was due to preach in the new meeting house at five p.m. when the mayor sent a message asking him to postpone the start until he and a number of his aldermanic colleagues had arrived.[5] The mayor of Cork took Wesley round the municipal buildings and also the poor-house.[6] In Guernsey Wesley and Coke dined with the Governor.[7] The first Methodist mayor was William Parker of Bedford, who was also a local preacher.[8]

Whilst we can rejoice that as the last years of his life were reached, Wesley was held in increasing honour, not only amongst his own societies, but both in Church and State, we must not forget that he remained a travelling evangelist to the end. He did not give up open-air preaching when the churches invited him inside. He contrived to maintain both types of ministry. The end came while he was still in harness. To his last breath, John Wesley was a missioner to the masses.

Although the years of recognition must have brought him pleasure, and eased his task, he was never tempted to trust in the approbation of men. Just before he died, he confided to Joseph Bradford: "I have been wandering up and down between fifty and sixty years, endeavouring in my poor way, to do a little good to my fellow-creatures; and now it is probable that there are but a few steps between me and death; and what have I to trust to for salvation? I can see nothing that I have done or suffered that will bear looking at. I have no other plea than this:

> I the chief of sinners am,
> But Jesus died for me."[9]

---

[1] Moore, *op cit.*, Vol. II, p. 218.
[2] Seymour, *op. cit.*, Vol. I, pp. 477 n., 478 n.
[3] *Journal*, Vol. VII, p. 463. 16th March, 1788. The church was St. Mark, College Green.
[4] *Ibid.*, Vol. VII, p. 14. 3rd April, 1774.
[5] *Ibid.*, Vol. VII, p. 240. 11th February, 1787.
[6] *Ibid.*, pp. 274–275. 12th May, 1787.
[7] *Ibid.*, p. 314. 18th August, 1787.
[8] *Ibid.*, Vol. VII, p. 35. 30th December, 1784, and n. 2.
[9] Moore, *op. cit.*, Vol. II, p. 389.

PART III
THE MESSAGE OF AN EVANGELIST

CHAPTER XIX

THE ONLY STANDARD OF TRUTH

"I BEGAN not only to read, but to study, the Bible, as the one, *the only standard of truth*, and the only model of pure religion." *Works* 11: 367.

"THE FIRST AXIOM OF EFFECTIVE EVANGELISM," ACCORDING TO Prof. James S. Stewart of Edinburgh, "is that the evangelist must be sure of his message. Any haziness or hesitation there is fatal."[1] John Wesley emerges from an examination on this count with first-class honours. No man could have been more certain of what he had to say, for it was burned into his mind and heart in dramatic personal experience. As we saw whilst we traced the several stages in the making of an evangelist, Wesley's pilgrimage before 1738 was leading him towards the discovery of his message—in existential terms as well as intellectual. It was not until he had laid hold of the gospel because the gospel had laid hold of him, that he was ready for his mission.

Before we proceed, in the remaining chapters, to consider the content of Wesley's evangelistic proclamation, we must start by noting its source. Wesley was a biblical preacher *par excellence*. What he had to declare to the paganized masses of the people was not a human theory, but a divine revelation. His message was not from below but from above. It did not represent the latest theological innovation, but the everlasting and unalterable truth of God. Although its language and application were geared to the outlook of the age, its core was the timeless offer of redemption in Christ. Wesley's message was taken straight from the authoritative record of salvation-history to be found in the pages of Holy Writ. He was not ashamed to be known as a Bible preacher. This, indeed, was the secret of his effectiveness.

On the 2nd of November, 1772, Wesley went by chaise to Bury St. Edmunds. There he expounded the Word to "a little cold company," with 1 Corinthians 13 as his chosen chapter. This love was what the congregation lacked, so he revealed in his *Journal*, although they did not like to be told so. "But I cannot help that," he added characteristically. "I must declare just what I find in the Book."[2] That was his invariable principle. As a preacher he never departed from his brief. He knew that his commission was to unfold the whole counsel of God. Like P. T. Forsyth

[1] James S. Stewart, *A Faith to Proclaim* (1953), p. 12.
[2] *Journal*, Vol. V, p. 488. 2nd November, 1772.

after him, he recognized the Bible as "the one Enchiridion of the preacher still."[1] It was at once the source of his message and the criterion by which all teaching was to be judged.

In *A Short History of Methodism* (1765), Wesley showed how soon the Bible became central in his thinking. It was so even before his conversion, and was the means of bringing him to that transforming experience. As leader of the Holy Club at Oxford, he had already begun to take the Scriptures as his guide. These men who first bore the nickname of Methodist, he explained, were all zealous members of the Church of England and tenacious not only of her doctrines but also of her discipline. They were similarly scrupulous in their observance of the University statutes, for conscience' sake. "But they observed neither these nor anything else further than they conceived it was bound upon them by their one book, the Bible; it being their one desire and design to be downright Bible Christians; taking the Bible, as interpreted by the primitive Church and our own, for their whole and sole rule."[2] In *A Plain Account of Christian Perfection* (1766), Wesley fixed on the year 1729 as the time when he "began not only to read, but to study, the Bible, as the one, the only standard of truth, and the only model of pure religion."[3]

Those who stood with Wesley from the start of his mission in 1738 were described by him as "of one heart, as well as of one judgement, resolved to be Bible Christians at all events; and, wherever they were, to preach with all their might plain, old, Bible Christianity."[4] This emphasis on the fact that Wesley and his colleagues sought above all else to be Bible Christians was reiterated in succeeding paragraphs.[5] Wesley went out of his way to make it clear that the basis of his work from the beginning was the Word of God. It was by accepting this standard that he himself had entered into the knowledge of salvation, and it was from this fountain that he derived all his refreshing, soul-converting messages. The sermons which changed a nation came straight from the Book of books.

This was one of the primary reasons why the Puritans appealed so much to Wesley when he turned to their writings, as Dr. J. A. Newton brings out. He commended them because "next to God Himself, they honour His Word. They are men mighty in the Scriptures, equal to any of those who went before them, and far superior to most that have followed them. They prove all things hereby. Their continual appeal is, 'To the law and to the testimony.' Nor do they easily form a judgement of a thing, till they have weighed it in the balance of the sanctuary."[6] In his refusal to recognize any other norm of truth than Scripture, Wesley stood clearly in the

---

[1] Peter Taylor Forsyth, *Positive Preaching and the Modern Mind* (1907), p. 38.
[2] *Works*, Vol. VIII, p. 348. *A Short History of Methodism* (1765).
[3] *Ibid.*, Vol. XI, p. 367. *A Plain Account of Christian Perfection* (1766).
[4] *Ibid.*, Vol. VIII, p. 349. *A Short History of Methodism* (1765).   [5] *Ibid.*, p. 350.
[6] *Christian Library*, Vol. IV, p. 107. Cf. J. A. Newton, *op. cit.*, p. 12.

line of the Puritans and the Reformers. When he spoke of the Bible being interpreted by the tradition of the primitive Church and of the Anglican communion, he was not suggesting a rival or even a collateral standard of judgement. He was rather expressing the view that in point of fact the best tradition had indeed ranged itself on the side of Scripture, and not over against it.

Wesley rejoiced to depict himself as "a man of one book." He used the phrase elsewhere, but its most significant occurrence was in the Preface to his *Sermons*. In a passage which is full of autobiographical echoes, Wesley put himself in the place of the seeker after truth. "I am a spirit come from God, and returning to God: just hovering over the great gulf; till, a few moments hence, I am no more seen; I drop into an unchangeable eternity! I want to know one thing—the way to heaven; how to land safe on that happy shore. God Himself has condescended to teach the way; for this very end He came from heaven. He hath written it down in a book. O give me that book! At any price, give me the book of God! I have it: here is knowledge enough for me. Let me be *homo unius libri*."[1]

Then Wesley went on to show how that one Book was used. "Here then I am, far from the busy ways of men. I sit down alone: only God is here. In His presence I open, I read His book; for this end, to find the way to heaven. Is there a doubt concerning the meaning of what I read? Does anything appear dark and intricate? I lift up my heart to the Father of Lights: 'Lord, is it not Thy word, "If any man lack wisdom, let him ask of God"? Thou "givest liberally and upbraidest not." Thou hast said, "If any be willing to do Thy will, he shall know." I am willing to do, let me know Thy will.' I then search after and consider parallel passages of Scripture, 'comparing spiritual things with spiritual.' I meditate thereon with all the attention and earnestness of which my mind is capable. If any doubt still remains, I consult those who are experienced in the things of God; and then the writings whereby, being dead, they yet speak. And what I thus learn, that I teach."[2]

This was how Wesley received his message. No passage could be more explicit than what has just been quoted. It lets us into the holy of holies. Here we see the secret of an evangelist's power and persuasiveness. To borrow another arresting phrase from Forsyth, the effective preacher "must speak from within the silent sanctuary of Scripture."[3] That was always Wesley's way. Those who heard him sensed immediately that here was a man who had been with God and who now came to them with

---

[1] *Sermons*, Vol. I, pp. 31–32. Preface. *Homo unius libri*—"a man of one book." Cf. *Works*, Vol. VII, p. 203, Sermon CVII, God's Vineyard; Vol. XI, p. 373. *A Plain Account of Christian Perfection* (1766); *Letters*, Vol. IV, p. 219. To John Newton 14th May, 1765; *Proc. W.H.S.*, Vol. V, p. 50.
[2] *Sermons*, Vol. I, p. 32. Preface.
[3] Forsyth, *op. cit.*, p. 38.

His message. Only preaching of that supernatural calibre could have
produced the results which Wesley saw.

Wesley's objective was disclosed in the next paragraph from the Preface: "I have accordingly set down in the following sermons what I find
in the Bible concerning the way to heaven; with a view to distinguish this
way of God from all those which are the inventions of men. I have endeavoured to describe the true, the scriptural, experimental religion, so as
to omit nothing which is a real part thereof, and to add nothing thereto
which is not."[1] "What I find in the Bible"—that was Wesley's sole concern. Not that he read nothing else, but that he assessed all else by this. The
Bible was his constant yardstick. "My ground is the Bible," he declared.
"Yea, I am a Bible bigot. I follow it in all things, both great and small."[2]
"The Scriptures are the touchstone whereby Christians examine all, real
or supposed, revelations," he explained. "In all cases they appeal 'to the
law and testimony,' and try every spirit thereby."[3] "Receive nothing un-
tried, nothing till it is weighed in the balance of the sanctuary," he advised:
"believe nothing they say, unless it is clearly confirmed by plain passages
of holy writ. Wholly reject whatsoever differs therefrom, whatever is not
confirmed thereby. And, in particular, reject, with the utmost abhorrence,
whatsoever is described as the way of salvation, that is either different
from, or short of, the way our Lord has marked out."[4]

Wesley was content that his preaching should stand or fall by the test of
Scripture. If anyone could show that what he said was contrary to revelation, he was quite prepared to alter it. "I trust, whereinsoever I have mistaken, my mind is open to conviction. I sincerely desire to be better informed. I say to God and man, 'What I know not, teach thou me!' Are
you persuaded that you see more clearly than me? It is not unlikely that
you may. Then treat me as you would desire to be treated upon a change
of circumstances. Point me out a better way than I have yet known.
Show me it is so, by plain proof of Scripture."[5] This was the only criterion
he was prepared to accept. He believed "the written Word of God to be
the only and sufficient rule both of Christian faith and practice."[6]

[1] *Sermons*, Vol. I, p. 32. Preface.
[2] *Journal*, Vol. V, p. 169. 5th June, 1766.
[3] *Letters*, Vol. II, p. 117. To Thomas Whitehead(?), 10th February, 1748; cf. Vol.
III, p. 172. To William Dodd, 12th March, 1756. "I try every Church and every
doctrine by the Bible."
[4] *Sermons*, Vol. II, p. 20. Sermon XXVII. Upon our Lord's Sermon on the Mount
XII.
[5] *Ibid.*, Vol. I, p. 33. Preface.
[6] *Works*, Vol. VIII, p. 340. *The Character of a Methodist* (1742). Cf. Vol. VII, p. 198,
Sermon CVI, On Faith: "The faith of the Protestants, in general, embraces only those
truths, as necessary to salvation, which are clearly revealed in the oracles of God.
Whatever is plainly declared in the Old and New Testament is the object of their
faith. They believe neither more nor less than what is manifestly contained in, and
provable by, the Holy Scriptures. The Word of God is 'a lantern to their feet, and a

In a letter to the anonymous "John Smith," on the 28th September, 1745, Wesley agreed with his correspondent that the ultimate appeal must always be to the Scriptures. The apostles substantiated their assertions from the sacred writings. "You and I are to do the same. Without such proof I ought no more to have believed St. Peter himself than St. Peter's (pretended) successor."[1] Then he added categorically: "I receive the written Word as the whole and sole rule of my faith."[2] So loyal was he to this axiom that he took care "always to express Scripture sense by Scripture phrase."[3] Writing to John Newton on the 1st April, 1766, Wesley said that he had told the Moravians: "The Bible is my standard of *language* as well as sentiment. I endeavour not only to think but to speak 'as the oracles of God.' "[4] He still kept to his "old way" and sought to "speak neither better nor worse than the Bible."[5]

In his sermon on "The Witness of our own Spirit," Wesley referred to the Word of God as "the Christian rule of right and wrong," and then defined it as "the writings of the Old and New Testament; all that the prophets and 'holy men of old' wrote 'as they were moved by the Holy Ghost;' all that Scripture which was 'given by inspiration of God' and which is indeed 'profitable for doctrine,' or teaching the whole will of God; 'for reproof' of what is contrary thereto; for 'correction' of error; and 'for instruction,' or training us up 'in righteousness' (II Timothy 3: 16)."[6] In the Preface to his *Notes on the New Testament* (1754) Wesley introduced the Bible in these terms: "Concerning the Scriptures in general, it may be observed, the Word of the living God, which directed the first patriarchs, also was, in the time of Moses, committed to writing. To this were added, in several succeeding generations, the inspired writings of the other prophets. Afterwards, what the Son of God preached, and the Holy Ghost spake by the apostles, the apostles and evangelists wrote. This is what we now style the Holy Scripture: this is that 'Word of God which remaineth for ever;' of which, though 'heaven and earth pass away, one jot or tittle shall not pass away.' "[7] For Wesley, "to preach Christ, is to preach what He hath revealed either in the Old or New Testament."[8]

Wesley held the Bible to be inspired in the fullest sense. It came to us

light in all their paths.' They dare not, on any pretence, go from it, to the right hand or to the left. The written Word is the whole and sole rule of their faith, as well as practice. They believe whatsoever God has declared, and profess to do whatsoever He hath commanded. This is the proper faith of Protestants: by this they will abide, and no other."
[1] *Letters*, Vol. II, p. 244. To "John Smith," 28th September, 1745.
[2] *Ibid.*
[3] *Ibid.*
[4] *Ibid.*, Vol. V, p. 8. To John Newton, 1st April, 1766.
[5] *Ibid.*
[6] *Sermons*, Vol. I, pp. 225-226. Sermon XI. The Witness of our own Spirit.
[7] John Wesley, *Explanary Notes upon the New Testament* (1754), Preface, para. 10.
[8] *Sermons*, Vol. II, p. 66. Sermon XXX. The Law Established by Faith.

in "words . . . taught by the Spirit" (I Corinthians 2: 13), not by human
wisdom. "Such are all the words of Scripture," commented Wesley.
"How high a regard ought we, then, to retain for them!"[1] He could insist
hat it was "the Holy Spirit who gave the Scripture," and that the words
were Spirit-dictated.[2] The authors were "purely passive" as they were
borne along by the Holy Ghost.[3] Wesley often referred to biblical passages
as being the words of the Spirit Himself.[4] The letters to the seven churches
of Asia in Revelation were dictated verbatim by the living Lord Jesus
Christ Himself.[5] John acted simply as His secretary. All this suggests that
Wesley's view of inspiration was static rather than dynamic, but, as Dr.
John Deschner argues, this verdict may require some modification.[6] Yet
whilst there may be room for further discussion as to how Wesley conceived the mode of inspiration, there can be no doubt as to what he took
to be the effect of inspiration. He received the Bible as from God Himself.
Beside it, all other literature faded into insignificance. "In the language of
the sacred writings we may observe the utmost depth, together with the
utmost ease. All the elegancies of human composures sink into nothing
before it; God speaks, not as man, but as God. His thoughts are very deep,
and thence His words are of inexhaustible virtue."[7]

It is evident that for Wesley inspiration extended not only to the general
content and concepts of revelation, but to the precise vocabulary. The
actual terminology of Scripture was accurately supplied by the Holy
Spirit. Hence Wesley could quote Luther with approval: "Divinity is
nothing but a grammar of the language of the Holy Ghost."[8] For this
reason "we should observe the emphasis which lies on every word."[9] Nothing can be discarded or denied. The words of God must not be treated
as if they are the words of men. " 'All Scripture is given by inspiration of
God,' " Wesley contended; "consequently, all Scripture is infallibly
true."[10] "If there be any mistakes in the Bible," he averred, "there may as
well be a thousand. If there be one falsehood in that book, it did not
come from the God of truth."[11] Hence "nothing which is written therein

---

[1] *Notes*, 1 Corinthians 2: 13.
[2] *Ibid.*, Galatians 3: 8; John 19: 24.
[3] *Ibid.*, 2 Peter 1: 21.
[4] *Sermons*, Vol. I, p. 250. Sermon XII, The Means of Grace: "The Holy Ghost
expressly declares"; *Notes*, Titus 1: 6—"Surely the Holy Ghost by repeating this so
often, designed to leave the Romanists without excuse;" Hebrews 3: 14—"A supposition made by the Holy Ghost is equal to the strongest assertion."
[5] *Notes*, Rev. 2: 1.
[6] John A. Deschner, *Wesley's Christology: An Interpretation* (1960), pp. 90, 110, n. 5.
[7] *Notes*, Preface, para. 12.
[8] *Ibid.*
[9] *Ibid.*
[10] *Sermons*, Vol. I, pp. 249–250. Sermon XII, The Means of Grace.
[11] *Journal*, Vol. VI, p. 117. 24th August, 1776. This was in answer to Soame Jenyns'
A view of the Internal Evidence of the Christian Religion (1756). Jenyns was one of the com-

can be censured or rejected."[1] "We may not, therefore, lay these expressions aside, seeing they are the words of God and not of man."[2] One of Wesley's favourite names for the Scriptures was to call them "the oracles of God."[3] We can only conclude, with Dr. Frank Baker, that, "Wesley was one with the Reformers in the tendency to substitute an infallible Book for an infallible Church."[4]

This fidelity to the principles of Protestantism is also reflected in Wesley's method of interpretation. His hermeneutical presuppositions were identical with those of Luther and Calvin. His basic insistence was on the primacy of the literal sense, which was one of the major gains of Reformed exegesis. His suspicion of mysticism arose from this prior conviction. "The general rule of interpreting Scripture is this," he told Samuel Furly: "the literal sense of every text is to be taken, if it be not contrary to some other texts; but in that case the obscure text is to be interpreted by those which speak more plainly."[5] The latter part of that quotation indicates Wesley's acceptance of a further axiom of Protestant hermeneutics, namely, that Scripture is its own best interpreter. "That is the true method of interpretation," asserted Luther, "which puts Scripture alongside of Scripture in a right and proper way."[6] *Scriptura sui ipsius interpres* was one of the Reformation slogans: Wesley was a convinced exponent of it.[7]

On the other hand, he was fully aware that, even where these principles are applied, human interpretations of the Bible will nevertheless be liable to variation. The seat of authority lies in the Word itself, not in any man-made glosses. "Nay, with regard to the holy Scriptures themselves, the best of men are liable to mistake, and do mistake day by day; especially

misioners of the Board of Trade who, after imbibing and promulgating rationalist principles, returned in some measure to the Christian faith. Wesley wrote: "He is undoubtedly a fine writer, but whether he is a Christian, Deist or Atheist I cannot tell. If he is a Christian, he betrays his own cause by averring that 'all Scripture is not given by inspiration of God, but the writers of it were sometimes left to themselves, and consequently made some mistakes' " (*ibid.*).

[1] *Notes*, John 10: 35.

[2] *Sermons*, Vol. II, p. 151. Sermon XXXV. Christian Perfection.

[3] *Journal*, Vol. II, p. 419. 28th January, 1741; *Sermons*, Vol I, p. 63. Sermon II, The Almost Christian; p. 245. Sermon XII, The Means of Grace; Vol. II, p. 96. Sermon XXXII, The Nature of Enthusiasm; p. 151. Sermon XXXV, Christian Perfection; p. 474. Sermon LI, The Good Steward; *Notes*, Romans 12: 6, *et al.*

[4] Frank Baker, "John Wesley's Churchmanship," *London Quarterly and Holborn Review*, October, 1960, p. 270.

[5] *Letters*, Vol III, p. 129. To Samuel Furly, 10th May, 1755. Cf. Vol. I, p. 234. To Lady Cox, 7th March, 1738: "We have no principles but those revealed in the Word of God; in the interpretation whereof we always judge the most literal sense to be the best, unless where the literal sense of one contradicts some other scripture."

[6] *Works of Martin Luther* (Philadelphia Edition), Vol. III (1930), p. 334. *Answer to Emser* (1521).

[7] *Works*, Vol. X, p. 483. *An Address to the Clergy* (1756); cf. p. 142, *Popery Calmly Considered* (1779); *Notes*, Romans. 12: 6.

with regard to those parts thereof which less immediately relate to practice. Hence, even the children of God are not agreed as to the interpretation of many places in holy writ; nor is their difference of opinion any
proof that they are not the children of God, on either side; but it is a proof
that we are no more to expect any living man to be infallible, than to be
omniscient."[1] This was the nub of Wesley's objection to Roman claims.
The Church of Rome, he declared, had no right to require anyone to
believe what she taught on her sole authority. The Pope was no more
infallible than any other believer. In every instance, the Church was to be
judged by the Scripture, and not the Scripture by the Church.[2]

This realization also helps to explain Wesley's attitude to current biblical scholarship. It must not be imagined that he retreated into some
obscurantist hide-out, and refused to open his mind to the access of new
knowledge. On the contrary, with the measuring-line of Scripture itself
in his hand, Wesley was ready to keep abreast with the most recent research. The Reformation had led to a remarkable renascence of biblical
studies: indeed it has been claimed that these were pursued in the previous
century with an intensity of application unequalled before or since.[3]
Something of this was carried over into the eighteenth century, and
manifested itself in the fields of textual criticism and of exegesis. In 1707
John Mills had completed his notable new edition of the New Testament
in Greek.[4] Amongst the learned commentators may be listed Daniel
Whitby, whose *Paraphrase and Commentary on the New Testament*, in two
volumes, appeared in 1703, and William Lowth, whose exposition of the
Old Testament prophecies was issued in parts between 1714 and 1725.[5] In
the Preface to his *Notes on the New Testament*, Wesley acknowledged his
indebtedness to other English exegetes: Philip Doddridge, John Guyse and
John Heylin.[6]

[1] *Sermons*, Vol. II, p. 154. Sermon XXXV. Christian Perfection.

[2] *Works*, Vol. X, pp. 141–142. *Popery Calmly Considered* (1779).

[3] Cf. Foster Watson, *The Cambridge History of English Literature*, ed. A. W. Ward
and A. R. Waller (1911), Vol. VII, p. 324.

[4] Mills was Principal of St. Edmund Hall, Oxford, from 1685. His edition of the
Greek New Testament was a great advance on any of its predecessors, for he added
the readings of nearly one hundred manuscripts. He was the first to lay down the
principles of sound textual criticism. His name was sometimes rendered as Mill.

[5] Whitby, Prebendary of Salisbury and Rector of St. Paul in that city, was noted
for his opposition to Romanism and his desire for reconciliation between Anglicans
and nonconformity. Latterly he drifted towards unitarianism.

Lowth was Chaplain to the Bishop of Winchester and Rector of Buriton. His first
work, *A Vindication of the Divine Authority of the Old and New Testaments* (1692), was
intended to counteract the critico-rationalistic theories of Jean Leclerc, a Swiss
Arminian who taught at the Remonstrant College in Amsterdam.

[6] Doddridge was one of the foremost Dissenters in the second quarter of the
eighteenth century. He was pastor of a large Independent congregation at Northampton, and also Principal of the theological academy there. His *Family Expositor* was
published in 1745.

But it was to the Lutheran scholar, Johannes Albrecht Bengel, that Wesley owed most. Bengel was a brilliant pioneer in the realm of textual criticism. His text and *apparatus criticus* of the New Testament, published in 1734, marked the beginning of the modern scientific approach. His contribution to biblical exegesis in the shape of his pertinent *Gnomon Novi Testamenti* (1742) was scarcely less significant. Wesley hailed him as "that great light of the Christian world," and proceeded to draw freely on his resources.[1] In his *Notes on the Old Testament*, Wesley went back to Matthew Henry, the Presbyterian commentator, whose work still lives today.[2]

It is fashionable to dismiss Wesley's undeniable biblicism on the score that he lived in pre-critical times, and even to claim that nowadays he would have embraced much more liberal views.[3] As Dr. Franz Hildebrandt reminds us, it is futile to speculate about historical impossibilities, and since Wesley belonged to the eighteenth century we can only properly assess him in his own context.[4] But when we do that, it is not to be assumed that he was altogether unconscious of the issues later raised in more acute form by the development of Higher Criticism. The French Oratorian, Richard Simon, has been identified as the father of biblical criticism, and his epochal works were written before the end of the seventeenth century.[5] In 1753, Jean Astruc published his *Conjectures sur les Mémoires originaux dont il paroît que Moyse s'est servi pour composer le Livre de la Genèse*, which heralded the onset of Pentateuchal criticism.[6] Astruc surmised that Genesis was a patchwork of earlier documents because of the variant names for God—Elohim and Jehovah. The upshot of the celebrated dispute over the Phalaris letters, between Charles Boyle and

Guyse was a Dissenting minister in London. He became the first pastor of the New Broad Street Chapel in 1727. He published *A Practical Exposition of the Four Gospels* in 1739.

Heylin was Rector of St. Mary-le-Strand, see above, p. 85. His *Theological Lectures at Westminster Abbey, with an Interpretation of the Four Gospels* appeared in 1749.

[1] *Notes*, Preface, para. 7. Bengel was appointed Professor at the Lutheran seminary at Denkendorf in 1707. He later became a General Superintendent in the Lutheran Church.

[2] Matthew Henry, son of the Puritan, Philip Henry, was a Presbyterian minister at Chester from 1687 to 1712. His *Exposition of the Old and New Testaments* (1708–1710) is, of course, a classic.

[3] E.g. E. H. Sugden: "Wesley was a critic, both higher and lower, before those much misunderstood terms were invented" (*Sermons*, Vol. I, p. 21. Introduction).

[4] Franz Hildebrandt, *From Luther to Wesley* (1951), p. 25.

[5] Simon was expelled from his order on account of his unorthodox views. In his *Histoire Critique du Vieux Testament* (1678) he denied the Mosaic authorship of the Pentateuch and paved the way for the documentary hypothesis. His stress on the grammatico-historical sense of Scripture was, however, commendable. (Cf. Daniel-Rops, *op. cit.*, pp. 34–36).

[6] Astruc was the son of a Protestant pastor, but seceded to Rome in his youth. He was eventually appointed as Professor of Medicine at the royal college in Paris.

Richard Bentley, was that "historians thereafter began to raise for all the writings of antiquity the preliminary question of their origin."[1]

An omnivorous reader like Wesley could hardly have been unaware of these preliminary rumblings. The storm was not to break until the next century, but the Bible was already under attack. Wesley's convictions were not held in an atmosphere of undisturbed calm. His belief in the reliability of Scripture was tested by the rationalistic climate of his age. In 1773 he looked into a volume of theological *Dissertations* (possibly from the pen of the eccentric Capel Berrow) in which the doctrine of eternal punishment was challenged. "It would be excusable if these menders of the Bible would offer their hypotheses modestly," was Wesley's comment. "But one cannot excuse them when they not only obtrude their novel scheme with the utmost confidence, but even ridicule that scriptural one which always was, and is now, held by men of the greatest learning and piety in the world. Hereby they promote the cause of infidelity more effectually than either Hume or Voltaire."[2]

In view of Wesley's attitude to the Scriptures, we are not surprised to learn that his message was entirely and exclusively derived from them. Not only was his preaching textual and expository: the whole tenor and tone of his sermons was biblical. His citation of proof-texts was prolific and his sole and sufficient appeal was to what stood revealed in God's Book. What Spurgeon once said of Bunyan is equally true of Wesley: his very blood was bibline. "His constant reference to the authority of the Bible reflects his conviction that this book was literally given by God to man," writes Dr. L. M. Starkey, "and contains all those things necessary for the salvation of all mankind."[3] For Wesley, the Bible was the unique repository of inspired doctrine from which the preacher could draw an inexhaustible supply of ammunition to arm him in his battle for souls. "The Scripture, therefore, of the Old and New Testament is a most solid and precious system of divine truth. Every part thereof is worthy of God; and all together are one entire body, wherein is no defect, no excess. It is the fountain of heavenly wisdom, which they who are able to taste prefer to all writings of men, however wise or learned or holy."[4]

Having traced the source of Wesley's message, we must now go on to indicate its content. This will be done in the chapters which follow. We do not propose to attempt an exhaustive review of Wesley's theology. Our

[1] Joseph Coppens, *The Old Testament and the Critics* (E.T. 1942), p. 6. Cf. Stromberg, *op. cit.*, p. 30. In 1699 Richard Bentley, the distinguished classicist, exposed the spuriousness of the so-called Phalaris Letters, which Charles Boyle had edited in 1695, by showing conclusively that they had been written hundreds of years later than the death of the Sicilian tyrant.

[2] *Journal*, Vol. V, p. 523. 8th August, 1773. *Proc. W.H.S.*, Vol. IV, p. 205.

[3] Lycurgus M. Starkey, *The Work of the Holy Spirit: A Study in Wesleyan Theology* (1962), p. 87.

[4] *Notes*, Preface, para. 10.

restricted concern is with his evangelistic preaching. We are out to discover what was Wesley's gospel. From the much wider range of his total
output of teaching, we confine ourselves strictly to this. And the evidence
will be drawn only from his sermons, although it may be clarified occasionally by reference to other writings. Of the latter, special attention will
be paid to Wesley's *Notes on the New Testament*, since these, together with
his standard sermons, formed the definitive *corpus* of Methodism. It was
altogether typical of John Wesley that he should take the unusual step of
elevating a collection of evangelistic messages to the position of a doctrinal norm. Like Principal James Denney later, he had no use for a theology unless it could be preached.[1] It is, then, not to the theology itself, but
to the theology as preached, that we now turn.

[1] James Denney, *Studies in Theology* (1899), p. 127.

CHAPTER XX

THE STANDING TOPIC

"MEANTIME, they began to be convinced, that 'by grace we are saved through faith;' that justification by faith was the doctrine of the Church, as well as of the Bible. As soon as they believed, they spake; salvation by faith being now their *standing topic*." *Works* 8: 349.

IN MAY 1766 JOHN WESLEY HAD OCCASION TO REAFFIRM HIS basic theological position. His views were under fire, and he felt it necessary to remind his critics that the heart of his message lay in the insistence on salvation by grace through faith only. He explicitly repudiated the unscriptural fallacy of works-righteousness. He maintained that this had been his consistent emphasis since his conversion in 1738. "I believe justification by faith alone, as much as I believe there is a God. I declared this in a sermon, preached before the University of Oxford, eight-and-twenty years ago. I declared it to all the world eighteen years ago, in a sermon written expressly on the subject. I have never varied from it, no, not an hair's breadth, from 1738 to this day."[1]

Nowhere was Wesley more obviously in line with the Protestant Reformers than in his recognition that the doctrine of justification lies at the centre of biblical theology. *Sola gratia* and *sola fide* were the twin watchwords of the Reformation, and they found an echo in Wesley's preaching. Despite the fact that at times Wesley took issue with what Luther taught—or more often, with what some who claimed to be exponents of Luther misrepresented as his teaching—he nevertheless found himself at one with the pioneer Reformer in his definite insights.[2] "Wesley stands together with Luther," affirms Prof. Philip S. Watson, "on the same solid ground of the doctrine of salvation by faith, about which the two men often speak in identical terms."[3] Dr. Watson goes on

[1] *Works*, Vol. X, p. 349. *Some Remarks on "A Defence of the Preface to the Edinburgh Edition of Aspasio Vindicated"* (1766). For the sermons mentioned, cf. *Sermons*, Vol. I, pp. 37–52, Sermon I, Salvation by Faith, pp. 114–130; Sermon V, Justification by Faith. This latter actually appeared in the first volume of Wesley's sermons in 1746. The tract to which Wesley replied was written in 1765 by John Erskine, then minister of the New Greyfriars Church, Edinburgh, who had republished James Hervey's letters to Wesley.

[2] Cf. *Journal*, Vol. II, p. 467. 15th June, 1741; p. 468. 16th June, 1741; Vol. III, p. 409. 19th July, 1749; *Letters*, Vol. III, p. 159, To Richard Tompson. 5th February, 1756; *Works*, Vol. XIII, p. 267, *A Plain Account of Kingswood School* (1781).

[3] Philip S. Watson, *Let God be God! An Interpretation of the Theology of Martin Luther* (1947), p. 4.

to cite some instances, culled from scores of similar passages.

Writing in 1740, Wesley described this central doctrine as "the *old way*, of salvation by faith only" and opposed it to "the *new path* of salvation by *faith and works*."[1] Two hundred years earlier, Luther was urging the defence of "the old faith against new articles of faith" and of "the old good works against the new good works."[2] In the first of his standard sermons, Wesley declared: "Never was the maintaining this doctrine more seasonable than at this day. Nothing but this can effectually prevent the increase of the Romish delusion among us. It is endless to attack, one by one, all the errors of that Church. But salvation by faith strikes at the root, and all fall at once where this is established. It was this doctrine, which our Church justly calls *the strong rock and foundation of the Christian religion*, that first drove Popery out of these kingdoms; and it is this alone can keep it out."[3] Luther used the same argument: "The doctrine of faith and justification, or how we become righteous before God . . . drives out all false gods and idolatry; and when that is driven out, the foundation of the Papacy falls, whereon it is built."[4]

Wesley was at one with the Reformers in regarding justification not simply as the most important tenet of Christian belief, but also as that which controls all the rest. "Wesley's doctrine of justification," asserts Prof. William R. Cannon, "was the measure and determinant of all else."[5] This was altogether in the manner of the Reformers. "This doctrine, as Luther found it expounded in St. Paul's Epistles," explained Charles Beard, "furnished the standard to which all other scriptural statements of the method of salvation were brought to be judged."[6] That was why Luther referred to this as "the article of a standing or falling Church."[7] He described justification as "master and prince, lord, ruler, and judge over all kinds of doctrine, which preserves and governs all ecclesiastical doctrines."[8] It is "the chief of the whole Christian doctrine, to which all divine disputations must be directed. . . . For when this article is kept fast and sure by a constant faith, then all other articles draw

[1] *Journal*, Vol. II, p. 354. 22nd June, 1740.

[2] *Works of Martin Luther* (Philadelphia Edition), Vol. V (1931), p. 256. *On the Councils and the Churches* (1539).

[3] *Sermons*, Vol. I, p. 50. Sermon I, Salvation by Faith. "The strong rock and foundation of the Christian religion" is from the Homily *Of Justification*.

[4] Martin Luther, *Tischreden* (ed. H. Borcherdt and W. Rehm, n.d.), Bd. 31, nr. 43; cf. Watson, *Let God be God!*, p. 4.

[5] William Ragsdale Cannon, *The Theology of John Wesley* (1946), p. 14.

[6] Charles Beard, *The Reformation of the Sixteenth Century* (1883), p. 128.

[7] *Articulus stantis et cadentis ecclesiae* (Schmalkald Articles II. i), *Die Symbolischen Bücher der Evangelische Kirche*, ed. J. T. Müller, p. 300 (1869); cf. *Sermons*, Vol. II, p. 425, Sermon XLIX, The Lord our Righteousness; *Works*, Vol. XI, p. 391. *Some Remarks on Mr. Hill's "Review of all the Doctrines taught by Mr. John Wesley"* (1772); *Journal*, Vol. V, p. 244, 1st December, 1767.

[8] *Luthers Werke* (Weimar Gesamtausgabe), Bd. XXXIX, p. 205.

on softly after. . . . God has declared no article so plainly and openly as this, that we are saved only by Christ. . . . He dwells continually upon this article of the salvation of our souls; other articles are of great weight, but this surpasses all."[1] Wesley clearly stood in this Protestant succession, for such a recognition not only directed his thinking but dominated his message.

As we have seen, this magisterial truth of justification was first accepted as revealed in God's Word and then transposed into the key of Christian experience. It was when the doctrine caught fire in his heart that Wesley became an evangelist. What Wesley learned at Aldersgate Street, according to Dr. Harmon L. Smith, was "that man is justified by grace alone and that this grace is given only through faith."[2] This was when salvation by grace became his "standing topic," shared with his fellow-labourers in the gospel of Christ.[3] Here was the fulcrum of his whole career. His ministry was revolutionized when he took up this stance. And it is important to note, as Dr. Cannon brings out, that Wesley's doctrinal conversion radically altered his conception not only of works but also of faith.[4] He no longer thought of salvation in terms of good deeds and pious practices, and even the faith which replaced them was now seen, not as an effort of man, but as a gift from God. It was perhaps more at this point than at any other that the essence of Wesley's reorientation could be recognized. It was here, too, that the plainly broke with the current Anglican interpretation, which was a legacy from the Caroline divines, and went back behind Laud to Cranmer and the Reformation.

It was such considerations as these which led Prof. George Croft Cell to the conclusion, in a masterly analysis, that it was this theologico-experiential *volte face* which gave the eighteenth-century awakening its remarkable dynamic. "The spring of religious energy in the Revival lay in Wesley's essential concurrence with the Luther-Calvin doctrine of salvation by faith; it lay in the Luther-Calvin doctrine how that faith is given and on the Luther-Calvin thesis that a God-given faith is the sole and abiding principle of all Christian experience; it is witnessed in the revolution wrought in Wesley's preaching by his abandonment of the libertarian theology and his adoption of the Luther-Calvin position."[5]

Wesley realized that the biblical centrality of this doctrine was related to the assumption of divine sovereignty which lay behind it. The whole stress of salvation by grace rests on God's initiative. It takes man's hand off his own redemption, and shows it to be altogether the supernatural work of God. Commenting on Ephesians 1: 9, Wesley explained "the mystery

[1] Luther, *Tischreden*, nr. 305.
[2] Harmon L. Smith, "Wesley's Doctrine of Justification," *London Quarterly and Holborn Review*, April, 1964, p. 120.
[3] *Works*, Vol. VIII, p. 349. *A Short History of Methodism* (1765).
[4] Cannon, *op. cit.*, pp. 77–78.
[5] Cell, *op. cit.*, p. 272.

of His will" as "the gracious scheme of salvation by faith, which depends on His own sovereign will alone. This was but darkly discovered under the law; is now totally hid from unbelievers; and has heights and depths which surpass all the knowledge even of true believers."[1] In view of this repeated emphasis in Wesley, Cell repudiates the charge, renewed of late, that he was guilty of synergistic compromise. Indeed, he goes so far as to claim that Wesley's thought was even more strictly monergistic in regard to its expression of grace than that of some later Calvinists. His rejection of the extreme logic of predestination (and more particularly in its corollary of reprobation), did not imply that he allowed even a minimal element of human co-operation in the matter of salvation. "The Wesleyan doctrine of saving faith . . . is a complete renewal of the Luther-Calvin thesis that in the thought of salvation God is everything, man is nothing."[2] "Wherein may we come to the very edge of Calvinism?" was a question discussed at the Conference of 1745. Here is the answer: "In ascribing all good to the free grace of God. In denying all natural free will, and all power antecedent to grace. And in excluding all merit from man; even for what he has or does by the grace of God."[3]

Wesley's teaching on justification, as reflected in his sermons, to which we must now rigidly confine ourselves, must be set in the context of his covenant theology. It was, of course, the Puritans who had elaborated this aspect of Reformed doctrine. It sprang from the reiteration of the Protestant emphasis on grace. The Puritans distinguished two covenants —that of works and that of grace. One of the major expositions was John Preston's *The New Covenant, or the Saint's Portion* (1630), which Dr. Monk shows must have been familiar to Wesley, for he republished part of it in his *Christian Library*.[4] Preston elucidated the distinction between the two covenants like this: "The covenant of works runs in these terms, Do this, and thou shalt live, and I will be thy God. This is the covenant that was made with Adam, and the covenant that is expressed by Moses in the moral law, Do this, and live. The second is the covenant of grace, and that runs in these terms, Thou shalt believe, thou shalt take my Son for thy Lord and thy Saviour, and thou shalt likewise receive the gift of righteousness."[5]

---

[1] *Notes*, Ephesians 1: 9.
[2] Cell, *op. cit.*, p. 271, cf. p. 256.
[3] *Works*, Vol. VIII, p. 285. *Minutes of Some Late Conversations II* (1745). Cell claimed that Wesley's thought actually touched "the very edge of predestination" (*op. cit.*, p. 244). Wesley himself declared that he was altogether at one with Calvin's teaching on justification (*Journal*, Vol. V, p. 116. 14th May, 1765).
[4] Monk, *op. cit.*, p. 97.
[5] John Preston, *The New Covenant, or the Saint's Portion* (1630), pp. 317–318. Preston was one of the most intellectually brilliant of the Puritans. He was Master of Queens' College, Cambridge before his ordination. In 1622 he succeeded John Donne in the preachership of Lincoln's Inn.

Wesley's fullest endorsement of the Puritan covenant theology is to be found in one of his early sermons, that on "The Righteousness of Faith" (from Romans 10: 5–8) which he preached at Epworth on the 12th June, 1742.[1] In his opening paragraph, Wesley showed that Paul was setting the covenant of grace over against the covenant of works—the latter "made with Adam while in paradise, but commonly supposed to be the only covenant which God had made with man."[2] Later, in the solid core of the discourse, Wesley expatiated on the dissimilarity between these respective covenants. "What is the difference then between the 'righteousness which is of the law,' and the 'righteousness which is of faith'? between the first covenant, or the covenant of works, and the second, the covenant of grace? The essential, unchangeable difference is this: the one supposes him to whom it is given, to be already holy and happy, created in the image and enjoying the favour of God; and prescribes the condition whereon he may continue therein, in love and joy, life and immortality: the other supposes him to whom it is given, to be now unholy and unhappy, fallen short of the glorious image of God, having the wrath of God abiding on him, and hastening, through sin, whereby his soul is dead, to bodily death, and death everlasting; and to man in this state it prescribes the condition whereon he may regain the pearl he has lost, may recover the favour and image of God, may retrieve the life of God in his soul, and be restored to the knowledge and love of God, which is the beginning of life eternal."[3]

In a passage which epitomizes the essence of Wesley's evangelistic message, he proceeded: "Again: the covenant of works, in order to man's *continuance* in the favour of God, in His knowledge and love, in holiness and happiness, required of perfect man a *perfect* and uninterrupted *obedience* to every point of the law of God. Whereas, the covenant of grace, in order to man's *recovery* of the favour and the life of God, requires only *faith*; living faith in Him, who, through God, justifies him that obeyed not.

"Yet, again: the covenant of works required of Adam, and all his children, to pay the price themselves, in consideration of which they were to receive all the future blessings of God. But in the covenant of grace, seeing we have nothing to pay, God 'frankly forgives us all:' provided only, that we believe in Him who hath paid the price for us; who hath given Himself a 'propitiation for our sins, for the sins of the whole world.' "[4]

It is not surprising that Wesley could use this distinction as the springboard, as it were, to make a powerful evangelistic appeal. "Thus the first covenant required what is now *afar off* from all the children of men; namely, unsinning obedience, which is far from those who are 'conceived

[1] *Journal*, Vol. III, p. 23. 12th June, 1742.
[2] *Sermons*, Vol. I, pp. 132–133. Sermon VI. The Righteousness of Faith.
[3] *Ibid.*, p. 138. [4] *Ibid.*, pp. 138–139.

and born in sin.' Whereas the second requires what is nigh at hand; as though it should say, 'Thou art sin! God is love! Thou by sin art fallen short of the glory of God; yet there is mercy with Him. Bring then all thy sins to the pardoning God, and they shall vanish away as a cloud. If thou wert not ungodly, there would be no room for Him to justify thee as ungodly. But now draw near, in full assurance of faith. He speaketh, and it is done. Fear not, only believe; for even the just God justifieth all that believe in Jesus.'"[1] In the same vein, Wesley met the objection of those who still supposed that they must do something to win salvation. "Nay, but *first believe*! Believe in the Lord Jesus Christ, the propitation for thy sins. Let this good foundation first be laid, and then thou shalt do all things well."[2] Wesley spoke from his own bitter experience as he warned against the folly of trusting in works-righteousness: those who accept the premiss, "Do this, and live," "set out wrong; their very first step is a fundamental mistake."[3]

It is not accidental that the initial sermon in the standard collection, intended both to reflect and to indicate the essence of effective gospel preaching, should deal with "Salvation by Faith" from Ephesians 2: 8. Like the strong, opening chords of a Beethoven symphony, Sermon One announced the theme which dominated the whole of Wesley's message, and which largely accounted for its impact. This was how his evangelical manifesto before the University of Oxford, on the 11th June, 1738, stated the presupposition of the gospel in its introductory paragraph. "All the blessings which God hath bestowed upon man are of His mere grace, bounty, or favour; His free, undeserved favour; favour altogether undeserved; man having no claim to the least of His mercies. It was free grace that 'formed man of the dust of the ground, and breathed into him a living soul,' and stamped on that soul the image of God, and 'put all things under his feet.' The same free grace continues to us, at this day, life, and breath, and all things. For there is nothing we are, or have, or do, which can deserve the least thing at God's hand. 'All our works, Thou, O God, hast wrought in us.' These, therefore, are so many more instances of free mercy: and whatever righteousness may be found in man, this is also the gift of God."[4]

Wesley went on to demonstrate the utter incapacity of man to atone for the least of his sins. So, having nothing to plead, neither righteousness nor works, "his mouth is utterly stopped before God."[5] "If then sinful men find favour with God, it is 'grace upon grace.' "[6] Wesley thus based his evangel on grace—"the most important word in the Protestant vocabulary," according to Robert McAfee Brown.[7] "Grace is both the begin-

---

[1] *Ibid.*, p. 139.   [2] *Ibid.*, p. 144.
[3] *Ibid.*, p. 139.   [4] *Ibid.*, p. 37. Sermon I. Salvation by Faith.
[5] *Ibid.*, p. 36.   [6] *Ibid.*
[7] Robert McAfee Brown, *The Spirit of Protestantism* (1961), p. 53.

H

ning and end" of salvation, Wesley declared.[1] "Our justification comes freely of the mere mercy of God," he reiterated from the Anglican Homilies.[2] From a host of similar affirmations it is clear that, as Dr. Starkey concludes, "Wesley retains the pronounced Pauline-Protestant emphasis on the unmerited, transcendent favour of God toward man in Christ."[3]

Such grace is "free in all, and free for all."[4] This dual proposition Wesley elaborated in a celebrated sermon preached at Bristol in 1740 from Romans 8: 32. "It is free in all to whom it is given. It does not depend on any power or merit in man; no, not in any degree, neither in whole, nor in part. It does not in any wise depend either on the good works or righteousness of the receiver; not on anything he has done, or anything he is. It does not depend on his endeavours. . . . Whatsoever good is in man, or is done by man, God is the author and doer of it. Thus is His grace free in all; that is, no way depending on any power or merit in man, but in God alone, who freely gave us His own Son, and with Him 'freely giveth us all things.' "[5]

The second item Wesley maintained in face of those who pressed the extremes of predestinarianism. The decree to which he appealed was that by which "whom God did foreknow, He did predestinate."[6] As an evangelist, he feared lest the ultimate logic of ultra-Calvinistic rigidity might inhibit the preaching of the gospel and the free offer of grace to all. It may well have been that some of his apprehensions were unjustified, for George Whitefield, from whom he parted company on this issue, was equally zealous in evangelism and reaped a proportionate harvest of souls within the shorter span of his ministry.

Wesley was far from supposing, however, that the natural man possessed any capacity to respond to the gospel apart from enabling grace. "Salvation begins with what is usually termed (and very properly) *preventing grace*; including the first wish to please God, the first dawn of light concerning His will, and the first slight transient conviction of having sinned against Him. All these imply some tendency toward life; some degree of salvation; the beginning of a deliverance from a blind, unfeeling heart, quite insensible of God and the things of God. Salvation is carried on by *convincing grace*, usually in Scripture termed *repentance*; which brings a larger measure of self-knowledge, and a farther deliverance from the heart of stone. Afterwards we experience the proper Christian salvation, whereby 'through grace' we 'are saved by faith.' "[7]

[1] *Notes*, Ephesians 2: 8. "This text lays the axe to the very roots of spiritual pride, and all glorifying in ourselves."
[2] *Sermons*, Vol. II, p. 431. Sermon XLIX, The Lord our Righteousness.
[3] Starkey, *op. cit.*, p. 36.
[4] *Works*, Vol. VII, p. 373. Sermon CXXVIII. Free Grace.
[5] *Ibid.*
[6] *Ibid.*, p. 385.
[7] *Ibid.*, Vol. VI, p. 509. Sermon LXXXV. Working out our own Salvation.

If "grace is the source of salvation, faith is the condition."[1] It is so, however, not at all in the sense that it represents something still to be done by man, which would make faith itself a kind of work. Wesley was particularly careful to guard his stress on faith as the condition of salvation from any sort of semi-Pelagian misunderstanding. He knew very well that the true gospel invitation is not an easy or uneasy believism. Faith is not man's contribution to his own salvation: it is itself a gift from God. "Of yourselves cometh neither your faith nor your salvation," Wesley stressed: " 'it is the gift of God'; the free, undeserved gift; the faith through which ye are saved, as well as the salvation which He of His own good pleasure, His mere favour annexes thereto. That ye believe, is one instance of His grace; that believing ye are saved, another."[2]

All Wesley meant, then, by describing faith as the condition of salvation was simply that there is no justification without it. He who does not believe is already condemned.[3] Faith, moreover, so Wesley preached, is the sole condition of salvation. "We mean thereby thus much, that it is the only thing without which no one is justified; the only thing that is immediately, indispensably, absolutely requisite in order to pardon. As, on the one hand, though a man should have everything else without faith, yet he cannot be justified; so, on the other, though he be supposed to want everything else, yet if he hath faith, he cannot but be justified. For suppose a sinner of any kind or degree, in a full sense of his total ungodliness, of his utter inability to think, speak, or do good, and his absolute meetness for hell fire; suppose, I say, this sinner, helpless and hopeless, casts himself wholly on the mercy of God in Christ (which indeed he cannot do but by the grace of God), who can doubt but he is forgiven in that moment? Who will affirm that any more is *indispensably required*, before that sinner can be justified?"[4]

This "divine faith wrought by the Holy Ghost" is more than "a bare assent to the truth of the Bible," or some credal definition.[5] "It is a confidence in a pardoning God. It is a divine evidence or conviction that 'God was in Christ reconciling the world to Himself, not imputing to them their' former 'trespasses'; and in particular, that the Son of God hath loved *me*, and given Himself for *me*; and that I, even I, am now reconciled to God by the blood of the Cross."[6] The striking repetition of personal pronouns vividly recalls Wesley's conversion testimony. It is to be found again and again as Wesley dealt with the nature of faith. He obviously had in mind his own heart-warming as he pleaded with others. "Justifying

[1] *Sermons*, Vol. I, p. 38. Sermon I. Salvation by Faith.
[2] *Ibid.*, p. 48.
[3] *Ibid.*, p. 126. Sermon V. Justification by Faith (cf. John 3: 18).
[4] *Ibid.*, p. 127.
[5] *Notes*, Romans 4: 5; *Sermons*, Vol. I, pp. 159–160, Sermon VII. The Way to the Kingdom.
[6] *Sermons*, Vol. I, p. 160.

faith implies, not only a divine evidence or conviction that 'God was in Christ, reconciling the world unto Himself,' but a sure trust and confidence that Christ died for *my* sins, that He loved *me*, and gave Himself for *me*."[1] And, in the best-known passage of all dealing with this topic: "Christian faith is, then, not only an assent to the whole gospel of Christ, but also a full reliance on the blood of Christ; a trust in the merits of His life, death, and resurrection; a recumbency upon Him as our atonement and our life, *as given for us*, and *living in us*. It is a sure confidence which a man hath in God, that through the merits of Christ, *his* sins are forgiven, and *he* reconciled to the favour of God; and, in consequence hereof, a closing with Him, and cleaving to Him, as our 'wisdom, righteousness, sanctification, and redemption,' or, in one word, our salvation."[2]

The object of saving faith is Christ Himself, as the last quotation made unusually specific. "Faith justifies only as it refers to, and depends on, Christ," Wesley insisted.[3] Hence his appeal was always in personal terms. He did not call on men in the first place to embrace truth, but to trust in the Saviour. His sermon on "Justification by Faith" closed with an invitation to "look unto Jesus."[4] "Thou ungodly one, who hearest or readest these words! thou vile, helpless, miserable sinner! I charge thee before God the Judge of all, go straight to Him, with all thy ungodliness. Take heed thou destroy not thine own soul by pleading thy righteousness, more or less. Go as altogether ungodly, guilty, lost, destroyed, deserving and dropping into hell; and thou shalt then find favour in His sight, and know that He justifieth the ungodly. As such shalt thou be brought unto the 'blood of sprinkling,' as an undone, helpless, damned sinner. Thus 'look unto Jesus!' There is 'the lamb of God,' who 'taketh away' thy 'sins.' Plead thou no works, no righteousness of thine own, no humility, contrition, sincerity! In no wise. That were, in very deed, to deny the Lord that bought thee. No: plead thou singly the blood of the covenant, the ranson paid for thy proud, stubborn sinful soul. . . . O come quickly! Believe in the Lord Jesus, and thou, even thou, art reconciled to God."[5]

In dealing with the actual nature of justification, Wesley correctly explained that in Scripture this does not mean being made righteous, but simply being declared righteous and treated as such.[6] Thus the line between justification and sanctification is sharply drawn and the two are not confused. Nor does justification involve a legal fiction, still less any self-deception on God's part.[7] "The plain scriptural notion of justification is pardon, the forgiveness of sins. It is that act of God the Father, whereby, for the sake of the propitiation made by the blood of His Son, He 'showeth

---

[1] *Ibid.*, p. 125. Sermon V. Justification by Faith.
[2] *Ibid.*, pp. 40–41. Sermon I. Salvation by Faith.
[3] *Notes*, Hebrews 11: 1. Cf. Acts 3: 16.
[4] *Sermons*, Vol. I, p. 129. Sermon V. Justification by Faith (cf. Hebrews 12: 2).
[5] *Ibid.*   [6] *Ibid.*, p. 119.   [7] *Ibid.*, p. 120.

forth His righteousness' (or mercy) 'by the remission of the sins that are past.' "[1] Again: "Justification is another word for pardon. It is the forgiveness of all our sins; and, what is necessarily implied therein, our acceptance with God. The price whereby this hath been procured for us (commonly termed 'the meritorious cause of our justification'), is the blood and righteousness of Christ."[2] Only on the ground of Christ's sacrifice for us on the cross can God declare repentent sinners to be righteous in His sight.[3] Wesley repudiated any idea of what Dietrich Bonhoeffer called "cheap grace."[4] He knew that the great slogan of Scripture with regard to redemption from sin is "not without blood."[5] The exceeding sinfulness of sin demanded a Lamb without blemish and without spot by way of atonement. But of this vital element in an evangelist's message we must speak in the chapter that follows.

[1] *Ibid.*, pp. 120–121.
[2] *Ibid.*, Vol. II, p. 445. Sermon L. The Scripture Way of Salvation.
[3] *Ibid.*, p. 431. Sermon XLIX. The Lord our Righteousness.
[4] Dietrich Bonhoeffer, *The Cost of Discipleship* (1951), p. 1.
[5] Cf. Hebrews 9:22.

CHAPTER XXI

THE LOATHSOME LEPROSY

"HE is convinced that he is spiritually poor indeed; having no spiritual good abiding in him. 'In me,' he saith, 'dwelleth no good thing,' but whatsoever is evil and abominable. He has a deep sense of *the loathsome leprosy* of sin, which he brought with him from his mother's womb, which overspreads his whole soul, and totally corrupts every power and faculty thereof." *Sermons* 1: 323.

IT HAS BEEN NEATLY SAID THAT THE CHRISTIAN MESSAGE IS BAD news before it is good news. It tells man he is a sinner, who is altogether helpless in himself and incapable of achieving salvation. He is a fallen creature with a built-in tendency to sin. If he persists in going his own way, he will only store up frustration and misery in this life and face eternal punishment in the next. It is solely on this assumption that the gospel offer is made. The cure is prescribed to the patient who recognizes his sickness. Christianity is optimistic about grace, but pessimistic about human nature.

These were the underlying presuppositions of Wesley's evangelistic proclamation. He cherished no illusions. His view of man was biblically realistic. He wasted no time in looking for the angel in the clay. He knew from the Word that in God's sight no man living is justified. The bias towards evil has affected all humanity. To build on any imagined natural goodness is to construct a house on the sand. Only on the basis of Christ's sufficiency can a new structure be raised. The starting-point of the gospel is the total inability of the sinner to make the tiniest contribution towards his own salvation. This was Wesley's position. But it was tempered by his teaching on prevenient grace, which he saw as operative in the heart even of the most degraded. The natural man is indeed dead in trespasses and sins, but he is not left there. In his low estate, God still deals with him. It was this conviction which quickened Wesley's evangelistic zeal. He could not dismiss even the worst of sinners as being altogether beyond redemption.

But Wesley was in no doubt concerning the abject condition of man, apart from this prevenient grace of God. "The unrenewed will is wholly perverse, in reference to the end of man. Man is a merely dependent being; having no existence or goodness originally from himself; but all he has is from God, as the first cause and spring of all perfection, natural and moral. Dependence is woven into his very nature; so that, should God withdraw from him, he would sink into nothing. Since then whatever man is, he is of Him, surely whatever he is, he should be to Him; as the waters which came out of the sea return thither again. And thus man was created looking directly to God, as his last end; but, falling into sin, he fell off from God, and turned into himself. Now, this infers a total apostasy and universal corruption in man; for where the last end is changed, there can be no real goodness. And this is the case of all men in their natural state: they seek not God, but themselves. Hence though many fair shreds of morality are among them, yet 'there is none that doeth good, no, not one.' For though some of them 'run well,' they are still off the way; they never aim at the right mark. Whithersoever they move, they cannot move beyond the circle of self. They seek themselves, they act for themselves; their natural, civil, and religious actions, from whatever spring they come, do all turn into, and meet, this dead sea."[1]

This picture of man "turned into himself" is reminiscent of Luther's phrase *incurvatum in se*.[2] Wesley's delineation of the sinner in his natural state was altogether in line with the Reformers. He differed from them, however, in extending the operation of prevenient grace to include more than the elect (since he did not take such grace to be irresistible), and to reach back into a man's past so that he was always without excuse. Wesley, nevertheless, is again at one with the Reformers in attributing the present plight of unregenerate man to original sin. Dr. Harmon Smith is quite justified in claiming that Wesley's thought here "strongly parallels that of both Luther and Calvin."[3] Moreover, as Dr. Monk points out, "Wesley's defence and use of Puritan expressions of the Protestant doctrine of original sin indicate his recognition of a theological affinity in this doctrine."[4] Or, to trace it further back, Wesley's view of original sin stemmed from the Augustinian federal theory of the fall. Man's "heart is altogether corrupt and abominable."[5] He "is still a 'child of wrath,' still under the curse, till he believes in Jesus."[5] Hence, Wesley was completely sceptical of any humanistic optimism. "How utterly needless is either the knowledge or the grace of God (consequently, how idle a book is the

---

[1] *Works*, Vol. IX, p. 456. *The Doctrine of Original Sin* (1756).

[2] *Luthers Werke* (Weimar Gesamtausgabe), Bd. LVI, p. 356. *Römerbriefvorlesung* (1515-1516). "And this agrees with Scripture, which describes man as bent upon himself (*incurvatum in se*) in such a way that he turns to his own account not only bodily, but even spiritual goods, and seeks himself in all things. And this crookedness is now natural, the natural vice and natural evil."

[3] Harmon L. Smith, "Wesley's Doctrine of Justification," *London Quarterly and Holborn Review*, April, 1964, p. 121. Wesley accepted without qualification the anthropological definitions of the Westminster Catechism, cf. Wesley's *Revision of the Shorter Catechism*, ed. J. A. MacDonald (1906); Starkey, *op. cit.*, p. 117.

[4] Monk, *op. cit.*, p. 133.

[5] *Sermons*, Vol. I, p. 38. Sermon I. Salvation by Faith.

[6] *Ibid.*, p. 127. Sermon V. Justification by Faith.

Bible), if a man be all-accomplished that has no more knowledge of God than a horse, and no more of His grace than a sparrow!"[1]

Wesley realized that original sin is "the general ground of the whole doctrine of justification."[2] In his sermon on "Justification by Faith," he proceeded to explain what he meant by that assertion. "By the sin of the first Adam, who was not only the father, but likewise the representative, of us all, we all fell short of the favour of God; we all became children of wrath; or, as the apostle expresses it, 'judgement came upon all men to condemnation.' Even so, by the sacrifice for sin made by the second Adam, as the representative of us all, God is so far reconciled to all the world, that He hath given them a new covenant; the plain condition whereof being once fulfilled, 'there is no more condemnation' for us, but 'we are justified freely by His grace, through the redemption that is in Jesus Christ.' "[3]

Since it was so closely bound up with the definitive doctrine of justification, Wesley regarded the article of original sin as a test of evangelical faith. In 1764 he met a group of like-minded clergymen in Bristol. The fellowship they enjoyed prompted him to disclose something which had evidently been on his heart for some time. "I have long desired that there might be an open, avowed union between all who preach those fundamental truths, original sin and justification by faith, producing inward and outward holiness; but all my endeavours have been hitherto ineffectual. God's time is not fully come."[4] Passing over the remarkable percipience of Wesley in seeing the need for such an association so far ahead of his time, we are struck by his selection of basic doctrines. He correctly linked justification by faith with original sin. These two belong inseparably together. Where the second is abandoned, the first is in jeopardy.

In his sermon on "Original Sin," from Genesis 6: 5, Wesley went so far as to claim that this is "the first grand distinguishing point between heathenism and Christianity."[5] "Many of the ancient heathens have largely described the vices of particular men. They have spoken much against their covetousness, or cruelty; their luxury, or prodigality. Some have dared to say, that 'no man is born without vices of one kind or another.' But still, as none of them were apprised of the fall of man, so none of them knew of his total corruption. They knew not that all men were empty of all good, and filled with all manner of evil. They were wholly ignorant of the entire depravation of the whole human nature, of every man born into the world, in every faculty of his soul, not so much by those particular vices which reign in particular persons, as by the general flood of atheism and idolatry, of pride, self-will, and love of the world."[6]

[1] *Journal*, Vol. VII, p. 464. 16th January, 1789.
[2] *Sermons*, Vol. I, p. 119. Sermon V. Justification by Faith.   [3] *Ibid.*
[4] *Journal*, Vol. V, p. 47. 16th March, 1764.
[5] *Sermons*, Vol. II, p. 222. Sermon XXXVIII. Original Sin.   [6] *Ibid.*

Wesley pressed the argument still more keenly. He made the charge that all who deny the reality of original sin, whatever title they may use, "are but heathen still, in the fundamental point which differences (*sic*) heathenism from Christianity. They may, indeed, allow that men have many vices; that some are born with us; and that consequently, we are not born altogether so wise or so virtuous as we should be; there being few that will roundly affirm, 'We are born with as much propensity to good as to evil, and that every man is, by nature, as virtuous and wise as Adam was at his creation.' But here is the *shibboleth*: Is man by nature filled with all manner of evil? Is he void of all good? Is he wholly fallen? Is his soul totally corrupted? Or to come back to the test, is 'every imagination of the thoughts of his heart only evil continually'? Allow this, and you are so far a Christian. Deny it, and you are but a heathen still."[1] Wesley continued his sermon by showing that the acceptance, or otherwise, of the biblical teaching about original sin affects our conception of the gospel, and what it is intended to do. A radical disease demands a radical cure. Only the cross can supply the antidote to sin. But, of course, if the seriousness of sin is questioned, the need for a desperate remedy is likewise rendered less certain. It is not difficult to recognize how crucial is the doctrine of original sin in the work of evangelism.

When Wesley spoke so strongly in his sermon on "Original Sin," he was meeting a particular situation. The seeds of doubt had been sown by an erudite Presbyterian minister in Norwich, Dr. John Taylor. He leaned heavily toward Socinianism, denying the divinity of our Lord, although he conceded that He was "a person of consummate virtue."[2] In 1740 Taylor published a treatise entitled *The Scripture Doctrine of Original Sin Proposed to Free and Candid Examination*, in which he put forward blatantyl Pelagian opinions.[3] He refused to believe that man entered the world with a sinful nature. He repudiated the relationship between Adam and his descendants. He admitted that men were degenerate, but he held that they failed to do what was right because they were unwilling rather than because they were unable. On the 28th August, 1748, Wesley reached Shackerley in Lancashire and found in his congregation many "disciples of Dr. Taylor, laughing at original sin, and, consequently, at the whole frame of Scriptural Christianity."[4] It is noticeable that, once again,

[1] *Ibid.*

[2] *Ibid.*, Vol. I, p. 207. Notes. Taylor, a noted Hebraist, went to Norwich in 1733 and founded the Octagon Chapel in 1754. He was appointed divinity tutor at Warrington Academy, which opened in 1757. (Tyerman appears to have been mistaken in describing Taylor as such so early as 1748, cf. *Life of John Wesley*, Vol. II, p. 18.) Wesley told A. M. Toplady: "I verily believe no single person since Mahomet has given such a wound to Christianity as Dr. Taylor" (*Letters*, Vol. IV, p. 48. To A. M. Toplady, 9th December, 1758).

[3] Telford gave the date as 1736, but the first edition was in 1740 (*Letters*, Vol. IV, p. 66. Notes).

[4] *Journal*, Vol. III, p. 374. 28th August, 1748.

Wesley regarded original sin as an essential premiss to the entire Christian faith. Omit it, and everything collapses. His further comment was characteristic. "Oh what a providence is it which has brought us here also, among these silver-tongued antiChrists! Surely a few, at least, will recover out of the snare, and know Jesus Christ as their wisdom and righteousness!"[1]

Wesley's sermon on "Original Sin," which he included amongst the forty-four which were prescribed as enshrining the doctrinal standards of Methodism, has been the subject of much theological discussion. We are in a better position today to receive and understand its contents than those who lived in a more sanguine period. Perhaps the somewhat unsympathetic comments of Dr. Sugden are explicable in such terms. He felt that Wesley had vastly exaggerated his case.[2] But that was in 1921. The insights of recent theological research enable us to reassess Wesley's thoroughgoing pessimism so far as unaided man is concerned. We see that he was speaking strictly of man *coram deo*, as the Reformers did: that is to say, of man in the presence of God. Interpreted in this light, Wesley's account is by means so bizarre as some would still have us conclude. Indeed, it ties in with the philosophy of Christian existentialism. It was Søren Kierkegaard himself who referred to the great "edification implied in the thought that against God we are always in the wrong."[3] Bishop Aulén reminds us that "sin is a concept which belongs entirely within the religious sphere."[4] "If we do not hold fast to this religious context, the viewpoint of Christian faith in regard to man's situation would be misinterpreted. It could then easily be accused of painting the situation in too dark colours and of being therefore monotonous and unrealistic. . . . *In naturalibus* there is room for a variety of human moral actions. It is only in respect to religion, *coram deo*, that all such relative judgements cease. *Coram deo* all human boasting ceases (I Corinthians 1: 29), man stands before God uncovered, naked, without protection and without any possibility of justifying himself."[5]

Enough has been quoted from Wesley already to indicate that for him the core of sin is pride. It is that fatal egoism which pits itself even against God. As Dr. Vincent Taylor has arrestingly expressed it, sin is self-coronation.[6] As such, Wesley argued, it is a form of idolatry, indeed its

---

[1] *Ibid.*

[2] *Sermons*, Vol. I, p. 208. Notes. Sugden also rightly observed that what Wesley said here about original sin needs to be balanced by his teaching elsewhere on prevenient grace.

[3] Søren Kierkegaard, *Either/Or* (E.T. 1944), Vol. II, p. 287; cf. Williams, *op. cit.*, p. 47.

[4] Gustaf Aulén, *The Faith of the Christian Church* (E.T. 1954), p. 269.

[5] *Ibid.*

[6] Vincent Taylor, *The Apostolic Gospel* (1952), pp. 8, 9. "Self-coronation, including subtle, unconscious self-coronation—that is the essence of sin."

grossest form. "In his natural state, every man born into the world is a rank idolater. Perhaps, indeed, we may not be such in the vulgar sense of the word. We do not, like the idolatrous heathens, worship molten or graven images. We do not bow down to the stock of a tree, to the work of our own hands. . . . But what then? We have set up our idols in our hearts; and to these we bow down, and worship them: we worship ourselves, when we pay that honour to ourselves which is due to God only. Therefore, all pride is idolatry; it is ascribing to ourselves what is due to God alone. And although pride was not made for man, yet where is the man that is born without it? But hereby we rob God of His inalienable right, and idolatrously usurp His glory."[1] This pride compels man to seek happiness in the creature rather than in the Creator. It is this fixation on the finite which makes him a prey to sensual appetites. "They lead him captive; they drag him to and fro, in spite of his boasted reason."[2] The sins of the flesh are the children, not the parents of pride; and self-love is the root, not the branch of all evil.[3]

It is this damaging connexion between original sin and actual sin which makes it impossible for man to evade responsibility for his own misdeeds. Wesley did not hesitate to confront the sinner with the fate that he deserved, and which would surely await him unless he repented and believed the gospel. "And knowest thou not that 'the wages of sin is death'?—death, not only temporal, but eternal. 'The soul that sinneth, it shall die;' for the mouth of the Lord hath spoken it. It shall die the second death. This is the sentence, to 'be punished' with never-ending death, 'with everlasting destruction from the presence of the Lord, and from the glory of His power'. . . . Thou art guilty of everlasting death. It is the just reward of thy inward and outward wickedness. It is just that the sentence should now take place. Dost thou see this, dost thou feel this? Art thou thoroughly convinced that thou deservest God's wrath, and everlasting condemnation? Would God do thee no wrong, if He now commanded the earth to open, and swallow thee up?—if thou wert now to go down quick into the pit, into the fire that shall never be quenched? If God hath given thee truly to repent, thou hast a deep sense that these things are so; and that it is of His mere mercy that thou art not consumed, swept away from the face of the earth."[4] Here is the cutting-edge of faithful evangelistic preaching.

Whilst many of the hearers were pierced to the heart, and led to cry for mercy, others were offended and resisted such an incisive message.

---

[1] *Sermons*, Vol. II, p. 218. Sermon XXXVIII. Original Sin.

[2] *Ibid.*, p. 219.

[3] *Ibid.*, Vol. I, p. 156, Sermon VII, The Way to the Kingdom; p. 534. Sermon XXVI, Upon our Lord's Sermon on the Mount XI; *Works*, Vol. VI, pp. 216–217. Sermon LVII, The Fall of Man; cf. Cannon, *op. cit.*, p. 193.

[4] *Sermons*, Vol. I, p. 157. Sermon VII. The Way to the Kingdom.

Wesley was preaching at Bath in 1743 to a congregation which included "some of the rich and great."[1] In his *Journal* he outlined the substance of his sermon. He "declared with all plainness of speech: (1) that, by nature, they were all children of wrath; (2) that all their natural tempers were corrupt and abominable; and (3) all their words and works, which could never be any better but by faith; and that (4) a natural man has no more faith than a devil, if so much." One of the hearers, a peer of the realm, stuck it out until Wesley reached the middle of his final point. Then, jumping up, he muttered, " 'Tis hot! 'tis very hot!" and hurried away as fast as he could. But others found the same word "a fragrance from life to life" (II Corinthians 2: 16) instead of from death to death. Several of the gentry asked to stay to the society meeting, where Wesley explained "the nature of inward religion."[2] One notorious sceptic, who may have been Dr. William Oliver, the eminent physician, was completely broken down and "hung over the next seat in an attitude not to be described."[3]

It was a feature of Wesley's preaching that, like the wise evangelist God had made him, he never submitted a diagnosis without at the same time prescribing the necessary treatment. His ruthless exposure of sin in all its repulsive putrefaction was always accompanied by the offer of God's remedy. The "proper nature of religion, of the religion of Jesus Christ" is "θεραπεία ψυχῆς—God's method of healing a soul which is thus diseased. Hereby the great Physician of souls applies medicines to heal this sickness; to restore human nature, totally corrupted in all its faculties."[4] To Wesley the gospel was the panacea for the ills of the soul. He saw himself as a dispenser of the most precious medicament in the world—that which cures a man from the malady of sin. He knew that there was a balm in Gilead, and he delighted to show how it could be applied.

The only remedy for "the loathsome leprosy of sin" is to be found at the Cross.[5] Here is the heart of Wesley's gospel and the final clue to his effectiveness. No evangelism will succeed which does not set the Cross in the centre. And the message of what happened there must be proclaimed in all the fulness with which Scripture itself has invested it. In the New Testament, as Prof. James S. Stewart reminds us, the Cross is set forth as the climax of revelation.[6] In consequence, thus to present it must always be the primary concern of the gospel preacher. That was Wesley's consuming preoccupation. Cell says that the atonement was the "burning focus of faith" for Wesley: as such it became also the incandescent nucleus

[1] *Journal*, Vol. III, p. 65. 24th January, 1743.
[2] *Ibid.*
[3] *Ibid.* Oliver had the leading practice in Bath from 1725. He invented the "Bath Oliver" biscuit. Cf. Vol. II, p. 206, n. 1; Seymour, *op. cit.*, Vol. I, p. 451 n.
[4] *Sermons*, Vol. II, pp. 223–224. Sermon XXXVIII. Original Sin.
[5] *Ibid.*, Vol. I, p. 323. Sermon XVI. Upon our Lord's Sermon on the Mount I.
[6] Stewart, *op. cit.*, p. 79.

of his missionary message.[1] It was with the *kerygma* of the Cross that he set out to reach Britain for Christ.

Wesley recognized that the atonement cannot be *discovered* from the incarnation, in the context of which it was historically located, but he nevertheless concentrated on the death of Christ as the essence of the saving proclamation. With the apostle Paul, he was prepared to strip his message of all that was peripheral, and to know nothing among his hearers except Jesus Christ and Him crucified (I Corinthians 2:2). "*The gospel* (that is, good tidings, good news for guilty, helpless sinners), in the largest sense of the word, means the whole revelation made to men by Jesus Christ; and sometimes the whole account of what our Lord did and suffered while He tabernacled among men. The substance of all is, 'Jesus Christ came into the world to save sinners;' or, 'God so loved the world, that He gave His only-begotten Son, to the end that we might not perish but have everlasting life;' or, 'He was bruised for our transgressions, He was wounded for our iniquities; the chastisement of our peace was upon Him; and with His stripes we are healed.' *Believe* this, and the kingdom of God is thine."[2] And again: "It is the blood of Christ alone, whereby any sinner can be reconciled to God; there being no other propitiation for our sins, no other fountain for sin and uncleanness."[3]

Wesley was content to by-pass the historical theories of atonement and construct his doctrine straight from Scripture.[4] He was more interested in announcing biblically-revealed facts than in spinning intricate webs of hypothesis and conjecture. After the manner of the apostolic preaching of the gospel, he simply rehearsed the salvation-event, namely, that, "Christ died for our sins in accordance with the Scriptures" (I Corinthians 15:3). Karl Heim declares that Christianity rests on "the majesty of what has happened," and Wesley fixed principally on that.[5] However, Dr. Williams is right in affirming that "the central point of the Penal Substitutionary theory was of great importance to Wesley."[6] This he proclaimed, not as a theological theory, but as a plain truth of Scripture. The satisfaction for human sin and guilt was provided by the sinless One as He bore our punishment on the Cross. But, as Williams explains, Wesley did not

---

[1] Cell, *op. cit.*, p. 297.

[2] *Sermons*, Vol. I, p. 159. Sermon VII. The Way to the Kingdom.

[3] *Ibid.*, pp. 243–244. Sermon XII. The Means of Grace.

[4] *Letters*, Vol. VI, p. 298. To Mary Bishop, 7th February, 1778. "Our *reason* is here quickly bewildered. If we attempt to expatiate in this field, we 'find no end, in wandering mazes lost.' But the question is (the only question with me; I regard nothing else), What saith the Scripture? It says, 'God was in Christ, reconciling the world unto Himself;' that, 'He made Him, who knew no sin, to be a sin-offering for us.' It says, 'He was wounded for our transgressions and bruised for our iniquities.' It says, 'We have an Advocate with the Father, Jesus Christ the righteous; and He is the atonement for our sins.'"

[5] Karl Heim, *Jesus der Weltvollender* (1952), p. 77.

[6] Williams, *op. cit.*, p. 85.

set this element of his teaching inside a legal framework, in which God is made subject to an eternal, unalterable order of justice.[1] The covenant of grace transcends finite limitations, and lifts us to a new realm of sovereign liberty.

Wesley did not shrink from the biblical emphasis on propitiation as the appeasement of divine wrath. It is noticeable how often he resorted to this factor in atonement.[2] It is clear that he considered it to be pivotal. In his comment on Romans 3 : 25, in the *Notes on the New Testament*, Wesley interpreted propitiation as a means to placate an offended God. "But if, as some teach, God never was offended, there was no need of this propitiation. And, if so, Christ died in vain."[3] It is significant that current research tends to restore the full biblical connotation of Christ's propitiatory sacrifice as repairing a mutual alienation.[4] Not only does man need to be reconciled to God: God has to be reconciled to man. Sin alienated man from God, but also God from man. Reconciliation must deal with both parties. Prof. A. B. Crabtree challenges Ritschl's thesis that only a change of attitude by man is involved. "Reconciliation consists equally, and indeed primarily, in a change of attitude on the part of God, a change from wrath to kindness, from condemnation to pardon, from rejection to acceptance. God turns to man in grace and man turns to God in faith. That is reconciliation as the New Testament understands it."[5] That is how Wesley understood it too.

The nub of Wesley's appeal to the sinner lay here. It was as he pointed to the One who took the place of those who deserved to die, that he found a responsive chord even in hardened hearts. It was as he spoke of a God now reconciled by the sacrifice of His Son, that those who were at enmity with God felt the need to be at peace with Him. It is in this mysterious

[1] *Ibid.*, p. 84.
[2] Cf. *Sermons*, Vol. I, p. 42. Sermon I. Salvation by Faith; pp. 118, 121, 123. Sermon V. Justification by Faith; p. 139. Sermon VI. The Righteousness of Faith; p. 328. Sermon XVI. Upon our Lord's Sermon on the Mount I; Vol. II, p. 59. Sermon XXX. The Law Established through Faith; p. 393. Sermon XLVII. The Repentance of Believers, *et al.* In a letter to Mary Bishop, Wesley took issue with William Law on this very point. In denying God's wrath, Law struck at the root of the atonement, in Wesley's view. "Had God never been angry, He could never have been reconciled. . . . Although, therefore, I do not term God, as Mr. Law supposes, 'a wrathful being,' which conveys a wrong idea; yet I firmly believe that He was angry with all mankind, and that He was reconciled to them by the death of His Son. And I know that He was angry with me till I believed in the Son of His love; and yet this is no impeachment to His mercy, that He is just as well as merciful." (*Letters*, Vol. VI, p. 298. To Mary Bishop, 7th February, 1778.)
[3] *Notes*, Romans 3 : 25.
[4] Cf. C. Kingsley Barrett, *The Epistle to the Romans* (1957), pp. 77–78; Leon Morris, *The Apostolic Preaching of the Cross* (1955), pp. 138–140; Leon Morris, *The Cross in the New Testament* (1965), pp. 348–350; C. Spicq, *L'Épître aux Hébraux* (1952), Vol I, p. 304.
[5] Arthur B. Crabtree, *The Restored Relationship* (1963), p. 46.

area of atonement at the Cross that the agelong appeal of the gospel lies. "Sinner, awake!" cried Wesley, in one of his sermons. "Know thyself! Know and feel that thou wert 'shapen in wickedness' and that 'in sin did thy mother conceive thee;' and that thou thyself hast been heaping sin upon sin, ever since thou couldest discern good from evil! Sink under the mighty hand of God, as guilty of death eternal; and cast off, renounce, abhor, all imagination of ever being able to help thyself. Be it all thy hope to be washed in His blood, and renewed by His almighty Spirit, who Himself 'bare all our sins in His own body on the tree.' Art thou unable to atone for the least of thy sins?—'He is the propitiation for' all thy 'sins.' Now believe on the Lord Jesus Christ, and all thy sins are blotted out! . . . Now cry out from the ground of thy heart:

> 'Yes, I yield, I yield at last,
>   Listen to the speaking blood;
> Me, with all my sins, I cast
>   On my atoning God.' "[1]

A friend of Principal James Denney who was a keen fisherman, told him how once he had the misfortune to lose his bait without catching anything with it. The reason was that, by some mishap, the barb had been broken from the hook. Denney's friend was a Christian and an evangelist, and it was he himself who said that this was exactly what happened when the love of God was preached without reference to the essential truth of the gospel that Christ died on the Cross in the place of sinners. "In other words," continued Denney, "the condemnation of our sins in Christ upon His Cross is the barb on the hook. If you leave that out of your gospel, I do not deny that your bait will be taken; men are pleased rather than not to think that God regards them with goodwill; your bait will be taken, but you will not catch men. You will not create in sinful human hearts that attitude to Christ which created the New Testament. You will not annihilate pride, and make Christ the Alpha and Omega in man's redemption."[2]

That was a lesson Wesley learned well. We need to relearn it today.

[1] *Sermons*, Vol. I, pp. 326–328. Sermon XVI. Upon our Lord's Sermon on the Mount I.

[2] Denney, *op. cit.*, p. 128.

CHAPTER XXII

PROPERLY SAID TO LIVE

"AND now he may be *properly said to live*: God having quickened him by His Spirit, he is alive to God through Jesus Christ. . . . From hence it manifestly appears what is the nature of the new birth. It is that great change which God works in the soul when He brings it into life; when He raises it from the death of sin to the life of righteousness." *Sermons* 2: 234.

"WESLEYANISM IS SOMETIMES CLASSED WITH ARMINIANISM," wrote Prof. James Orr, "but it essentially differs from it in the central place it gives to the work of the Spirit of God in regeneration."[1] One of the distinctive marks of Wesley's evangelistic message was the emphasis he placed on the new birth. He saw it as the entrance into Christian life and the evidence that the Spirit's operation in a man's heart had taken full effect. But Wesley's reiterated teaching about the necessity of regeneration, and his recognition that it is solely the result of the Spirit's supernatural activity, must be considered in the context of his overall doctrine of the Holy Spirit. The third person of the Trinity was given the honour that is due to Him as the executive of the Godhead, and thus the dynamic force in all Christian experience. What God the Father has done for man and his salvation was done once for all in Jesus Christ His Son. What God the Father now does for man and his salvation is done through the Holy Spirit, as He applies the benefits of the Saviour's atoning death.

Wesley did not hesitate to ascribe every item in the experience of redemption to the action of the Holy Ghost. "It is certain all true faith, and the whole work of salvation, every good thought, word, and work, is altogether by the operation of the Spirit of God."[2] From the initial stirrings of common grace (which Wesley held to be related to the basic need of man to be saved) to the moment of regeneration, and all through the

[1] James Orr, *The Progress of Dogma* (1897), p. 300. The extent to which Wesley's theology may properly be regarded as Arminian needs to be defined with some care. He was certainly at one with Arminius in his reaction against what he took to be the deterministic logic of high Calvinism. Without infringing on the Divine sovereignty, room was found for human responsibility (as in Calvin himself). But in seventeenth-century England, the theology of Laud and his supporters was loosely called Arminian, as was that of the Latitudinarians. In the eighteenth century the term was associated with Socinianism. Wesley, needless to say, was far removed from such Pelagian and Unitarian tendencies. Cf. Harrison, *op. cit.*, p. 210.

[2] *Works*, Vol. VIII, p. 49. *A Farther Appeal to Men of Reason and Religion* (1745).

Christian's growth in holiness, the Spirit is the agent of enablement. He is "the Inspirer and Perfecter, both of our faith and works. 'If any man have not the Spirit of Christ, he is none of His.' He alone can quicken those who are dead unto God, can breathe into them the breath of Christian life, and so prevent, accompany, and follow them with His grace, as to bring their good desires to good effect."[1] And again, earlier in the same sermon: "Without the Spirit of God, we can do nothing but add sin to sin; it is He alone who worketh in us by His almighty power, either to will or to do that which is good; it being as impossible for us even to think a good thought, without the supernatural assistance of His Spirit, as to create ourselves, or to renew our whole souls in righteousness and true holiness."[2]

Wesley described the Holy Ghost as "the fountain of all spiritual life."[3] His constant formula was to refer all merit to Christ and all power to the Spirit. "There is no more of power than of merit in man. As all merit is in the Son of God, in what He has done and suffered for us, so all power is in the Spirit of God."[4] As Dr. Starkey observes, this might lead us to suppose that the Holy Spirit is inoperative in justification, but that was not what Wesley intended to convey.[5] He strongly stressed the historical atonement as the meritorious cause and ground of pardon; but the indispensable condition and vehicle of pardon is faith, which is itself a work of the Spirit.[6] It is, moreover, the Spirit who actually applies the gains of Christ's death to the believer, so that he is thus justified in God's sight.

In his sermons Wesley spoke of the Spirit's gracious activity at every stage of man's experience of God. If in his insistence on justification Wesley trod in the steps of Martin Luther, in this repeated emphasis on the Holy Spirit as the prior agent of effectual calling he was reminiscent of John Calvin. But whereas Calvin and his disciples regarded regeneration as the initial work of the Spirit as He implants new life in the soul, Wesley resorted to the doctrine of prevenient grace, in which the Spirit exerts what might be described as pre-natal influences.[7] To press the analogy of natural birth, as Wesley himself did, we might say that in his view prevenient grace represents the quickening of the Spirit from the moment of conception. Wesley believed, however, that these influences of the Spirit were at work even earlier still, "in every child of man—although it is true, the generality of men stifle them as soon as possible, and

[1] *Sermons*, Vol. I, p. 276. Sermon XIII. The Circumcision of the Heart.
[2] *Ibid.*, p. 268.
[3] *Works*, Vol. VI, p. 394. Sermon LXXIV. Of the Church.
[4] *Ibid.*, Vol. VIII, p. 49. *A Farther Appeal to Men of Reason and Religion* (1745).
[5] Starkey, *op. cit.*, p. 46.
[6] *Works*, Vol. VIII, pp. 56–57. *A Farther Appeal to Men of Reason and Religion* (1745).
[7] The Reformers in general employed the term regeneration in a broader sense to include both the begetting and the bringing forth of new life: Wesley kept it for the actual birth.

after a while forget, or at least deny, that they ever had them at all."[1]

What Wesley called convicting grace, leading to repentance, he also saw as being bestowed by the Holy Spirit, according to Scripture.[2] Indeed, he considered it to be "the peculiar work of the Holy Ghost."[3] He can bring this conviction "without any means at all, or by whatever means it pleaseth Him, however insufficient in themselves, or even improper to produce such an effect."[4] Some may be broken in pieces in a moment, in sickness or in health, without any visible cause.[5] This Wesley referred to as "an immediate stroke of His convincing Spirit."[6] Others may be moved when God comes upon them unawares in "an awakening sermon or conversation," or "by His Word applied with the demonstration of His Spirit."[7] Again, it could be "by some awful providence."[8] Through these and other means, or directly, the sinner may be awakened to a consciousness of his plight and brought to the place of repentance.

But, declared Wesley, "it is the ordinary method of the Spirit of God to convict sinners by the law."[9] This introduces us to one of the salient features of Wesley's mission preaching. It was his invariable method to present his hearers with the demands of the moral law, before he announced the good news of salvation in Christ. In this way he made men aware of their need, as disobedient sinners in God's sight, before he spoke of the Saviour who had paid the price of their release. "I think the right method of preaching is this," he explained, with the antinomian so-called "gospel preachers" obviously in mind.[10] "At our first beginning to preach at any place, after a general declaration of the love of God to sinners and His willingness that they should be saved, to preach the law in the strongest, the closest, the most searching manner possible; only intermixing the gospel here and there, and showing it, as it were, afar off. After more and more persons are convinced of sin, we may mix more and

[1] *Sermons*, Vol. II, p. 445. Sermon L. The Scripture Way of Salvation. Cf. Vol. I, p. 196, Sermon XI, The Spirit of Bondage and of Adoption: "As the Spirit of God does not 'wait for the call of man,' so, at some times He *will* be heard. He puts them in fear, so that, for a season at least, the heathen 'know themselves to be but men.' They feel the burden of sin, and earnestly desire to flee from the wrath to come. But not long: they seldom suffer the arrows of conviction to go deep into their souls; but quickly stifle the grace of God, and return to their wallowing in the mire."

[2] *Ibid.*, Vol. II, p. 52. Sermon XXIX. The Original, Nature, Property and Use of the Law.
[3] *Ibid.*
[4] *Ibid.*
[5] *Ibid.*
[6] *Ibid.*, Vol. I, p. 257. Sermon XII. The Means of Grace.
[7] *Ibid.*, p. 185. Sermon IX. The Spirit of Bondage and of Adoption.
[8] *Ibid.*
[9] *Ibid.*, Vol. II, p. 52. Sermon XXIX. The Original, Nature, Property and Use of the Law.
[10] *Letters*, Vol. III, p. 80. To Ebenezer Blackwell(?), 20th December, 1751.

more of the gospel, in order to *beget faith*, to raise into spiritual life those whom the law hath slain; but this is not to be done too hastily neither."[1] This, of course, was altogether in the manner of the Reformers. "The law revealeth the disease," declared Luther; "the gospel ministereth the medicine."[2] Law and gospel were always associated like this in Luther's preaching. Both were regarded as works of Christ, to be applied by the Spirit. Law is His *opus alienum*: gospel is His *opus proprium*.[3]

In his sermon on "The Original, Nature, Property, and Use of the Law" Wesley expanded this theme. "It is this which, being set home on the conscience, generally breaketh the rocks in pieces. It is more especially this part of the Word of God which is ζῶν καὶ ἐνεργὴς—'quick and powerful,' full of life and energy, 'and sharper than any two-edged sword.' This, in the hand of God and of those whom He hath sent, pierces through all the folds of a deceitful heart, and 'divides asunder even the soul and spirit;' yea, as it were, the very 'joints and marrow.' By this is the sinner discovered to himself. All his fig-leaves are torn away, and he sees that he is 'wretched, and poor, and miserable, and blind, and naked.' The law flashes conviction on every side. He feels himself a mere sinner. He has nothing to pay. His 'mouth is stopped,' and he stands 'guilty before God.' To slay the sinner, then, is the first use of the law; to destroy the life and strength wherein he trusts, and convince him that he is dead while he liveth; not only under the sentence of death, but actually dead unto God, void of all spiritual life, 'dead in trespasses and sins.' "[4]

Thus the unbeliever is prepared to enter into new life in Christ in what the Bible calls regeneration. Wesley reserved this term for the actual moment of birth, which he took to be instantaneous. The prior process of gestation he preferred to regard as the work of prevenient grace, though still performed by the Holy Spirit. Hence he could refer to the regenerate man now being "properly said to live," having been quickened by the Spirit of God.[5] He is alive in Christ. "God is continually breathing, as it were, upon the soul; and his soul is breathing unto God. Grace is descending into his heart; and prayer and praise ascending to heaven: and by this intercourse between God and man, this fellowship with the Father and the Son, as by a kind of spiritual respiration, the life of God in the soul is sustained; and the child of God grows up, till he comes to the 'full measure of the stature of Christ.' "[6]

Wesley supplied a memorable definition of the new birth. "It is that

---

[1] *Ibid.*, cf. p. 82. See *Journal*, Vol. III, p. 16, 2nd June, 1742.
[2] *Sermons of Martin Luther* (E.T. ed. James Kerr, 1875), p. 219.
[3] "His strange work" and, "His proper work."
[4] *Sermons*, Vol. II, p. 52. Sermon XXIX. The Original, Nature, Property and Use of the Law.
[5] *Ibid.*, Vol. II, p. 234. Sermon XXXIX. The New Birth.
[6] *Ibid.*

great change which God works in the soul when He brings it into life; when He raises it from the death of sin to the life of righteousness. It is the change wrought in the whole soul by the almighty Spirit of God when it is 'created anew in Christ Jesus;' when it is 'renewed after the image of God in righteousness and true holiness;' when the love of the world is changed into the love of God; pride into humility; passion into meekness; hatred, envy, malice, into a sincere, tender disinterested love for all mankind. In a word, it is that change whereby the earthly, sensual, devilish mind is turned into the 'mind which was in Christ Jesus.' This is the nature of the new birth: 'so is every one that is born of the Spirit!' "[1] In another sermon, on "The Great Privilege of those that are Born of God," Wesley described regeneration as "a vast inward change, a change wrought in the soul by the operation of the Holy Ghost; a change in the whole manner of our existence; for, from the moment we are born of God, we live in quite another manner than we did before; we are, as it were, in another world."[2]

Regeneration was classed by Wesley, along with justification by faith, as one of the two basic factors in the Christian faith. "If any doctrines within the whole compass of Christianity may be properly termed fundamental, they are doubtless these two—the doctrine of justification, and that of the new birth: the former relating to that great work which God does *for us,* in forgiving our sins; the latter, to the great work which God does *in us,* in renewing our fallen nature."[3] A similar distinction was made by Wesley in another sermon. "Justification implies only a relative, the new birth a real, change. God in justifying us does something *for* us; in begetting us again, He does the work *in* us."[4]

Wesley, however, made a logical but not a chronological differentiation between justification and the new birth. In terms of timing he regarded them as simultaneous. "In order of time, neither of these is before the other; in the moment we are justified by the grace of God, through the redemption that is in Jesus, we are also 'born of the Spirit;' but in order of *thinking,* as it is termed, justification precedes the new birth. We first conceive His wrath to be turned away, and then His Spirit to work in our hearts."[5] This does not mean that the sinner can be justified without being

---

[1] *Ibid.,* cf. p. 227: "the great work which God does *in us,* in renewing our fallen nature." As Monk points out (*op. cit.,* p. 145), the Puritans used strikingly similar language.

[2] *Sermons,* Vol. I, p. 300. Sermon XV. The Great Privilege of those that are Born of God. Cf. *Works,* Vol. VII, p. 205. Sermon CVII. On God's Vineyard.

[3] *Sermons,* Vol. II, pp. 226–227. Sermon XXXIX. The New Birth.

[4] *Ibid.,* Vol. I, p. 299. Sermon XV. The Great Privilege of those that are Born of God.

[5] *Ibid.,* Vol. II, p. 227. Cf. Vol. I, pp. 299–300, Sermon XV, The Great Privilege of those that are Born of God; *Works,* Vol. VII, p. 205, Sermon CVII. On God's Vineyard.

reborn. Rather, unless the new birth accompanies belief in Christ, it is not the living faith which alone can justify, but a dead speculative assent.[1] Wesley also looked on regeneration as being closely connected with conversion, although he did not treat these as synonymous. He made comparatively little mention in his sermons of conversion as such. He saw that it is an effect rather than a cause. When a man has been born again and has trusted in Christ, it will be recognized that he has been completely turned round. Conversion is thus the observed evidence of regeneration.

The new birth was regarded by Wesley as instantaneous.[2] It happens in the twinkling of an eye. Once again the analogy of natural birth holds good. A baby is born in a recorded moment of time. The period of gestation is protracted: even the labour may last for some hours: but the birth itself is not registered until the child emerges from the womb and draws the first breath of air. From that moment of birth the little one must grow, and this again will occupy a lengthy span. Wesley was fond of employing this analogy when explaining regeneration. The new birth he saw as a crisis, preceded by the gradual preparatory work of the Spirit in prevenient grace, and followed by the developing life of holiness. Wesley was careful to circumscribe the actual instant of regeneration. For this reason, we find it hard to accept John Parris's theory that it is closer to Wesley's maturer theology "to interpret the new birth in the complete and post-baptismal sense as being accomplished, not in the moment of conversion, but in the life of holiness."[3]

The fullest sermonic treatment of the subject is to be found in Wesley's sermon on "The New Birth," which, as the register shows, was a favourite with the evangelist.[4] In inquiring into the nature of regeneration, Wesley made it clear that we cannot expect any exact, philosophical account of its mode. This he took to be sufficiently evident from our Lord's discourse with Nicodemus in the Third Chapter of John, from which his text was taken at verse 7. "How the Holy Spirit works this in the soul," he said, "neither thou nor the wisest of the children of men is able to explain."[5] "However," he added, "it suffices for every rational and Christian purpose, that, without descending into curious, critical inquiries, we can give a plain scriptural account of the nature of the new birth. This will satisfy every reasonable man who desires only the salvation of his soul."[6]

Following the line of argument already set out in his previous sermon on "The Great Privilege of those that are Born of God," Wesley went on

---

[1] *Sermons*, Vol. I, p. 284. Sermon XIV. The Marks of the New Birth.

[2] *Works*, Vol. VII, p. 48. *A Farther Appeal to Men of Reason and Religion* (1745).

[3] John R. Parris, *John Wesley's Doctrine of the Sacraments* (1963), p. 49.

[4] *Sermons*, Vol. II, p. 226. Notes.

[5] *Ibid.*, p. 231. Sermon XXXIX. The New Birth.

[6] *Ibid.*, pp. 231–232.

to note the resemblances between natural and spiritual birth.[1] Before a child is born into the world, he has eyes but cannot see, he has ears but cannot hear, and he has a very imperfect use of any other sense. He has no idea what the world is like, nor any knowledge of any sort. To this uterine existence we do not rightly give the name of life. It is only when a man is born that we say he begins to live. Then he begins to see the light and to distinguish objects around him. His ears are opened and he hears the sounds which strike the drums. All his other senses begin to fulfil their function. He starts to breathe and live in a manner wholly different from what he did before.[2]

"How exactly doth the parallel hold in all these instances!" remarked Wesley. "While a man is in a mere natural state, before he is born of God, he has, in a spiritual sense, eyes and sees not; a thick impenetrable veil lies upon them: he has ears, but hears not; he is utterly deaf to what he is most of all concerned to hear. His other spiritual senses are all locked up: he is in the same condition as if he had them not. Hence he has no knowledge of God; no intercourse with Him; he is not at all acquainted with Him. He has no true knowledge of the things of God, either of spiritual or eternal things; therefore, though he is a living man, he is a dead Christian."[3] But as soon as he is born of the Spirit, there is a total change. Eyes and ears, heart and mind are opened. He sees the light of God's love in the face of Jesus Christ. He hears the inward voice of God, saying, "Be of good cheer; thy sins are forgiven thee." He feels in his heart the mighty working of the Spirit of God. He grasps with his mind the truth of the Word, and daily increases in knowledge. It is now that he is "properly said to live."[4]

Wesley proceeded to demonstrate the necessity of the new birth, by showing how essential it is in three particulars. It is the prerequisite of holiness. This was defined, not as "bare external religion, a round of outward duties," but as "no less than the image of God stamped on the heart."[5] It can have no existence until we are renewed by the Spirit. "It cannot commence in the soul till that change be wrought; till, by the power of the Highest overshadowing us, we are 'brought from darkness to light, from the power of Satan unto God;' that is, till we are born again; which, therefore, is absolutely necessary in order to holiness."[6]

Furthermore, the new birth is equally essential to eternal salvation. "Men may indeed flatter themselves (so desperately wicked and so deceit-

---

[1] *Ibid.*, pp. 232–233. Cf. Vol. I, pp. 300–302, Sermon XV. The Great Privilege of those that are Born of God.

[2] *Ibid.*, Vol. II, pp. 232–233. Sermon XXIX. The New Birth.

[3] *Ibid.*, p. 233.

[4] *Ibid.*, p. 234.

[5] *Ibid.*, p. 239.

[6] *Ibid.*

ful is the heart of man!) that they may live in their sins till they come to the last gasp, and yet afterwards live with God; and thousands do really believe that they have found a broad way which leadeth not to destruction. 'What danger,' say they, 'can a woman be in that is so *harmless* and so *virtuous*? What fear is there that so *honest* a man, one of so strict morality, should miss of heaven; especially if, over and above all this, they constantly attend on church and sacrament?' One of these will ask with all assurance, 'What! shall I not do as well as my neighbours?' Yes, as well as your unholy neighbours; as well as your neighbours that die in their sins! For you will all drop into the pit together, into the nethermost hell! You will all lie together in the lake of fire, 'the lake of fire burning with brimstone.' Then, at length, you will see (but God grant you may see it before!) the necessity of holiness in order to glory and, consequently, of the new birth, since none can be holy, except he be born again."[1]

Wesley's third count was that the new birth is essential to happiness. Even the secular poet Juvenal knew the melancholy truth that "no wicked man is happy."[2] Evil creates "a present hell in the breast," and even the softer passions, if left uncontrolled, spell more pain than pleasure. "Therefore, as long as these reign in any soul, happiness has no place there. But they must reign till the bent of our nature is changed, that is, till we are born again; consequently, the new birth is absolutely necessary in order to happiness in this world, as well as in the world to come."[3]

It will have been noted that Wesley's strictures were directed not only towards the irresponsible pagans of his century, but also at those who vainly sought to be saved (as he himself had once done) by moral behaviour and the scrupulous performance of ecclesiastical duties. How far Wesley was now removed from his former High Church reliance on sacramental grace as procuring salvation, may be judged from his vigorous insistence on the necessity of the new birth. As we shall see later, he did not discard the proper use of the sacraments, but here he dissociated both baptism and the Lord's Supper from the conditions of salvation. It is of the essence of High Church sacramentalism to maintain that these two ordinances are the "divinely given occasions and instruments for the bestowal of . . . regeneration, and the possession of the Spirit," as Bishop Gore expressed it.[4] Wesley's teaching on the new birth alone was sufficient to distinguish him from such a school of thought. He even went so far as to tell his nephew Samuel, who had become a Roman Catholic: "If you are not born of God, you are of no church."[5]

Amongst the inferences drawn from the scriptural truth of regeneration

[1] *Ibid.*, pp. 235–236.
[2] *Nemo malus felix.* Juvenal, *Satires*, IV, 1. 8.
[3] *Sermons*, Vol. II, p. 236. Sermon XXXIX. The New Birth.
[4] Charles Gore, *The Holy Spirit and the Church* (1924), p. 283.
[5] *Letters*, Vol. VII, p. 231. To Samuel Wesley (nephew), 19th August, 1784.

Wesley included the fact that baptism is not to be identified with the new birth.[1] The one is the sign, the other is the thing signified. The one is external and visible, the other is internal and invisible. Furthermore, since the new birth is not the same thing as baptism, so it does not always accompany baptism. The two do not belong inseparably together. It is possible to be "born of water" and yet not "born of the Spirit" (John 3: 5). It is a fact too obvious to be controverted that many of those who were children of the devil before they were baptized continue the same after baptism.[2] Wesley excepted the case of infants, considered *qua* infants, out of deference to the teaching of the Anglican Church, but it is nevertheless clear that the logic of his argument is retrospective in respect of those who survive. This becomes apparent as we listen to him addressing some who trusted in such baptism to save them.

"Say not then in your heart, 'I *was once* baptized, therefore I *am now* a child of God.' Alas, that consequence will by no means hold. How many are the baptized gluttons and drunkards, the baptized liars and common swearers, the baptized railers and evil-speakers, the baptized whore-mongers, thieves, extortioners? What think you? Are these now the children of God? Verily, I say unto you, whosoever you are, unto whom any one of the preceding characters belong, 'Ye are of your father the devil, and the works of your father ye do.' "[3] And again (more explicitly with reference to Wesley's concession to Anglican doctrine): "Lean no more on the staff of that broken reed, that ye *were* born again in baptism. Who denies that ye were then made children of God, and heirs of the kingdom of heaven? But, notwithstanding this, ye are now children of the devil. Therefore, ye must be born again."[4] It seems that here Wesley was not disputing the fact that by being baptized as infants his hearers had, according to the official teaching of the Church, actually become children of God. His argument stemmed from the realism of their condition as adults: whatever they might have been made by baptism, they were not now regenerate.

It must be admitted that Wesley's attempts to harmonize his convictions concerning the new birth with the formularies of the Anglican Church, to which he tried hard to be loyal, are singularly unconvincing. We are compelled to conclude, with Prof. Cannon, that, "Wesley's acceptance of the efficacy of infant baptism is just an acceptance, and nothing more. He affirms it as a teaching of the Church. Nowhere does he stress it as a fundamental of his own doctrine."[5] The logic of his preaching

[1] *Sermons*, Vol. II, p. 237. Sermon XXXIX. The New Birth; cf. Vol. I, p. 300. Sermon XV. The Great Privilege of those that are Born of God.
[2] *Ibid.*, Vol. II, pp. 238–239. Sermon XXXIX. The New Birth.
[3] *Ibid.*, Vol. I, p. 295. Sermon XIV. The Marks of the New Birth.
[4] *Ibid.*, p. 296.
[5] Cannon, *op. cit.*, p. 129. Parris, *op. cit.*, p. 58, does not deny that such an interpretation is possible, although he prefers to think that Wesley was seeking a *via*

about regeneration might have been expected to draw him away from the traditional Anglican belief about infant baptism. But he shrank from the full implications of his own message, since he felt that as an evangelist his point could still be made on the score of forfeited grace. Whether this latter argument was truly scriptural is open to question.

If, on analysis, a certain inconsistency and hesitation entered into Wesley's theological thinking here, it did not seriously inhibit his message. Let us close this chapter as we hear one of his trenchant perorations. " 'Nay, but I constantly attend all the ordinances of God: I keep to my church and sacrament.' It is well you do; but all this will not keep you from hell, except you be born again. Go to church twice a day; go to the Lord's table every week; say ever so many prayers in private; hear ever so many good sermons; read ever so many good books; still 'you must be born again:' none of these things will stand in the place of the new birth; no, nor anything under heaven. Let this, therefore, if you have not already experienced this inward work of God, be your continual prayer: 'Lord, add this to all Thy blessings—let me be born again! Deny whatever Thou pleasest, but deny not this; let me be 'born from above.' Take away whatsoever seemeth Thee good—reputation, fortune, friends, health— only give me this, to be born of the Spirit, to be received among the children of God! Let me be born, 'not of corruptible seed, but incorruptible, by the Word of God, which liveth, and abideth for ever;' and then let me daily 'grow in grace, and in the knowledge of our Lord and Saviour Jesus Christ!' "[1]

---

media between the Protestant and Catholic emphases. He admits that at times Wesley came "close to a sectarian position on Baptism" (p. 59).

[1] *Sermons*, Vol. II, p. 243. Sermon XXXIX. The New Birth.

CHAPTER XXIII

AN INWARD IMPRESSION ON THE SOUL

"The testimony of the Spirit is *an inward impression on the soul*, whereby the
Spirit of God directly witnesses to my spirit that I am a child of God; that
Jesus Christ hath loved me, and given Himself for me; and that all my sins are
blotted out, and I, even I, am reconciled to God." *Sermons* 1: 208.

DURING A VISIT TO BRISTOL IN JANUARY 1740, WESLEY WAS
approached by a man who had a question to ask. There must have
been many occasions in his evangelistic ministry when such informal interviews took place, although not more than a fraction of them have been
recorded. It is not clear from the *Journal* whether this inquirer was a recent
convert, or one who was seeking salvation.[1] He wanted to know if a
person could not be saved without the faith of assurance.

Wesley's reply shows how careful he was not to exceed the bounds of
scriptural restraint on this controverted subject. On the other hand, it is
clear that he held strongly to the doctrine of assurance, as he could
hardly fail to do after his own experience at Aldersgate Street. Here is his
answer: "(1) I cannot approve of your terms, because they are not scriptural. I find no such phrase as either 'faith of assurance' or 'faith of adherence' in the Bible. Besides, you speak as if there were two faiths in one
Lord. Whereas, St. Paul tells us there is but one faith in one Lord. (2) By,
'Ye are saved by faith,' I understand, ye are saved from your inward and
outward sins. (3) I never yet knew one soul thus saved without what you
call 'the faith of assurance;' I mean, a sure confidence that, by the merits
of Christ, he was reconciled to the favour of God."[2]

From the start of his mission, this was one of the major emphases of
Wesley's preaching. Although he modified his standpoint slightly in later
years, and allowed exceptions to the general rule, he nevertheless con-
sistently regarded the assurance of present salvation as the privilege of
believers, which they could and should claim if they lacked it. He went so
far as to select this as "the main doctrine of the Methodists" and, indeed,

[1] *Journal*, Vol. II, p. 333. 25th January, 1740. It would seem from the nature of his
inquiry that this man had come under the influence of some extremist Moravians,
who demanded the full assurance of faith as evidence of justification. This was not
official Moravian doctrine, for Wesley learned at Herrnhut that "being justified is
widely different from the full assurance of faith" (p. 20, 10th August, 1738).
[2] *Ibid.*, pp. 333–334. 25th January, 1740.

"the very foundation of Christianity."[1] In a letter to "John Smith"—the one where the two assertions just quoted are to be found—Wesley elaborated on this, and at the same time made it apparent that he closely linked the witness of the Spirit with the work of the Spirit in sanctification. "Therefore the distinguishing doctrines on which I do insist in all my writings and in all my preaching will lie in a very narrow compass. You sum them all up in Perceptible Inspiration. For this I earnestly contend; and so do all who are called Methodist preachers. But be pleased to observe what we mean thereby. We mean that inspiration of God's Holy Spirit whereby He fills us with righteousness, peace, and joy, with love to Him and to all mankind. And we believe it cannot be, in the nature of things, that a man should be filled with this peace and joy and love by the inspiration of the Holy Spirit without perceiving it as clearly as he does the light of the sun."[2]

From what Wesley said about it in this letter, it is plain that he extended the scope of assurance to include not only the certainty of sins forgiven, but also of the indwelling Spirit in the life which results from regeneration. Here he fixed his foot, and would not be moved. "This is the substance of what we all preach. And I will still believe none is a true Christian till he experiences it; and, consequently, 'that people at all hazards must be convinced of this—yea, though that conviction at first unhinge them ever so much, though it should in a manner distract them for a season. For it is better that they should be perplexed and terrified now than that they should sleep on and awake in hell.'

"I do not, therefore, I will not, shift the question; though I know many who desire I should. I know the proposition I have to prove, and I will not move a hair's breadth from it. It is this: 'No man can be a true Christian without such an inspiration of the Holy Ghost as fills his heart with peace and joy and love, which he who perceives it not has it not.' This is the point for which alone I contend."[3] He was persuaded that such teachings are fundamental and of the essence of the faith, and therefore he made no apology for preaching them "with such diligence and zeal as if the whole of Christianity depended on them," as his correspondent had objected.[4]

In his second sermon on "The Witness of the Spirit," composed as late as 1767, Wesley still laid the same stress on this vital matter. Looking back on almost thirty years of evangelism he could write: "It more nearly concerns the Methodists, so called, clearly to understand, explain, and defend this doctrine; because it is one grand part of the testimony which God has given them to bear to all mankind. It is by His peculiar blessing

[1] *Letters*, Vol. II, p. 64. To "John Smith," 30th December, 1745.
[2] *Ibid.*, pp. 63–64.
[3] *Ibid.*, p. 64.
[4] *Ibid.*

upon them in searching the Scriptures, confirmed by the experience of His children, that this great evangelical truth has been recovered, which had been for many years wellnigh lost and forgotten."[1] That is why Principal H. B. Workman could claim that the doctrine of assurance "was the fundamental contribution of Methodism to the life and thought of the Church."[2] It was at this point that Wesley significantly amplified the work of the Protestant reformers, by including within the orbit of salvation-theology the scriptural emphasis on certainty.

The modification introduced by Wesley has been exaggerated by some, as if to suggest that he left the whole issue quite open once again, as he did before his conversion. But that is to press the evidence too far. All he now conceded was that there were exceptions to the usual pattern. "Wesley never ceased to proclaim that it was the privilege of every believer to know his sins forgiven," declared Dr. Henry Bett, "and that this was the most vital fact in the experience of religion. But he came to see that there were many sincere followers of Christ who did not possess this great assurance, either because it had been doubted or denied as the normal privilege of the believing soul, or because it had been obscured by a superstitious stress upon the rites of the Church, as if the only assurance that a believer could have depended upon a priestly absolution. But Wesley and his followers have always maintained that every penitent and believing soul may possess, and ought to possess, an assurance of salvation."[3]

It was in writing to Prof. Rutherforth in March 1768 that Wesley clarified his position, by distinguishing between several types of assurance. This was his revised view, as he revealed, and one from which he does not seem to have departed. "I believe a few, but very few, Christians have an assurance from God of everlasting salvation; and that is the thing which the apostle terms the plerophory or full assurance of hope.

"I believe more have such an assurance of being now in the favour of God as excludes all doubt and fear. And this, if I do not mistake, the apostle means by the plerophory or full assurance of faith.

"I believe a consciousness of being in the favour of God (which I do not term plerophory, or full assurance, since it is frequently weakened, nay perhaps interrupted, by returns of doubt or fear) is the common privilege of Christians fearing God and working righteousness.

"Yet I do not affirm that there are no exceptions to this general rule. Possibly some may be in the favour of God, and yet go mourning all the day long. But I believe this is usually owing either to disorder of body or ignorance of the gospel promises. Therefore I have not for many years

---

[1] *Sermons*, Vol. II, pp. 343–344. Sermon XLV. The Witness of the Spirit.

[2] *New History of Methodism*, Vol. I, p. 19. This was not intended to imply that the doctrine of assurance is peculiar to Methodism, but that Wesley reasserted it at a time when it was regarded as a dangerous innovation.

[3] Bett, *op. cit.*, p. 37.

thought a consciousness of acceptance to be essential to justifying faith."[1]

These degrees of assurance were further clarified in later statements. They are said to correspond to the Johannine differentiation between children, young men, and fathers in Christ (I John 2: 12–14).[2] Elsewhere Wesley distinguished between a clear and a full assurance. "The one is an assurance that my sins are forgiven, clear at first, but soon clouded with doubt or fear. The other is such a plerophory or full assurance that I am forgiven, and so clear a perception that Christ abideth in me, as utterly excludes all doubt and fear, and leaves them no place, no, not for an hour. So that the difference between them is as great as the difference between the light of the morning and that of the midday sun."[3] All this, however, as Starkey is at pains to stress, "does not mean that Wesley dropped this doctrine in his later years; on the contrary, he continued to urge every Christian to seek assurance as his 'common' privilege."[4]

Wesley preached this truth as one who had himself entered into the enjoyment of such assurance. The language of his testimony as to what happened to him on the 24th May, 1738, was not accidental: "an assurance was given me that He had taken away *my* sins, even *mine*, and saved *me* from the law of sin and death."[5] In his second sermon on "The Witness of the Spirit," Wesley appealed to the evidence of Christian experience, including his own. It is this which confirms the teaching of Scripture: "the experience not of two or three, not of a few, but of a great multitude which no man can number. It has been confirmed, both in this and in all ages, by 'a cloud' of living and dying 'witnesses.' It is confirmed by *your* experience and *mine*. The Spirit itself bore witness to my spirit, that I was a child of God, gave me an evidence hereof; and I immediately cried, 'Abba, Father!' And this I did (and so did you) before I reflected on, or was conscious of, any fruit of the Spirit. It was from this testimony received, that love, joy, peace, and the whole fruit of the Spirit flowed. First, I heard

> 'Thy sins are forgiven! Accepted thou art!'—
> I listen'd, and heaven sprung up in my heart."[6]

---

[1] *Letters*, Vol. V, pp. 358–359. To Professor Thomas Rutherforth, 28th March, 1768. Rutherforth was Regius Professor of Divinity at Cambridge from 1745, and Archdeacon of Essex from 1752. In 1763 he published *Four Charges to the Clergy of the Archdeaconry of Essex*, the first three of which were directed against the Methodists. Cf. Tyerman, *Life of John Wesley*, Vol. II, pp. 490–491. For Scriptural references to πληροφορία see Colossians 2: 2, 1 Thessalonians 1: 5, Hebrews 10: 22 and 6: 11.

[2] *Letters*, Vol. VI, p. 146. To John Fletcher, 22nd March, 1775; Vol. V, p. 175. To Mary Bosanquet, 2nd January, 1770; p. 229. To Joseph Benson, 16th March, 1771.

[3] *Works*, Vol. VIII, p. 393. *An Answer to the Rev. Mr. Church's Remarks* (1745).

[4] Starkey, *op. cit.*, p. 68. Cf. Arthur S. Yates, *The Doctrine of Assurance* (1952), p. 72.

[5] *Journal*, Vol. I, p. 476. 24th May, 1738.

[6] *Sermons*, Vol. II, pp. 349–350. Sermon XLV. The Witness of the Spirit.

It was, of course, from the Moravians that Wesley had learned, prior to his own conversion, that one of the fruits of true faith in Christ was "constant peace," arising "from a sense of forgiveness."[1] But, as Monk has shown, the doctrine of assurance, conveying a sense of pardon and acceptance, was prominent in the Puritans. In the same passage from the *Journal* in which Wesley acknowledged his debt to the Moravians in this context, he also showed his awareness of the fact that the teaching was typical of the Puritans.[2] In his Fernley-Hartley Lecture on *Puritan Devotion*, Gordon Wakefield refers to the doctrine of assurance as a "distinctively Puritan and evangelical contribution."[3] He goes on to remind us that Wesley claimed that his teaching on the subject was the same as that of the Puritans.[4] And then he cites Wesley's syllogistic argument, in his first sermon on "The Witness of the Spirit," as being altogether in the manner of the Puritans.[5] But, of course, the origin of the doctrine can be traced even further back to the Reformers' rediscovery of Scripture. In a letter to Richard Tompson in 1756, Wesley revealed his awareness that "Luther, Melanchthon, and many other (if not all) of the Reformers frequently and strongly assert that every believer is conscious of his own acceptance with God, and that by a supernatural evidence."[6] He also believed that the ancient Fathers were "far from being silent on our question."[7]

To come to the doctrine as Wesley presented it in his preaching, it arose from his realization that the Holy Spirit illuminates His own work. "It is He that not only worketh in us every manner of thing that is good, but also shines upon His own work, and clearly shows what He has wrought. Accordingly, this is spoken of by St. Paul, as one great end of our receiving the Spirit, 'that we may know the things which are freely given to us of God.'"[8] Such illumination not only accompanies the initial work of salvation, but covers the whole ground of the Spirit's activity in

---

[1] *Journal*, Vol. I, p. 471. 24th May, 1738. Narrative.

[2] *Ibid.* "All the Scriptures relating to this I had been long since taught to construe away; and to call all Presbyterians who spoke otherwise."

[3] Gordon S. Wakefield, *Puritan Devotion* (1957), p. 124.

[4] *Ibid.*, p. 126. Cf. *Letters*, Vol. IV, p. 126. To the Editor of *Lloyd's Evening Post*, 20th December, 1760, where Wesley mentioned Robert Bolton, William Perkins, John Preston and Richard Sibbes amongst the Puritans who had anticipated his own teaching on assurance.

[5] Wakefield, *op. cit.*, p. 126. Cf. *Sermons*, Vol. I, p. 210. Sermon X. The Witness of the Spirit. "If, therefore, this be just reasoning,

He that now loves God, that delights and rejoices in Him with an humble joy, an holy delight, and an obedient love, is a child of God:

But I thus love, delight, and rejoice in God;

Therefore I am a child of God:—

Then a Christian can in no wise doubt of his being a child of God."

[6] *Letters*, Vol. III, p. 159. To Richard Tompson, 5th February, 1756.

[7] *Ibid.*

[8] *Sermons*, Vol. I, p. 209. Sermon X. The Witness of the Spirit. 1 Corinthians 12: 12.

the believer. Each aspect of the Spirit's operation is similarly authenticated. At every state, the Spirit graciously declares Himself. In Charles Wesley's line, the inward witness of the Holy Spirit is "strong, and permanent, and clear."[1]

Wesley's definition of the testimony of the Spirit as "an inward impression on the soul," first provided in his sermon on "The Witness of the Spirit" published in 1746, was exactly reproduced in his second sermon on the same text written in 1767.[2] "The testimony of the Spirit is an inward impression on the soul, whereby the Spirit of God directly witnesses to my spirit, that I am a child of God; that Jesus Christ hath loved me, and given Himself for me; and that all my sins are blotted out, and I, even I, am reconciled to God."[3] "After twenty years' further consideration, I see no cause to retract any part of this," Wesley commented, after transcribing his earlier definition. "Neither do I conceive how any of these expressions may be altered, so as to make them more intelligible. I can only add, that if any of the children of God will point out any other expressions which are more clear, or more agreeable to the Word of God, I will readily lay these aside."[4]

In the second sermon, Wesley proceeded to enlarge on the previous statement, however. "Meantime, let it be observed, I do not mean hereby, that the Spirit of God testifies this by any outward voice; no, nor always by an inward voice, although He does this sometimes. Neither do I suppose, that He always applies to the heart (though He often may) one or more texts of Scripture. But He so works upon the soul by His immediate influence, and by a strong, though inexplicable operation, that the stormy wind and troubled waves subside, and there is a sweet calm; the heart resting as in the arms of Jesus, and the sinner being clearly satisfied that God is reconciled, that all his 'iniquities are forgiven, and his sins covered.'"[5] Wesley contended that no one could deny the witness of the Spirit without flatly contradicting the Scriptures, and charging a lie on the God of truth. Indeed, it would be blasphemy against the Holy Ghost thus to disown His work. The crux of the matter, however, lay in Wesley's insistence on a direct witness of the Spirit, as distinct from the indirect evidence in the pacified conscience and the transformed life.

Without at all minimizing the importance of this indirect testimony, Wesley nevertheless claimed that the straightforward interpretation of Paul's words in Romans 8: 16 implies that the witness of the Spirit is immediate and unique. It is sharply differentiated from the witness of our

---

[1] *Wesley's Hymns*, Nr. 390, v. 5. l. 4.
[2] *Sermons*, Vol. I, p. 208. Sermon X. The Witness of the Spirit; Vol. II, p. 345. Sermon XLV. The Witness of the Spirit.
[3] *Ibid.*, Vol. I, p. 208. Sermon X. The Witness of the Spirit.
[4] *Ibid.*, Vol. II, p. 345. Sermon XLV. The Witness of the Spirit.
[5] *Ibid.*

own spirit, which answers to it without being identified with it. Wesley appealed to a parallel text in Galatians 4: 6: "Because ye are sons, God hath sent forth the Spirit of His Son into your hearts, crying, Abba, Father." "Is not this something *immediate* and *direct*, not the result of reflection and argumentation? Does not this Spirit cry, 'Abba, Father,' in our hearts, the moment it is given, antecedently to any reflection upon our sincerity; yea, to any reasoning whatsoever? And is not this the plain, natural sense of the words, which strike any one as soon as he hears them? All these texts, then, in their most obvious meaning, describe a direct testimony of the Spirit."[1]

In commenting on Hebrews 6: 11 in his *Notes on the New Testament*, Wesley spoke of the full assurance both of faith and of hope as being "wrought in the soul by the same immediate inspiration of the Holy Ghost" and "not an opinion, not a bare construction of Scripture," but as "given immediately by the power of the Holy Ghost, and what none can have for another, but for himself only."[2] "The testimony now under consideration is given by the Spirit of God to and with our Spirit: He is the Person testifying."[3] That is the premiss on which Wesley built his teaching. He recognized the joint testimony of the Spirit with our spirits. He did not decry the means of grace. But he staunchly maintained that behind all this there stands the immediate, authentic witness of the Spirit, prior to any consciousness on our part and independent of any mode or rite. "Whatever voice, or word, or ordinance may be employed," declared William Burt Pope explaining Wesley's position, "—each and all may be employed, and the Word in some form always—the assurance must ultimately be conveyed direct from Spirit to spirit."[4]

We pass from the nature of this testimony to its content. How did Wesley in his preaching describe the effect of assurance? It is simply "to evince the reality of our sonship."[5] The witness of the Spirit tells me "that I am a child of God."[6] That is precisely what Paul affirms in Romans 8: 16. Assurance is related to the pardon of sin and acceptance into a filial relationship with the Father. This is the double seal on the believer's salvation. In debate with William Warburton, the learned Bishop of Gloucester, who had taken exception to his teaching on the Spirit, Wesley adroitly quoted at some considerable length from John Pearson's *An Exposition of the Creed* (1659), which was accepted as a classic statement of the Anglican position. Bishop Pearson had plainly asserted: "It is the

[1] *Ibid.*, p. 349.
[2] *Notes*, Hebrews 6: 11.
[3] *Sermons*, Vol. II, p. 344. Sermon XLV. The Witness of the Spirit.
[4] William Burt Pope, *A Compendium of Christian Theology* (2nd edn. revised, 1880), Vol. III, p. 129.
[5] *Sermons*, Vol. I, p. 210. Sermon X. The Witness of the Spirit.
[6] *Ibid.*, Vol. II, p. 345. Sermon XLV. The Witness of the Spirit.

office of the Holy Ghost to assure us of the adoption of sons, to create in us a sense of the paternal love of God towards us, to give us an earnest of our everlasting inheritance."[1] Wesley ingeniously impaled Warburton on the horns of a theological dilemma. "It now rests with your Lordship to take your choice; either to condemn or to acquit both. Either your Lordship must condemn Bishop Pearson (a man no ways inferior to Bishop Chrysostom), or you must acquit me. For I have his express authority on my side. . . ."[2]

Wesley was firm in his conviction that those who are indeed the children of God will not be left in doubt by the Holy Spirit. The notion of unconscious faith, favoured by some theologians today, would scarcely have appealed to him. To Wesley it would have seemed incredible that a man should be born again and not know it. He did not hesitate to make this a criterion by which the genuine Christian can be distinguished from the nominal. No doubt he had his own previous experience in mind. Speaking of those whose religion had not advanced beyond the form of godliness to the essential power, Wesley said: "Many of these have a desire to please God: some of them take much pains to please Him: but do they not, one and all, count it the highest absurdity for any to talk of *knowing* his sins are forgiven? Which of *them* even pretends to such a thing? And yet many of them are conscious of their own sincerity. Many of them undoubtedly have, in a degree, the testimony of their own spirit, a consciousness of their own uprightness. But this brings them no consciousness that they are forgiven; no knowledge that they are the children of God. Yea, the more sincere they are, the more uneasy they generally are, for want of knowing it; plainly showing that this cannot be known in a satisfactory manner, by the bare testimony of our own spirit, without God's directly testifying that we are His children."[3]

Whilst the way in which the Spirit imparts this assurance remains cloaked in mystery, like the new birth itself, the fact is nevertheless indisputable. Too much curiosity about the medium of operation must not prevent us from recognizing the reality of its results. As Luther puts it, there are times when too inquisitive minds must learn to "crucify the how."[4]

[1] John Pearson, *An Exposition of the Creed* (1659), Article VIII, p. 501. Pearson was Lady Margaret Professor of Divinity at Cambridge from 1661, and Bishop of Chester from 1673. "He was perhaps the most erudite and profound divine of a learned theological age" (*Oxford Dictionary of the Christian Church*, p. 1037). For Wesley's admiration of him, cf. *Journal*, Vol. III, p. 391, 23rd March, 1749; *Letters*, Vol. IV, p. 243. To Cradock Glascott, 13th May, 1764.
[2] *Letters*, Vol. IV, p. 378. To William Warburton, 26th November, 1762. Warburton became Dean of Bristol in 1757 and Bishop of Gloucester in 1759. He published *The Doctrine of Grace* against Wesley in 1759. Professor R. W. Greaves dubs him "that rumbustious ecclesiastical and literary controversialist" (*Essays in Modern English Church History*, p. 163).
[3] *Sermons*, Vol. II, p. 352. Sermon XLV. The Witness of the Spirit.
[4] Cf. *Luhter's Works*, ed. Jaroslav Pelikan (1957), Vol. XXII, p. 304.

I

That was Wesley's attitude too. "The manner how the *divine* testimony is manifested to the heart, I do not take upon me to explain. Such knowledge is too wonderful and excellent for me: I cannot attain to it. The wind bloweth, and I hear the sound thereof; but I cannot tell how it cometh, or whither it goeth. As no one knoweth the things of a man, save the spirit of a man that is in him; so the *manner* of the things of God knoweth no one, save the Spirit of God. But the fact we know; namely, that the Spirit of God doth give a believer such a testimony of his adoption, that while it is present to the soul, he can no more doubt the reality of his sonship, than he can doubt of the shining of the sun, while he stands in the full blaze of its beams."[1]

Wesley was careful in his preaching to indicate how the witness of the Spirit may be distinguished "from the presumption of a natural mind, and from the delusion of the devil."[2] The eighteenth century shrank from anything savouring of enthusiasm. Nowadays the validity of assurance is queried on psychological grounds. We must not conclude, Wesley argued, that because certain mad French prophets imagined that they had experienced the impression of the Spirit on their hearts, that therefore others may not have known the reality which Satan so cleverly counterfeits. The fact that a madman thinks he is a king does not prove that there are no real monarchs. "Religion is the spirit of a sound mind; and, consequently, stands in direct opposition to madness of every kind."[3] The Spirit brings sanity and balance. His witness within is not to be confused with the frenzied ravings of an ecstatic.

In his first sermon on "The Witness of the Spirit" Wesley set out the scriptural marks which identify genuine assurance. In it the comfortable sense of pardon is always preceded by deep conviction of sin and real repentance. Those who have never experienced these necessary prerequisites cannot enjoy the peace which flows from them.[4] Again, the witness of the Spirit must stem from the "vast and mighty change" of regeneration.[5] Those who do not show evidence of such a transformation cannot rightly claim assurance. They see no need for the new birth: they say they have always been Christians: they cannot point to a time when they received life from above.[6] Furthermore, the child of God is known from a presumptuous self-deceiver by his humble joy. In its train there follows meekness, patience, gentleness, long-suffering. There is "a soft, yielding spirit; a mildness and sweetness, a tenderness of soul, which

[1] *Sermons*, Vol. I, p. 210. Sermon X. The Witness of the Spirit. On p. 234 Wesley explained that the joy brought by the Spirit "does not arise from any natural cause: not from any sudden flow of spirits."
[2] *Ibid.*, p. 211.
[3] *Ibid.*, Vol. II, p. 90. Sermon XXXII. The Nature of Enthusiasm.
[4] *Ibid.*, Vol. I, pp. 211–212. Sermon X. The Witness of the Spirit.
[5] *Ibid.*, p. 213.
[6] *Ibid.*

words cannot express."[1] The false testimony produces just the reverse effect. It makes a man haughty and incapable of receiving reproof. Most important of all, the witness of the Spirit will be shown in obedience and love. "Love rejoices to obey; to do, in every point, whatever is acceptable to the beloved. A true lover of God hastens to do His will on earth as it is done in heaven."[2] This is the indirect testimony of our own spirit to the direct testimony of the Holy Spirit.

At the close of his second sermon on the subject, Wesley drew two inferences.[3] "Let none ever presume to rest in any supposed testimony of the Spirit, which is separate from the fruit of it. . . . Let none rest in any supposed fruit of the Spirit without the witness."[4] Fruit and witness belong together. Man must not divide what God has united. Only as this admirably scriptural equilibrium is preserved is the doctrine of assurance safeguarded on the one hand from the excesses of fanatical emotion, and on the other from the snare of justification by works. Whilst urging his converts to claim the privilege of a pardon that can be known, Wesley also taught them that profession has to be supported by character and conduct. Such counsel could hardly be bettered in any age.

[1] Ibid., p. 214.
[2] Ibid., pp. 214–215.
[3] Ibid., Vol. II, pp. 358–359. Sermon XLV. The Witness of the Spirit.
[4] Ibid., p. 358.

CHAPTER XXIV

THE GRAND DEPOSITUM

"I AM glad Brother D—— has more light with regard to full sanctification. This doctrine is *the grand depositum* which God has lodged with the people called Methodists; and for the sake of propagating this chiefly He appeared to have raised us up." *Letters* 8: 238.

ACCORDING TO BISHOP PAUL TAYLOR, IT WAS THE DISTINCTIVE commission of John Wesley to recover and restore "the masterpiece called 'Holiness unto the Lord,' which through many years had gathered dust and discoloration in the attic of the Church."[1] Wesley himself was in no doubt as to what had been his chief concern from the start. In the *Large Minutes* the question was asked: "What was the rise of Methodism, so called?" The answer given was this: "In 1729, two young men, reading the Bible, saw they could not be saved without holiness, followed after it, and incited others so to do. In 1737 they saw holiness comes by faith. They saw likewise, that men are justified before they are sanctified; but still holiness was their point. God then thrust them out, utterly against their will, to raise a holy people."[2] Wesley's objective throughout his career as an evangelist was "to spread scriptural holiness over the land."[3]

In recognizing this he conceded that it is insufficient for the gospel preacher to confine himself to the bare message of salvation. Even in addressing the unconverted, it is necessary to stress the resultant life of holiness. Those who are being invited to tread the Christian way have a right to know where they are going. The impression must not be conveyed that conversion is an end in itself. It is incumbent upon the evangelist to indicate the nature of the new life which follows the new birth. All this was part of Wesley's preaching, not only to his societies, but also to the crowds of as yet uncommitted hearers. "This is no esoteric message for the few," explained Dr. Newton Flew.[4] The need for sanctification was urged from the first, even on those who were still only seekers.

"To retain the grace of God is much more than to gain it"—so Wesley told Adam Clarke.[5] This was why what would nowadays be termed his

---

[1] J. Paul Taylor, *Holiness: The Finished Foundation* (1963), p. 14.
[2] *Works*, Vol. VIII, p. 300. *Large Minutes* (1789).
[3] *Ibid.*, p. 299.
[4] R. Newton Flew, *The Idea of Perfection in Christian Theology* (1934), p. 330.
[5] *Letters*, Vol. VIII, p. 249. To Adam Clarke, 26th November, 1790.

follow-up programme laid so much weight on the upward call of holiness. He knew that the mortality rate in evangelism can be high, and he was determined to take every precaution. He was aware, of course, that God can care for His own, but he was equally convinced that He often does so through human channels. He wanted to be clear of the blood of all to whom he preached, and his conscience was not content merely to rest in the fact that he had faithfully declared the truth as it is in Christ Jesus. He must also make every provision for their growth in grace, and warn them in advance that their profession of faith must be evidenced in sanctity of living.

On Friday the 30th April, 1773, a solemn watch-night service was held at Cork.[1] "I believe the confidence of many was shaken while I was enforcing, 'Though I had all faith, so as to remove mountains, and have not love, I am nothing.' A hard saying! but yet absolutely necessary to be insisted on, particularly among the people called Methodists. Otherwise, how many of them will build on the sand, on an unloving, unholy faith!"[2] Wesley was determined to lay a surer foundation than that. Evidently what he had said sank in, for after his visit to the city he was able to write: "I left Cork with must satisfaction, having seen the fruit of my labour."[3]

In Wesley's eyes, the work of evangelism and the urging of holiness went hand in hand. Where the latter was neglected, the former would inevitably suffer. In September 1765 he examined the society at Bristol, and was perturbed to find fifty members fewer than the previous year. He quickly pointed to one reason for the decline: "Christian Perfection has been little insisted on; and wherever this is not done, be the preachers ever so eloquent, there is little increase, either in the number or the grace of the hearers."[4] It was from such a conviction that Wesley continually exhorted his preachers to emulate him in never failing to press home this teaching. "Speak, and spare not," he told George Merryweather. "Let not regard for man induce you to betray the truth of God. Till you press the believers to expect *full salvation* now you must not look for any revival."[5] It is not

[1] The watch-night service was not then confined to New Year's Eve, as it almost always is in Methodism today, but could be held at any time when an act of reconsecration was demanded.
[2] *Journal*, Vol. V, p. 504. 30th April, 1773. Cf. Vol. IV, p. 529. 15th September, 1762.
[3] *Ibid.*, Vol. V, p. 504. 30th April, 1773.
[4] *Ibid.*, p. 149. 30th September, 1765.
[5] *Letters*, Vol. IV, p. 321. To George Merryweather, 8th February, 1766. Evidently Jacob Rowell, the assistant at Yarm, had not been giving scriptural holiness as much prominence as he should, and Wesley therefore pressed Merryweather to "supply his lack of service" (*ibid.*). He had started the letter by saying: "Where Christian perfection is not strongly and explicitly preached there is seldom any remarkable blessing from God, and consequently little addition to the Society and little life in the members of it" (*ibid*). Cf. Vol. VI, p. 42. To John Bredon, 18th September, 1773: "Be all a Methodist; and strongly insist on full salvation to be received now by simple faith."

difficult to see why Wesley maintained the pressure at this vital point. "When we think of the passionate evangelism of the early Methodists," explained Dr. Bett, "we must remember that it would simply have gone for nothing if the holy lives of the early Methodists had not backed up the evangelistic appeal."[1]

The sources of Wesley's teaching on sanctification have been the subject of scholarly scrutiny in recent years. The theory propounded by Cell, that Wesley's theology represents a "necessary synthesis of the Protestant ethic of grace with the Catholic ethic of holiness," has come under fire.[2] Cell's judgement at this point is open to serious question. It is being realized that, as Dr. Williams puts it, the "Catholic view of holiness cannot be moulded on to the Protestant view of grace."[3] The Roman doctrine of sanctification assumes the ability of man, with the aid of grace, to climb up the ladder of merit. He will ultimately reach the goal of perfection as a result of his own efforts, supplemented by the enabling power of God only when this is thought to be required. Hence sanctification, though not altogether by works, is not altogether by grace either.

Now, whilst Wesley placed perhaps greater emphasis than did the Reformers on the need for an actual righteousness to be displayed as the evidence of saving faith, his teaching nevertheless remained strictly within Protestant categories, as Williams rightly affirms.[4] "Wesley's view is one of sanctification by faith alone. In other words, Wesley put his doctrine within the Protestant framework of justification by faith, not within the Roman framework of justification by faith and works. He put it within the order of personal relationship to Christ, not within the order of a legal relationship to a moral standard."[5] And, as Monk makes clear, Wesley was not only in line with the Reformation in this, but also an heir of the Puritans.[6] "For Wesley," declares Prof. Outler, "the doctrine of perfection was yet another way of celebrating the sovereignty of grace."[7]

Wesley's preaching of holiness was set in the broader context of the Spirit's total operation. We have noted the agency of the Third Person of the Trinity in prevenient grace, in conviction, in regeneration, in applying the merit of Christ in justification, in leading to repentance and faith, and

---

[1] Bett, op. cit., p. 157.
[2] Cell, op. cit., p. 361. Cf. E. Gordon Rupp, *Principalities and Powers* (1952), p. 82; Monk, op. cit., p. 110; Williams, op. cit., pp. 174–175.
[3] Williams, op. cit., p. 175.
[4] *Ibid.*
[5] *Ibid.*
[6] Monk, op. cit., p. 68. Cf. Newton, op. cit., p. 19. Wesley wrote: "There appears μεγα χάσμά (a great gulf) a huge chasm between the first and the perfect love. Now this Mr. Bolton, Dr. Preston, Dr. Sibbes, and their contemporaries, above all others, instruct us how to pass through: how to use the faith which God has given, and to go from strength to strength." (*Christian Library*, Vol. IV, pp. 107–108.)
[7] Outler, op. cit., p. 253.

in bringing assurance to the child of God. Wesley's doctrine of sanctification found its place in the same area, as related to the Spirit's continuing
work in the believer. But he was careful not to divorce it from the redemption wrought by Christ on the Cross. He kept close to Scripture in
regarding holiness as being one of the benefits of Christ's death. Indeed, he
could affirm that it was "the peculiar business of Christ" thus to establish
His kingdom in the hearts of men.[1]

In his sermon on "The Lord our Righteousness," in which he claimed
that he said nothing which he had not repeated at least fifty times that very
year (1765), Wesley went out of his way to underline the link between
what Christ has done for us on the Cross and what He will do in us
through the Spirit. The second would not be possible without the first.
No doctrine of holiness which does not see it as having its source in the
atoning sacrifice of Christ can be accepted as truly biblical. "The righteousness of Christ is the whole and sole foundation of all our hope. It is by faith
that the Holy Ghost enables us to build upon this foundation. God gives
this faith; in that moment we are accepted of God: and yet, not for the
sake of that faith, but of what Christ has done and suffered for us."[2] On
the other hand, Wesley constantly warned against the danger of resting in
the imputed righteousness of Christ without any concern for the impartation of that righteousness to produce a holy life.[3]

Wesley's presentation of what he called "the grand depositum" also
stemmed from his view of regeneration.[4] It implies a real change, whereas
justification involves only a relative change.[5] Since the new birth is instantaneous, sanctification begins in that very moment, and continues
whilst the believer remains in the body. In it the Holy Spirit carries on
what was inaugurated by regeneration. In expounding Wesley's meaning,
Sugden said that "regeneration is the impartation of the new *life* through
the indwelling of the Holy Spirit; sanctification is the gift of holiness or
spiritual *health*, holiness and health being a derivation of the same. Of
course there can be no life without some measure of health; but we can
distinguish between life and health; and whilst there are no degrees in life
—a man is either alive or dead—there are degrees in health, and it is
capable of improvement."[6]

One of the features of the Puritan writers which most appealed to
Wesley, so he confessed, was that "they are continually tearing up the very
roots of Antinomianism, by showing at large, from the oracles of God,
the absolute necessity, as of that legal repentance which is previous to

---

[1] *Notes*, Matthew 4: 17.
[2] *Sermons*, Vol. II, p. 434. Sermon XLIX. The Lord our Righteousness.
[3] *Ibid.*, pp. 435–436.
[4] *Letters*, Vol. VIII, p. 238. To Robert Carr Brackenbury, 15th September, 1790.
[5] *Sermons*, Vol. II, p. 446. Sermon L. The Scripture Way of Salvation.
[6] *Ibid.*, p. 446, n. 4.

faith, so of that evangelical repentance which follows it, and which is essential to that holiness, without which we cannot see the Lord."[1] This recognition was basic to Wesley's teaching on holiness, and figured prominently in his sermons addressed to believers, many of whom were not long in the faith. Two of them must occupy as we consider the presuppositions of Wesley's message of holiness. One dealt with the need for evangelical repentance—the element Wesley noted in the Puritans—and the other, which precedes it in the standard collection, had to do with the prior issue of sin in the believer. To these we must now turn in some detail.

In the *Journal* for the 28th March, 1763, Wesley recorded: "I retired to Lewisham, and wrote the sermon on 'Sin in Believers' in order to remove a mistake which some were labouring to propagate—that there is no sin in any that are justified."[2] In the sermon itself Wesley wasted no time in beating about the bush. He came straight to the point at the start by posing three pertinent questions: "Is there then sin in him that is in Christ? Does sin *remain* in one that believes in Him? Is there any sin in them that are born of God, or are they wholly delivered from it?"[3] This is something which should concern every Christian.

Wesley believed that Scripture confirmed the statement of the Ninth Article, *Of Original or Birth Sin*, which he quoted, that "this infection of nature doth remain, yea, in them that are regenerated; whereby the lust of the flesh called in Greek φρόνημα σαρκὸς . . . is not subject to the law of God. And although there is no condemnation for them that believe, yet this lust hath of itself the nature of sin."[4] That two principles "contrary the one to the other" are at work even in the believer, Wesley proved conclusively from Scripture (Galatians 5: 17, *et al.*). "Indeed, this grand point, that there are two contrary principles in believers—nature and grace, the flesh and the Spirit—runs through all the Epistles of St. Paul, yea through all the Holy Scriptures; almost all the directions and exhortations therein are founded on this supposition; pointing at wrong tempers or practices in those who are, notwithstanding, acknowledged by the inspired writers to be believers. And they are continually exhorted to fight with and conquer these by the power of faith which was in them."[5]

This is corroborated by experience. Christians do in fact "feel an heart bent to backsliding; a proneness to depart from God, and cleave to the things of earth. They are daily sensible of sin remaining in their heart—pride, self-will, unbelief; and of sin cleaving to all they speak and do, even

[1] *Christian Library*, Vol. IV, p. 107.
[2] *Journal*, Vol. V, p. 10. 28th March, 1765. Wesley probably stayed at the home of his friend Ebenezer Blackwell, a partner in Martins Bank.
[3] *Sermons*, Vol. II, p. 361. Sermon XLVI. On Sin in Believers.
[4] *Ibid.*, pp. 360-361.
[5] *Ibid.*, p. 367.

their best actions and holiest duties. Yet at the same time they 'know that they are of God'; they cannot doubt of it for a moment. They feel His Spirit clearly 'witnessing with their spirit that they are the children of God.' They rejoice 'in God through Christ Jesus, by whom they have now received the atonement.' So that they are equally assured that sin is in them, and that 'Christ is in them the hope of glory.' "[1]

Wesley now reached the crucial question: "But can Christ be in the same heart where sin is?" His answer was a firm refutation of those—mainly misled Moravians—who spoke of sinlessness. "Undoubtedly He can; otherwise it never could be saved therefrom. Where the sickness is, there is the Physician,

> 'Carrying on His work within
> Striving till He cast out sin.[2]' "

But then Wesley went on with equal discernment to deal a blow at any antinomian laxity, and to prepare the ground for his call to holiness. "Christ indeed cannot *reign* where sin *reigns*; neither will He *dwell* where any sin is *allowed*. But He *is* and *dwells* in the heart of every believer, who is *fighting against* all sin; although it be not yet purified, according to the purification of the sanctuary."[3]

It is the realization that sin still persists in the heart even of the believer which leads to that evangelical repentance of which the Puritans wrote. Wesley's sermon on this subject was prepared in 1767 and published the next year. In it he spoke of repentance and faith as the gate of religion, but not only so. There is, of course, a repentance and faith which belong to the beginning of the Christian pilgrimage, leading to salvation. "But, not-withstanding this, there is also a repentance and a faith (taking the words in quite another sense, a sense not quite the same, nor yet entirely different) which are requisite after we have 'believed the gospel;' yea, and in every subsequent stage of our Christian course, or we cannot 'run the race which is set before us.' And this repentance and faith are full as necessary, in order to our *continuance* and *growth* in grace, as the former faith and repentance were, in order to our *entering* into the kingdom of God."[4]

Such evangelical repentance is defined as "one kind of self-knowledge, the knowing ourselves sinners, yea, guilty, helpless sinners, even though we know we are children of God."[5] It is the recognition that believers are at once redeemed from sin and yet not out of its grip. It is the acknow-ledgement that "they are no more able now *of themselves* to think one good thought, to form one good desire, to speak one good word, or to do one

---

[1] *Ibid.*, pp. 368–369. Cf. pp. 446–447. Sermon L. The Scripture Way of Salvation.
[2] *Ibid.*, p. 369. Sermon XLVI. On Sin in Believers.
[3] *Ibid.*
[4] *Ibid.*, p. 380. Sermon XLVII. The Repentance of Believers.
[5] *Ibid.* Cf. Vol. I, p. 268. Sermon XIII. The Circumcision of the Heart.

good work, than before they were justified."[1] There is no doubt that power is available to conquer sin, "but it is not from nature, either in whole or in part; it is the *mere* gift of God: nor is it given all at once, as if they had a stock laid up for many years; but from moment to moment."[2] It will be seen that in his doctrine of holiness, Wesley was as careful to exclude all reliance on any personal merit as in the case of justification. It is this thoroughly Reformed approach which marks him off from those who represented what Cell called "the Catholic ethic of holiness."[3] The mystic ladder is kicked from under the Christian's feet at the outset.

This evangelical repentance, which will manifest itself through good works of piety and mercy, though it does not rely on them, is the necessary prelude to that faith which alone secures sanctification. Wesley was often accused of preaching justification by faith yet sanctification by works: he rebutted the charge with vigour. "I have constantly declared just the contrary; and that in all manner of ways. I have continually testified in private and in public, that we are sanctified as well as justified by faith. And indeed the one of those great truths does exceedingly illustrate the other. Exactly as we are justified by faith, so are we sanctified by faith. Faith is the condition, and the only condition, of sanctification, exactly as it is of justification. It is the *condition*: none is sanctified but he that believes; without faith no man is sanctified. And it is the *only condition*: this alone is sufficient for sanctification."[4]

Later in his sermon on "The Scripture Way of Salvation," Wesley elucidated the nature of this sanctifying faith. "It is a divine evidence and conviction, first, that God hath promised it in Holy Scripture. Till we are thoroughly satisfied of this, there is no moving one step further."[5] Then, it is a persuasion that what God has promised He is able to perform. With God all things are possible. He can "purify the heart from all sin," and "fill it with all holiness."[6] If He speaks, it shall be done. Thirdly, it is faith that He is not only able but willing to do it, and do it now. "And why not? Is not a moment to Him the same as a thousand years? He cannot want more time to accomplish whatsoever is His will. And He cannot want or stay for any more *worthiness* or *fitness* in the persons He is pleased to honour."[7] To this confidence must be added one thing more—belief that God is actually doing it. In that hour it is done.

It is clear, then, that, though Wesley regarded sanctification as a process spanning the entire life of the believer from the moment of the new birth,

---

[1] *Ibid.*, Vol. II, p. 389. Sermon XLVII. The Repentance of Believers.
[2] *Ibid.*
[3] Cell, *op. cit.*, p. 361. Cf. above, p. 262.
[4] *Sermons*, Vol. II, p. 453. Sermon L. The Scripture Way of Salvation.
[5] *Ibid.*, p. 457.
[6] *Ibid.*
[7] *Ibid.*, pp. 457–458.

he nevertheless expected a crisis within that process, consequent upon the
exercise of evangelical repentance and faith. As Lindström brings out, this
is the hallmark of Wesley's teaching on holiness. "The gradual process is
interrupted . . . by the direct intervention of God, which in a single instant raises man to a higher plane. It is this combination of the gradual and
the instantaneous that particularly distinguishes Wesley's conception of
the process of salvation."[1] But these two aspects of sanctification were not
divorced in Wesley's thought. The process led to the crisis and then
flowed from it. Although he often referred to the crisis, he made it clear
in a letter to his brother Charles that he did not consider this to be his
special *forte*. "O insist everywhere on *full* redemption, receivable by *faith
alone*! Consequently to be looked for *now*. . . . Go on, in your *own way*,
what God has peculiarly called you to. Press the *instantaneous* blessing:
then I shall have more time for my peculiar calling, enforcing the gradual
work."[2]

The content of holiness had been indicated by Wesley in a sermon first
preached in the church of St. Mary the Virgin, Oxford, as early as 1733.
Its subject was "The circumcision of the Heart," which Wesley equated
with "that habitual disposition of soul which, in the sacred writings, is
termed holiness; and which directly implies, the being cleansed from sin,
'from all filthiness both of flesh and spirit;' and, by consequence, the being
endued with those virtues which were also in Christ Jesus; the being so
'renewed in the spirit of our mind,' as to be 'perfect as our Father in
heaven is perfect.'"[3] Wesley told John Newton in 1765 that this sermon
contained all that he still taught "concerning salvation from *all sin* and
loving God with an *undivided heart*."[4]

In 1739 Wesley defined holiness (with echoes of Scougal) as "the life of
God in the soul of man; a participation of the divine nature; the mind
that was in Christ; or, the renewal of our heart after the image of Him
that created us."[5] In 1741 he was encouraged to publish a sermon on
"Christian Perfection," after a conversation with Edmund Gibson, Bishop
of London, at Whitehall. This took place towards the end of 1740, so
Wesley revealed in his *A Plain Account of Christian Perfection* (1766).[6] The
Bishop asked what Wesley meant by Christian perfection. Wesley told
him, without any concealment or modification. When he had finished,
Dr. Gibson said, "Mr. Wesley, if this be all you mean, publish it to all the
world. If any one then can confute what you say, he may have free leave."
Wesley answered, "My Lord, I will," and accordingly wrote and printed

[1] Harald Lindström, *Wesley and Sanctification* (1946), p. 121.
[2] *Letters*, Vol. V, p. 16. To Charles Wesley, 27th June, 1766.
[3] *Sermons*, Vol. I, pp. 267–268. Sermon XIII. The Circumcision of the Heart.
[4] *Letters*, Vol. IV, p. 299. To John Newton, 14th May, 1765.
[5] *Journal*, Vol. II, p. 275. 13th September, 1739.
[6] *Works*, Vol. XI, p. 374. *A Plain Account of Christian Perfection* (1766).

the sermon on the subject now included in the standard selection.[1]

The sermon discussed perfection (from Philippians 3 : 12) in its negative and positive aspects. In a comprehensive series of denials Wesley spiked the guns of those who took exception to what they imagined his teaching to be, by showing that he shared their misgivings. Sanctified believers are not free from ignorance or from mistake. They are liable to error, though not in matters essential to salvation.[2] Nor are they free from infirmities— by which Wesley meant such physical weaknesses as are not of a moral nature. Freedom from temptation is not claimed either, for Christ Himself was subject to it.[3] Wesley strongly repudiated the notion of absolute perfection in man. "There is no *perfection of degrees*, as it is termed; none which does not admit of continual increase. So that how much soever any man has attained, or in how high a degree soever he is perfect, he hath still need to 'grow in grace,' and daily to advance in the knowledge and love of God his Saviour."[4] In *A Plain Account of Christian Perfection*, Wesley enlarged upon these reservations, and stressed that "the most perfect have continual need of the merits of Christ."[5] He envisaged no holiness which was independent of the Cross.[6] Sinless perfection he explicitly rejected. "I never contended for it," he maintained, ". . . seeing the term is not scriptural. A perfection that perfectly fulfils the whole law, and so needs not the merits of Christ? I acknowledge none such—I do now, and always did, protest against it."[7] And again: "Sinless perfection is a phrase I never use, lest I should seem to contradict myself."[8] He contented himself rather with speaking about salvation from sin—by which he meant "a voluntary transgression of a known law"—and leaving it at that.[9]

In the sermon Wesley next turned to the more positive aspect of perfection. After a lengthy examination of the relevant texts—especially those in the First Epistle of John—Wesley reached this considered conclusion, which he believed to be congruous with the whole tenor of the New Testament: "a Christian is so far perfect, as not to commit sin."[10] This is the glorious privilege of every Christian. There is no need for him to fall into evil. He may in fact do so, but that is not God's will for him. Nor can he complain that he had no alternative, for all the resources of grace are freely provided for him. Wesley did not claim that a Christian was not able to sin, but that by the indwelling Spirit he was able not to sin. More-

[1] Ibid. Cf. Sermons, Vol. II, pp. 150–174. Sermon XXXV. Christian Perfection.
[2] Sermons, Vol. II, pp. 152–155. Sermon XXXV. Christian Perfection.
[3] Ibid., pp. 155–156.
[4] Ibid., p. 156.
[5] Works, Vol. XI, p. 395. A Plain Account of Christian Perfection (1766).
[6] Ibid., pp. 395–396.
[7] Letters, Vol. IV, p. 213. To Mrs. Maitland, 12th May, 1763.
[8] Works, Vol. XI, p. 396. A Plain Account of Christian Perfection (1766).
[9] Ibid.
[10] Sermons, Vol. II, p. 169. Sermon XXXV. Christian Perfection.

over, those who are strong in the Lord will also be emancipated from evil thoughts and tempers.[1] Yet all this results from a maintained condition of holiness, rather than as the automatic entail of a crisis experience.

As a preacher, Wesley was content to declare the doctrine of holiness, from Scripture and as confirmed by Christian experience, without entering into a theological debate about the precise formulation of its contents. As a result, he left a number of ends untied, and it would be quite impossible to reduce his teaching to a neat, consistent scheme. Sometimes he placed his weight on this aspect, sometimes on that. Always what was said about the instantaneous work has to be seen in the context of the gradual, and what was said about the gradual has to be related to the instantaneous.[2] Moreover, the instantaneous must not be confused with the static, as if some high experience of the moment could control the future. In this sense, as Wesley saw it, sanctification differs from salvation.

The crisis of entire sanctification is never isolated from the process of spiritual development, which both precedes and follows it. Hence Wesley's constant exhortation was to press towards the mark and reach for the prize. "Yea, and when ye have attained a measure of perfect love, when God has circumcised your hearts, and enabled you to love Him with all your heart and with all your soul, think not of resting there. That is impossible. You cannot stand still; you must either rise or fall; rise higher or fall lower. Therefore the voice of God to the children of Israel, to the children of God, is, 'Go forward!' 'Forgetting the things that are behind, and reaching forward unto those that are before, press on to the mark, for the prize of your high calling of God in Christ Jesus!' "[3]

This intensive reiteration of the need to make progress was the best possible fellowship message for Wesley's converts. One of the reasons why such a high percentage of them stayed the course is to be found here. None of those who listened to Wesley's preaching could rest on their spiritual oars. As he mounted his horse and headed for his next location, they knew that they themselves must be on their way as they made for the Celestial City.

[1] *Ibid.*, pp. 169-171.
[2] *Works*, Vol. VI, p. 509. Sermon LXXXV. Working out our own Salvation. Wesley there defined "the proper Christian salvation" as consisting of "those two grand branches, justification and sanctification." "All experience, as well as Scripture, show this salvation to be both instantaneous and gradual. It begins the moment we are justified, in the holy, humble, gentle, patient love of God and man. It gradually increases from that moment, as 'a grain of mustard-seed, which, at first, is the least of all seeds,' but afterwards puts forth large branches, and becomes a great tree; till, in another instant, the heart is cleansed from all sin, and filled with pure love to God and man. But even that love increases more and more, till 'we grow up in all things into Him that is our Head;' till we attain 'the measure of the stature of the fulness of Christ.' "
[3] *Works*, Vol. VII, p. 202. Sermon CVI. On Faith.

CHAPTER XXV

THE WRATH TO COME

"THERE is only one condition previously required in those who desire admission into these Societies,—a desire 'to flee from *the wrath to come*, to be saved from their sins.' But where this is really fixed in the soul, it will be shown by its fruits." *Works* 8: 270.

IN A PERCEPTIVE ARTICLE ON "WESLEY'S DOCTRINE OF THE LAST Things," originally presented as a paper at the Institute of Methodist Theological Studies, Dr. William Strawson of Handsworth College issued a wise warning. "Two dangers connected with any consideration of the doctrine of the Last Things are isolation and exaggeration. On the one hand, it is fatally easy to isolate this doctrine from the whole Christian belief, which results in a wrong emphasis; on the other hand, by extracting references to the belief from the whole thought of a writer, one can easily give the impression that this belief was overwhelmingly significant, to the exclusion of all else. We shall do well to keep in mind these two dangers as we consider Wesley's views on eschatology."[1]

That is a shrewd and necessary *caveat*, which will be kept prominently in mind as we examine the place accorded in Wesley's evangelistic preaching to the sanctions of judgement and the events of the End. One would have felt, however, that the current tendency is rather to underrate than to exaggerate the incidence of this element in Wesley's message. Dr. Rattenbury dismissed the inquiry by asserting that "Wesley preached little on the subject."[2] Dr. Albert M. Lyles, whilst admitting that an emphasis on the necessity for conversion was connected in Wesley's mind with the horrors of impending judgement, thinks that his sermons were not minatory in character.[3] David Dunn Wilson, confining himself exclusively to the importance of hell in Wesley's preaching, finds that the actual references are comparatively few.[4]

[1] William Strawson, "Wesley's Doctrine of the Last Things," *London Quarterly and Holborn Review*, July, 1959, p. 240.
[2] Rattenbury, *op. cit.*, p. 106.
[3] Lyles, *op. cit.*, p. 76.
[4] *Proc. W.H.S.*, Vol. XXXIV, p. 12. Wilson apparently relied on the indices of the *Journal* and *Works*, which are by no means exhaustive. Moreover, he confined himself to the explicit allusions to hell: a survey of all the passages dealing with judgement to come would show that these factors occupied a more prominent place than he allows.

In an addendum to the chapter on "John Wesley's Subjects" in his study of Wesley as a preacher, W. L. Doughty confessed that honesty compelled him to make mention of this factor.[1] He felt obliged to take note of Wesley's appeal to what he himself described as "the terrors of the Lord," because to ignore it would expose him to a charge of *suppressio veri*.[2] He was candid enough to recognize that Wesley's awareness of the wrath to come was such as to ensure its inclusion amongst the ingredients of his evangelistic preaching. Doughty added, justifiably, that much more might be written on the matter, but he himself was content to deal with it in a couple of paragraphs.

No one can analyse the contents of Wesley's *Journal* without realizing that the theme of judgement was more than an occasional or incidental feature of his message. On the evening of the 8th September, 1749, Wesley took his stand in the market-place at Alnwick "and exhorted a numerous congregation to be always ready for death, for judgement, for heaven. I felt what I spoke; as I believe did most that were present, both then and in the morning, while I besought them to 'present' themselves 'a living sacrifice, holy, acceptable to God.'"[3] On the 16th May, 1774, Wesley was in Scotland. He preached twice in the Presbyterian Kirk at Port Glasgow. "My subjects were Death and Judgement," he reported, "and I spoke as home as I possibly could." In the evening at Greenock he "opened and enlarged these awful words, 'Strait is the gate, and narrow is the way, that leadeth unto life.'"[4] "I know not that ever I spoke more strongly," he added.[5] This particular sermon is preserved in the standard collection, and there we learn that Wesley also dealt with the previous verse in Matthew 7, referring to the wide gate and the broad way which leads to destruction.[6] The first part of his message was devoted to considering "the inseparable properties of the way to hell." And in his appeal at the close, Wesley built on this. "Settle it in your heart, and let it be ever

[1] Doughty, *op. cit.*, p. 101.

[2] *Ibid*. For Wesley's use of the phrase "the terrors of the Lord" (2 Corinthians 5: 11— where it is in the singular), cf. *Journal*, Vol. V, p. 45. 26th February, 1764; Vol. VI, p. 342. 14th January, 1782, *et. al.*

[3] *Ibid.*, Vol. III, p. 428. 8th September, 1749. Rattenbury remarked that Wesley's preaching of hell was not "vitalized by experience," in the nature of the case (*op. cit.*, p. 101), but this passage from the *Journal* shows that Wesley nevertheless spoke from deep personal conviction about the reality of judgement. What Simon wrote about the early Methodist preachers was also true of Wesley himself: they "spoke as men who had been down to the iron gates and had gazed upon the horrors of death eternal. Every appeal was pointed with their own experience; it winged every arrow that flew into the hearts of their hearers" (*Revival of Religion in the Eighteenth Century*, pp. 294–295).

[4] *Journal*, Vol. VI, p. 19. 16th May, 1774.

[5] *Ibid.*

[6] *Sermons*, Vol. I, pp. 533–536. Sermon XXVI. Upon our Lord's Sermon on the Mount XI.

uppermost in your thoughts, that if you are in a broad way, you are in the way that leadeth to destruction. If many go with you, as sure as God is true, both they and you are going to hell! If you are walking as the generality of men walk, you are walking to the bottomless pit! . . . In whatever profession you are engaged, you must be singular, or be damned! The way to hell has nothing singular about it; but the way to heaven is singularity all over. . . . It is far better to stand alone than to fall into the pit."[1] Wesley then went on to urge his hearers in a positive manner that they should "strive to enter in at the strait gate."[2]

When Wesley visited Kelso on the 14th June, 1782, he was cordially welcomed by the parish minister, Dr. Douglas. He "spoke strong words in the evening, concerning judgement to come; and some seemed to awake out of sleep. But how shall they keep awake, unless they 'that fear the Lord speak often one to another'?"[3] It would appear that Wesley regarded the preaching of judgement as part of the awakening ministry which paves the way for the gospel offer. "I preached at St. Ewen's church, but not upon Justification by Faith," he wrote from Bristol on the 23rd March, 1777.[4] "I do not find this to be a profitable subject to an unawakened congregation," he went on. "I explained here, and strongly applied, that awful word, 'It is appointed unto men once to die.' "[5]

At Sligo on the 6th May, 1769, preaching near the market-house, he soon found he was shooting over the heads of the hearers in talking about salvation by faith. So the next morning, he said, "I suited myself to their capacity by preaching on, 'Where their worm dieth not, and the fire is not quenched.' The effect was that the evening congregation was such as I had not seen here for many years."[6] He adopted similar tactics at the Masons' Lodge, Port Glasgow, on the 22nd April, 1772. The building was filled to capacity and most of the gentry of the district were present. "Resolving not to shoot over their heads, as I had done the day before, I spoke strongly of death and judgement, heaven and hell. This they seemed to comprehend; and there was no more laughing among them, or talking with each other; but all were quietly and deeply attentive."[7]

In February 1764 Wesley rode to Sundon and spoke in the evening "to a very quiet and very stupid people."[8] "How plain is it that even to enlighten the understanding is beyond the power of man!" he observed.

[1] Ibid., p. 541.
[2] Ibid., pp. 541–542.
[3] Journal, Vol. VI, pp. 357–358. 14th June, 1782.
[4] Ibid., p. 141. 23rd March, 1777. Rumney Penrose was Rector.
[5] Ibid., Hebrews 9: 27.
[6] Ibid., Vol. V, p. 317. 6th and 7th May, 1769. Mark 9: 48, Sermon LXIII. On Hell (Works, Vol. VI, pp. 381–391).
[7] Journal, Vol. V, p. 455. 22nd April, 1772. Cf. Vol. VI, p. 29. 22nd July, 1744; Vol. VII, p. 363. 16th March, 1768.
[8] Ibid., Vol. V, p. 45. 23rd February, 1764.

"After all our preaching here, even those who have constantly attended no more understand us than if we had preached in Greek."[1] A few days later, however, he tried another way to reach them. "I preached on, 'Where their worm dieth not, and the fire is not quenched;' and set before them the terror of the Lord, in the strongest manner I was able. It seemed to be the very thing they wanted. They not only listened with the deepest attention, but appeared to be more affected than I had ever seen them by any discourse whatever."[2]

A scrutiny of Wesley's texts, both in the *Journal* and the Sermon Register, reveals the fact that amongst those more frequently used were several which bore directly on this theme. These include the following: "And I saw the dead, small and great, stand before God" (Revelation 20: 12); "Therefore be ye also ready: for in such an hour as ye think not the Son of man cometh" (Matthew 24: 44); "It is appointed unto men once to die, but after this the judgement" (Hebrews 9: 27); "When the Lord Jesus shall be revealed from heaven with His mighty angels, in flaming fire taking vengeance on them that know not God, and that obey not the gospel of our Lord Jesus Christ, who shall be punished with everlasting destruction from the presence of the Lord, and from the glory of His power, when He shall come to be glorified in His saints" (II Thessalonians 1: 7-10); and, "Where their worm dieth not, and the fire is not quenched" (Mark 9: 48).[3] Wesley's sermon on "The Great Assize" (from Romans 14: 10) appears in the standard selection to represent this theme.[4] That on Mark 9: 48 is included as Number LXXIII ("On Hell") in the *Works*, whilst others bearing on eschatology are Numbers LXXXIV ("The Important Question," Matthew 16: 26), XCIX ("The Reward of the Righteous," Matthew 25: 1), CXII ("The Rich Man and Lazarus," Luke 16: 31), CXX ("On the Wedding Garment," Matthew 22: 12), LIV ("On Eternity," Psalm 90: 2), LXXI ("Of Good Angels," Hebrews 1: 14), and LXXII ("Of Evil Angels," Ephesians 6: 12).[5] There are, of course, many references in other sermons not directly concerned with the Last Things.

Sufficient evidence has been adduced to indicate that what Wesley

---

[1] *Ibid.*

[2] *Ibid.*, 26th February, 1764.

[3] Revelation 20: 12—*Journal*, Vol. VI, p. 20. 22nd May, 1774; p. 323. 23rd June, 1781; Vol. VII, p. 321. 29th August, 1787; Vol. VIII, p. 51. 18th March, 1790; Hebrews 9: 27—Vol. VI, p. 141. 23rd March, 1777; p. 156. 17th June, 1777; p. 251. 24th August, 1779 (whilst a funeral bell was tolling in Llanelly churchyard); Vol. VII, p. 309. 9th August, 1787; p. 382. 30th May, 1788; p. 430. 27th August, 1788; p. 519. 13th July, 1789; 2 Thessalonians 1: 7-10—Vol. VII, p. 362. 15th March, 1788, and Sermon Register *passim*; Mark 9: 48—*Journal*, Vol. V, p. 345. 16th October, 1769; Vol. VI, p. 20. May 22nd, 1774; p. 29. 27th July, 1774; p. 40. 29th October, 1774. For the Sermon Register (1747-1761), where each of these texts recur, see Vol. VIII, pp. 171-252.

[4] *Sermons*, Vol. II, pp. 401-419. Sermon XLVIII. The Great Assize.

[5] *Works*, Vol. VI, pp. 381-391, pp. 493-505; Vol. VII, pp. 127-138, pp. 244-255, dp. 311-317; Vol. VI, pp. 361-370, pp. 370-380.

called "the terrors of the Lord" formed a part of his preaching which cannot be ignored. As we shall show, he was restrained in his handling of it, and his ultimate appeal was not to fear. But in our eagerness to vindicate Wesley from the charge of a kind of spiritual blackmail—against which the evangelist must always be on his guard—we must not go so far as to deny that he approved or employed the legitimate sanctions of judgement. In replying to "John Smith," Wesley defended his use of this evangelistic weapon. "But may not love itself constrain us to lay before men 'the terrors of the Lord'? And is it not better that sinners 'should be terrified now than that they should sleep on and awake in hell'? I have known exceeding happy effects of this, even upon men of strong understanding."[1] But he agreed that in private conversation with critics little good is done by "the profuse throwing about hell and damnation," and that the best way of deciding the points in question is cool and friendly argumentation.[2]

In a careful review of the available facts, Dr. J. Cyril Downes concedes that Wesley did at times use the motive of fear, although, as the last quotation shows, it was not incompatible with genuine compassion and concern for those whom he sought to win. Wesley believed that preaching "the terrors of the Lord" "could serve to awaken those who were morally and spiritually asleep, and make them aware of their danger."[3] He also considered that it could bring his hearers to repentance. "When men feel in themselves the heavy burthen of sin, see damnation to be the reward of it, behold with the eyes of their mind the horror of hell, they tremble, they quake, and are inwardly touched with sorrowfulness of heart, and cannot but accuse themselves, and open their grief to Almighty God, and call unto Him for mercy,"[4] Wesley was there quoting, with obvious approval, from the Anglican Homilies. A distinction made by Tyerman reflects Wesley's own attitude to this matter: "It may be unreasonable to think of frightening a man to heaven; but it is not unreasonable to endeavour to frighten him away from hell."[5]

We must therefore proceed to examine the content of Wesley's preaching about the wrath to come. It is not without significance that this very phrase was incorporated into the basis of membership in the Methodist societies. The sole condition of admission was a desire "to flee from the

[1] *Letters*, Vol. II, p. 69. To "John Smith," 25th June, 1746.
[2] *Ibid.*
[3] J. Cyril T. Downes, *Eschatology Doctrines in the Writings of John and Charles Wesley*, unpublished Ph.D. thesis, University of Edinburgh 1960. Kindly loaned by the author.
[4] *Letters*, Vol II, p. 268 To Thomas Church, 17th June, 1746.
[5] Tyerman, *Life of John Wesley*, Vol. I, p. 468. Wesley's resolve on board the *Simmonds*, after the storm, must not be overlooked. When he saw how soon most of the passengers forgot their experiences, he wrote: "For the future, I will never believe them to obey from fear who are dead to the motives of love" (*Journal*, Vol. I, p. 139, 18th January, 1736).

wrath to come, to be saved from their sins."[1] That still stands in the
Methodist Church today. It suggests that for Wesley the whole of life was
visualized from the standpoint of the eternal. This indeed was his perspective. His evangelistic mission was carried on in the knowledge, akin to
that of the first emissaries of the gospel in New Testament times, that both
he and his hearers were living between the advents. The period in which
all the activity of the Church is set stretched from Christ's first coming to
His second. This awareness supplied a keen edge to Wesley's evangelism,
which is noticeably lacking in an age like ours which has largely discarded
the eschatological context, except perhaps as a speculative theory. But for
Wesley, it was no hypothesis: it represented the existential reality domi-
nating his whole concept of mission. He told "John Smith:" "I desire to
have both heaven and hell ever in my eye, while I stand on this isthmus of
life, between these two boundless oceans; and I verily think the daily
consideration of both highly becomes all men of reason and religion."[2]

For Wesley, the judgement was not taken to occur at the moment of
death, as some in his day surmised, but after the Parousia. He rejected the
Roman figment of purgatory, but believed that, even though judgement
is postponed, the soul must be aware of its final destination immediately
after death. "The moment a soul drops the body, and stands naked before
God, it cannot but know what its portion will be to all eternity. It will
have full in its view, either everlasting joy, or everlasting torment; as it is
no longer possible for us to be deceived in the judgement which we pass
upon ourselves. But the Scripture gives us no reason to believe, that God
will then sit in judgement upon us. There is no passage in all the oracles
of God which affirms any such thing. . . . The imagination therefore of
one judgement at death, and another at the end of the world, can have no
place with those who make the written Word of God the whole and sole
standard of their faith."[3]

In his sermon on "The Great Assize," Wesley rehearsed from Scripture
the sequence of events preceding the judgement. Clearly he associated
this with the return of Christ. It is He who must come who will act as
Judge, in terms of John 5: 22, 27.[4] Wesley made no chronological dis-
tinctions between the judgement of believers and unbelievers, nor did he
interpret Matthew 25: 31-46 as applying only to the Gentiles as over
against the Jews and the Church. As an evangelist, he confined himself to
the bold outlines of prophecy, rather than wrestling with the details of
debatable interpretation. The judgement itself will be of a most searching
character. God will expose not only the hidden worlds of darkness, but
also all the thoughts and intents of the heart. This is necessary for the

[1] *Works*, Vol. VIII, p. 270. *Large Minutes* (1789).
[2] *Letters*, Vol. II, p. 98. To "John Smith," 10th July, 1747.
[3] *Sermons*, Vol. II, pp. 473-474. Sermon LI. The Good Shepherd.
[4] *Ibid.*, p. 405. Sermon LVIII. The Great Assize.

vindication of the divine wisdom and justice. "And then only when God hath brought to light all the hidden things of darkness, whosoever were the actors therein, will it be seen that wise and good were all His ways; that He saw through the thick cloud, and governed all things by the wise counsel of His own will; that nothing was left to chance, or the caprice of men, but God disposed all strongly and sweetly, and wrought all into one connected chain of justice, mercy, and truth."[1] The sovereignty of God could hardly have been more vividly exhibited by Calvin himself.

The sentence of the Judge will be unambiguous. The righteous will "shine forth as the sun in the kingdom of their Father," whereas "the wicked shall be turned into hell" (Matthew 13: 43; Psalm 9: 17). But, whilst Wesley sufficiently indicated the awfulness of perdition, his final appeal in this sermon was not to fear. In a passage of unusual eloquence, even for him, Wesley depicted the advent of Christ in judgement. "See! See! He cometh! He maketh the clouds His chariots! He rideth upon the wings of the wind! A devouring fire goeth before Him, and after Him a flame burneth! See! He sitteth upon His throne, clothed with light as with a garment, arrayed with majesty and honour! Behold, His eyes are as a flame of fire, His voice as the sound of many waters!"[2]

Then, confronting his listeners with a personal challenge, Wesley moved into his customary appeal. It is to be remembered that this sermon was first preached on the 10th March, 1758, at the Bedford Assizes, in the church of St. Paul, before the Honourable Sir Edward Clive, Judge of the Common Pleas, and the High Sheriff of the County, William Cole.[3] The latter was a friend of Wesley, and it was through him that the opportunity came. Clive and the other judges would be present in all the colourful splendour of their scarlet and ermine, as Sugden reminded us, with their trumpeters, javelin-men, and others of their entourage.[4] They must have been astonished to hear themselves addressed like this: "How will ye escape? Will ye call the mountains to fall on you, the rocks to cover you? Alas, the mountains themselves, the rocks, the earth, the heavens, are just ready to flee away! Can ye prevent the sentence? Wherewith? With all the substance of thy house, with thousands of gold and silver? Blind wretch! Thou camest naked from thy mother's womb, and more naked into eternity. Hear the Lord, the Judge! 'Come, ye blessed of my Father, inherit the kingdom prepared for you from the foundation of the world.' Joyful sound! How widely different from that voice which echoes through the expanse of heaven, 'Depart, ye cursed, into everlasting fire, prepared for the devil and his angels!' And who is he that can prevent or retard the full execution of either sentence? Vain hope! Lo, hell is moved

[1] *Ibid.*, p. 410.
[2] *Ibid.*, p. 418.
[3] *Ibid.*
[4] *Ibid.*, p. 398. Notes.

from beneath to receive those who are ripe for destruction. And the everlasting doors lift up their heads, that the heirs of glory may come in!"[1]

Yet, whilst the alternatives were clarified for the congregation with uncompromising sharpness, the ultimate appeal was not to the instinct of fear but rather to the magnetism of love. Wesley reminded his hearers that the Judge of all is likewise the Saviour of all. "Hath He not bought you with His own blood, that he might not perish, but have everlasting life? O make proof of His mercy, rather than His justice; of His love, rather than of the thunder of His power! He is not far from every one of us; and He is now come, not to condemn, but to save the world. He standeth in the midst! Sinner, doth He not now, even now, knock at the door of thy heart? O that thou mayest know, at least in this thy day, the things that belong unto thy peace! O that ye may now give yourselves to Him who gave Himself for you, in humble faith, in holy, active, patient love! So shall ye rejoice with exceeding joy in His day, when He cometh in the clouds of heaven."[2] If that is a fair sample of Wesley's evangelistic preaching (and we have reason to believe that it is), then it is as evident that the sanctions of judgement were invoked as that they were biblically balanced with an even more powerful reminder of God's redeeming love. No doubt Wesley realized that the second gained force when it followed the first.

Beyond the judgement and its verdict, Wesley saw the irrevocable destinations of heaven and hell. He marked the scriptural insistence that each of these states is of eternal duration. In Matthew 25: 46 Jesus said that the wicked will go away to everlasting punishment, whilst the righteous will enjoy everlasting life. Wesley noted that the same Greek word $\alpha i \acute{\omega} \nu \iota o \varsigma$ is used in each clause. "It follows, that either the punishment lasts for ever, or the reward too will come to an end."[3] The latter is inconceivable, unless God could die and His mercy and truth could fail: hence the former is established in the divine nature itself. Thus, "the refusing a happy eternity implies the choosing of a miserable eternity. For there is not, cannot be, any medium between everlasting joy and everlasting pain."[4] Again, concerning the wicked, in the sermon "On Hell": "All those torments of body and soul are without intermission. They have no respite from pain; but 'the smoke of their torment ascendeth up day and night.' *Day and night!* that is, speaking according to the constitution of the present world. . . . But although the damned have uninterrupted night, it

---

[1] *Ibid.*, p. 418.
[2] *Ibid.*, p. 419.
[3] *Ibid.*, p. 411.
[4] *Works*, Vol. VI, p. 195. Sermon LIV. On Eternity. Cf. p. 210. Sermon LVI. God's Approbation of His Works; "As wicked spirits are tormented day and night without any intermission of their misery; so holy spirits enjoy God day and night without intermission of their happiness."

brings no interruption in their pain. No sleep accompanies that darkness.
. . . And be their suffering ever so extreme, be their pain ever so intense,
there is no possibility of their fainting away; no, not for a moment."[1]
There is a Dante-esque touch about that last inference which makes us
realize how harrowing such preaching could be.

But Wesley rose to a crescendo of horrific admonition in the subsequent paragraph. "And of this duration there is no end! What a thought
is this! Nothing but eternity is the term of their torment! And who can
count the drops of rain, or the sands of the sea, or the days of eternity?
Every suffering is softened, if there is any hope, though distant, of deliverance from it. but here,

> Hope never comes, that comes to all

the inhabitants of the upper world! What! sufferings *never* to end!

> NEVER!—Where sinks the soul at that dread sound?
> Into a gulf how dark, and how profound!

Suppose millions of days, of years, of ages elapsed, still we are only on the
threshold of eternity! Neither the pain of body or of soul is any nearer
an end, than it was millions of ages ago. When they are cast into τὸ πῦρ
τὸ ἄσβεστον. (How emphatical! 'the fire, the unquenchable') all is concluded: 'their worm dieth not, and the fire is not quenched.' "[2]

Curnock's verdict is categorical. That Wesley "regarded the future
punishment of the wicked as an article of the Christian creed," he declared, "there can be no question."[3] Equally indisputable is Williams's
observation that "Wesley's picture of hell is a literal transcription of the
New Testament language."[4] Those who quarrel with Wesley's presentation are compelled to reject his view of Scripture. That he himself saw
that these are interrelated is shown by what he wrote to William Law in
1756. After citing an impressive catena of scriptural texts, Wesley claimed
that they spoke of hell and its eternal punishment as a reality. "I would
then ask but one plain question: If the case is not so, why did God speak
as if it was? Say you, 'To affright men from sin'? What, by guile, by dis-
simulation, by hanging out false colours? Can you possibly ascribe this to
the God of truth? Can you believe it of Him? Can you conceive the Most

---

[1] *Ibid.*, p. 389. Sermon LXXIII. On Hell.

[2] *Ibid.*, pp. 389–390. The first poetical quotation is from John Milton's *Paradise
Lost*, Bk. I, 1. 65.

[3] *Journal*, Vol. I, p. 139. Notes. Curnock recognized that, as we have shown,
Wesley was restrained in his appeal to fear as a motive. He tried, however, to dismiss Wesley's sermon On Hell as having been "composed in pre-evangelistic days"
(*ibid.*). But Wesley continued to preach it with regularity, which he would hardly
have done had he altered his views, any more than he would have included it amongst
his published sermons.

[4] Williams, *op. cit.*, p. 199. Cf. *Proc. W.H.S.*, Vol. XXXIV, p. 13.

High dressing up a scarecrow, as we do to fright children? Far be it from Him! If there be, then, any such fraud in the Bible, the Bible is not of God. And, indeed, this must be the result of all: if there be 'no unquenchable fire, no everlasting burnings,' there is no dependence on those writings wherein they are so expressly asserted, nor of the eternity of heaven any more than of hell. So that if we give up the one, we must give up the other. No hell, no heaven, no revelation!"[1]

To Wesley, every sinner was "under the sentence of hell-fire," until he turned to Christ.[2] It was this uncomfortable conviction which added exceptional urgency to his evangelistic task. Like Richard Baxter, Wesley preached as "a dying man to dying men"—and he was certain that if they died in their sins they would be damned for ever.[3] It is fashionable now-adays to pour scorn on such a crude belief, as it is considered to be: but does any other presupposition provide such a compelling stimulus to the work of mission? Even love itself may grow cold, unless it is continually prompted by the solemn realization that if the watchman fails to warn the wicked, he will be taken away in his iniquity, and moreover, his blood will be required at the preacher's hand (Ezekiel 33: 7, 8). Wesley believed that those who failed to confront the sinner with the facts of life in the future, in terms of the indescribable agonies which await the impenitent, themselves stood under the judgement of Christ. He himself was determined to declare the whole counsel of God and, whilst he offered the love of God in Christ, also to impress on his listeners in no ambiguous terms the literally dreadful consequences of rejecting the gospel.

[1] *Letters*, Vol. III, p. 370. To William Law, 6th January, 1756.
[2] *Sermons*, Vol. I, p. 157. Sermon VII. The Way to the Kingdom.
[3] *The Autobiography of Richard Baxter, Being the Reliquiae Baxterianae*, ed. J. M. Lloyd Thomas (1925), p. 79.

EPILOGUE

IT HAS BEEN SHREWDLY STATED THAT TRUE GREATNESS GROWS. IT not only endures, but actually increases. The stature of those whose greatness springs from goodness (as the highest always does) is enhanced as the years go by, and succeeding generations recognize more and more of significance in their character and influence. This is a principle clearly distinguishable in the case of those whom God has chosen to be lights of the world in their several generations. "The path of the just is as the shining light, that shineth more and more unto the perfect day" (Proverbs 4: 18). It is so for him, as that Scripture suggests, but where greatness is allied to righteousness it seems as if the illumination is also conveyed to subsequent ages.

"Some men grow larger as they walk away from their own time"—so writes Ola Elizabeth Winslow in her perceptive study of Bunyan.[1] That is certainly true of John Wesley. He has always been known as an outstanding figure in the history of the Christian Church. But his stock improves as the march of time takes us further from his century, and it can be argued that never was he more discussed and appreciated than today. We are beginning to realize the measure of his greatness, under God. The judgements of Augustine Birrell that he was "the greatest force of the eighteenth century," and of Sir Charles Grant Robertson that he represents "the most striking of eighteenth-century figures," are widely accepted.[2] An editorial in The Times Literary Supplement has reaffirmed this conviction: "No historian can miss the immense raising of the nation's spiritual temper by Wesley in his own movement and through its effects in the Church of England. When we review the nineteenth century we find the evils which we criticize in our own, sometimes in worse shapes, but we see a high seriousness and far less confusion of mind. The recovery of the national mind and character started with Wesley."[3]

This acclaim is not confined to Great Britain, of course. Wesley's fame is universal. In the language of William Ewart Gladstone, his "life and acts have taken their place in the religious history not only of England,

[1] Ola Elizabeth Winslow, John Bunyan (1961), p. 20.
[2] Augustine Birrell, Miscellanies (1901), p. 34; Robertson, op. cit., p. 386.
[3] Cf. Times Literary Supplement, 21st May, 1938.

but of Christendom."[4] It is from this broad standpoint that Prof. Martin Schmidt has embarked on his recent theological biography, as he describes it.[2] He sees in Wesley a man who lived and acted as an ecumenical Christian, in the New Testament connotation of that much controverted adjective. He regards him as belonging to the whole Church, since the last of the major ecclesiastical organizations to have come into being in the development of Christianity originated with him. Although that was not what he intended at first, Wesley found himself borne along by the tide of the Spirit, and this factor unites him with all those significant figures before him (especially at the time of the Protestant Reformation) who found themselves in similar situations.[3] The man who took the world as his parish now has the eyes of the world upon him.

In our survey we have sought to analyse the distinctive contribution of John Wesley, not only to his own generation, but to those which have succeeded, and, in particular, ours today. This has been no strictly academic exercise: throughout we have been concerned to discover what can be learned from Wesley about the continuing task of evangelism. We have tried to show where Wesley's real significance lay. His genius was so many-sided that it is possible to overlook the essential factor—the more so if we are not interested in recognizing it. But in the preceding pages we have been sufficiently reminded that "Wesley was from the first the complete evangelist," as Richard Pyke rightly insisted.[4] No category is more expressive of his basic concern than this.

We have traced the providential steps in Wesley's training as an evangelist. The remarkable impact of his upbringing has been assessed. The combination of the best both in the Anglican and Puritans traditions helped to mould him into an apostle to the nation. The discipline of study equipped him intellectually to be a defender of the faith. But most of all, the abject failure of self-effort and ascetic rigorism to bring him either peace of soul or a sense of fulfilment in his ministry, ultimately led him to seek salvation where alone it can be found—namely, in an unconditional reliance on the merits of Christ the Redeemer. It was Wesley's conversion that made him an evangelist. Until the experience at Aldersgate Street on the 24th May, 1738, he was too preoccupied with the problem of saving his own soul to be effective in winning others. After that determinative encounter he resolved in his brother's words,

> "To spend, and to be spent, for them
> Who have not yet my Saviour known"[5]

Henceforward it was on these that he was to prove his lifelong mission.

[1] William Ewart Gladstone, *Gleanings of Past Years 1843–1878* (1879), Vol. VII, p. 205.
[2] Schmidt, *op. cit.*, Vol. I, p. 10. [3] *Ibid.*, p. 9.
[4] Pyke, *op. cit.*, p. 77.
[5] *Wesley's Hymns*, No. 433, v. 3, lines 5, 6.

According to Hugh of St. Victor, the medieval exegete, there are three stages of faith.[1] Wesley passed through each. The first consists in an acceptance of Christian teaching, without reflection or an understanding of why it is worthy of belief. On his own admission, this was Wesley's position as a schoolboy at Charterhouse. It would have been surprising at that age if he had advanced much further. Despite his candid confession, however, we can be sure that, since from childhood he always required a reason for all that he was asked to do, he had already begun to probe the rationale of belief. This process continued at Oxford. It led to a logical formulation which temporarily satisfied his mind, but, tied as he was to a virtually humanistic conception of justification by works, he lamentably failed to find that inner repose of soul which he so desperately sought.

The second stage of faith involves the approval of reason. In Wesley's case, it was through the guidance of the Moravians that he rediscovered the Reformed teaching on justification in the Anglican standards, and eventually embraced it mentally as an article of belief in March 1738. This was his intellectual conversion, as we have defined it. But the third stage of faith, declared Hugh of St. Victor, is only reached when a man inwardly experiences what he has believed with his mind. It is then that he comes into perfect union with God in Christ—a union mediated both by love and knowledge.[2] It was into this experiential appropriation of salvation by grace through faith alone that Wesley entered at Aldersgate Street. It supplied the capstone of conviction, and at the same time fired him with missionary zeal. He had sailed to Georgia three years before, but his motive then was primarily to save himself. Now his own account was settled, and he could devote himself with a single eye to the redemption of his fellows.

We would therefore wish to qualify the contention of Prof. Umphrey Lee that "attempts to interpret that experience as an evangelical conversion which transformed Wesley from a sinner to a saint, or from a naturalistic humanist into a Christian, are in contradiction to Wesley's own judgement and misreadings of the facts."[3] This is not to deny that Wesley had been devoutly religious at least since 1725, and that his practical humanism was set within a framework of supernatural revelation. But for all that, it is surely plain beyond argument that the pre-Aldersgate Wesley would never have turned Britain upside down. He was still *homo perturbatus*, and as such quite unready to undertake the mission God had for him. He lacked a sense of acceptance and consequently a sense of dynamic. His conversion alone brought deliverance, confidence and direction. Wesley became the man he is now hailed as being through divine intervention. No doubt many of his qualities already lay hidden within his personality, but it was only at the touch of the Spirit that they sprang to

---

[1] Hugo de S. Victor, *De Sacramentis Christianae Fidei*, I.x.4 (J. P. Mique, *Patrologia Latina*, Vol. CLXXVI, p. 232.   [2] *Ibid.*

[3] Umphrey Lee, *John Wesley and Modern Religion* (1936), pp. 101–102.

life and received their necessary integration. All that Wesley was and did can be traced back to that transforming experience. If the Damascus road explains Paul the apostle; if the Milanese garden accounts for Augustine of Hippo, the doctor of the Church; if the Black Tower at Wittenberg gave birth to Martin Luther as the pioneer Reformer; then Aldersgate Street, London, produced John Wesley the evangelist.[1]

Wesley had now found his *forte*. He was not to spend his days in academic seclusion as a university don. He was not to exercise a parochial ministry in the Anglican Church. He was to become an evangelist at large. "If either by a natural or an acquired power of persuasion I can prevail upon sinners to turn to God, am I to bury even that talent in the earth?" Wesley inquired of "John Smith." " 'No; but try if you cannot do more good in a college or in a parish.' I have tried both, and I could not do any substantial good, either to my pupils or my parishioners. Among my parishioners in Lincolnshire I tried for some years; but I am well assured I did far more good to them by preaching three days on my father's tomb than I did by preaching three years in his pulpit."[2]

As we have seen, it was when the doors of the churches were shut on him, as he preached what was considered to be dangerously innovative doctrine, that in April 1739 he was constrained to take to the open air. This was the decisive step which inaugurated the mission to Britain. Already George Whitefield had anticipated it, and the pair of them, despite their variant emphases, were to be the twin instruments of the Spirit in the awakening of thousands. There was a divine overruling in the restrictions which drove Wesley to operate outside the orbit of the Established Church. The need of the hour was for the adaptation of the Christian strategy to reach out to the people where they were, and, as F. J. Snell observed, "the ossified Church of England had lost this faculty."[3] Dissent was in little better shape: according to Halévy it "had lost all capacity for propaganda."[4] Wesley was propelled by the Spirit into the true sphere of evangelism. He took the message to the people where they were. He refused to be shackled by ecclesiastical proprieties. He cheerfully abandoned his own reputation for respectability in a way which would have been inconceivable before his evangelical conversion. He addressed himself wholeheartedly to the central task of the true Church—namely, the preaching of the gospel to those who most need to hear it. He embarked upon his incredible itinerancy, becoming, in the vivid words of Rupp, "a human sputnik, a Don Quixote for Christ's sake."[5]

Wesley achieved what must always be the first objective of an evan-

[1] Cf. A. Skevington Wood, "Lessons from Wesley's Experience," *Christianity Today*, Vol. VII (1963), p. 721.

[2] *Letters*, Vol. II, p. 96. To "John Smith," 25th March, 1747.

[3] F. J. Snell, *Wesley and Methodism* (1900), p. 117.   [4] Halévy, *op. cit.*, p. 407.

[5] E. Gordon Rupp, "The Future of the Methodist Tradition," *London Quarterly and Holborn Review*, 1959, p. 266.

gelist. He actually got in touch with the people, and managed to communicate his message to them. We have indicated the means by which this was done and the heterogeneous character of his audiences. But his heart went out to the underprivileged. It was his overriding concern that the poor should have the gospel preached to them. In this, he was eminently successful and the fruit was plentiful. Although it is fictional, a letter in Samuel Richardson's novel *Sir Charles Grandison*, written in 1753, reflects what must have been happening in fact. "Mrs. O'Hara is turned *Methodist*. . . . Thank God she is anything that is serious. Those people really have great merit with me in *her* conversion. I am sorry that our own clergy are not as zealously in earnest as they. They have really given a face of religion to subterranean colliers, tinners, and the most profligate of men, who hardly ever before heard either of the word or the thing."[1] Historians today continue to underline the beneficial effect of Wesley's preaching to the depressed classes. "A feeling of purpose, a trust in Providence, was thus given to those who might otherwise have been filled only with the violence of despair," explains J. Steven Watson in a recent volume in the *Oxford History of England*.[2]

Tribute is also paid to the efficiency of Wesley's follow-up programme. Prof. R. W. Greaves refers to the fact that "in a lifetime of immense pastoral activity, in the course of great journeys all over the British Isles, and by a vast correspondence," Wesley "had been the leader in creating a great, flexible, and effective organization."[3] Prof. Basil Williams declared that "John Wesley's greatness consisted not only in his power as a preacher, but also in his initiation of the vast system by which his teaching was to be kept alive and vigorous."[4] It could well be claimed that Wesley was a pioneer in modern methods of post-natal care in evangelism.

We have devoted considerable space to an examination of Wesley's message and its biblical presuppositions. It is fashionable to suggest that here Wesley was a man of his age, and that neither his view of Scripture nor his presentation of the gospel is viable today. Sufficient evidence has been produced to warn us against so facile a judgement. The Bible was already under rationalistic fire in the eighteenth century, and there were many who found it more convenient to modify the less palatable elements in the Christian message. Indeed it was the contrast between Wesley's vibrant, incisive exhortations and the innocuous tepidity of the average discourse of the day which arrested attention. Before the revival, preaching in England had declined into intolerable dullness.[5] "The more doc-

[1] Samuel Richardson, *The History of Sir Charles Grandison* (1752), Vol. VI. Letter 9.
[2] J. Steven Watson, *The Reign of George III 1760–1815* (1960), p. 38.
[3] *New Cambridge Modern History*, Vol. VII, p. 138.
[4] Basil Williams, *The Whig Supremacy 1714–1760* (1939), p. 97.
[5] Stephen, *op. cit.*, Vol. II, p. 337. Referring to the sermons of the period, Stephen wrote: "Dull, duller and dullest are a sufficient critical vocabulary to describe their merits."

trinal aspects of religion were softened down, or suffered silently to recede,"
according to Lecky, "and, before the eighteenth century had much
advanced, sermons had very generally become mere moral essays, characterized chiefly by a cold good sense, and appealing almost exclusively to
prudential nature."[1]

It was the fear of causing offence which robbed the contemporary
pulpit of its pungency, and reduced the saving message to a colourless
apology. The scandal of the Cross is also its power. To trim the gospel is
to devitalize it. As Canon Overton observed, with reference to the Tillot-
sonian type of preaching, "what is intended to offend nobody is apt also
to affect nobody."[2] An extreme instance of such reticence is to be found in
the career of Dr. Knightly Chetwood, Dean of Gloucester from 1707
to 1720. On one occasion he was preaching at court, and somewhat diffi-
dently threatened sinners with punishment "in a place which he thought
it not decent to name in so polite an assembly."[3] This prompted Alexander
Pope's reference to "the soft Dean . . . who never mentions Hell to ears
polite."[4] It is not difficult to appreciate that Wesley's full-blooded proclamation of an uncompromising gospel, together with the sanctions of
judgement to come, produced a startling effect on his hearers, who were
struck by such unaccustomed frankness. It still remains true that those
who shrink from declaring the whole counsel of God, defeat their own
ends. The aim of the evangelist is not to please his hearers, but to save
them. That can only be done through the offence of the Cross.

As Alan Walker puts it, evangelism is still "God's word for this hour."[5]
Wesley's task is ours. We live in a world of which he could hardly have
dreamed. Yet even in a technological society, man without God is as lost
as ever he was. His environment may differ, but his fundamental need is
the same. He may reach the moon, but he will still be a sinner when he
gets there. We can only agree with General Omar Bradley's assessment
that modern man is "a nuclear giant and an ethical infant."[6] It must be the
major strategy of the Church to reach him with the good news of Christ.

[1] Lecky, op. cit., Vol. I, p. 84.
[2] John H. Overton, The Evangelical Revival in the Eighteenth Century (1886) p. 4.
[3] The Poems of Alexander Pope, Vol. III, i, ed. F. W. Bateson (1951), p. 152, n. 150.
[4] Ibid., p. 152, lines 149, 150. Epistles IV, To Richard Boyle, Earl of Burlington.
The Dean would appear to be the same person as the "eminent divine" mentioned by
Richard Steele (The Guardian, No. 17, 31st March, 1713) who "told his congregation
at Whitehall that if they did not vouchsafe to give their lives a new turn, they must
certainly go to a place which he did not think fit to name in that courtly audience."
Professor Williams (op. cit., p. 95, n. 1) identified the Dean with White Kennett of
Peterborough, but this does not seem to be in character (cf. G. V. Bennett, White
Kennett 1660–1728, Bishop of Peterborough (1957), p. 184). As Bateson points out, a
letter of Pope in the Daily Journal, 23rd December, 1731, supplies the likely clue,
with a mention of Dean Chetwood and "his courtly sermons."
[5] Alan Walker, The Whole Gospel for the Whole World (1958), p. 13.
[6] Cf. Leighton Ford, The Christian Persuader (1966), p. 26.

To have been reminded of one who bridged the gap in a bygone century should confirm the conviction that it can still be done today. The population explosion daily increases the magnitude of the mission. But the God who raised up Wesley and his colleagues can call out a task-force in our time too. That He may do so with similar effect must surely be the prayer of every Christian.

SELECT BIBLIOGRAPHY

Place of publication is London unless otherwise specified.

PRIMARY AUTHORITIES

The Works of the Rev. John Wesley, A.M., 3rd Edition, ed. Thomas Jackson, 14 vols., 1829–1831.
The Journal of the Rev. John Wesley, A.M., Standard Edition, ed. Nehemiah Curnock, 8 vols., 1909–1916.
The Letters of the Rev. John Wesley, A.M., Standard Edition, ed. John Telford, 8 vols., 1931.
The Standard Sermons of John Wesley, ed. Edward H. Sugden, 2 vols., 1921.
Sermons on Several Occasions by the Rev. John Wesley, A.M., 9th Edition, 2 vols., 1824.
Wesley, John, *Explanatory Notes upon the Old Testament*, 3 vols., Bristol, 1765.
Wesley, John, *Explanatory Notes upon the New Testament*, 1754.
Wesley's Revision of the Shorter Catechism, ed. James Alexander MacDonald, Edinburgh, 1906.
A Christian Library: Consisting of Extracts from and Abridgments of the Choicest Pieces of Practical Divinity which have been published in the English Tongue, 50 vols., Bristol, 1749–1755.
A Compend of Wesley's Theology, ed. Robert W. Burtner and Robert E. Chiles, New York, 1954.
John Wesley, ed. Albert C. Outler (*A Library of Protestant Thought*), New York, 1964.
The Message of the Wesleys, ed. Philip S. Watson, 1965.
The Journal of the Rev. Charles Wesley, M.A., ed. Thomas Jackson, 2 vols., 1849.
A Collection of Hymns for the Use of the People Called Methodists, 1780.
Green, Richard, *The Works of John and Charles Wesley: A Bibliography*, 1896.
Osborn, George, *Outlines of Wesleyan Bibliography*, 1909.
George Whitefield's Journals, ed. Iain Murray, 1960.
Lives of the Early Methodist Preachers, ed. Thomas Jackson, 6 vols., 1871–1872.
Arminian Magazine, 1778–1797.
Methodist Magazine, 1798–1821.

SECONDARY AUTHORITIES
THE EIGHTEENTH CENTURY IN BRITAIN

(a) *General*
Ayling, S. E., *The Georgian Century 1714–1837*, 1966.
George, M. Dorothy, *London Life in the Eighteenth Century*, 1925.
Halévy, Élie, *A History of the English People*, Vol. I, E.T. 1924.
Humphreys, A. R., *The Augustan World: Life and Letters in Eighteenth Century England* 1954.
Lecky, William Edward Hartpole, *A History of England in the Eighteenth Century*, 7 vols., 1892.
Lindsay, J. O. (ed.), *The old Regime 1713–1763*, Vol. VII in the New Cambridge Modern History, Cambridge, 1957.

Marshall, Dorothy, *The English Poor in the Eighteenth Century*, 1926.
Marshall, Dorothy, *The English People in the Eighteenth Century*, 1956.
Marshall, Dorothy, *Eighteenth Century England*, 1962.
Nicolson, Harold, *The Age of Reason 1700–1789*, 1960.
Petrie, Sir Charles, *The Four Georges: A Revaluation of the Period from 1714–1830*, 1936.
Plumb, J. H., *England in the Eighteenth Century*, 1950.
Richardson, A. E., *Georgian England: A survey of Social Life, Trade, Industries and Art*, 1931.
Robertson, Sir Charles Grant, *England Under the Hanoverians*, Vol. VI in *A History of England*, ed. Sir Charles Oman, 1911.
Stephen, Leslie, *A History of English Thought in the Eighteenth Century*, 2 vols., 1876, 1881.
Turberville, A. S., *English Men and Manners in the Eighteenth Century*, 1929.
Turberville, A. S. (ed.), *Johnson's England. An Account of the Life and Manners of His Age*, 2 vols., Oxford, 1933.
Watson, J. Steven, *The Reign of George III 1760–1815*, Vol. XII in the Oxford History of England, ed. G. N. Clark, Oxford, 1960.
Willey, Basil, *The Eighteenth Century Background: Studies in the Idea of Nature in the Thought of the Period*, 1950.
Williams, Basil, *The Whig Supremacy 1714–1760*, 2nd Edition, Vol. XI in the Oxford History of England, ed. G. N. Clark, 1962.
Williams, E. Neville, *Life in Georgian England*, 1962.

(b) *The Church of England*
Abbey, Charles J., *The English Church and its Bishops 1700–1800*, 1887.
Abbey, Charles J., and Overton, John H., *The English Church in the Eighteenth Century*, 2 vols., 1878.
Carpenter, S. C., *Eighteenth Century Church and People*, 1959.
Carter, C. Sydney, *The English Church in the Eighteenth Century*, 1948.
Clarke, W. K. Lowther, *Eighteenth Century Piety*, 1944.
Cragg, Gerald R., *The Church and the Age of Reason 1648–1789*, Vol. IV in the Pelican History of the Church, 1960.
Davies, G. C. B., *The Early Cornish Evangelicals 1735–1760*, 1951.
Elliott-Binns, Leonard E., *The Early Evangelicals: A Religious and Social Study*, 1953.
Greaves, R. W., Chapter VI, "Religion," in *The Old Regime 1713–1763*, ed. J. O. Lindsay, Vol. VII in The New Cambridge Modern History, Cambridge, 1957.
Legg, J. Wickham, *English Church Life from the Restoration to the Tractarian Movement*, 1914.
Overton, John H., *The Evangelical Revival in the Eighteenth Century*, 1886.
Overton, John H., and Relton, Frederic, *The History of the English Church from the Accession of George I to the end of the Eighteenth Century 1714–1800*, Vol. VII in *A History of the English Church*, ed. W. R. W. Stephens and William Hunt, 1906.
Plummer, Alfred, *The Church of England in the Eighteenth Century*, 1910.
Reynolds, John S., *The Evangelicals at Oxford 1735–1871*, Oxford, 1953.
Simon, John S., *The Revival of Religion in the Eighteenth Century*, n.d. (c. 1907).
Stromberg, Roland N., *Religious Liberalism in Eighteenth Century England*, Oxford, 1954.
Sykes, Norman, *Church and State in England in the Eighteenth Century*, Cambridge, 1934.

(c) *Methodism*
Bett, Henry, *The Spirit of Methodism*, 1937.
Davies, Rupert E., *Methodism*, 1963.
Davies, Rupert E., and Rupp, E. Gordon (eds.), *A History of the Methodist Church in Great Britain*, Vol. I, 1966.

Dimond, Sidney G., *The Psychology of the Methodist Revival*, Oxford, 1926.
Gill, Frederick C., *Charles Wesley*, 1964.
Harrison, Archibald W., *The Separation of Methodism from the Church of England*, 1945.
Jackson, Thomas, *The Life of Charles Wesley*, 2 vols., 1841.
Myles, William, *A Chronological History of the People Called Methodists*, 1800.
Stevens, Abel, *The History of the Religious Movement of the Eighteenth Century called Methodism*, 3 vols., 1858–1861.
Townsend, W. J., Workman, H. B., and Eayrs, G. (eds.), *A New History of Methodism*, 2 vols., 1909.
Tyerman, Luke, *The Oxford Methodists*, 1873.
Wearmouth, Robert F., *Methodism and the Common People of the Eighteenth Century*, 1945.
Workman, Herbert B., *Methodism*, Cambridge, 1912.

(d) *Dissent*
Colligan, J. Hay, *Eighteenth Century Nonconformity*, 1915.
Coomer, Duncan, *English Dissent under the Early Hanoverians*, 1946.
Cowherd, Raymond G., *The Politics of English Dissent*, New York, 1956.
Curteis, George Herbert, *Dissent in its Relation to the Church of England*, 1873.
Davies, Horton, *Worship and Theology in England: From Watts and Wesley to Maurice 1690–1850*, Princeton, 1961.

WESLEY'S LIFE AND WORK

Bready, J. Wesley, *England Before and After Wesley, The Evangelical Revival and Social Life*, 1939.
Doughty, W. Lamplough, *John Wesley: Preacher*, 1955.
Edwards, Maldwyn L., *John Wesley and the Eighteenth Century: A study of His Social and Political Influence*, 1933.
Edwards, Maldwyn L., *After Wesley*, 1935.
Fitchett, W. H., *Wesley and His Century: A Study in Spiritual Forces*, 1906.
Green, Richard, *John Wesley: Evangelist*, 1905.
Green, Vivian H. H., *The Young Mr. Wesley*, 1961.
Hutton, William Holden, *John Wesley*, 1927.
Haddal, Ingvar, *John Wesley. A Biography*, E.T. 1961.
McConnell, Francis J., *John Wesley*, New York, 1939.
Marshall, Dorothy, *John Wesley*, 1965.
Moore, Henry, *The Life of John Wesley*, 2 vols., 1824–1825.
Nottingham, Elizabeth K., *The Making of an Evangelist*, Columbia, 1938.
Overton, John H., *John Wesley*, 1891.
Piette, Maximin, *John Wesley in the Evolution of Protestantism*, E.T. 1937.
Pyke, Richard, *John Wesley Came This Way*, 1938.
Rattenbury, J. Ernest, *Wesley's Legacy to the World*, 1928.
Rattenbury, J. Ernest, *The Conversion of the Wesleys*, 1938.
Rigg, James H., *The Living Wesley*, New York, 1874.
Rigg, James H., *The Churchmanship of John Wesley*, 1878.
Schmidt, Martin, *John Wesley: A Theological Biography*, Vol. I, E.T. 1962.
Schmidt, Martin, *The Young Wesley: Missionary and Theologian of Missions*, E.T. 1958.
Simon, John S., *John Wesley and the Religious Societies*, 1921.
Simon, John S., *John Wesley and the Methodist Societies*, 1923.
Simon, John S., *John Wesley and the Advance of Methodism*, 1925.
Simon, John S., *John Wesley, The Master Builder*, 1927.
Simon, John S., *John Wesley, The Last Phase*, 1934..
Telford, John, *The Life of John Wesley*, 1899.

K

Thompson, Edgar W., *Wesley: Apostolic Man; Some Reflections on Wesley's Consecra-tion of Dr. Thomas Coke*, 1957.
Tyerman, Luke, *The Life and Times of the Rev. John Wesley*, 3 vols., 1870–1871.
Urlin, R. Denny, *John Wesley's Place in Church History*, 1870.
Urlin, R. Denny, *The Churchman's Life of Wesley*, 1880.
Vulliamy, C. E., *John Wesley*, 1931.

WESLEY'S THEOLOGY

Bowmer, John C., *The Sacrament of the Lord's Supper in Early Methodism*, 1951.
Cannon, William Ragsdale, *The Theology of John Wesley, with Special Reference to the Doctrine of Justification*, New York, 1946.
Cell, George Croft, *The Rediscovery of John Wesley*, New York, 1935.
Deschner, John A., *Wesley's Christology: An Interpretation*, Dallas, 1960.
Downes, J. Cyril T., *Eschatological Doctrines in the Writings of John and Charles Wesley*, Unpublished Ph.D. Thesis, Edinburgh, 1960.
Faulkner, John A., *Wesley as Sociologist, Theologian, Churchman*, New York, 1918.
Hildebrandt, Franz, *From Luther to Wesley*, 1951.
Hildebrandt, Franz, *Christianity According to the Wesleys*, 1956.
Lawson, Albert B., *John Wesley and the Christian Ministry*, 1963.
Lawson, John, *Notes on Wesley's Forty-Four Sermons*, 1946.
Lindström, Harald, *Wesley and Sanctification*, Stockholm, 1946.
Monk, Robert C., *John Wesley: His Puritan Heritage*, Nashville, 1966.
Parris, John R., *John Wesley's Doctrine of the Sacraments*, 1963.
Perkins, Harold W., *The Doctrine of Christian or Evangelical Perfection*, 1927.
Sangster, W. E., *The Path to Perfection: An Examination and Restatement of John Wesley's Doctrine of Christian Perfection*, 1943.
Starkey, Lycurgus M., *The Work of the Holy Spirit: A Study in Wesleyan Theology*, Nashville, 1962.
Turner, George Allen, *The More Excellent Way: The Scriptural Basis of the Wesleyan Message*, Winona Lake, 1952.
Williams, Colin W., *John Wesley's Theology Today*, 1960.
Yates, Arthur S., *The Doctrine of Assurance*, 1952.

EVANGELISM AND CONVERSION

Allan, Tom, *The Face of My Parish*, 1954.
Ford, Leighton, *The Christian Persuader*, New York, 1966.
Green, Bryan S. W., *The Practice of Evangelism*, 1948.
Green, E. M. B., *The Meaning of Salvation*, 1965.
Hartt, Julian A., *Toward a Theology of Evangelism*, Nashville, 1955.
Jones, W. Lawson, *A Psychological Study of Religious Conversions*, 1937.
Kantonen, T. A., *The Theology of Evangelism*, Philadelphia, 1954.
Kuiper, R. B., *God-Centered Evangelism. A Presentation of the Scripture Theology of Evangelism*, Grand Rapids, 1961.
Lang, L. Wyatt, *A Study of Conversion. An Enquiry into the Development of Christian Personality*, 1931.
Nygren, Anders, *The Gospel of God*, Philadelphia, 1951.
Packer, James I., *Evangelism and the Sovereignty of God*, 1961.
Sweaze, George, *Effective Evangelism*, New York, 1953.
Underwood, Alfred Clair, *Conversion: A Comparative and Psychological Study*, 1925.
Walker, Alan, *The Whole Gospel for the Whole World*, 1958.
Williams, Colin W., *Where in the World? Changing Forms of the Church's Witness*, 1965.
Williams, Colin W., *What in the World?*, 1965.
Wingren, Gustaf, *Gospel and Church*, Philadephia, 1965.

INDEX OF NAMES

INDEX OF PLACES

INDEX OF SUBJECTS